Lady Bird Johnson
and the
Environment

Lady Bird Johnson
and the
Environment

Lewis L. Gould

University Press of Kansas

For Helen Keel

Published by the University Press of Kansas (Lawrence, Kansas 66045), which was
organized by the Kansas Board of Regents and is operated and funded by Emporia
State University, Fort Hays State University, Kansas State University, Pittsburg State
University, the University of Kansas, and Wichita State University

All photos except that on p. 11 are courtesy of the Lyndon B. Johnson Library.

Library of Congress Cataloging-in-Publication Data

Gould, Lewis L.
  Lady Bird Johnson and the environment.
  Bibliography: p.
  Includes index.
  1. Johnson, Lady Bird, 1912–   —Views on
environmental protection. 2. Environmental protection—
United States. I. Title.
E848.J64G68 1988   973.923'092'4   87-25331
ISBN 0-7006-0336-0

British Library Cataloguing in Publication Data is available.

Printed in the United States of America
10 9 8 7 6 5 4 3 2 1

Contents

List of Illustrations

Preface

This study of Lady Bird Johnson and beautification began in 1982 when I offered a course at the University of Texas at Austin on "First Ladies in the Twentieth Century." Lady Bird Johnson attended one session of the undergraduate honors seminar in November 1982, when she talked about her own perceptions of her role as First Lady. At about this time my colleague Robert A. Divine decided to prepare a second volume of scholarly essays on the Johnson years, based on his very successful book *Exploring the Johnson Years,* published that same year. He invited me, because of my new interest in First Ladies, to look at some aspect of Mrs. Johnson's years in the White House.

Her work on beautification seemed a likely and manageable topic for the kind of exploratory essay that Divine had in mind. I had some general sense of the range of her involvement, or so I thought, and the materials in the Johnson Library were relatively untapped for such a project. So, in the late spring of 1983, under the guidance of the staff of the Johnson Library, I began to examine what the White House Central Files and the files of presidential aides contained on highway beautification, the First Lady's efforts in Washington, D.C., and her national impact on conservation questions. These sources were rich and informative but also somewhat scattered. What was there in Lady Bird Johnson's own White House Social Files on her beautification campaign? These files were in the library but had not yet been opened for scholarly research.

Through the help of the library's staff, which reviewed and processed these materials, and with the kind consent of Lady Bird Johnson herself, I was allowed to scrutinize, for research purposes, the various series within the Social Files. Early in 1984 I began to examine the twenty-six boxes of the Beautification Files in the Social Files. It rapidly became evident that there was much more to Lady Bird Johnson's campaign for beautification than a single forty-page essay could encompass. Telling the story of how the Highway Beautification Act of 1965 evolved would require an extended treatment of the subject, as would the different levels of her First Lady's Committee for a More Beautiful Capital in Washington, D.C. This book is the result of my realization that the record of Mrs. Lyndon B. Johnson and beautification in the 1960s needed a more elaborate and complete analytic investigation.

The nature of the research and writing for this narrative warrants discussion. After I began to work in the Social Files on beautification, the Johnson Library's staff began to process review requests from me and other scholars in other sections of the Social Files than just the Beautification Files series. Because there are, for example, more than two thousand boxes in the Alphabetical Files series, this work is ongoing, and members of the library's staff treat these requests in the same manner that they handle all review requests for all materials in the Johnson Library. In screening, the library's staff looks for items that have been specified in a donor's deed of gift as causing embarrassment, injury, or harassment to any living person; materials dealing with national-security issues; and papers relating to the Johnsons' family or private matters. Otherwise the result of the reviewing work is that new information becomes available for scholars as that process continues.

Every file that I have seen is now open to all other researchers on the basis of the Johnson Library's normal rules and procedures. No part of the sources of this book is off-limits to any other researcher, and I have received no special access to documents that other scholars may not see. Some sources that I have located, such as the legal records relating to the Taylor family in Marshall, Texas, and Lady Bird Johnson's early life are in the Lewis L. Gould Papers at the library and may be seen by any interested investigator. I also intend to donate to this collection in the library as many as possible of the documents and letters that this study has generated.

This is not an authorized or official study of Lady Bird Johnson, nor is it a biography. She would prefer, as I understand, that no biographies be written during her lifetime, and I have tried to respect that position. This study necessarily has biographical elements as they relate to beautification. Mrs. Johnson granted me an interview in September 1984, and she was most hospitable and informative on that occasion. She has not, however, read any part of this book before its publication, except as she may have read the parts that have appeared in print elsewhere. The views expressed are mine, and no inference or conclusion should be drawn that Mrs. Johnson or members of the Johnson family agree, disagree, or have any opinion about the facts or conclusions that the book contains.

The Lyndon B. Johnson Foundation provided financial support for the research that resulted in the article for Professor Divine's book. For participants in the volume who came to Austin from other cities, this support consisted of transportation expenses and some photocopying of documents. Those of us who live in Austin received about the same amount of funds for the copying of source material, or about $500 in all. Each author also received an honorarium from the foundation. No representative or agent of the foundation has seen either the article or this book, and no one has attempted in any way to influence the content or interpretation of the research and writing that I have done.

As the reader of the book will quickly discover, I have reached a favorable conclusion in general about the worth and value of Lady Bird Johnson's beautification endeavors. Colleagues have asked, as they so often do about women's history, whether the record of what Lady Bird Johnson did reveals anything that was not already known or that is not "trivial" and "cosmetic." While the First Lady's commitment to beautification was well known during the 1960s, the range and variety of what she tried to accomplish has not at all been documented. The degree of her involvement with billboard control exceeds what researchers on this subject have previously discussed, and the complexity of the story says much about why highway beautification has taken the direction it has during the past two decades. Similarly, the work that she encouraged in Washington's black community and the support that she gave to the initiatives of Lawrence Halprin to reshape Capitol Hill and other parts of the city reveal the errors that occur if a historian looks only at what took place in the floral and monumental sections of the nation's capital.

On the question of importance as opposed to "triviality," the issue itself embodies the assumption of a male-oriented history that what men do is significant and what women do is less relevant and consequential. If a man in the 1960s had been involved with an environmental issue such as highway beautification, had changed the appearance of a major American city, had addressed the problems of black inner-city youth, and had campaigned tirelessly to enhance national concern about natural beauty, no doubts would be raised that he was worthy of biographical and scholarly scrutiny. Lady Bird Johnson's accomplishments as a catalyst for environmental ideas during the 1960s and thereafter entitle her to an evaluation of what she tried to do and what she achieved.

As was the case for Lyndon Johnson as well, the record she made is impressive. Martin V. Melosi has shown that Lyndon Johnson's contribution to conservation and environmentalism was substantial. Lady Bird Johnson was a significant element in what her husband's presidency achieved in these areas. While the Highway Beautification Act of 1965 was imperfect legislation that did not bring about the sweeping regulation of billboards, Mrs. Johnson's identification with the cause made the appearance of the roadside a national issue and kept it in the public eye. Her work in Washington, D.C., improved that city's condition in an enduring way and contributed to a similar beautification and restoration impulse in cities large and small during that same decade. Most of all, she made citizen concern about the environment a legitimate position in the letters and statements that went out from her office promoting beautification campaigns and supporting efforts to preserve the California redwoods and the Grand Canyon.

Because of their situation as political celebrities, First Ladies have inherent difficulties in championing any policy initiatives that involve specific programs or controversial issues. Lady Bird Johnson overcame this obstacle because she deftly blended public occasions, where her beautification objectives received positive attention from the press, with the careful use of her influence as First Lady within the Johnson administration to promote the environmental causes she favored. She did so while simultaneously acting as a counselor to her husband, an advocate of the Head Start program, the coordinator of plans for a presidential library, and White House hostess. Among modern First Ladies for whom the historical record is open, only Eleanor Roosevelt surpasses Lady Bird Johnson in importance as the wife of the president.

My most important debt is to Harry Middleton, director of the Lyndon B. Johnson Presidential Library, and his staff for their generous and untiring cooperation with my research and writing. Harry Middleton encourages scholarship on Lyndon Johnson with admirable objectivity and provides a friendly and harmonious environment in which historical research can go forward productively. His associates, Charles Corkran, Lawrence Reed, and Gary Yarrington, were always prepared to provide support and understanding in abundance.

Michael Gillette ably directs the library's Oral History project, but his enthusiasm for this book went well beyond his specific responsibilities. He guided me toward rewarding sources, helped arrange interviews, and listened patiently to drafts of early chapters and reports of research findings. The Oral History staff was always patient and kind, and I am grateful to Christie Bourgeois, Gina Gianzero, Theodore Gittinger, Regina Greenwell, Joan Kennedy, and Lois Martin.

In the archives section of the library, I was the beneficiary of the impressive talents of Claudia Anderson, Shellynne Eickhoff, Linda Hanson, David Humphrey, Tina Lawson, and Robert Tissing. I owe a special word of thanks to Nancy Smith of the archives. She was responsible for the opening, reviewing, and handling of Lady Bird Johnson's White House Social Files. To that task she brought superb skills as an archivist, which enabled me to consult relevant materials with an ease that otherwise would have been impossible. Nancy's infectious enthusiasm as an archivist, combined with her imposing mastery of the sources in her charge, made a significant contribution in the book's progress toward completion.

Philip Scott and Frank Wolfe of the library's audio-visual section were most cooperative in helping me select illustrations for the book.

Those who participated in Lady Bird Johnson's beautification endeavors responded with warmth and kindness to my inquiries. Elizabeth C. ("Bess") Abell talked about her years as the White House social secretary during a lunch at her Washington home, which made it easy to understand her success as a hostess and her reputation as a witty and incisive observer of the political scene. Elizabeth S. ("Liz") Carpenter extended her hospitality, helped to set up interviews, commented on portions of an early version of the study, and taught me much about her own unique personality. Cynthia Wilson put original materials at my disposal, gave perceptive critiques of my writing, and was always helpful and kind. Sharon Francis graciously shared her insights with me as well. I am indebted to Mayor Walter E. Washington and his wife for their hospitality in 1984.

Stewart L. Udall gave me an interview during the early stages of the book with characteristic generosity, and he remained interested and responsive as the work went on. Lawrence Halprin was most thoughtful and generous when I visited his office in San Francisco. Ross Netherton gave me valuable help with the issues of billboard regulation. Phillip Tocker shared his expertise on outdoor advertising with me in several long interviews at his home and at the LBJ Library. I learned much from his prodigious command of the workings of the billboard industry.

For other materials provided or interviews given, I am in the debt of Nash Castro, Mr. and Mrs. Willard Deason, Jerry English, Ruth R. Johnson, Katherine Louchheim, George McInturff, Yale Maxon, Elizabeth Rowe, Spencer Smith, Clay Speake, and Senator Robert Stafford.

Librarians and colleagues at other institutions were of crucial aid in helping me gather information. John Simpson at the University of Oregon did thorough research in the Maurine Neuberger Papers. Susan Jackson at the Montana Historical Society provided me with copies of relevant documents from the Lee Metcalf Papers. William Cooper of the University of Kentucky pulled together significant data from the papers of John Sherman Cooper. William H. Wilson provided a careful reading and helpful comments on the chapters regarding billboard regulation. Other scholars were generous as always with comments and suggestions—Thomas H. Appleton, Jr., Robert Dallek, Charles Floyd, Daniel Flores, Gary

Gallagher, Hugh D. Graham, Gene Gressley, Paul Holbo, Herbert F. Margulies, and Ingrid Scobie.

Students at the University of Texas were valued participants in the book during all stages of its preparation. The members of the First Ladies seminar in 1982 and those in the classes on Lyndon Johnson in 1986 and 1987 refined my ideas with their comments and questions. I owe special and individual thanks to Nancy Beck, Christie Bourgeois, Joseph Louis Brown, Catherine Collins, Judi Doyle, Louis Gomolak, Sally H. Graham, Dorothy Lane, John Leffler, Lois Martin, Janet Mezzack, Joseph Monticone, Craig H. Roell, and Stacy Rozek.

Two of my colleagues in the History Department at the University of Texas at Austin were of special assistance as friends and co-workers in the Johnson field. Robert A. Divine asked me to write the essay from which this book grew, and he was both a valued critic and warm supporter of my efforts. Clarence G. Lasby shared the insights he gained from his important research on the history of heart disease and Lyndon Johnson's health, and he gave generously of his wise counsel and insights into modern American history.

Two scholars who read my manuscript for the University Press of Kansas—Martin V. Melosi and Joanna Schneider Zangrando—offered criticisms that made the book better, and I am in their debt. I also wish to acknowledge the professional care shown to my work by the staff of the University Press of Kansas at every stage of the publishing process.

My mother-in-law, Helen Keel, has been an enthusiastic participant in the project since it began. She has been an expert proofreader and has always shared readily her good sense. Karen Gould gave beyond measure of her care, good humor, and affection, qualities that sustained me in the difficult passages of the book's emergence. Her own scholarship was always an example of what I should strive to achieve.

For permission to publish materials that had already appeared in print and for their helpful editorial contribution in the articles themselves, I am indebted to Joseph Epstein and the *American Scholar* for passages that appear in chapter 2 and to Caryn Bernart and William D. Robbins of *Environmental Review* for portions of chapters 7 and 8.

Again, because of the nature of this book, it is important to reiterate that all of the judgments and opinions expressed in this study are mine alone and should not be construed as representing those of the Lyndon Baines Johnson Library, the Johnson family, or Lady Bird Johnson herself.

Nor are any of the people mentioned in these pages responsible for the strengths and weaknesses of this book. Those qualities are the result of my work, for which I am responsible.

15 May 1987   *Lewis L. Gould*
                                                     Austin, Texas

1

Introduction:
Women in Conservation

The dominant role in many evaluations of Lady Bird Johnson's work as a beautifier of the nation's environment is one of skepticism or sarcasm. Writing about Nancy Reagan as First Lady, Garry Wills said in passing that "Ladybird pitted daisies against billboards." In the 1970s, Barbara Howar mused that Mrs. Johnson might have had more impact on her husband and his administration "had she used her influence in matters more crucial than beautifying a troubled nation." Myra MacPherson, in her examination of political marriages, noted that "Lady Bird was caricatured for her accent and her 'beautification' projects" and suggested that she, like other wives of public men, "may have been reaching out" in her own way "to compensate for an incomplete private life."[1]

There have been more favorable appraisals of Lady Bird Johnson's motives and actions. Abigail McCarthy said that beautification, "despite the somewhat gimmicky tone of its title," had a real impact in directing attention to the quality of the environment. Accounts of Lyndon Johnson's presidency are now granting his wife a more central role in the area of conservation. June Sochen's 1973 assessment seems likely to reflect an emerging consensus: "Lady Bird's concern for the natural environment foreshadowed the much publicized ecology movement of the late sixties."[2]

What all these judgments, positive and negative, do not recognize is the tradition of women in the conservation movement during the first half of this century and their equally important part in modern environmentalism. When Lady Bird Johnson launched her campaign for natural beauty in 1964/65, she was taking her place among other female advocates of the environment in the United States who had been a positive force in improving the quality of the nation's life since the late nineteenth century. Her efforts need first to be placed in the context of the feminine conservationists who had preceded her.

1

Though there has been some scholarly inquiry into the extent to which women brought a distinctly female view to the American landscape and environment before 1900, evidence is abundant regarding the results of the campaigns that women organized to beautify cities and towns and to address issues of sanitation and health between 1890 and 1920. What American women did during those decades, said one contemporary writer, represented "an uncharted but highly contagious epidemic of civic righteousness." Through such bodies as the General Federation of Women's Clubs, the Daughters of the American Revolution, the Audubon Society, the National Congress of Mothers, and the Women's National Rivers and Harbors Congress, women sought to teach the lesson that "bad physical environment means bad moral environment." The result would be, added Imogen B. Oakley, "the more civic work, the less need of philanthropy."[3]

In the field of urban sanitation and in the campaigns against pollution, women achieved an extensive involvement and notable success before 1920. Katherine L. Bowlker led the Women's Municipal League of Boston, which sought cleaner streets and the rating of the city's shops and markets for healthful conditions between 1908 and 1915. Caroline Bartlett Crane of Kalamazoo, Michigan, was a Unitarian minister, a champion of meat inspection, and a national advocate of cleaner city streets. After her record in Kalamazoo, Crane became a popular speaker and a well-traveled consultant to cities and states on street-cleaning practices. She called her work "Municipal Housekeeping!" and hoped it would "make women feel their share of responsibility for the cleanliness of their city." In Chicago, Mary McDowell was known as the "Garbage Lady" who taught that "women must come to regard their city as their home." Her City Waste Committee led in 1913 to the establishment of the Chicago City Waste Commission and to the eventual improvement in the city's handling of waste and sewage. The most authoritative student of this aspect of women in urban conservation, Suellen M. Hoy, says that they were "particularly instrumental in making the urban environment a healthier and more comfortable place in which to live."[4]

Women also formed the large membership base of the City Beautiful movement that flourished during the first two decades of the century. "Women must now learn to make of their cities great community homes for all the people," wrote Katherine Bowlker in 1912. Women criticized the proliferation of billboards along city streets and highways, they cleaned up parks and alleys, and they planted trees. "There is no doubt," wrote Mrs. J. J. Levinson of New York, "that women are the natural leaders for the realization of the city beautiful—beautiful not with a lot of expensive cut stone, formidable fences or marble columns, but beautiful with natural parks, with avenues lined with fine trees and with front yards covered with verdure and blossoms, and beautiful with children, healthy mentally and physically." The range of City Beautiful activities was so diverse that towns and cities of every size—from Daytona Beach, Florida, and its Palmetto Club to Roseville, California, and its Women's Improvement Club—saw organized women laboring to upgrade the appearance of their localities. "Hundreds of cities that have distinguished themselves for notable achievements," observed a male writer, "can point to some society or several societies of women that have been the first inspiration to do things."[5]

Most of the women who pursued beautification and sanitation causes during the Progressive Era came from the middle class or the upper class of their communities. They were also usually middle-aged, with their children grown and with time to do good works. Their instincts were conservative, and they did not challenge the assumption that men should be the leaders of the conservation movement. "There is one thing women can bring to a movement of this kind," said a member of the Daughters of the American Revolution at a National Conservation Congress in 1911—namely, "an atmosphere that makes ideas sprout and grow, and ideals expand and develop and take deeper root in the subsoil of the masculine mind." The masculine mind was often unreceptive to these suggestions when they disagreed with what men wished to do. In the fight over the Hetch Hetchy Valley and creating a lake for San Francisco's water supply, the city engineer complained of "short-haired women and long-haired men" who were members of "so-called nature-loving societies" and who resisted his idea of progress. Despite male bias, women in conservation made important contributions to the achievements of this far-reaching social movement. They helped to preserve species of birds from extinction, fought against dams and against forest cutting in the West, and provided mass support for an improved environment.[6]

After World War I, the conservation impulse became less focused and more diffused during the 1920s and 1930s. Nonetheless, women remained a significant component in the areas of natural-resource policy that were active. In the cause of scenic beauty, garden clubs and state roadside councils waged a running battle against the billboard industry, in which women took a highly visible role as advocates of "roadside control." The leading proponent of this program was Elizabeth B. Lawton, who first became angered about outdoor advertising in 1923, when workmen began to dig holes for billboard structures near her home in upstate New York. Opposition to billboards became for her "virtually a life work," and she built a network of garden clubs and roadside councils that struggled to impose restrictions on what Lawton termed a "parasitic industry." One ally, Hilda Fox in Pennsylvania, used publicity tactics to identify "Blot of the Month" billboards in her state.[7]

In Florida between the wars, May Mann Jennings, the wife of a former governor, sought to preserve the Everglades and to beautify highways by means of the Florida Federation of Women's Clubs, the Florida Federation of Garden Clubs, and several state beautification conventions in the 1920s. Jennings argued that it was "vital to the future of the state" that the government have "a definite policy in regard to road beautification and plan for rights-of-way suitable to such need." Jennings also endeavored to save Florida's beaches, and during the 1950s, when she was in her eighties, she labored against litter with Keep America Beautiful. When Jennings died in 1963, a Florida newspaper paid tribute to her decades of conservation activity when it inquired: "Who will step forward to take her spade?"[8]

During the 1930s, Rosalie Edge turned her interests in suffrage politics and the fate of birds into a deepening participation in the affairs of the then male-dominated, stodgy, and ineffective Audubon Society. She launched a sustained assault on the organization's leadership through her Emergency Conservation Committee. In her campaigns against the killing of migrating hawks and in her labors for national parks, she won the grudging admiration of her male adversaries as "the only honest, unselfish, indomitable hellcat in the history of conservation." Later in life she remarked that she wished "more women would work for conservation. Most of the conservation measures are so closely related to business that it is sometimes difficult for men to take a strong stand on the side of the public interest. But women can do it, and they should."[9]

In fact, the presence of women in conservation battles was still evident during the years after World War II. The fight to control billboards went on, with Hilda Fox and Helen Reynolds of California carrying on the work of Elizabeth Lawton. A co-worker later wrote that Reynolds was "the leading spirit and chief dynamo of the California Roadside Council" as its executive vice-president. When national billboard legislation came before Congress in the late 1950s, women from garden clubs and roadside councils were present to testify on behalf of "man's innate desire for beauty in the landscape" and to prevent the new interstate highway system from "becoming a billboard canyon." Similarly, in New York City, women such as Mary Lasker and Anna Rosenberg decided "that the downtown streets of our American cities should be made more attractive and livable—with flowers." Lasker contended that the tulips and daffodils along Park Avenue and other thoroughfares in Manhattan made the city "gay and pleasant, and is good commercially." In 1965, at the White House Conference on Natural Beauty, John E. Terrell, the director of community improvement for Sears, Roebuck, said: "The doers in beautification projects have been and are the women of America. They make up a great many of our volunteer organizations. The National Council of State Garden Clubs, the General Federation of Women's Clubs, etc., have been for decades our 'outdoor housekeepers.' "[10]

By the early 1960s a new feminine voice had been added to the conservation cause, and the work of Rachel L. Carson would help to launch the moden environmental movement. In 1962 Carson published *Silent Spring,* in which she wrote: "Along with the possibility of the extinction of mankind by nuclear war, the central problem of our age has therefore become the contamination of man's total environment with such substances of incredible potential for harm"—namely, pesticides, insecticides, and, especially, DDT. The book was a best seller, and one historian of American conservation has called it the "*Uncle Tom's Cabin* of modern environmentalism."[11]

Carson received her scientific education in the fields of zoology and genetics, and she spent most of her professional life as a biologist and editor in the United States Fish and Wildlife Service. By the early 1950s her book *The Sea Around Us* had achieved record sales, and in 1952 she left governmental service to write independently. About her book, one reader said "I assume from the author's knowledge that he must be a man." In the 1950s she worked on other books while taking care of her mother and a grandnephew, whom she later adopted. When she began to do research on the subject of pesticides, Carson was in her early fifties, a single woman living on the coast of Maine. A friend told her about how a private bird sanctuary had been sprayed with DDT and asked Carson for help. From that request and from her own growing awareness of the pesticide problem, Carson began a book that she first called *Man against the Earth.* The time had come, she believed, to make her views known. "There would be no peace for me if I kept silent."[12]

The book was published as *Silent Spring,* and the ensuing controversy about its merits has not yet abated.[13] Carson's indictment of the pesticide products made by the chemical industry evoked bitter and sometimes unseemly comments from the men who made and used these substances. An agent of the government's pest-control program said: "I thought she was a spinster. What's she so worried about genetics for?" If her book received mixed appraisals within the scientific community, it was more favorably assessed by the general public, governmental officials, and the conservation establishment. Carson was named Conservationist of the Year by the National Wildlife Federation and was given the highest honor of the Audubon Society. Already ill with cancer when she began her book, she struggled on during the early 1960s, in spite of pain and infirmity, to testify before Congress and to spread her findings. "The 'control of nature,' " she wrote at the end of *Silent Spring,* "is a phrase conceived in arrogance, born of the Neanderthal age of biology and philosophy, when it was supposed that nature exists for the convenience of man." Rachel Carson succumbed to cancer in April 1964 at the age of fifty-six.[14]

By assembling a lucid and easily understood indictment of pesticides and the pollution they caused, Rachel Carson focused public concern on whether American technology and its influence on national politics was threatening the general health and safety of the nation's people and the future of the land itself. She did not create the ecological revolution all by herself, but she was a powerful catalyst for change in attitudes toward the environment. She was also the most celebrated and most effective woman in the field of American conservation during this century.

Rachel Carson was not, however, a solitary figure among women in the conservation cause. She had done in her way what women had been seeking to accomplish for seventy-five years, in city parks, along roadsides, and in the wilderness. The derision that Carson encountered from men in industry and science mirrored the treatment that women had often received when they had involved themselves in questions of resource policy. To speak of natural beauty, to worry about the appearance of a roadside or a scenic view, to question the actions of hard-headed and cynical men in making decisions about streams and forests—these were things that women did at the risk of being called sentimental and soft-headed. "Get back in your kitchen, lady, and let me build my road," said one highway engineer to a San Mateo County, California, housewife who was protesting road construction in 1966.[15]

Stephen Fox, a careful student of the American conservation impulse, has correctly recognized that most treatments of the topic, even his own, "have understated the participation of women in the movement." Wives such as Avis De Voto and Anne Morrow Lindbergh seconded the efforts of their husbands in conservation, and other women encouraged men in subtle and private ways. Women, Fox concludes, "deserve a large chapter in conservation history"; and he is exactly right.[16] By the time her husband was elected to the presidency in his own right in 1964, Lady Bird Johnson was ready to make her own powerful addition to the strong record that women had already achieved in conservation. She had come to this point from a girlhood in East Texas and a marriage to the Democratic politician who now gave her the opportunity, as First Lady, to apply on a national scale what had been private feelings for the land and the environment.

2

From East Texas
to the White House

"My interest in beauty dates way, way back to my girlhood," Mrs. Lyndon B. Johnson told an interviewer in 1965. "Some of the most memorable hours I've ever spent have been in the out-of-doors, communing with nature and reveling in the scenic beauty which abounds."[1] Though these comments served at that time to advance the cause of beautification that Mrs. Johnson and President Lyndon B. Johnson had launched a few months earlier, they also reflected the genuine life experience of a woman from East Texas who now intended to use the influence of a First Lady on behalf of the land and its natural beauty. In the family background and the formative years of Claudia Alta Taylor, the shaping effect of an interest in the environment expressed itself in her concern for flowers, trees, and the appearance of the landscape.

She was born on 22 December 1912 in Karnack, Texas, a small town of six hundred people in Harrison County, near the Louisiana border. Her parents, Thomas Jefferson Taylor and Minnie Patillo Taylor, had been married for twelve years; earlier they had had two sons, Tom, Jr., now eleven, and Antonio, who was eight. The little girl acquired her lifelong nickname in infancy. A black cook called her "as purty as a lady bird," referring to the ladybird beetles of the region. "It was very early in life and people began to call her Lady Bird," Tony Taylor later recalled; "the poor gal tried to shake it but in vain."[2]

Her parents had divergent personalities, and the marriage experienced some degree of strain. T. J. Taylor put his robust energies into a flourishing cotton business and general store, where he proclaimed himself a "Dealer in Everything." Moneylending at 10 percent brought him good returns from those who could pay. He foreclosed on those who could not and thus acquired thousands of acres of land during the first twenty years of the century. His daughter grew up in the comfortable life style of the "Brick House," whose two stories made it distinctive in Karnack. T. J. also supplied her with a model of assertive masculinity that later shaped her choice of a husband. Friends remembered Taylor as a "ladies' man," and Claudia said that "he was head man in his tiny world." When she met Lyndon Johnson in 1934, she informed a college friend that "he's the only man I've ever met who is taller than my daddy."[3]

Minnie Taylor conveyed a different set of messages in the almost six years that she spent with Claudia. An aura of culture, eccentricity, and aloofness from the ways of Karnack surrounded Mrs. Taylor. She had her own car and chauffeur, and she owned an ample library of the books that middle-class Americans regarded as classics in those years. Food fads regularly captured her allegiance, and she avoided meat. Veils and turbans provided relief from migraine headaches and gave her a distinctive appearance in little Karnack.[4]

After her native Alabama, East Texas provided a cloistered life for Minnie Taylor, and she escaped it whenever she could. During the opera season she went to Chicago, and there were other visits to sanitariums in the Middle West. Her sons spent time away from home at boarding schools, and it is not clear how often the whole family was together during the years before Claudia was born. Minnie's resistance to life in Karnack may also have expressed itself in her invitations to local blacks to visit her home. She went out in pursuit of black culture in precincts where other whites never ventured. Residents remembered that Minnie organized a drive to protect local quail against excessive hunting. In the last summer of her life, she dabbled in local politics. Women could now vote in the Democratic primary, and Mrs. Taylor campaigned against a candidate who had received a draft deferment. He was, she told other women, "a slacker," and he lost.[5]

Claudia had only fleeting impressions of her mother. She was "tall, graceful, wore white quite a lot, and went around the house in a great rush and loved to read." Her daughter also recalled: "She used to read me Greek, Roman and Teutonic myths. Siegfried was the first romantic hero I ever loved." But their time together was cut short. Minnie's health worsened during the years after Claudia was born, the boys went back to private schools, and their mother's nervous breakdown took her again to a sanitarium in Battle Creek, Michigan. After returning home, at the age of forty-four, Mrs. Taylor became pregnant. In the late summer of 1918, the family dog tripped her on the stairs. The fall caused a miscarriage, blood poisoning, and death in September. Claudia at first was "quite sure" that her mother was "going to come back," but in time, with the resilience of children, "I quit even thinking about it at all."[6]

After a year as a single parent, T. J. Taylor found that he could not raise the little girl by himself, so he accepted the advice of relatives that Effie Patillo, his wife's unmarried sister, should take care of Claudia. Aunt

Effie, "a lovely little spinster lady," came to Karnack and stayed on as a surrogate mother. "She was delicate and airy and very gentle," her niece later said, "and she gave me many fine values which I wouldn't trade for the world." Among these gifts were a feeling for nature and a devotion to reading, akin to that of Claudia's mother. Effie was less successful on the practical side of life, and young Claudia grew up having to depend on herself in school and with friends of her own age she made in both Texas and Alabama.[7]

Much of her time was spent alone out-of-doors. "When I was a little girl," she said in 1976, "I grew up listening to the wind in the pine trees of the East Texas woods." On Caddo Lake, which was very near the Brick House and Karnack, she "loved to paddle in those dark bayous, where time itself seemed ringed round by silence and ancient cypress trees, rich in festoons of Spanish moss. Now and then an alligator would surface like a gnarled log. It was a place for dreams." On her walks she watched the wild flowers and "the daffodils in the yard. When the first one bloomed, I'd have a little ceremony, all by myself, and name it the queen."[8] From her earliest years her relationship with the landscape was comfortable and sympathetic. It was not something to be conquered or transformed; it could be enjoyed for its own sake.

Claudia went to a one-room schoolhouse in Karnack, and she spent time in Alabama through the seventh grade. She then attended school in nearby Jefferson, Texas, for two years. At about this time she "spelled my middle name Byrd, after I had given up ever managing to be called Claudia!" She went to Marshall, the county seat, for high school, where she graduated at fifteen. Fifty years later, she recalled for her classmates "our school newspaper, The Parrot, and my pleasure in seeing my name on a by-line no matter how inconsequential" and the prophecy in the yearbook that she "would become a second Halliburton, poking her nose in unknown places of Asia." Her high grades made her a likely choice as valedictorian or salutatorian, and she feared having to make an address before an audience; but she came in third in the class by one point.[9]

Her father and her Aunt Effie decided that she was too young for college and that she should attend St. Mary's School for Girls in Dallas. "There is a certain stark loneliness in any boarding school," she later remembered, "especially for someone as shy as I." In two years at St. Mary's, she intensified her love of the theater by seeing such plays as "They Knew What They Wanted" and by taking roles in school productions, including an appearance as Sir Toby Belch in *Twelfth Night*. Her shyness eased while she was in Dallas. She read voraciously, walked with her friend Emily Crow, and chafed at the restrictions that a girls' school imposed on its students.[10]

There was never any question about her desire to go to college, and as a testament to her affluence, she flew down to Austin in 1930 to look over the University of Texas. "I fell in love with Austin the first moment that I laid eyes on it and that love has never slackened," she said later. Part of the city's appeal was its natural beauty. "There were Bluebonnets with red poppies and primroses among them," she wrote in 1966, "I remember them like a friend!" Despite the depression, T. J. Taylor provided his daughter with her own car, an old Buick, and charge accounts at Neiman-Marcus; but he refused to let her join Alpha Phi sorority, which she pledged as a freshman.[11]

In four active years at the university, Claudia Taylor revealed her determination to excel and demonstrated a widening range of interests. She had studied history at St. Mary's with Frances Miller, who instilled in Claudia a regard for the subject that put her "on a lifetime program—as a history student." To her history major, she added a concentration in journalism; she also took a course in geology, "which stretched my perspective of the life of man on this physical planet."[12]

A journalism assignment on the poems of John Keats, which she wrote at the Wrenn Library, appeared in the *Daily Texan* in 1933, and she served first as assistant publicity manager and then as publicity manager for the University of Texas Sports Association, which oversaw women's athletics at Texas. In the picture of the association in the *Cactus,* a slim stylish Claudia Taylor joined her fellow members under a spreading tree. At the university, she believed, "all the doors of the world suddenly were swung open to me."[13]

Her social life was more active than later accounts that depict a shy, reclusive coed would suggest. "She always had a lot of young men, you know, beaus in those days," her friend Eugenia ("Gene") Boehringer has said. The men she went out with found, as one of them put it, that "we had been doing what she wanted to do." Claudia made it clear, Emily Crow concluded, that she was "really never serious about anybody who she thought wouldn't amount to something, wouldn't work hard and get there." As evidence of her commitment to succeed, Taylor decided to stay on in Austin after she received her Bachelor of Arts degree, with honors, in June 1933 and secured a journalism degree as well. Newspaper people, she thought, "went more places and met more interesting people, and had more exciting things happen to them." She also studied shorthand. In June 1934 she earned a Bachelor of Journalism degree, again with honors, and prepared to spend a little time in Karnack, supervising the redecoration of the Brick House and seeing her father. But after that she intended to use the teaching certificate that she had also acquired or, as an alternative calling, to try to become a drama critic on a newspaper.[14]

Council of the University of Texas Sports Association in the 1933 yearbook *Cactus*. Back row: Betty Coburn, Rosalie Robinson, Margaret Grasty, Eileen Crain; front row: Claudia Taylor, Florence Parke, Adrian Rose, Elizabeth Bentley, Amanda Gatour (courtesy of Barker Texas History Center, University of Texas at Austin).

Marriage to Lyndon Johnson in November 1934 took her life on a new course. Some of the details of their brief courtship are well known. They met through Gene Boehringer, who was now working for the Texas Railroad Commission. Introduced to Claudia Taylor on August 31, Johnson met her the next morning for breakfast. She said years later: "He was excessively thin but very, very good looking, with lots of black wavy hair, and the most outspoken, straightforward, determined manner I had ever encountered. I knew I had met something remarkable, but I didn't quite know what." Lyndon Johnson left no comparable record of his initial reaction to her. Contemporary photographs show a slender woman, five feet four inches in height, with dark hair and a simple but attractive taste in clothes. She had, as she put it, made peace with her nickname by this time, and her personalized stationery carried the name "Bird Taylor."[15]

They spent the day together, driving around Austin, and then he proposed to her. "I thought it was some kind of a joke," she said later, but something had passed between them. Johnson gave her a book to mark the occasion. Inside the cover of *Nazism: An Assault on Civilization,* he wrote: "To Bird—In the hope within these pages she may realize some entertainment and find reiterated here some of the principles in which she believes and which she has been taught to revere and respect." The book was a serious study of the Germany of Adolf Hitler during its early stages. Such a gift indicated that something more than infatuation and calculation had occurred when Taylor and Johnson first met.[16]

In the week after this encounter, Johnson took her to San Marcos to meet his parents and to the King Ranch in South Texas to see his boss, Congressman Richard M. Kleberg. When Johnson had to go back to Washington, he visited her in Karnack to meet her father. T. J. Taylor was impressed: "You've been bringing home a lot of boys. This one looks like a man." Biographers of Lyndon Johnson focus on Taylor's second sentence. Biographers of Lady Bird Johnson should give equal weight to the first in evaluating her popularity and relative shyness. Her life had not been empty of male friends before she met Johnson, and she compared him both with her other suitors and with her father.[17]

An intense long-distance romance followed, by mail and by telephone. "This morning I'm ambitious, proud, energetic and very madly in love with you," Johnson wrote her on 24 October 1934, and in letter after letter he urged her to agree to marriage. She told him about the books she was reading and about the flowers that she and her friend Dorris Powell had seen as they had walked around Karnack. She was establishing the landscape as her domain and her particular interest. At the old Haggerty place, she said, "There are the tallest magnolias I've ever seen, and great live oaks, and myriads of crepe myrtle, and a carpet of jonquils and flags in the spring." But she also spoke to his personal concerns. "I would hate for you to go into politics," she told him, but then she added immediately, "Don't let me get things any more muddled for you than they are though, dearest!" As she read through old letters in December 1967, it all came back to her about the days when she had been "doing over the Brick House, with all of my days and half of my mind, and with the other half trying to decide whether to marry Lyndon, while we wrote and he telephoned and we headed toward marriage."[18]

Letters and phone calls were not enough for the ardent Lyndon Johnson, so he drove to East Texas in early November to plead his case

Lyndon and Lady Bird Johnson on their honeymoon in Mexico, November 1934.

in person. Bird insisted that she go first to Alabama, to consult with Aunt Effie. Ailing as usual, Effie told her niece to wait. Claudia also shopped for wedding clothes with a friend. When she got back to Karnack, Johnson asked her father for his advice. T. J. Taylor said that Effie had "no right" to ask his daughter "to sacrifice her life and happiness to wait on her." In the end, he told Lyndon, "you and Bird do as you think best." The couple decided to drive the several hundred miles to Austin to see Gene Boehringer. On the way, Johnson persuaded Claudia to get married. He called friends in San Antonio, arranged for a license, and they were married there on the evening of 17 November 1934. "Lyndon and I committed matrimony last night," the new Mrs. Johnson told Boehringer by phone the next morning, before the couple left on a Mexican honeymoon.[19]

Several biographers of Lyndon Johnson, most notably Robert A. Caro, argue that his sudden and passionate pursuit of Claudia Taylor continued a pattern in his life by trying to find a wealthy girl to marry. No doubt Johnson was aware in a general sense that his bride was financially secure in a way that his own family had not been since the early 1920s. It is unlikely, however, that Bird Taylor, who was anything but the dowdy wallflower portrayed in some accounts, would have been taken in by a selfish suitor who had only mercenary motives. Both parties gained from the union. Lyndon Johnson had, as a biographer later put it, found "the one possible wife" for him, but he also "had the ideal helpmate for a going places politician." For Bird Taylor, Lyndon Johnson, a congressional aide with a political future, represented a way out of Karnack and the invisible constraints that restricted intelligent women in Texas during the early 1930s. The bridegroom was clearly going somewhere and seemed likely "to get there." The woman who married him made as shrewd a judgment about his prospects as he made about her family's resources.[20]

During the early years of the marriage, Mrs. Lyndon Johnson adjusted to the habits and demands of a hard-driving, self-centered husband.* He criticized her taste in clothes, often in front of their friends, and he used

---

*What to call Lyndon Johnson's wife after her marriage troubled her and to a degree must confront any student of her life. Her given name, Claudia, was almost never used. A few intimate friends addressed her as Bird. Once she became First Lady, the title Lady Bird was often employed by those who did not know her well. Even those who now work with her closely call her Mrs. Johnson. In the ensuing narrative, I will use the terms Lady Bird Johnson and Mrs. Johnson interchangeably, reflecting the usage she seems to prefer. By describing her as Mrs. Johnson, there is the problem of defining her in terms of her husband, but the wishes of the person involved ought to be the decisive element in this matter.

to say to her, "You don't sell for what you're worth." She had to bring him breakfast in bed, and he did little of the traveling, sightseeing, or reading that they had discussed while courting. There were times when his abrasive tongue and manner toward her embarrassed onlookers. Because the marriage endured for almost four decades, however, excessive emphasis on the inevitable strains in the relationship overlooks a reality of affection and respect to which both Johnsons contributed.[21]

Yet Lyndon Johnson has a reputation as a man who was, at intervals during his marriage, unfaithful to his wife. He is supposed to have had an affair with Alice Glass Marsh between 1938 and 1941; and one other involvement is depicted as having shaped his presidential plans in 1960.[22] Talk about additional relationships with the wives of aides and friends drifts across his life at other times. Extramarital romances are easy to believe but, by their nature, hard to document. Mrs. Johnson seems to have taken the position that her husband's dalliances, if any, were inherently temporary. Patience and calm were the best answer to any rival. "In her realm," Nancy Dickerson observed, "she had no peer; she knew it, he knew it, and so did everybody else." How long it took and how painful a process it was to reach this degree of self-assurance no one but Lady Bird Johnson will ever know. In the absence of credible documentation, such matters are perhaps best left to the "confidential sources" and "anonymous informants" from whence they usually come. The evolution of Mrs. Johnson's character as a wife and public figure emerges clearly enough without them.[23]

After their honeymoon in Mexico, the Johnsons lived in a Washington apartment throughout the first half of 1935. Then in the summer, Lyndon was offered the position of Texas administrator for the National Youth Administration (NYA). His wife was in Karnack when he called her to ask, "How would you like to live in Austin?" It was as if he had said, she recalled, "How would you like to go to Heaven?" They spent nearly two years in Austin for the NYA. One of the important contributions of Johnson's tenure was a system of roadside parks. Thirty years later he said that the idea was a joint inspiration with his wife. Other accounts place the credit with Gladys Montgomery, the wife of a University of Texas professor. Mrs. Johnson, who told her husband and friends the names of trees and flowers as they drove through Texas, probably made some contribution to the conception of the program. "Not many things have ever meant so much to us as the NYA," she believed, "brief though it was."[24]

In February 1937 the congressman from the Tenth District, James P. Buchanan, died of a heart attack, and Lyndon Johnson wanted to run in the special election to be held in early April. Among the central problems, and there were many with his candidacy, was the need for enough money to launch the campaign until fund raising from other sources could begin. After talking with former state senator Alvin J. Wirtz, one of her husband's mentors, Lady Bird Johnson, convinced that Lyndon had a chance to win in the crowded field, called her father and arranged to obtain ten thousand dollars of her share of her mother's estate over that weekend. In the campaign itself, she largely played the supporting role that custom still demanded of political wives and "kept the home fires burning." On election day, Lyndon was in the hospital with appendicitis, and she occupied her time, as he suggested, "by taking friends and kinfolks and homebound elderly citizens to the polls and telephoning." Johnson defeated his opponents "and that ushered in a new chapter in our lives."[25]

Over the next four years, Lyndon poured his energies into work for the Tenth District and into the pursuit of his ambition for higher political office. For his wife, "the biggest word in my vocabulary, the most important was 'constituency,' which one spelled in capitals." She took visitors from the Tenth District around to the tourist attractions of Washington, "and I spent my hours going to innumerable weddings, gatherings, and in the first year or so paying calls." Friends recalled Mrs. Johnson as "a sweet-looking, dark-haired, dark-eyed girl who seemed to adore her husband and let him have the floor." The Johnsons wanted to have children, but Mrs. Johnson suffered several miscarriages in the prewar period. The picture of her as a "drab" person afflicted with "terrible shyness" is overdrawn and misleading in regard to the part that she played in Lyndon Johnson's life. Despite Lyndon's flirtations and his demanding political quest, Lady Bird Johnson was not an anomaly in his career; she was a central aspect of it.[26]

When Johnson ran for the Senate in 1941, his wife accompanied him on the campaign trail and took home movies that recorded the pageantry of her husband's well-financed canvass. Despite support from President Franklin D. Roosevelt and despite a statewide effort, Lyndon lost narrowly to Governor W. Lee ("Pappy") O'Daniel. The Johnsons returned to Washington in the autumn of 1941 and soon found their lives overtaken by the march of impending war. Soon after Pearl Harbor, Lyndon Johnson went on active duty as a naval-reserve officer. In the next several months, the congressman lobbied for an assignment in the war zone, while his wife assisted with the operation of his Washington office. By late April 1942, Commander Johnson was on his way to the South Pacific.[27]

Lady Bird Johnson took over the work at the capital that her husband had left. "The office is so stimulating and interesting," she said on March 3, "that I 'graduated myself' from business school and now get down here about eight-thirty every morning and stay until our Lyndon Johnson quitting time—which is when everything is done." She dealt with an array of problems—the status of the city abattoir in Austin, the location of an Army Air Support Command there as well, and the impact of rationing and housing policies in the district. Always there were the lists of people to write, congratulating them on weddings, graduations, or local honors and, in regard to the war, providing news about heroism, wounds, and death. During these months, Lady Bird Johnson received a political education. She wrote to a friend that she had learned more in three months than in four years in college.[28]

Only a few of her letters to her husband are available. They reveal her energy and commitment to the work she had taken on and the affection of a couple separated by war. "Never do I seem to catch up!" she told him, "There are always things left over to talk to you about." In return, he urged her, in the marginal notes that he scribbled on her letters, to "Write Write Long Long Letters." The men around Johnson conveyed to him their high opinion of her contribution. "She is doing a bang up good job," J. J. ("Jake") Pickle wrote to him from Austin, "and the people are beginning to realize it." Looking back on the whole experience, she recalled, "It gave me a sense of, sort of reassurance about myself because I finally emerged thinking that—well, I could make a living for myself."[29]

Her own views on issues, and some wry humor, also emerged as the days passed. "When I think of Lyndon's being captured by the Japs," she wrote to Emily Crow in May 1942, "I think of O'Henry's 'Ransom of Red Chief.' " To another correspondent she remarked that "China must be kept free because it offers one of the best bases of operations for the United Nations." She was also involved in deciding whether Lyndon should enter the Senate primary against O'Daniel, who was now seeking a full six-year term. Her judgment was that her husband should opt for reelection to the House, because it was unlikely that he would defeat the popular O'Daniel. Other friends of Johnson's agreed, and they helped her secure the petitions that put the congressman on the primary ballot without opposition. By mid July, Johnson had returned from the South Pacific on what his wife then described as "the grandest day of my life." She also said to the new bride of an old Johnson friend, somewhat in jest: "Isn't housekeeping fun. It is my all time favorite of jobs and I yearn to get back to figuring on menus, bargains at the grocery, and the prettiest combinations of linens and china, instead of the vagaries and shortcomings of the OPA, ODT, and WPB."[30]

Actually, Lady Bird Johnson had begun to assume a more active role in her husband's career. Jonathan Daniels, an aide to the president, noted in his diary for 10 October 1942: "Lyndon Johnson's wife is the sharp-eyed type who looks at every piece of furniture in the house, knows its period and design—though sometimes she is wrong. She is confident that her husband is going places and in her head she is furnishing the mansions of his future." After Lyndon returned from the war, she persuaded him that they should use money that she was receiving from her inheritance to buy a house in Washington. When he imperiled the sale by dickering about the price, she erupted before a startled Lyndon and John B. Connally, Jr.: "I want that house! Every woman wants a home of her own. I've lived out of a suitcase ever since we've been married. I have no home to look forward to. I have no children to look forward to, and I have nothing to look forward to but another election." As she left the room, Johnson asked Connally: "What should I do?" Connally's answer was, "I'd buy the house."[31]

Once the home was acquired, she turned with particular pleasure to the yard and her garden. "The sunshine was so inviting," she wrote to friends in March 1943, "that I spent a couple of more enthusiastic than useful hours digging in my flower garden." Eventually the garden became "quite a remarkable" one, "about 30 by 30 in the backyard of my little house," where she raised zinnias and peonies. She took friends to the Botanical Gardens and carefully noted the periods of each year when the cherry blossoms and the tulips came out in Washington. As she drove back and forth from Washington in the prewar years and later after the war had ended, she also marked the changes in the landscape, the junkyards, the billboards, and the impact of development on natural beauty. "I loved the trips across the country to Washington," she later said, "and I never got too many of them."[32]

By the spring of 1943, however, Lady Bird Johnson had commenced another project, which took her back to Austin regularly and also stretched her abilities. The Johnsons bought radio station KTBC in Austin, from which grew an extensive investment in radio and television stations in Texas over the next twenty years. The impulse that put the Johnsons into this new venture arose from the uncertainties of the political profession. "Both Lyndon and I were interested in having a little piece of the communications world," she said, and they explored the possibility of acquiring a country newspaper in East Texas. Then the opportunity arose to purchase the Austin station. "I had a degree in journalism and we knew a lot of folks in the business. It just held an attraction for us, and we thought it was a coming industry."[33]

The place of KTBC in the life of the Johnsons remains controversial and murky. Corporate records are not now available, and the issue of the extent to which Lyndon Johnson employed his political influence to achieve success in broadcasting still arouses passions among his biographers. During the 1960s it was widely believed that "the Senate Majority Leader could make a success of a television station in the Gobi Desert," and there is evidence that Johnson knew precisely how to exert pressure in order to produce advertising revenues. Corporate sponsors found it advantageous, for example, to buy time on Johnson's radio station, even though the size of the Austin market, in comparison to other cities, was still relatively modest.[34]

The issues for those who are interested in Lady Bird Johnson is the actual extent of her participation in the management of these media holdings from 1943 onward. All sources agree that her inheritance was crucial in providing the money to acquire KTBC in early 1943. In a draft of a radio address for the 1946 Democratic primary campaign, in words that were prepared for her to deliver, she says that she had received about $40,000 from her Uncle Claude Patillo and had also secured a loan of $40,500 from her Aunt Effie. From that total of $80,500, she paid for a house that they bought in Austin, the house in Washington, and the $17,500 that was required to buy KTBC in January 1943. Her application to the Federal Communications Commission (FCC) listed her net worth at $64,332, and a supporting document noted that "she has recently served approximately a year as the secretary for the Congressman." In one sense, of course, Mrs. Johnson clearly did not have the extensive background in business to manage a radio station, but few women in the 1940s would have qualified for a license under such criteria. On its merits, it would have been striking had the license been refused. Her husband's political standing with the Roosevelt administration explains the speed with which the proposal went through. It does not account for the approval itself. And while the license laid the basis for the Johnsons' fortune, it did not in itself guarantee prosperity. The Johnsons still had to make a success of what an employee dubbed "a very run-down station."[35]

Lyndon told his wife, "You have to go down there and take that place over." When she walked into the station, two blocks off Congress Avenue, she found "that the place was *real* dirty. I mean cobwebs on the windows and the floor was grimy." Employees remembered that she scrubbed the floor herself. More important, she brought in new staff members, including Harfield Weedin, to manage the station first, later Pat Adelman, and finally Jesse C. Kellam. She set about paying off old bills and working through the accounts receivable. The station was in the red during the first half of 1943, and Lyndon complained to a family friend in May that "the radio station is pulling me down for the third time." Mrs. Johnson's efforts enabled the station to be "in the black in August to the tune of eighteen dollars," and from then on the station was consistently profitable.[36]

The key to its initial success was her ability to persuade the Federal Communications Commission to grant KTBC the right to broadcast twenty-four hours a day and to increase its transmitting power to one thousand watts. She also obtained network affiliation with the Columbia Broadcasting System, beginning long friendships with William S. Paley and Frank Stanton. Mrs. Johnson received detailed weekly reports about the station's progress, along with monthly budgets, when she was back in Washington. Associates reported that she was, on the business side, "any man's equal; she reads a balance sheet like most women examine a piece of cloth." If the chauvinism implicit in such judgments ever bothered her, she did not show it. When she moved into the White House and had to relinquish her interest in the station and her other media properties, she wrote to Jesse Kellam in nostalgic terms about ending her formal connection with KTBC: "Trading in a twenty-two year love and work for the months that lie ahead brought a torrent of thoughts and emotions in its wake. . . . How I shall miss the plans, the people—even the problems—the affiliates conventions, yes, even the thick Saturday morning reports, the Christmas party, and perhaps even more, the summer parties with everybody's children."[37]

By 1952 the Johnsons had applied for a television-station license in Austin, and their application showed that KTBC was worth almost half a million dollars. The FCC granted the license, and the station enjoyed a monopoly of television coverage in the Austin area for more than a decade. During this same period the holdings of the Johnsons included stations in Waco and Corpus Christi, as well as other properties in land and businesses in the Austin area amounting to more than $10 million. No precise record is available as to how much Mrs. Johnson's business sense, compared with her husband's political clout, made possible such an impressive growth. That they were a partnership in the most meaningful and profitable sense is undeniable.[38]

During the first decade of their marriage, the Johnsons tried unsuccessfully to have children, but in March 1944 their first daughter was born. "I wanted to name her Lady Bird," Lyndon told one of his friends, "but her mother preferred Lynda Bird, and since she is the boss I had to compromise." Mrs. Johnson was reported to be seriously ill in the summer of 1945, and she lost a baby because of a tubal pregnancy in

1946. A year later, however, in July 1947, the Johnsons had their second daughter, Lucy Baines Johnson.[39]

During the latter part of the 1940s, Mrs. Johnson also became more centrally involved with her husband's political career. Hardy Hollers, Lyndon's opponent in the 1946 Democratic primary campaign for the House, made the Johnson family's finances a crucial theme in his race. So bitter did the contest become that the Johnson camp considered having Mrs. Johnson rebut the allegations in a radio address of her own. The speech writers wanted her to say that "I have been happy in the role of housewife trying to keep a home for him while he battled on the stormy seas of politics." The text then went over her inheritance in detail and also disputed the charge that her father's construction company had profited from contracts that Lyndon had directed to it. Apparently, in the end, the speech did not need to be given. On election day, Johnson overwhelmed Hollers by more than two to one. By raising the issue of the Johnsons' finances, the 1946 campaign left the congressman with a political stigma from which he never entirely escaped.[40]

Two years later, in Lyndon's Senate race against Coke Stevenson, Mrs. Johnson was an even more active participant in the campaign. She helped Marietta Brooks organize the Women's Division, and they toured the state together, meeting groups of women. One newspaper called the candidate's wife "An Able Vote-Getter," though the reporter found her "a rather modest woman" who "used to even be on the shy side." Lyndon ran second to Stevenson in the first primary, and the two men fought out the runoff in August 1948. A special session of Congress took Johnson out of the state, and his wife wrote to friends in his absence to convey "our deep appreciation for your faithful and untiring work in his behalf" and to urge them to get out the vote in the next round. The night before the election, Lady Bird Johnson rode to San Antonio to join Lyndon. The car in which she was riding had two accidents, but despite the resulting bruises, she went on to San Antonio, "made a fine speech," and then returned to Austin, where she telephoned voters throughout election day. The results gave Johnson a controversial and contested eighty-seven-vote victory, which kept the Johnsons in court and in suspense until the new senator took the oath in January 1949. "The 1948 campaign was one that just didn't end," Lady Bird Johnson later said, "it just went on and on."[41]

Election to the Senate made Lyndon Johnson a national figure. For his wife the most tangible impact of his new position came when he maneuvered to acquire the Martin place from his aunt. Located on the Pedernales River between Johnson City and Fredricksburg, the property was in dilapidated condition, and Lady Bird Johnson responded with a reaction of "complete withdrawal" when she saw it. "I was aghast! How can you *possibly* do this to me?" she asked him. In the end her husband's enthusiasm and the pull of the landscape of the Hill Country overcame her qualms: "I gradually began to get wrapped up in it myself. I always have loved living on the land. It was just that I had grown up in such a completely different sort of land."[42]

While redecorating the inside of the house, she also spread seventy-five pounds of bluebonnet seeds on both sides of the river. She also put in other wild-flower seeds and asked advice from seed dealers about the best time to plant—"whether or not to scratch the surface of the ground with a cultivator, water it well beforehand, simply broadcast them in among the grass or whatever." She reported "very minimum results from the considerable amounts I have planted in the past," and she wondered whether "it's a lost cause to try to plant wildflower seeds in an area where either cattle or sheep occasionally graze?" As the 1950s unfolded, the ranch frequently became a place for their guests, entertainment, and "a good visit" with friends from everywhere. It served these important purposes because Mrs. Johnson had applied the talent she had developed as a gardener and her affinity for the landscape to improve the ranch that her husband had purchased.[43]

In the summer of 1955, Lyndon Johnson suffered a serious heart attack. A heavy smoker, Johnson drove himself hard, ate irregularly, and had gained forty pounds above his optimal weight. On July 2, while driving to the home of George Brown in Virginia, he experienced severe chest pains, which doctors quickly diagnosed as a heart attack. Mrs. Johnson received a phone call that told her: "Lyndon's on his way to Bethesda Naval Hospital in an ambulance. Our local doctor thinks it may be a heart attack." She was at the hospital when he arrived, and he said to her: "And you stay here. I'd rather fight with you beside me. I'm sure we'll lick this." She remained at the hospital until he was released five weeks later. As he recovered, Mrs. Johnson grappled with "the difficulties of breaking the smoking habit and going on this dismal low-calorie/low fat diet." Lyndon got his weight back down to 180 pounds, and in the process she dropped 14 pounds herself.[44]

She also sought to make changes in his life style. "My husband was always a taut, driving perfectionist who lived with constant tension," she said in 1956; and she hoped that the needed rest might impel him to find other sources of interest and diversion. One positive result of his illness, she wrote to Senator Styles Bridges, might be "his discovery of the very real pleasure there is in reading books." Her hopes that he might change in this direction were disappointed despite public assurances to the contrary. As she said to Thomas G. Corcoran, a Washington lawyer and friend since the 1930s, in a moment of candor, Lyndon "has no natural cultural bent," though she hoped he might listen to some music as he recuperated. The heart attack did not change his intellectual habits, but it did alter their mutual sensitivity about his health. As the diary she kept during the presidency indicates, she was conscious of his medical condition and vigilant about it throughout the rest of their life together.[45]

By early 1956, Lyndon had resumed his Senate duties and had begun to be talked about as a presidential or vice-presidential hopeful. At the Democratic National Convention in August 1956 he made an abortive attempt to stop Adlai E. Stevenson's candidacy. Mrs. Johnson laughed when reporters asked her how she would feel about being First Lady. "That's a long way into the distant future in that vast convention of folks," she responded, and she was equally skeptical about her husband's chances against Stevenson: "I no more expect it to happen than I do to walk out that door and have lightning strike me."[46]

Nineteen fifty-six was not Johnson's year, but the prospect of national office and future campaigning for them was more likely as the decade ended. Mrs. Johnson enrolled in a formal public-speaking course at the Capital Speakers Club in 1959. The experience helped to relieve some of her anxieties about speaking in public as she learned to talk more slowly and to pitch her voice lower. By the spring of 1960 she was able to introduce her husband to a women's conference as "an exciting man to live with; an exhausting man to keep up with; a man who has worn well in the twenty-five years we have been together." Speaking still made her nervous, and "her hands shook so she could barely hold her speech notes" before a campaign appearance in October 1960. Continued practice and her own determination had enabled her to develop a comfortable and effective style of public speaking by the time she came to the White House in 1963.[47]

In 1960, Lyndon Johnson made another try for the presidency. Mrs. Johnson prepared to campaign for him and to set up a women's organization for his run at the nomination. The senator waited until just before the Democratic National Convention in July 1960 to make a formal announcement of his candidacy. His passivity, which allowed John F. Kennedy to build up a large lead, may have stemmed from personal considerations as much as from a strategy of emphasizing his Senate duties and avoiding the primaries. Aides later recalled his infatuation for a woman who was working in his office and intimated that he had given thought to breaking up his marriage. In any case, the majority leader's indecisive course kept his wife limited to making occasional public comments about him before the party assembled in Los Angeles. Johnson's candidacy then fell before the better-organized and nationally based Kennedy campaign on the first ballot. Mrs. Johnson told the press that while "Lyndon would have made a noble President," she had "a sizable feeling of relief" at the result.[48]

The events of the next two days, which involved Johnson's being selected as Kennedy's running mate, remain confused about the details of how the individual actors behaved. What is striking about Mrs. Johnson is her closeness to the center of her husband's decision about accepting a place on the ticket. She took the first phone call from Kennedy on Thursday morning July 14, when he asked for a meeting with Johnson. "I know he's going to offer the Vice Presidency, and I hope you won't take it," she said. Mrs. Johnson was there when Philip Graham, publisher of the *Washington Post*, arrived. "Lady Bird tried to leave," Graham recalled in a famous memorandum about the vice-presidential decision, but "Johnson and I lunged after her, saying she was needed on this one." She advised Lyndon not to see Robert F. Kennedy, who was then talking in another room with Sam Rayburn; she advised him to speak only to the nominee. When the confusion worked itself out and Johnson finally made a statement to the press that he would accept the second spot on the ticket, he and his wife stood there, in Graham's words, "looking as though they had just survived an airplane crash." That impression probably related more to the tumult of the occasion than to an earlier sense on her part that Lyndon should not take the vice-presidency. She posed the choice that they had both confronted when she said later, in a characteristically lucid way, "it was not a spot he would have sought; he had just not thought about it, but the way it was put to him—that the Party needed him—struck a responsive chord."[49]

In the ensuing campaign, Lady Bird Johnson was the most visible woman that the Democrats put before the voters. Jacqueline Kennedy was pregnant and was therefore little disposed to conduct an active canvass. Mrs. Johnson announced her plans to tour Texas in late August with Eunice Shriver (Kennedy's sister) and Ethel Kennedy (Robert Kennedy's wife). When a questioner at the press conference raised the issue of opposition to Kennedy's Catholicism in Texas, Mrs. Johnson replied: "There is such a thing as a religious issue. That we all know. But the more deeply one reads the Bible, the more fair one is going to be. And so, I do not believe it will be a decisive issue in our State." She also deftly answered a probe about medical care for the elderly. Her father's private resources had enabled him to afford the nursing care that an eighty-six-year-old man required; people without that advantage would confront "financial ruin" when illness came. To another inquiry about Mrs. Kennedy's hair style, the crisp response was: "I think it's more important what's inside the head than what's outside."[50]

Lady Bird Johnson emerged as a major force in the Democratic effort in 1960. The wife of the vice-presidential candidate became central in the appeal to southern voters, whose Democratic allegiance had slipped during the Eisenhower years. She crisscrossed the region in tours that represented the largest part of the 35,000 miles she traveled in all. "Campaigning might be tiring, if it weren't so much fun," she said in Charlotte, North Carolina. She urged voters in Corpus Christi, Texas, to do "five things" for her husband and the Democrats: "He wants you to write a card to all your kinfolks, have a coffee or tea party for your friends, phone ten people and ask each of them to phone ten more, write a letter to the editor of your newspaper, and drive a full car to the polls on November eighth." Campaigning in a red dress, she used chartered planes to reach the rallies, but she was most in her element on the whistle-stop tours of "cold hotcakes and early sunrises" through Alabama and the Deep South. When she traveled with Lyndon, she reminded him if he was speaking too long, and she mended his split pants in Albuquerque after he rode a horse in a parade.[51]

Two events punctuated the campaign. T. J. Taylor, who had been ill for some time, began to fail in late September, and Mrs. Johnson interrupted her schedule in order to go to Marshall. Three weeks later his condition again worsened, and she returned to his hospital. He died on 22 October 1960. After the funeral she went back to the hustings, but she retained a keen interest in her hometown, her father's house, and the life he had made in Karnack.[52]

Four days before the voting, the Johnsons were to address a luncheon of Democrats at the Adolphus Hotel in Dallas. As their motorcade reached the downtown area, it encountered several thousand Republican partisans who had just seen Richard M. Nixon off at the airport. The sign-waving crowd forced the Johnsons to leave their car at the Baker Hotel, on the other side of Commerce Street. Inside the Baker the sound of the chanting mob could still be heard, and the couple decided that they had to go back across to the Adolphus, lest the Republicans claim success for their intimidation tactics.[53]

It was a difficult moment. Mrs. Johnson was spit upon, and one member of the crowd hit her with a sign. "I just had to keep on walking and suppress all emotions," she recalled, "and be just like Marie Antoinette in the tumbrel." One witness said that Mrs. Johnson nearly lost her temper and tried to answer one of the "young, Junior League types," but Lyndon "put his hand over her mouth and stopped that and brought her right along." His height enabled him to see above the crowd; "she could only see up." The episode backfired on the Republicans and may have added to the narrow victory that put Texas in the Democratic column. Robert F. Kennedy put Mrs. Johnson's contributions to the campaign in a larger context, in a way that also diminished her husband's role on the ticket: "Lady Bird carried Texas for us."[54]

The three years that Lady Bird Johnson spent as Second Lady proved to be useful preparation for the duties she assumed after November 1963. Her goal was "helping Lyndon all I can, helping Mrs. Kennedy whenever she needs me, and becoming a more alive me." Mrs. Kennedy regarded the ceremonial duties of a president's wife as burdens that she discharged when it suited her other priorities. As a result, Mrs. Johnson often found herself called upon as a surrogate for the First Lady. She became, as one journalist said, "Washington's No. 1 pinch hitter." She greeted women delegates from the United Nations in December 1961, accepted an Emmy award for Mrs. Kennedy in May 1962, and stood in for her in April 1963 at a luncheon of the Senate Ladies Red Cross group. "I don't know how we could get along without Lady Bird," said one White House aide in these years.[55]

To meet the increased responsibilities of the vice-presidency, the Johnsons moved to a larger house that they had purchased from the perennial Washington hostess Perle Mesta. "The Elms" had sufficient space for entertaining and an office for Mrs. Johnson. She also acquired the beginnings of a personal staff. Bess Abell, the daughter of Senator Earle C. Clements of Kentucky, was her secretary, and Elizabeth ("Liz") Carpenter handled press relations. The two women made an effective team. Abell was quiet and understated, with a dry wit and a close knowledge of the Washington scene. A graduate of the University of Texas like her employer, Carpenter supplied an infectious ebullience that endeared her to the reporters who covered Mrs. Johnson. She also understood, from her own background as a Washington journalist, about deadlines, access, and candor.[56]

The foreign travel and the ceremonial duties that fell to her husband during this period of his political eclipse as vice-president offered Mrs. Johnson an impressive exposure to new cultural and public experiences. They went to Senegal in April 1961, and in her account of the trip, she picked out as the symbol of that African nation "the strange but fascinating baobab tree which stands sturdily all over the landscape and in the lives of the people." That same spring the Johnsons traveled to six Asian nations, and the flowers that she saw remained a vivid memory: "Exquisite orange trees full of blossoms greeted us first at Hawaii and kept appearing along the way; only when we got to Pakistan, with the countryside and climate not unlike Texas, did the lowly zinnia and petunia show up." In Pakistan they also met Bashir Ahmad, a camel driver, who came to Washington later in 1961 as their guest and whom Mrs. Johnson entertained with characteristic dignity and respect.[57]

Other vice-presidential trips included a tour of the Mediterranean and the Middle East in the late summer of 1962 and a final trip to Scandinavia in September 1963. "We tromped through the forests of Sweden and Finland, picking lingonberries," Mrs. Johnson reported. "As I travel around the world with Lyndon," she told one interviewer, "I often think of that funny old sign on my daddy's store, 'Thomas Jefferson Taylor, Dealer in Everything.' Now science and time and necessity have propelled the United States to be the general store for the world, dealers in everything. Most of all, merchants for a better way of life, I hope."[58]

At home, Lady Bird Johnson was finding her own voice and role in Washington. She saw to it that women in the labor movement, who were visiting the city for a strategy conference in January 1962, had an entertaining tea at the Elms, including a talk from the vice-president. In one of her speeches she argued: "American women are undergoing a great revolution in our lifetime. We have learned to master dishwashers, typewriters and voting machines with reasonable aplomb. We must now try to make our laws catch up with what has happened to us as we bounce in and out of the labor market and raise a family." In the pocket notebook that she carried during those years, "I make little lists and scratch 'em off" as she moved through days as varied as a visit to a Peace Corps center in Oklahoma, a ground-breaking ceremony for a public-works facility in West Virginia, or the Spanish lessons that she was taking.[59]

Gradually the public realized that the vice-president's wife was a singular individual. The chairman of the Indiana Public Service Commission, publicly announcing his criteria for a secretary, included "the charm of Lady Bird Johnson" among his desired specifications. The *Washington Post* called her "a lady of exceptional grace" who had rendered "unstinting and indefatigable public service." As the fall of 1963 began, she told columnist Ruth Montgomery that she relished her role as Second Lady: "I'd be a vegetable if I didn't! I have an omnivorous curiosity about the wide, wide world, and Lyndon's position has given me an unparalleled opportunity to be exposed to it both at home and abroad."[60]

The woman who was preparing to welcome President and Mrs. Kennedy to the LBJ Ranch in November 1963 had come a long distance from the little girl who had walked in the forests near Caddo Lake four decades earlier. Through the years of college and early marriage, motherhood and political campaigns, business and notoriety, she had maintained her own identity against what Anne Morrow Lindbergh called, in a phrase that Lady Bird Johnson quoted, "the fragmentation of self."[61] Whereas her husband never read books, she was bookish, almost intellectual. He had no time for the theater; she loved Broadway and saw plays alone in Washington. Lyndon's volatility made working for him alternately a stimulus and an ordeal. Her calmness soothed pained feelings and eased the hurts that he inflicted. They were a team of two strong individuals, and they were now about to become among the most famous people in the world.

In the autumn of 1963, Lady Bird Johnson was not yet an active conservationist. The potential existed, however, for her interest in public life to have that emphasis. She later wrote that she was "an 'enjoyer,' somebody who gets pleasure from the beauty around me. It had not yet occurred to me that I could *do* anything about making sure that the beauty remained here for our children and our grandchildren or about trying to see that there was even more of the beauty, but that would come."[62] The process began during the first full year of Lyndon Johnson's presidency, when his wife's lifelong sensitivity to the landscape interacted with the "New Conservation" policies that foreshadowed the emergence of environmentalism during the 1960s.

3

Becoming First Lady

The events of 22 November 1963 and the circumstances under which the Johnsons came to the White House were so traumatic that consideration about what the president's wife might do publicly as First Lady was deferred in the weeks after John F. Kennedy was killed. "Oh, Mrs. Kennedy," Mrs. Johnson said on the plane that flew back from Dallas, "you know we never even wanted to be Vice President and now, dear God, it's come to this." Like other Americans on that grim weekend, Mrs. Johnson had the sense "that I was moving, step by step, through a Greek tragedy" as the funeral procession made its way through the streets of Washington.[1]

Amidst the sad mood of those days, the relentless pressure of the presidency gave Mrs. Johnson things to do for her husband. She saw Katharine Graham, publisher of the *Washington Post,* on November 23, at the president's request. By Tuesday, 26 November, the new First Lady had confronted other choices that would affect the White House years ahead. After she and Mrs. Kennedy had met that afternoon, reporters wanted to know when the Johnsons would move in and when Mrs. Kennedy would leave. The First Lady issued a statement: "I would to God I could serve Mrs. Kennedy's comfort; I can at least serve her convenience." By 7 December 1963 the move to the White House had taken place, and she entered it with the Johnsons' favorite picture of Sam Rayburn in hand.[2]

In her little notebook, the First Lady wrote: "Sell House, arrange for own household staff, sell station—Leonard Marks, get some one to brief me on so much." Methodically, she moved through that agenda. The Elms was sold, her television interests were placed in a blind trust, and advice was sought from Mrs. Kennedy's former social secretary, Letitia ("Tish") Baldridge, and numerous others. Liz Carpenter became the director of Mrs. Johnson's staff and the first officially designated press secretary to the First Lady. Bess Abell continued as the social secretary.[3]

29

Lady Bird Johnson's background in journalism, television, and politics gave her an acute sensitivity to the needs of the working press. She also understood that the women journalists who covered the First Lady had the power to define the success or the failure of the programs that she might pursue. The appointment of Carpenter, a Washington newswoman, underscored Mrs. Johnson's perception that press relations would be central to her success. It was "a whole new adjustment for me—having every move watched and covered and considered news," but she adapted readily to the presence of reporters and the trappings of celebrity that accompanied the First Lady. "She knew the language of the trade," Liz Carpenter recalled, "the difference between an A.M. and P.M. deadline, that it is better to be accessible than evasive." Mrs. Johnson also knew about the growing influence of television. Network news programs had gone from fifteen minutes to half an hour in the autumn of 1963, and their cameras and crews were more visible components of the White House scene as coverage of the presidency expanded. Simone Poulain joined Liz Carpenter's operation to handle the First Lady's relations with television.[4]

After Eleanor Roosevelt left the White House in April 1945, her immediate successors as First Lady had abandoned Mrs. Roosevelt's practice of holding regular news conferences for the women reporters who were assigned to the president's wife. Mrs. Johnson had no inclination to return to the Roosevelt example. She met with the press corps on 10 January 1964 for tea, "to set the tenor of press conferences—not as conferences but informal meetings—as an invitation to a relaxed and pleasant atmosphere with an opportunity to meet somebody else who was newsworthy." This approach evolved into "Women Doer" luncheons, where the guests heard an active woman discuss public questions, with one or more press representatives in attendance.[5]

The new First Lady enjoyed a good press almost from her earliest days in the White House. "She treated reporters with warmth and respect," Liz Carpenter said, and the female press contingent that reported on the First Lady during those years responded in kind. Unlike her husband, she paid little attention to what was written about her. Nan Robertson once remarked that Mrs. Johnson had "an instinctive sense of public relations polished during nearly 28 years of public life. . . . She is sympathetic to reporters' problems and needs." The frequent trips that she made helped to create a rapport with the newswomen who accompanied her.[6]

During the first days in the White House, Mrs. Johnson also decided to create a formal record of her time near the presidency. The diary that she began keeping in late November 1963 eventually reached nearly

1,750,000 words. Sometimes on the same day, sometimes a day or a week later, she would sit down with files and clippings that were designed to prod her memory, and she would dictate her recollections into a tape recorder. Most of the recording occurred "in a small room in the southwest corner of the second floor of the White House." A sign on the door, "a tiny pillow about the size of an eyeglass case," carried the words "I want to be alone."[7]

After the Johnson presidency, one-seventh of Lady Bird Johnson's diary was published in 1970 under the title *A White House Diary*. Though there are gaps and some subjects, such as beautification, are only sporadically covered, the *Diary* is a valuable record of what the First Lady did and how she operated in the White House. It is the most complete account of its kind for a presidential wife, and it remains the place to begin in appraising her performance.

Though Lady Bird Johnson emerged as an advocate for programs and as a presidential partner behind the scenes, she was also the mother of two young women who came under the same kind of media scrutiny and popular interest that their parents experienced. Lynda Bird Johnson was nineteen when her father became president. She was attending the University of Texas at Austin and was majoring in history, as her mother had done. Tall and straight like her father, Lynda had a rapid-fire intelligence and a dry, understated wit. She became engaged to a midshipman at the Naval Academy in the spring of 1963, but the romance ended in 1964. During the 1960s she had not yet blossomed into the attractive woman she would become two decades later. Her father said, with mingled pride and unconscious chauvinism, "Lynda Bird is so smart that she will always be able to make a living for herself." At the White House she took full advantage of the opportunities to meet the famous and celebrated, including the movie actor George Hamilton. She married Charles S. Robb, a Marine officer, in 1967.[8]

In 1963, Lucy Baines Johnson (it became Luci during the presidency) was an exuberant, outgoing sixteen year old, who seemed, on the surface, a teenager of the 1960s. Her father believed that she was "so appealing and feminine there will always be some man around wanting to make a living for her." She was attending the National Cathedral School in Washington, from which she graduated in 1965. Later that summer she met Patrick J. Nugent of Wisconsin, and they were married in a White House wedding in 1966. Luci's energy and flair made her a media favorite. She also had a serious side, which her mother and father saw. Personal searching led to her conversion to Catholicism, and her marriage encountered internal stresses that foreshadowed its later breakup.[9]

The most important familial role that Mrs. Johnson had to play was being wife of the president. Her diary offers continuing evidence of her alertness for fluctuations in Lyndon Johnson's health and personal sense of well-being. "I wish we could do something about these sleepless nights," she said in January 1966. In November 1982 she told students at the University of Texas how she came to dislike the pile of reading that appeared on the president's pillow each evening and how good she felt when there was only a small amount for her husband to do.[10]

The First Lady herself made sure that she was well informed about the issues that the president's nightly reading contained. When she traveled, she received briefings from the White House staff, including its senior members, about such issues as nuclear policy and the future of the economy. There are other indications of her curiosity regarding substantive issues. In March 1968 she had copies of congressional hearings on wiretapping and gun control sent to her. Similarly, in December 1967, Harry C. McPherson, Jr., prepared a long memorandum for her on the president's statements about "family planning and population control." During the administration she had an important role in the creation of the presidential library, kept current on such issues as the promotion of literacy and Head Start, and had a detailed grasp of environmental policy issues in areas outside of her own beautification cause.[11]

How large a part Mrs. Johnson played in the decision making of Lyndon Johnson as president cannot easily be reconstructed from the materials that are now available. When the full text of her diary is available, it may be possible to take a more precise measure of her impact. As the years progressed, the Johnsons talked often "in the early hours of the morning." There are also signs that show her contributions of language and thoughts to important statements. She provided a draft proposal regarding the seating of the Mississippi delegation in 1964, which recommended in favor of the white Democrats and against the Mississippi Freedom Democratic party. In 1966 she read the "final draft of the domestic part" of the State of the Union speech and "suggested a little sentence about thrift and common sense in the conduct of the war on poverty, with due respect for spending the taxpayer's dollar." Often the president involved her as part of a "collective judgment" regarding press stories, and she reminded him about opportunities to meet White House visitors whom she had assembled.[12]

Throughout the White House years she identified with the purposes of her husband's administration and hoped for its success. She played a decisive part in his decision to run for a full term in 1964, and she was equally important in his judgment that he should step aside four years later. The Johnsons had their disagreements over issues and strategy, and he teased her publicly and privately about her beautification campaign. But she remained the one person in whom he confided with complete trust because she had, in Wilbur Cohen's words, "no ulterior purpose." Her influence was large, and her part in the administration was important. "He trusted her advice and judgment," said his aide Harry McPherson; and as Hubert H. Humphrey noted, "In her quiet way she made him come to heel."[13]

Beyond her duties as mother, wife, and political partner lay the question of what her role as First Lady should be. "I feel as if I am suddenly on stage for a part I never rehearsed," Mrs. Johnson told a friend in the early days of her husband's presidency. Friends and the writers of early essays about her assured the public that she would find important things to do. Katie Louchheim said that Mrs. Johnson was "by disposition, experience, and inclination what President Johnson calls a 'can-do' woman" and predicted that the First Lady would consider ways in which "she might make the White House a showcase for women of achievement." Anne Morrow Lindbergh saw Mrs. Johnson as a blend of the traditional southern woman, who is concerned about family values, and of the pioneering heritage of the Southwest, which made her a partner for her husband. "That same spirit we think of as pioneer—independent, active, positive, with something of a crusading tinge—has been strong in Mrs. Johnson's life," Lindbergh concluded. "Lady Bird is still growing," wrote columnist Ruth Montgomery, who cited friends as forecasting "that she will one day take her place as one of America's great First Ladies."[14]

The question was which model among the previous First Ladies she should emulate. The institution of presidential wife had evolved a great distance from the passivity and reclusiveness that marked White House spouses in the nineteenth century. During the first thirty years of the twentieth century, First Ladies had gradually become more active and more visible on the Washington social scene. Some of them, such as Edith Carow Roosevelt and Grace Goodhue Coolidge, had been cultural and social leaders of Washington. Edith Roosevelt had begun to hold evening musicales at the White House. Other wives had been important influences on their husbands outside of the public gaze. Before her crippling illness in the spring of 1909, Helen Herron Taft had pushed her husband's candidacy, advised him on appointments, and consulted about his legislative program. Edith Bolling Wilson had appeared to some to have served as an acting president when Woodrow Wilson's stroke disabled him between October 1919 and March 1921. All of these women had taken on some of the attributes of celebrities as popular interest in the First Lady and the family of the president quickened after 1900.[15]

In the early 1930s, Eleanor Roosevelt transformed the role of First

Lady into a combination of ombudswoman to the nation, an advocate
for the disadvantaged, and an agent of the president. Though her impact on President Roosevelt's decisions was limited, she acted as a gad-
fly and stimulus to him. She used her fame and influence to stretch the
boundaries of the New Deal in her commitment to black Americans,
the young, and the less privileged. As the wife of a congressman between 1937 and 1945, Lady Bird Johnson saw Eleanor Roosevelt in action and felt an empathy for her that never diminished. "I had an awful
lot of respect for her hard work, and her caring, and her knowledge,"
Mrs. Johnson said, though she told the same interviewer that she had
similar feelings about Dolley Todd Madison and Abigail Smith Adams.
Mrs. Johnson once walked the alleys of Washington with Mrs. Roosevelt,
and she saw the First Lady come to a benefit luncheon in 1939 at which
only one person could be helped. "But where else do you start except
with one person?" Mrs. Johnson recalled when she spoke about the occasion in April 1964.[16]

Lady Bird Johnson was astute enough to recognize, however, that Mrs.
Roosevelt's independent style had often brought political difficulties for
her husband. Some of the projects and people that Eleanor Roosevelt
endorsed during the 1930s and 1940s had proved misguided, as in the
case of the abortive Arthurdale project in West Virginia. Moreover, Mrs.
Roosevelt's ample energies had often been diffused into too many causes
and too much activity, as her fame became a substitute for a clear focus
on which priorities were best to pursue. Franklin Roosevelt had endured
the resultant controversies with a calm that Lyndon Johnson could not
hope to match. A First Lady in the Eleanor Roosevelt vein would have
to find a direction for activism that gave her programs coherence and
political appeal.[17]

After Eleanor Roosevelt's tenure, the institution of First Lady had re-
ceded from the high point of public interest. Bess Wallace Truman
deliberately made herself a retiring contrast to her predecessor. Such a
posture well suited Mrs. Truman's dislike of public attention; it also enabled her to exercise a good deal of quiet influence on the president in
their private conferences. Mamie Doud Eisenhower had no ambitions
to sway her husband on substantive questions, and a chronic illness
limited her commitments while she was in the White House. "She was
very much against pushing forward into public view," Dwight D.
Eisenhower said after he had left the presidency.[18]

The three years that Jacqueline Kennedy spent as First Lady revitalized the institution and made the wife of the president a figure of glamour
and sophistication. The legacy that Mrs. Kennedy left to her successor
was an image of beauty, culture, and good taste that no other woman

could easily attain. As a high-school history teacher in Maine said of Mrs. Johnson in 1967, "What she suffers from is having had to follow a goddess." The components of Mrs. Kennedy's aura as First Lady arose initially from her personal allure and her experience in the White House, "the mystical nimbus of tragedy and beauty" that she possessed. Added to it were memories of the dazzling parties and the artistic occasions that she and President Kennedy had provided. Her sponsoring of the restoration and renewal of the mansion in the style of the early-nineteenth-century United States enhanced the image of gentility and elegance that she conveyed. Mrs. Johnson liked and admired Mrs. Kennedy and felt deeply for her in her grief. They remained friends throughout the Johnsons' White House years and beyond.[19]

If Lady Bird Johnson knew about the less happy side of Jacqueline Kennedy's years as First Lady, she never mentioned such facts publicly or privately. Early in her diary, Mrs. Johnson noted that Mrs. Kennedy achieved on the day of her husband's funeral "something she had never quite achieved in the years she'd been in the White House—a state of love, a state of rapport between herself and the people of this country." There was more of an ambivalent character about Mrs. Kennedy's approach to her duties at the time than would be evident twenty-five years later. She said that her relations with the newspaper women who covered the White House would be "minimum information given with maximum politeness," and she treated her encounters with the public in much the same way.[20]

When it suited Mrs. Kennedy as First Lady, she could be very visible and seemingly accessible. Her televised tour of the White House in 1962 was a triumph in the ratings and with the critics. Similarly, her travels with the president or by herself received ecstatic responses in the United States and overseas. But if she chafed at the ceremonial duties of the president's wife, then she simply did not do them, and she often relied on Mrs. Johnson to act in her stead. Beyond the restoration of the White House and a general appreciation of the arts, Mrs. Kennedy pursued no programs and mobilized no constituencies. This stance accorded with her dislike of politics and kept her at a distance from her husband, whose chronic infidelities persisted even when he was president. These aspects of Mrs. Kennedy's life, however, were not available to Mrs. Johnson as guides to her own conduct or as reasons for her to follow a different path as First Lady. She had to be herself but to do so in ways that would not cast even an implied rebuke on the woman who had preceded her.[21]

Mrs. Johnson began to evolve her own style as First Lady in mid January 1964 with her initial trip on behalf of the president and the "unconditional war on poverty" that he had declared in his State of the Union

address. On January 11 she flew to Wilkes-Barre, Pennsylvania, to visit
a depressed coal-mining region where the Area Redevelopment Administration was seeking, in her words, "to substantially reduce unemployment and defeat the common enemy." As she flew over the country,
she remarked on its beauty, "but when you saw the vast scars across
the landscape from the mining that is literally a surface mining, you
couldn't keep from thinking that God had done his best by this country, but Man had certainly done his worst, and now it is up to Man
to repair the damage."[22]

Once she had arrived in Pennsylvania, it became "a day of running"
for her. She spent six hours touring the countryside, seeing what she
labeled "the first battleground" of the war on poverty and telling her
listeners that education was central to any long-range solutions for
unemployment and economic difficulties. "We cannot rest easy when
$5\frac{1}{2}$ percent of the American people are unemployed," she said. The ARA
administrator concluded that her visit had been "a real tonic for the people
of the area." For her, "it was a day I loved living," composed of "a montage of faces, outstretched hands in the biting cold, children wanting
autographs, roses." The event foreshadowed the similar well-organized,
highly publicized trips that would mark her career as First Lady and the
persisting popular interest in the president's wife as a celebrity. At the
end of January, *U.S. News and World Report* said that "Lady Bird Johnson
is setting a pace as First Lady that hasn't been matched since Eleanor
Roosevelt's day."[23]

In the ensuing months, Lady Bird Johnson kept up the same active
schedule. She made a trip to Huntsville, Alabama, to visit the Space Flight
Center in late March, where she told the audience that "the South has
hitched its wagon to the stars." She went with the president in April
on a five-state swing that included the Appalachian region of Kentucky.
She returned the next month to the "beautiful but economically depressed Cumberland Plateau" of the same state. She delivered the bac-
calaureate address at Radcliffe College in early June. It was a speech "that
I had worked harder on than any other." She told the women graduates:
"If you achieve the precious balance between women's domestic and
civic life, you can do more for zest and sanity in our society than by
any other achievement."[24]

She espoused a mild and cautious feminism in 1964 as she searched
for a theme to guide her years in the White House. "A quite remarkable
young woman has been emerging in the United States," she said at
Radcliffe; "she might be called the natural woman, the complete woman."
The First Lady added that this new woman did not "want to be the
long-striding feminist in low heels, engaged in a conscious war with men,"

but rather hoped to become "pre-eminently a woman, a wife, a mother, a thinking citizen." She believed that American women held "a tremendous potential of strength for good" when they exerted their force as "we mark a ballot, teach our children, or work for a better community."[25]

For the most part, the general response to Lady Bird Johnson during these early months was positive. Republican congressmen went to Alabama in the spring and found black tenant farmers living in poverty on the land that the First Lady owned in that state. *U.S. News and World Report* gave their discovery national attention. The implied contrast between the "War on Poverty" and the squalid state of the tenants did not have any lasting political impact. Otherwise, the First Lady drew friendly crowds and admiring reviews. Biographies appeared that brought a sense of her life and her style to the public. "You're doing a wonderful job. Everybody says so," Robert Kennedy said to her at General Douglas MacArthur's funeral in April.[26]

There remained the question of what she would do with herself in a programmatic way in the White House. Her Women Doer Luncheons provided a means to put talented women before the press, but these gatherings were not in themselves a substitute for a coherent agenda of action. Until the president's political future had been decided, the First Lady stayed within the boundaries of what was already being done. She endeavored to carry on Mrs. Kennedy's restoration work for the mansion itself, "to make sure that there *is* continuity in all of the good things that have been done, preservation of everything that has gone forward." Working with Clark Clifford, she proceeded with the creation of the office of curator of the White House and the establishment of the Committee for the Preservation of the White House. Mrs. Johnson also helped Mrs. Paul Mellon bring to fruition her plans to rename the East Garden the Jacqueline Kennedy Garden.[27]

Amid the tumult of the election year and becoming accustomed to the presidency, the background for the First Lady's interest in beautification slowly came together. The process was gradual and to a degree unplanned, but it underlay what happened once the election of 1964 had been won. In February 1964 the Cincinnati Park Commission wrote to the president about planting a tree in his honor in that city's Eden Park. "The President has turned your letter over to me," Mrs. Johnson replied, "because I am more of a gardener than he is." First she suggested a dogwood and then settled on a live oak, as being "close to my husband's boyhood." Later in the summer, at the suggestion of Secretary of the Interior Stewart Udall, she opened the American Landmarks Celebration on the garden steps of Woodrow Wilson's home in Washington. "How many times in the past 25 years I've driven past this house," she said, "to show constituents the house where President Wilson spent his last years." She spoke of "this age of vast and constant change," when it was "more important than ever that we preserve our rich inheritance and remember its significance—both for the present and for our future."[28]

At the White House in 1964 there were other occasions when her interest in natural resources, environmental questions, and the quality of life appeared in her diary. In mid April, Lady Jackson (Barbara Ward) talked of how model cities and traffic experiments might flow from closed military bases. Later in the month the First Lady and Mrs. J. Frank Dobie took time to "talk of Texas wildflowers." Lunching with Udall, Secretary of Commerce Luther H. Hodges, and other cabinet members on June 14, she listened as the talk turned to the Interstate Highway System and its impact on national parks and historic places along its way. She noted that Udall and his Interior Department constituted "a loud voice for preserving the wilderness, the National Parks, the shrines, the jewels of America."[29]

Two days later, Jane Jacobs, who had written *The Death and Life of Great American Cities,* spoke at a Women Doer Luncheon. Lady Bird Johnson asked her "how to keep size from smothering the individual, crowding him into an impersonal and uncomfortable mold, and how to make a city beautiful." Jacobs's comments about the lack of money "for the upkeep of an existing park" clearly impressed Johnson, whose speeches during these months also suggested something of her future concern for the environment. At Radcliffe she urged the young women "to im- prove the esthetics of our cities where 70% of the people now live. More than 90% of our population growth will occur in our metropolitan areas. If our cities are cement and asphalt jungles, the children may be wolf- cubs." She told the YWCA National Convention earlier in the spring that women "want a good home environment for our children. And, if we mean this and strive for it effectively, it encompasses a really massive attack on the part of city dwellers to demand long-range, imaginative efforts to make our cities clean, functional and beautiful."[30] There is no direct evidence of how these events and remarks flowed into her later thinking about the environment, but with her acute memory and ten- dency to think ahead, it is interesting that such concepts were in her mind.

The policies of the Johnson administration provided another push in the same direction during the spring and summer of 1964. In his "Great Society" speech of 22 May 1964 at Ann Arbor, Michigan, President Johnson proclaimed the need "to prevent an ugly America" because "once our natural splendor is destroyed, it can never be recaptured. And once man can no longer walk with beauty or wonder at nature his spirit will wither and his sustenance be wasted." The language came from speechwriter Richard Goodwin, who in turn took some of his ideas from James Reston, Jr., then an assistant to Secretary of the Interior Udall. Reston argued that the concern over the destruction of the environment was largely centered at the local level and lacked a unifying "focal point." He then contended that "if public consciousness were aroused by a strong Presidential speech, giving some initiative to a movement for esthetic awareness, the battlers in the little fights all over the country would find their position vastly enhanced." In the Ann Arbor speech, Goodwin's sentences on the environment and its quality marked precisely the kind of presidential endorsement that Reston had proposed.[31]

To carry forward the ambitious agenda of the Great Society, the president set up individual task forces to evaluate major issues and to offer policy recommendations that could be pursued after the election. Bill D. Moyers and Richard Goodwin were in charge of organizing these task forces in the wake of the Ann Arbor address. It fell to Goodwin to assemble a task force on what he described as "this thing they were trying to put together. They weren't quite sure what it was. It was the environment, it was the quality of life, it was beauty, and it was a very amorphous and difficult subject."[32]

Goodwin drew some of his ideas together in the Task Force Issue Paper "Preservation of Natural Beauty," which was given to Moyers in mid June. "The Federal Government has not developed comprehensive policies on the preservation of the natural beauty of the nation," he argued, and "a *laissez-faire* approach has characterized our attitude" toward the issue. There did not as yet exist organized support for the preservation of natural beauty, the costs of which would be large, and the political backing for federal control of zoning and land use probably did not exist. Goodwin recommended that the administration push for additions to the National Parks System, endorse legislative efforts to create a fund for land and water conservation, and seek laws to set up wilderness areas and wild-river systems. Other individual proposals included the control of billboard advertising along the highways and the regulation of strip mining. He then discussed how the task force might proceed to define its mission and whom its membership might include.[33]

The Johnson administration's impulse to promote natural beauty in 1964 was part of a general revival of the conservation movement that had begun in the late 1950s and had gathered momentum during the years of Kennedy's presidency. In its beginning phase, the agenda for action centered on questions relating to "natural environmental values" that involved the preservation of wilderness areas, the providing of room for recreation, and the general claims of open space against the advance of developments, roads, and construction. When Lyndon Johnson became president, Stewart Udall submitted a memorandum on "The Administration and Conservation—A Look at Programs and Priorities." The document emphasized the Land and Water Conservation Fund, the Wilderness bill, water projects, national parks and seashores, and plans for the conversion of salt water and the transmission of electrical power. Udall also recommended that a presidential message be devoted to "an appeal to protect the quality of American life," but there was not yet, inside or outside of the federal government, what could rightly be called an ecological or environmental movement as such.[34]

Some of the basic aspects of that social and political force were in the process of formation by 1964. The older style of conservation, associated initially with Theodore Roosevelt and Gifford Pinchot, which stressed the efficient use of natural resources and opposed the preservation of wilderness areas, came to seem, by the 1950s, narrowly focused and insensitive to the threats that man-made pollution and a growing population posed to the environment. During the postwar years, Americans saw themselves as potential users or consumers of the beauty and integrity of the land, and they worried about the quality of their lives as the natural world became degraded. Progress that might destroy the Indiana Dunes, that imperiled Storm King Mountain on the Hudson River, or that endangered the Grand Canyon had to be resisted. Those who mounted protests against local examples of pollution and environmental decay also swelled the membership lists of the Sierra Club and the Audubon Society during the late 1950s and early 1960s. In these years, argues Samuel P. Hays, Americans "came to value natural environments as an integral part of their rising standard of living."[35]

The publication of Rachel Carson's *Silent Spring* in 1962, which alerted a national audience to the dangers of DDT and other pesticides, was only the most celebrated event of a rising consciousness about the environment in the decade before Lyndon Johnson came to office. "The problem of air pollution has become so widespread that no section of the United States is immune from it," Thomas H. Kuchel (R, Calif.) told the Senate in 1955. In 1959, David Brower of the Sierra Club complained that California freeways were draining productive resources and yet the roads "become obsolete before the ribbon is cut in our standard opening ceremony." Stewart Alsop evoked the thrust of the quality-of-life impulse in an article in the *Saturday Evening Post* in 1962. He called the nation "America the Ugly" and he assaulted the "way we Americans are turning our lovely country into a garish, brassy, neon-lit, billboard-ridden, slummish, littered, tasteless and, above all, *messy* place." The picture that Alsop offered contrasted sharply with a mounting desire among young, educated, affluent citizens for a natural environment that would afford them access to "new 'amenity' and 'aesthetic' goals and desires" that were symbolic of a good and harmonious society. Their status as consumers gave them not only a shared commitment "to protect community environmental values against threats from external developmental pressures" but also the political energy to mobilize their power as voters. The basis was present in these forces for a shift from the attention on the "natural environmental values" of the late 1950s and early 1960s to the ecological thrust of the latter part of the 1960s. The Johnson administration's conservation program and Lady Bird Johnson's campaign for beautification would both grow from and become a part of this transformation of American conservation.[36]

John F. Kennedy supplied more vigorous presidential leadership in the conservation field than the nation had seen since Franklin D. Roosevelt. He supported federal action on the problems of the environment through a special message about conservation to Congress in February 1961, and he called a White House Conference on Conservation in May 1962. Most of all, Kennedy encouraged his secretary of the interior, Stewart Udall, and wrote a preface to Udall's book *The Quiet Crisis* (1963). "New technical processes and devices litter the countryside with waste and refuse," the president wrote, which "contaminate our air and water, imperil wildlife and man and endanger the balance of nature itself."[37]

Kennedy's most significant long-range contribution was his reassertion of the concept that the federal government has a primary responsibility to exercise its authority on issues involving natural resources and the environment. During the 1960s the development of policy in this area would more and more become the province of the national government, and Kennedy was instrumental in the adoption of the idea of an expanded federal role and a higher level of funding. The Johnson administration had a direct legacy from its predecessor in conservation matters, an important consideration for a new president who wished to emphasize the continuities between his White House and the Kennedy years.

In the months after Lyndon Johnson became president, Udall pressed him to become more openly involved "with the fight for his conservation program." The secretary sent editorials that urged Johnson to "lift the hearts of conservationists and the hearts of all citizens" by supporting the pending Wilderness Bill and the Land and Water Bill in Congress. As it happened, the president needed little convincing in the area of conservation. In 1964 and ensuing years, this Texas politician showed a commitment to the future of the nation's natural heritage that enabled him to rival Theodore Roosevelt among conservationist presidents.

Part of his concern came from his innate love of the land, originally the Texas Hill Country, but now the broader national landscape. "I have a lot of land," he told his Task Force on Natural Beauty in July 1964, "and I only wish that all the people could have the chance to experience the same joys that I can. I am concerned with the erosion of natural beauty in this country. I know that this is a problem which cuts across many lines."[38]

Beyond this aspect of his conservation spirit, Lyndon Johnson saw himself as both carrying forward Franklin Roosevelt's tradition of support for natural resources and extending the Kennedy legacy. And the program coincided with the impulse of the Great Society, which also spoke about the overall quality of national life. As one early student of the environmental movement recognized, Johnson's espousal of the issue "added status and dignity to the efforts of those who sought to better the public environment and who had characteristically been dismissed by practical politicians as ineffectual nature lovers and utopians."[39]

How much did Lady Bird Johnson have to do with the Natural Beauty initiative in 1964? In later years, Stewart Udall believed that "she influenced the President to demand—and support—more far-sighted conservation legislation"; he was also convinced that "Ladybird's pushing" made her husband more receptive to conservation initiatives. To avoid claiming credit for herself about legislation or ideas that were properly those of Lyndon Johnson, his wife, in the postpresidential years, rarely made direct connections about her influence on specific conservation decisions. There would be, on occasion, brief flashes of expertise that indicated how much she knew and how closely she followed the field. Given the reciprocal influence between the Johnsons, it is logical to conclude that her impact in 1963/64 was significant.[40]

Richard Goodwin's suggestions to Bill Moyers formed the basis for the composition of the Task Force on Natural Beauty, and he also recruited its chairman, Charles M. Haar of Harvard University, to serve on the panel. The eleven-member task force, which included Jane Jacobs, Loren Eisley, Laurance S. Rockefeller, John Kenneth Galbraith, and William H. Whyte, met with President Johnson on 31 July 1964. James Reston, Jr., who was there as an observer for Secretary Udall, captured the flavor of the president's charge to the task force. Johnson wanted them "to paint me a picture . . . of how we can preserve a beautiful America." They should not worry about how their recommendations might fare in Congress. He would consider their ideas and send to Capitol Hill "what I think is fitting." Reston was impressed: "He was power, embodied in a man—the kind of power that God could never have intended for a mortal man to wield. And yet he was talking about human things—about a ranch, and about trees and rocks."[41]

After the president had left, the group began to define its areas of interest and responsibility. Haar later recalled that they concluded that their task was "really to raid the capital that already existed, to tap it and put it into some legislative do-able form for the president." They had a tentative schedule of two months, a budget of $50,000, and the need, as Haar put it, "to capture the conscience of the king." They did not yet know, he added, "of the great interest of Mrs. Johnson in this operation, nor that the President was going to make this one of his very carefully nurtured babies." So by midsummer 1964 the Task Force on Natural Beauty was assembling the elements of a new conservation impetus for the Johnson Administration.[42]

At almost the same time, Mrs. Johnson made a trip through the Rocky Mountain West to visit Indian reservations and national parks in the region. As a collateral purpose, the trip was designed to help such Democratic senators in the area as Gale McGee of Wyoming and Frank Moss of Utah, who were up for reelection in states where Barry M. Goldwater seemed strong. The tour accomplished both of those aims. It also served to give the First Lady time to discuss conservation issues with an important participant in her beautification campaign, because Secretary Udall accompanied her in this country that he knew well. As they sat together on the propeller-driven plane, they talked about the landscape that lay below them.[43]

Stewart Lee Udall was forty-four years old that summer. Born in St. Johns, Arizona, to Mormon parents, he had attended the University of Arizona and been an air gunner in Europe during World War II. After returning to Arizona, he finished college and obtained a law degree. In 1954 he ran for Congress and served three terms. His ability to deliver the Arizona delegation for Kennedy at the Los Angeles convention led to selection for the cabinet. "I was a great booster of him as was Teddy," Robert Kennedy later wrote. Udall's wiry hair and quick movements evoked memories of his years as a guard on the Arizona basketball team.[44]

Udall brought energy and a commitment to conservation to the Interior Department, but it took him some years to become an effective administrator. In his spare moments, usually on long plane trips, he found time to write the book *The Quiet Crisis*, which made him a national figure in conservation. "America today stands poised on a pinnacle of wealth and power," he contended in the foreword, "yet we live in a land of vanishing beauty, of increasing ugliness, of shrinking open space, and of an overall environment that is diminished daily by pollution and noise and blight."[45]

Because he had blocked Lyndon Johnson's bid to secure Arizona's seventeen delegates, Udall expected that he would be an early casualty of a cabinet shakeup. Johnson had a "long memory," and Udall, who "loved my job," worried about his chances of survival. To Udall's suprise, though the president teased him about 1960, Johnson also wanted Udall to stay on, in part to preserve the continuity that he so prized in 1964. More important, the two men found that they shared a feeling for the land of the Southwest. This bond drew them together in a way that Udall had not experienced with Jack Kennedy, a man of the sea and the shore.[46]

Udall came to be the significant spokesman for the environment in the Johnson administration. He recalled later that under both of the presidents he served, he "had pretty much of a free hand." While he was glad from an institutional perspective that "there was very little that was initiated at the White House in my area," Udall also kept himself in presidential favor by his support of the First Lady's urban-beautification efforts and his endorsement of billboard control. Like President Johnson himself, Udall was in transition from the older style of conservation to the new rhythms of environmentalism. As Martin Melosi has said, Udall's language spoke of "a concern for quality-of-life issues, and a commitment to environmental protection." Udall's actual policies often looked back to the more usual conservation matters of land and water and of resource management. His partnership with the Johnsons was strong and productive until it frayed at the end of the administration.[47]

In April 1964, Liz Carpenter suggested that Lady Bird Johnson make a western trip to see Indian reservations and national parks, and Udall took up the idea enthusiastically. "No First Lady within memory has gone to an Indian reservation to make a survey of conditions," he said to Carpenter. The trip was scheduled for August 14-17, with ceremonies to include the dedication of a dam, a speech at the University of Utah, and political appearances, in addition to the visits to the Indian reservations. James Reston, Jr., began to draft some speeches for the First Lady that would address regional and conservation themes.[48]

The remarks that Mrs. Johnson made in the West were sprinkled with thoughts about the quality of the landscape. "The interesting thing about Park City," she told residents of that Utah community, "is that you have developed the one resource that is least exhaustible, your natural beauty." At the University of Utah on August 15, she asserted: "This American society can never achieve [the] destiny it seeks, can never remove the slums or the prejudice, or the ugliness, unless citizens join in the great adventure of our time." She told her listeners at the dedication of Flaming Gorge Dam: "Enjoy the beauty of your hills, and protect it for your children." The result of the trip was what Udall called a political tour de force, especially in regard to a stop with Democratic women in Wyoming. "Mrs. Johnson was extremely effective on her 'land and people' tour in the West last week," the secretary told Lyndon Johnson. Her interest in the out of doors and her concern for conservation have a national impact that is the finest kind of Presidential politics."[49]

The conversations that Udall and the First Lady had on the western tour produced a lasting impact on their future working relationship. They found, Udall said, an "instant rapport" on conservation issues, and Mrs. Johnson displayed "an instinctive feeling for the beauty of the country." She asked him countless questions, and Udall became convinced that she decided then to make "a major commitment of her time" to the cause of conservation and beautification. For the present, however, the western visit indicated that the First Lady could be a potent campaigner. "I think she came back with considerable confidence" was Udall's verdict.[50]

A week after the trip, on August 24, the Democratic National Convention opened in Atlantic City, New Jersey. As Lyndon Johnson prepared to go to the convention, he was still saying to his wife "the same old refrain" that "he did not believe he should accept the nomination." She had "reason to think he didn't want to run previous to 1964," and now "he was wrestling with that demon very hard." As early as mid June he had showed her a statement taking himself out of the race. After long talks with him on August 25 and much walking, she wrote to her husband: "To step out now would be wrong for your country, and I can see nothing but a lonely wasteland for your future. Your friends would be frozen in embarrassed silence and your enemies jeering." The extent to which Lyndon Johnson was serious about withdrawal is questionable. His wife's letter provided some degree of reassurance, once it had been, in her words, "put in front of him, sort of inescapable.[51]

Mrs. Johnson's faith in herself, which had been reinforced in the West, was evident during the rest of the ensuing campaign. On the hustings with her husband or on her own, the First Lady displayed an ease with the public that enabled her to try out some ideas that revealed her affinity for the natural scenes around her. In Columbus, Ohio, on September 18 she said to the Federated Democratic Women of that state: "We are—and women particularly are—cleaning up the cities of our country"; she also praised "those who make the small places greatly to blossom—the backyard, the schoolyard, the town park." When she and the president stumped through New England, her brief introductory words never failed to speak about the hues of the season. "We saw the beautiful autumn face of Connecticut," she told a crowd in front of the

Hartford Times Building, "those lovely golds and reds of the trees, the most charming memory one could have."[52]

The high point of her campaign experience in 1964 came in early October, when the "Lady Bird Special" made a whistlestop tour through the heart of the South. The Civil Rights Act of 1964 and the racial liberalism of the Johnson administration had loosened the Democratic allegiance of Dixie, and passions for Goldwater ran high. After a two-week drive along the Gulf Coast, a southern woman reported that "she never saw anything but Goldwater bumper stickers any place on the trip."[53]

Despite the surge of Republican sentiment, the Johnsons did not intend to let their native region slip away without a struggle. Their own experience and the rising force of the civil-rights movement had led both of them away from the prejudices that still motivated many white Southerners in 1964. The frequent automobile rides from Washington to Texas with their black household employees had shown the Johnsons the personal dimensions of segregation. In Memphis, on one trip, Mrs. Johnson asked a woman motel operator whether her maid Zephyr Wright and another black person who was traveling with them might stay over night. "No," responded the woman, "we work 'em but we don't sleep 'em." Mrs. Johnson replied, "That's a nasty way to be," and drove on. Still, the First Lady believed that the South should not be ignored in the Democratic canvass. "We must go," she said, "We must let them know that we love the South." She convinced the president, against his initial political instincts to let her make the trip. For Lady Bird Johnson, it was to be "a journey of the heart."[54]

She approached the campaign with her usual thoroughness. "Don't give me the easy towns, Liz," she informed Carpenter; "anyone can get into Atlanta—it's the new, modern South. Let me take the tough ones." With the resources of the Democratic National Committee, the White House, and seventy men and women who were doing advance work in the South, Carpenter and the First Lady mapped out nearly seventeen hundred miles through Virginia, the Carolinas, Florida, Georgia, Alabama, Mississippi, and Louisiana. Mrs. Johnson said to the advance staff: "I feel at home in the small towns, and I want my speeches to make the people feel I am at home too." She intended to defend the president's policies because "I know the Civil Rights Act was right and I don't mind saying so. But I'm tired of people making the South the whipping boy of the Democratic Party." Before the trip had been publicly announced, she called all the governors and senators of the states that she would visit, to invite them on board the train and to ask for their support. Senator Willis Robertson of Virginia had planned "antelope hunting," and another politician was still mourning his wife, who had died two years earlier. Mrs. Johnson's calls did induce five governors to join her, and four senators signed on as well.[55]

The trip grew in size and popular interest as October 6 approached. "Everyone seems to be caught up in the spirit of the project," the First Lady was told on October 1, and she could expect "large crowds and a warm reception." Three hundred people, including a press contingent of over two hundred, left on the nineteen cars of the Lady Bird Special from Union Station around seven in the morning on October 6. The car from which Mrs. Johnson would speak had been painted red, white, and blue, provided with an awning, and decorated with flowers by Bess Abell and her associates. The president made the first stop in Alexandria, Virginia, and joined them again later, once in North Carolina and at the end in New Orleans. After he had left the first time, the train was off on a rollicking and exciting old-time stump swing. Reporters munched LBJ's pickled okra, enjoyed the daily happy hour, and read Liz Carpenter's "Dixie Dictionary," which defined "Kissin' kin" as "anyone who will come to the depot."[56]

At each stop, Mrs. Johnson made a set speech that contained deft local touches. "The law to assure equal rights passed by Congress last July with three fourths of the Republicans joining two thirds of the Democrats has been received by the South for the most part in a way that is a great credit to local leadership," she said in Alexandria, Virginia; and she stressed economic prosperity as being a more important asset to the region than clinging to racial prejudices. In Virginia and North Carolina, she argued, per capita income was up over 1960, and "I would be remiss if I did not point out that these were Democratic years." As the audiences responded to her, she exclaimed to Liz Carpenter: "I love it. I'm like Br'er Rabbit in the briar patch." Congressman Hale Boggs of Louisiana, warming up the crowds, shouted that the Johnsons were as "much a part of the South as tobacco and cotton and peanuts and grits and redeye gravy." Southern politicians found that being seen on the train had become the thing to do.[57]

It was not a love fest at every stop. In the Carolinas, hecklers appeared with posters reading "Lady Bird, Lady Bird, Fly away"; and in Charleston, signs on the homes announced "This House Is Sold on Goldwater." Male politicians on the train wanted to strike back when interruptions and jeering occurred during Mrs. Johnson's speeches. She declined that advice: "I know you're chivalrous and they make you mad, but I didn't expect this would be an easy assignment. I'll handle it." Her answer was to stop her speech, look at the hecklers, and say: "I respect your right to think as you do. Now I'm asking you to be quiet while I finish what

Lynda Bird Johnson, Liz Carpenter, Lady Bird Johnson, an unidentified man, and Bess Abell on the Lady Bird Special, October 1964.

I have to say." Usually she obtained silence, and Republican leaders asked publicly that the taunting stop.[58]

After four days of towns, speeches, grimy reporters, and a carnivallike atmosphere, the Lady Bird Special ended its run in New Orleans. President Johnson joined his wife and made a major speech on civil rights that night. The First Lady's campaigning had been a decided success.

"Not since the days of Franklin Roosevelt have so many Southern Democratic leaders openly thrown their lot in with the national ticket," wrote one reporter. Nevertheless, the trip did not reverse Goldwater's inroads or Republican sentiment in the South, and four states in which she had campaigned went for the GOP in the fall election. Her appearances did, however, underscore Democratic interest in the South and may have minimized defections from the party. For Mrs. Johnson herself, the Lady Bird Special was a sign of her clear emergence as a public figure on her own terms. No First Lady before her, not even Eleanor Roosevelt, had campaigned by herself for her husband. The organizational skills that Carpenter, Abell, and Mrs. Johnson's staff had shown would also carry over into the beautification work ahead. The trip had been, Mrs. Johnson wrote later, "those four most dramatic days in my political life."[59]

Mrs. Johnson displayed another side of her character a few days after the trip ended. Presidential assistant Walter W. Jenkins had been arrested at the Washington YMCA and had been charged with having had homosexual relations with a sixty-year-old man on October 7. A week later the incident came to light, along with a previous episode in 1959. While the president said nothing publicly, the First Lady immediately issued a statement: "My heart is aching today for someone who has reached the end point of exhaustion in dedicated service to his country." President Johnson released his own statement later that same day, and the incident rapidly faded from public attention. By her independent action, his wife had done what was right under the circumstances and had also prevented a minor flap from becoming a major embarrassment.[60]

During the last three weeks of the campaign, Mrs. Johnson stumped with the wives of three cabinet members, Mrs. W. Willard Wirtz, Mrs. Robert S. McNamara, and Mrs. Orville L. Freeman, through the Southwest, and made other stops in Pennsylvania, Kentucky, and Indiana. In the final days she joined the president in crisscrossing the West and the Midwest before the voting on November 3. They celebrated the landslide victory over Goldwater at the Municipal Auditorium in Austin, and then they returned to the LBJ Ranch for ten days, to rest from the campaign and to plan for the term ahead. "My chief emotions," Mrs. Johnson wrote later, "were simply satisfaction in people's faith in Lyndon and a renewed determination to help him use the next four years to the best of his ability and to make some steps forward."[61]

Her own first year in the White House had been a time of beginnings and testing. She and her staff had learned about the demands of organizing trips, having speeches prepared, and accommodating to the needs of the press. Mrs. Johnson had overcome her earlier fears of public speaking and had succeeded, on the Lady Bird Special, in establishing herself as a skilled campaigner. It now remained for her to identify issues and subjects that she could pursue during a full presidential term. To that question she turned within a few days of the election and soon concluded that natural beauty, or "beautification," had the capacity to "make my heart sing." Beginning in Washington, D.C., she launched a movement that became an important element in the heightened conservation spirit of the 1960s and helped her to expand the horizons of the institution of the First Lady.[62]

4

Ways to Beautify America

In the weeks after the 1964 election, as the president went back and forth from LBJ Ranch to the White House, Lady Bird Johnson focused on the subjects she now wanted to pursue as First Lady. She gave much attention to the Head Start program for preschool children and provided a general sponsorship for that activity in 1965/66 with Sargent Shriver of the Office of Economic Opportunity.[1] She decided, however, that "the whole field of conservation and beautification" had "the greatest appeal." Within a few days of the election, probably on November 6, she induced the president to call Secretary of Commerce Luther Hodges about junkyards along the highways, and she launched what in time became the effort to enact highway-beautification legislation.[2]

The Johnsons returned to Washington on November 15 for a four-day stay. In that period, the Task Force on Natural Beauty submitted its report to the president. In his cover letter, Charles Haar cited "a great and growing popular demand for an improvement in the quality of the environment." The report itself argued that "the time was never better for action to conserve the natural beauty of this land." The task force recommended that the federal government have a specific focus for natural beauty, as well as national programs for the preservation of landscape and open space. Highways should be beautified, and billboards should be regulated. Parks and forest lands should be made more useful to Americans, and the cities should rehabilitate their park systems. In addition to measures to stimulate private efforts to promote beauty, the task force urged President Johnson to call a White House conference on "America the Beautiful." Udall told Haar that it was "the most perceptive and creative of the task force reports we have scrutinized."[3]

Lady Bird Johnson saw the task force's report at this time. The president had digested its contents within a few days and had discussed its implementation with Udall and Hodges at the Ranch on November 19 and 20. Stewart Udall recalled that the First Lady was familiar with the contents of the report when they talked during his visit. He sent her a memorandum on November 19, suggesting that she make Washington, D.C., " 'a garden city' whose floral displays and plantings would make it a handsome model for America." The next day they met at the Ranch. He was on "cloud nine" when he received the invitation to come to Texas, and he became even happier as they discussed how to begin with Washington so as to make it an example for the rest of the nation. Udall set about developing ways in which the Interior Department could carry forward and participate in the First Lady's initiative.[4]

While Udall went forward with his program, friends of the First Lady were advising her to make Washington, D.C., a focus for her activities during the ensuing four years. A long-time confidante, Elizabeth ("Libby") Rowe, wrote to Lady Bird Johnson in early December to recommend "that you extend your interest in the White House's beauty and history to the entire city." The wife of James Rowe, a sometime political adviser to Lyndon Johnson, Libby Rowe was a native Washingtonian and the chairman of the National Capital Planning Commission. She proposed that a "White House Committee on Washington's appearance" be established, and she suggested names of city officials and public-spirited citizens who might serve as members. Rowe's letter was an important event in the early stages of beautification planning for Washington.[5]

Lady Bird Johnson rarely limited herself to one set of advisors or to one line of action. She enlisted Katherine ("Katie") Louchheim—an assistant deputy secretary in the State Department and a leading figure among Democratic women—and Antonia Chayes—a lawyer in the Kennedy White House and a consultant at the National Institute of Mental Health—to provide their ideas about the city's appearance. She also drew in Mary Lasker—a New York philanthropist, an advocate of urban beauty, and a diligent lobbyist for health legislation—as another possible source of concepts.

Ideas came in quickly. Louchheim suggested that the First Lady sponsor "America the Beautiful" awards for "preserving, improving or beautifying the American scene." In a memorandum of December 9, Udall noted that "no First Lady in all our history has ever provided sustained conservation leadership on behalf of our capital city." Like Rowe, he indicated that a committee under the First Lady's sponsorship should develop a beautification plan for the city. Chayes contended that cities "should offer people the chance to grow and live a full life," and she observed that playgrounds and parks belonged not only in the "good neighborhoods" but everywhere. "These are goals that go beyond survival—beyond breaking the circle of poverty. These goals reach for the 'Great Society.' "[6]

On December 11, Lady Bird Johnson talked with Louchheim at the White House about a "possible beautification campaign" for Washington. At this stage, her commitment was cautious and limited. There would be a committee under her guidance, and she would give awards. She would "not be the one to make the decision or plan the campaign because of her limited acquaintance with the subject matter." Four days later, Mrs. Johnson had lunch with Rowe and Louchheim, at which time the mandate of the committee grew more expansive. "Mrs. Johnson's sponsorship would inspire wide support of both a private and governmental nature and generally interest the Nation in this beautification and preservation process precisely as Mrs. Kennedy had done with the historic renovation of the White House." She would concentrate on Washington's parks, the Mall, historical landmarks, "and the beautification of all new urban renewal projects and public housing units." Improvement of the look of the city's highways and parks was discussed, along with an awards program. Finally, they considered who might be potential members of a First Lady's committee.[7]

The decision to focus first on Washington, D.C., was logical because of the attention that the nation's capital had already attracted for its deteriorating physical situation and its mounting social problems. "Washington is a shabby city," Udall told the First Lady; critics outside of the government spoke even more harshly. In 1963, Wolf Von Eckardt, who wrote about architecture and urban design for the *Washington Post,* said that among Washington's disgraces were its "many lawns, dilapidated sidewalks, ugly and confusing clutter of traffic signs, decrepit benches, forbidding trash baskets, hideous parking lots, poorly lit, deserted, and crime-ridden city parks, and a desperate dearth of amenities" for residents and tourists. There was the "Official Washington," of monuments, parks, and public buildings, and the "Other Washington," where most of the city's residents lived.[8]

Both Washingtons faced significant problems when the Johnson administration took power. Pollution, controversies over highway location and construction, inadequate public transportation, and a decaying inner city—all of these issues and more made Washington a case study of the urban dilemmas that convulsed the United States during the 1960s. To that mix was added the city's subordinate relation to Congress, which ran it "like some territorial possession." Even more significant was the presence of a black majority, impoverished and segregated, and a white minority in economic and political control. The black residents of Washington, Von Eckardt said, were "on a sidetrack of the American way of life."[9]

President John Kennedy took an interest in Washington, which he hoped would develop into, "to a degree, a showcase of our culture." There was both an enhanced respect for older buildings in the city and a desire within the administration to upgrade the quality of federal edifices. A long-range plan to improve Pennsylvania Avenue, through a commission chaired by the architect Nathaniel Alexander Owings, provided further evidence of Kennedy's intentions. The president's wry remark that "Washington has the charm of a Northern city and the efficiency of a Southern one" underlined his concern for the capital's affairs, as did the appointment of a presidential assistant for District of Columbia policy, Charles Horsky. Nonetheless, in the mid 1960s, Washington was still very much "a lost colony still surviving—barely—on the American continent."[10]

By December 1964, Mrs. Johnson had several personal campaigns under way regarding beautification. Improvement of the look of the nation's highways had begun, and negotiations over the control of junkyards and billboards were in motion. This important issue would run parallel to her other work on natural beauty in 1965.[11] The preliminary discussions over the First Lady's Committee were nearly completed by early January 1965, and preparations went ahead to issue invitations and call the panel together. Simultaneously, President Johnson was readying his State of the Union message for delivery on 4 January 1965. In that speech, too, the administration's new emphasis on beauty would be apparent.

When he addressed Congress that evening, the president said that "for over three centuries the beauty of America has sustained our spirit and enlarged our vision." Now the nation had to act to "protect this heritage." In the first State of the Union speech to mention natural beauty, Johnson advocated more parks; improved landscaping on highways, streets, and open spaces; and the legal authority for the government to block air and water pollution "before it happens." He hoped to make the Potomac River "a model of beauty" and to protect streams in a wild rivers bill. At the end of this section, he announced that he would shortly call a White House Conference on Natural Beauty.[12]

After the speech, reporters asked the First Lady how much influence she had on its drafting. "I have lived with it and helped hammer it out," she said, "I can't say I helped write it, but some of my own thoughts and hopes came through," particularly "the exciting vistas that beautification opens up." In her diary she noted, after discussing passages about beauty, including "the green legacy for tomorrow": "I hope we can do something about that in our four years here."[13]

Throughout the rest of January and into February the preparations for the first meeting of the First Lady's Committee went ahead in tandem with the president's message on natural beauty, which was scheduled for transmission to Congress in early February. Mrs. Johnson sent out letters of invitation to prospective committee members on January 30, asking them to come to the White House on February 11 "to discuss the formation of a Committee for a More Beautiful Capital." She told them that "it is in our own communities that we can best participate in creating an environment which has beauty, joyousness, and liveliness, as well as dignity"; she also wanted them to "stimulate new interest in making our city truly beautiful for the people who live here and come here."[14]

As the date for the president's message and the launching of her committee approached, the First Lady reached out for more advice on her program. On February 3 she talked with the Laurance Rockefellers about his role in coordinating the projected White House Conference on Natural Beauty. "Getting on the subject of beautification is like picking up a tangled skein of wool—all the threads are interwoven," she wrote in her diary entry for that day, "recreation and pollution and mental health, and the crime rate, and rapid transit, and highway beautification, and the war on poverty, and parks—national, state, and local." As she thought about Rockefeller and the conference, she added: "There are many of us desperately interested in something positive coming out of this program, something besides a lot of words and proliferation of committees."[15]

President Johnson did his part on February 8 with his message on natural beauty: "A growing population is swallowing up areas of natural beauty with its demands for living space, and is placing increased demand on our overburdened areas of recreation and pleasure." The solution was "a new conservation" that would emphasize "restoration and innovation." Concerned with the dignity of man's spirit, this new "creative conservation" meant "that beauty must not be just a holiday treat, but a part of our daily life." He asserted that the nation could "introduce into all our planning, our programs, our building and our growth, a conscious and active concern for the values of beauty." Specific programs included highway beautification, clean-air legislation, an array of other conservation measures, and a White House Conference on Natural Beauty, to meet in May.[16]

Three days later, at 4 o'clock in the afternoon, the First Lady's Committee assembled in the Blue Room of the White House. Elizabeth Rowe, Katie Louchheim, Mary Lasker, and Stewart Udall were there from the organizing group; they were joined by national figures who were identified with conservation and by representatives from the Washington community. Over the next four years, some who attended, such as Laurance Rockefeller, Walter Washington, and Nathaniel Owings, would play large

Lady Bird Johnson and Mary Lasker at the White House on 5 February 1965, when Lasker spoke at the Women Doer Luncheon.

roles in Mrs. Johnson's work. Others, such as William P. Rogers, Adm. Neill Phillips, and Mrs. Kit Haynes, would be less significant. Mrs. Johnson also made sure that Walter Tobriner, a District of Columbia commissioner; Charles Horsky; and representatives of the business community were present.[17]

Lady Bird Johnson began by reading from a description that the British ambassador, Lord Bryce, had written about Washington in 1913, which emphasized the possibilities that existed for the city's beauty. She said that her committee should have as its goal "to implement what is already underway, supplement what should be underway, and to be the catalyst

Lady Bird Johnson, Secretary of the Interior Stewart Udall, Walter Washington, and others at the White House meeting of the Committee for a More Beautiful Capital, 11 February 1965.

for action." The members agreed to plant flowers in the traffic triangles and squares of Washington, to give awards for neighborhood beautification, and to endorse existing projects, such as the revitalization of Pennsylvania Avenue and the preservation of Lafayette Park. The First Lady then turned the meeting over to Udall, who appointed several subcommittees to work on specific topics and bring back suggestions for the next meeting the following month.[18]

On February 8, Mrs. Johnson met with six reporters from *U.S. News and World Report* to talk about the beautification program. Coverage in a national news magazine would provide the public exposure that could launch her initiative in the most visible manner. The resulting story came out in the issue dated February 22 under the title "Ways to Beautify America." She said to the interviewers: "There is a great interest in beautifying the landscape. It seems to me to represent a basic hunger, or yearning, that has spread throughout the whole country." When they asked her the predictable question if there was more to beautification than "beauty for beauty's sake," she responded: "Ugliness is so grim. A little beauty, something that is lovely, I think, can help create harmony which will lessen tensions." She was cautious about billboard control because "it's a big industry," but she predicted that "public feeling is going to bring about regulation, so that you don't have a solid diet of billboards on all the roads." After ranging over numerous related subjects, she concluded: "The time is ripe—the time is now—to take advantage of this yeasty, bubbling desire to beautify our cities and our countryside. I hope all Americans will join in this effort."[19]

The general popular response to the First Lady's interview, the convening of her committee, and the president's message on natural beauty was enthusiastic. Calls poured into the White House from Washingtonians on the days when plans for the committee were announced, and the national reaction seemed equally positive. "Bravo Mr. President," said the Women's Chamber of Commerce of Atlanta. "Natural Beauty is a Political Natural," wrote James M. Perry in the *National Observer*, citing the remark of "a Presidential supporter" that "there's intellectual interest in all of this and there's interest from the four-buck-an-hour factory worker who has an out-board in the garage." Perry also noted that Mrs. Johnson's "rebellion against ugliness" seemed "as genuine and deep-seated as the President's, and surely she is as influential with her husband as any First Lady we've seen in this century."[20]

In the spring of 1965, few commentators examined the origins of the term *beautification* or considered the feelings and attitudes that it aroused among those who were concerned professionally with the city, its appearance, and the general nature of the American landscape. The word itself, which Mrs. Johnson never liked and which she sought to jettison for a more precise label, conveyed to the popular mind an image of triviality and cosmetic effort. Wolf Von Eckardt said that the term "scares me a little." While helpful as a means of involving citizens, he argued, beautification left "our real problems" unsolved if all that occurred was "sprinkling wildflower seeds along highways, getting rid of automobile junkyards, billboards, overhead wiring, smog and water pollution alone—important as all this is." He did not believe that "the planting of azaleas in neglected old city parks, or even the creation of new ones," would "cure our urban malaise."[21]

The references that Stewart Udall made to Washington as a potential "garden city" and Von Eckardt's comments to Udall in a memorandum about the "City Beautiful" indicated how Mrs. Johnson's proposed work in Washington evoked the legacy of an earlier emphasis on beautification. At the turn of the century the City Beautiful movement flourished in the United States. Involving "organized, dedicated, and informed laymen," rather than professional city planners, the City Beautiful effort had "pioneered in comprehensive planning, in the regularity and monumentality of building design, and in the fusion of naturalistic park systems with classicistic civic centers."[22]

Students of the City Beautiful impulse argue that it operated on several different levels. In the area of large city planning, the McMillan Plan for Washington, outlined in 1902, established that city's monumental character through the work of Daniel H. Burnham and Frederick Law Olmsted, Jr. The White City of Chicago's World's Fair of 1893 also impressed architects and citizens with the possibilities of designing a metropolis that kept aesthetic elements in mind. As one writer put it in *Municipal Affairs:* "Beauty in high places is what we want; beauty in our municipal buildings, our parks, squares, and courts; and we shall have a national school when, and not until when, art, like a new Petrarch, goes up to be crowned at the capitol." In numerous American cities between 1900 and 1915, this spirit found expression in parks, railroad stations, public buildings, and broad avenues.[23]

At the same time, the City Beautiful spirit arose first in smaller localities and had a large component of lay participation, with women being strongly represented among the improvement associations and civic leagues that were the core of the effort. A student of civic-improvement groups in 1900 wrote: "No task is too great for these associations to undertake. . . . They create sentiment in favor of ornamental backyards and tidy alleys. Indeed, they offer you prizes for the prettiest backyard and neatest alley." These exponents of the City Beautiful did not regard their improvements to be an end in themselves, as their critics often charged. Their purpose, wrote a leading spokesman, J. Horace McFarland, was "to make our America a better and more beautiful place to live in." One count identifies more than twenty-four hundred "improvement societies" in the nation by 1905 and links the City Beautiful campaigns to the optimistic reformism of the Progressive Era.[24]

Related to and sometimes competing with the City Beautiful idea was the concept of the clean and efficient city, which also gained favor in the early twentieth century. Again, women were among the leaders of citywide cleanup campaigns. Children were enlisted in the Junior Sanitation League in Philadelphia, and there were Junior Health Leagues in other cities. The program spread to elaborate city-cleanup days and extensive antilitter efforts under such titles as Municipal Housekeeping Day in Pennsylvania. The national Clean Up and Paint Up bureau coordinated five thousand local campaigns in 1915. A woman in Binghamton, New York, said: "We must picture to our children . . . how each one of us has pride in his home, and wants it to be as perfect as possible, and how that feeling extends to its surroundings, to the lawns and streets in the vicinity. Then in a broader way we think of the city as our home." Some of these programs proved to be transitory, of course, and their orientation toward women and children kept them separated from the predominantly male professions of sanitary and technical engineers that actually made city policy during those years. Nonetheless, the aesthetic reformers of the years 1900 to 1920 had identified serious environmental issues that would be present for Lady Bird Johnson half a century later.[25]

The City Beautiful idea itself had faltered by the time of World War I. Architects and the emerging profession of city planning assailed beautification as a matter of "superficialities." Cass Gilbert exhorted his fellow architects: "Let us have the city useful, the city practical, the city livable, the city sensible, the city anything but the city beautiful." The City Beautiful was too simple an idea, many planners concluded, to deal with the hard issues of zoning, sanitation, and housing. As city planners become more professional and scientific, beautification seemed less and less relevant. "Can we with equanimity stand by and help the city spend its money on . . . frills and furbelows when only a step away the hideous slum, reeking with filth and disease, rotten with crime, is sapping the very life-blood of the city?" was how George B. Ford posed the issue before the American Civic Association.[26]

During the 1920s and 1930s, the City Functional replaced the City Beautiful, and *beautification* became a term that evoked an outmoded and discredited creed to the professionals who designed and operated the nation's cities. Because the advocates of beautification were usually women, often organized in garden clubs and roadside councils, it was even more likely that the male-dominated professions of architecture and city planning would react negatively to the word. This skepticism about the capacity of females to understand the complexities of the urban situation persisted into the 1960s and provided an unstated but pervasive background for Lady Bird Johnson's campaign. She understood this intuitively when she said of the word that "it sounds cosmetic and trivial and it's prissy."[27]

The problem of what to call her campaign would plague the First Lady over the next four years. "We all, I believe," said her aide Sharon Francis, "suffered from the wrong word, and Mrs. Johnson asked us to use the word beautification as little as possible." Liz Carpenter said of the term: "It just seemed to rise up, and it was never a word we were totally satisfied with, but the alternatives were stodgy and they didn't sound like anything new. Conservation. Environmental beauty. Nothing." The heart of the problem was that Lady Bird Johnson and those around her shared the view, well expressed by Charles Haar of the Task Force on Natural Beauty, that beautification "sort of has a feminine aura to it, you know, and it's something sissy-like." When Lyndon Johnson talked about beauty, Haar added, "it became a much more masculine approach, and it became much more talking of natural parks and society. It became much more acceptable."[28]

As a woman of her time and her region, Lady Bird Johnson accepted the idea that the feminine implications of beautification had to be muted and restrained. Unaware of the tradition of women in conservation and as yet not a feminist herself, she tacitly concurred in the attribution of inferiority toward women that the word beautification implied. She and her associates sometimes spoke of "garden club ladies" and invoked the stereotypes of "old ladies in tennis shoes or puttering gentlemen in tweeds with a rose cutting in their hands." Given the political role she had chosen as First Lady, her husband's chauvinistic attitudes, and the real constraints of a male-dominated Washington and nation, her attitude toward beautification as a word apparently made sense in the short run. There were lasting negative consequences. Since beauty was such an ill-defined and easily mocked concept, it meant that her program could be treated with heavy masculine sarcasm whenever its opponents wished to make cheap points. Male supporters could only respond in a tentative and uneasy manner, lest they seem unmanly in their views. There was always an undeserved tone of apology and supplication about what Lady Bird Johnson did for the environment; this arose from the label beautification. In its way, her campaign became an instructive lesson in how constricted a role women could play in American public life in the 1960s.[29]

If the mainstream of American city planning, architecture, and landscape architecture criticized beautification for doing too little to address the ills of the urban environment, another criticism of the idea of cleaning up highways and cities was gaining adherents during the 1950s and 1960s. This school of thought had less influence at the time than it has achieved over the last twenty years, but it has become an important perspective on whether beautification is worth doing. It is unlikely that either of the Johnsons knew about a critical evaluation of their beautification program that appeared in a small journal called *Landscape* in its spring 1965 issue. The editor, John Brinckerhoff Jackson, had been developing a view of the American landscape that saw the spread of highways, drive-ins, billboards, and road signs as expressions of the vitality of the national culture.[30]

Beautification, as Mrs. Johnson and the president envisioned it, struck Jackson as a "hopelessly superficial" attitude. On the one side, the regulation of billboards and junkyards was too timid: "The billboard is an affront not merely because it is ugly but because it is a form of economic parasitism, depending on the presence of the highway with no service in return." At the same time, in Jackson's mind, beautification failed to recognize the evolving quality of the landscape "where land and buildings are increasingly thought of in speculative terms, where families move on the average of once every five years, where whatever is old is obsolete, and whatever is obsolete is discarded." What the Johnsons proposed, Jackson concluded, "is not a permanent alteration in the environment, but a disguising of the ugliness, like a gangster's coffin under a mass of greenery and flowers."[31]

There was a sound element in Jackson's thinking. The American landscape had emerged in response to strong currents within society that expressed deeply held national values. The changing of behavior and attitudes would not be simple, and some aspects of beautification would require the affected individuals to sacrifice their own personal interests for an elusive aesthetic goal. In the case of billboards, for example, roadside signs provided direct economic gain to all who were involved in leasing them, creating them, or displaying products on them. Regulation meant financial loss to those people in order to obtain intangible assets for those who were traveling through a less cluttered landscape.

The thrust of Jackson's analysis was that fundamental changes in American attitudes were required; anything else was essentially cosmetic. Unless policy makers were ready to make the tough policy decisions necessary to clean up the country in a sweeping way, they should not interfere with the native expressions of popular culture. Jackson's radical critique of beautification actually would have had very conservative consequences if it meant that politicians should refrain from doing anything until they could accomplish everything. When Jackson said that the philosophy of beautification was "little more than a collection of tired out middle class platitudes about the need for beauty, greenery, and the wickedness of bad taste," he neglected to specify what alternative policies might preserve the best of the existing landscape and the urban environment while reducing pollution and ugliness. To talk of restricting the oil companies, "the trucking companies, the utilities and the larger chain stores" by means of legislation was impressive but rather impractical.[32]

Despite her initial lack of sophistication about the range of issues that beautification would touch, Mrs. Johnson operated from as sound environmental premises as either J. B. Jackson or the city planners did, with their scorn for "cosmetic" or "garden club" solutions. The First Lady never believed that simple cleanups would be enough. In 1965 she told a financial columnist that she wanted to move "from the garden club to the hardware stage of the problem," and she sought to address the impact of business on the landscape as much as she could. Moreover, her emphasis on the urban dimension of the environmental problem represented an important and decided shift from the rural focus of the early twentieth century. She wanted to involve as many citizens as possible in beautification, and she rejected few remedies and left few options unexplored. She also believed that something accomplished was better than an uncompleted vision, however powerful it might be on paper. In that way, her campaign, even in its initial stages, looked back to the citizen idealism that had first sparked the City Beautiful movement, while it simultaneously tapped the local consciousness about environmental deterioration that would spur the ecological movement in the next decade.[33]

In 1965, popular interest in the First Lady's appeal for beautification produced an upsurge in her mail at the White House. To answer the correspondence, Mrs. Johnson's staff was expanded with the addition of two women who became key participants in the beautification work. Sharon Francis was the first to be enlisted in the campaign. After a childhood in Seattle, where she had seen "one too many Douglas fir trees chopped down between me and my mountains," she came east to Mount Holyoke College. After graduating in 1959, she worked for the Wilderness Society until 1961, when she joined Stewart Udall's staff. Francis helped Udall in the preparation of *The Quiet Crisis*. In December 1964 she attended a planning meeting for the First Lady's Committee at the White House, where she met Mrs. Johnson for the first time. When the First Lady entered the room on that cold, snowy afternoon, the singing of civil-rights marchers outside the fence was audible. Mrs. Johnson asked "What are they doing?" and Francis responded "They're singing 'We Shall Overcome,' and they're kneeling in the snow, Mrs. Johnson." As Francis turned around to look at the First Lady, she saw "a tear coming down the side of her face."[34]

On 17 March 1965, Francis received a call from Udall about Mrs. Johnson's mail. Could she help with the overflow? From an informal arrangement in regard to sorting these letters, Francis's duties expanded to a full-time position that was involved entirely with beautification. Eventually, she obtained her own office, and by September 1965 she was officially a "staff assistant for beautification." Assistants assigned to program objectives were a new development for a First Lady; they reflect how Mrs. Johnson was stretching the institution to accommodate her own goals and priorities. Liz Carpenter called Francis the "East Wing Egghead." Francis became a combination speech writer, link with conservation groups, and source of ideas for her boss. Francis's influence would be important in the beautification campaign in Washington, D.C., and on such national issues of the period as the Grand Canyon and the California redwoods.[35]

Cynthia Wilson became part of the First Lady's operation in much the same way that Francis did. Work on an M.A. in journalism at the University of Texas brought Wilson to the attention of Carpenter and Mrs. Johnson, and she came to the White House in early 1965, also to respond to the mail. Wilson, who was devoted to conservation causes and was energetic, functioned as an all-purpose "inside" implementer for the First Lady. She wrote press releases, did advance work on trips, and monitored the incoming correspondence for information about controversies and possible problems. Wilson and Francis made a solid team, and the staff in the East Wing operated smoothly over the ensuing four years.[36]

The spring of 1965 was a period of testing and experimentation for Mrs. Johnson as the new campaign got under way. At its second meeting, on 9 March 1965, her committee heard architect Nathaniel Owings discuss his ideas for improving the Mall. After listening inside, the members got into minibuses for a tour of the Mall and "our first planting." Later, at the triangle between Maryland and Independence avenues, at Third Street, S.W., Mrs. Johnson put in the first azaleas. At the urging of Walter Washington, the "entourage of committee and press" went to Greenleaf Gardens, a black housing area. Two school bands serenaded the minibuses, and then Mrs. Johnson spoke briefly. Afterwards she told Udall "that all of our efforts will fail unless people in these neighborhoods can see the challenge and do the work in their own front yards."[37]

Behind the public face of the committee there were some questions among those who were not close to Mrs. Johnson regarding the focus of the panel. An associate of Udall's, John Carver, argued that the smaller subject committees that were formed at the first meeting "do not have well-defined responsibilities, and there are some omitted areas." In addition, the assignments of Walter Washington, the only black member, to poor neighborhoods, and of Mrs. Kit Haynes of the National Capital Garden Club League to well-to-do neighborhoods struck Carver as "patently indefensible." Victor Gruen of the committee also told Udall that there was "a danger that one of these days the work of this committee could be attacked in the press and elsewhere as being only superficially concerned with cosmetics, flowers, trees and bushes, etc." He suggested that some official statement be issued "to anticipate this type of criticism" and to indicate that the committee understood that environmental problems had deep roots and that Mrs. Johnson was trying in the short run to "create that atmosphere of hope and optimism which is necessary in order to attack the deep-seated problems successfully."[38]

Lady Bird Johnson plants "a symbolic few" pansies as Secretary of the Interior
Stewart Udall looks on, 9 March 1965.

Mrs. Johnson was already addressing these issues. She met for two hours
on March 17 with the Udalls, Elizabeth Rowe, Nash Castro, Sharon Francis, and Liz Carpenter to discuss what beautification "could mean for
the United States in five or ten years." The First Lady stressed that her
mail indicated that the American people were "ready for higher aesthetic
standards" and that the committee could be a means to "express these
thoughts." She wanted to act as an inspirational and encouraging force
to persuade citizens to beautify their own surroundings. Cleanup programs and projects, such as the ones that Walter Washington had proposed, improved the physical environment and resulted "in an increased
sense of neighborliness and community pride among the participants."

As these comments showed, the popular response to the beautification campaign had taken her well beyond the limited role that she had set for herself the previous December.[39]

By the third meeting of the committee on April 8, the work of the group had become more institutionalized. Udall provided a stenographer, who prepared a transcript of the session, and that practice continued for the life of the committee. There was much to announce. Mary Lasker had donated more than nine thousand azaleas for the refurbishing of Pennsylvania Avenue. From the Japanese government came four thousand cherry trees, though in the end the trees had to be American plants grown from Japanese roots, because the native Japanese trees carried a dangerous virus. The largest single gift was $100,000 from Laurance Rockefeller, some of which was to be allocated to the improvement of the Watts Branch area, consisting of thirty-six acres in a low-income part of Northeast Washington; the rest was to be used in cleaning green oxide from statues in the city.[40]

The committee also listened to reports on improvements for downtown Washington from Knox Banner of Downtown Progress, National Capital Downtown Committee, and reviewed a program of beautification awards that Katie Louchheim had put together. Walter Washington discussed what his Subcommittee on Neighborhoods and Special Projects proposed to accomplish in "the blighted areas where the conditions are gray and dismal." In her comments, Mrs. Johnson said that the demand for speakers on beautification had grown to a point that Lee Udall, Stewart's wife, had arranged a speakers bureau composed of Senate and cabinet wives to fill the out-of-town requests that Mrs. Johnson could not meet. Sharon Francis and Liz Carpenter had assembled kits of background materials for the speakers to use, and in the spring of 1965 there was an abundance of opportunities for these volunteers to spread the First Lady's message.[41]

The campaign received an additional impetus in April 1965 when the *Reader's Digest* reprinted in its May issue the *U.S. News and World Report*'s interview. The magazine wanted to make a formal presentation of the issue to Mrs. Johnson, a move that the White House forestalled, lest she become too associated with an individual commercial enterprise. Instead, the Let's Beautify America forum and workshop was held in Washington on April 28, with eleven local and national beautification figures exchanging ideas about strategies for improving the nation's appearance. On that same day the First Lady held a Women Doer luncheon on neighborhood beautification.[42]

In the middle of May, Mrs. Johnson made the first tour devoted explicitly to beautification in what would become a pattern during the rest of her years in Washington. She believed that it was necessary to bring her ideas and her presence to areas of the nation that had scenic beauty or where problems afflicted the environment. Also, she knew that she needed, as Liz Carpenter put it, "to escape from behind that big iron fence around the White House once in awhile and get the feel of the country." For her it was good "to get out in the open and come to terms with things." The first region selected was close-by, the historic sites in Virginia that constituted "Landscapes and Landmarks." On May 11 she set out with a company of the Udalls, the Rockefellers, the wife of Vice-President Humphrey, several cabinet wives, and assorted highway and beautification experts, including Rex Whitton of the Bureau of Public Roads, Nash Castro of the National Park Service, and state senator Fred Farr of California. Behind the First Lady's party came a press bus, with some forty press reporters and crews from all the major television networks.[43]

As the bus rolled along, Mrs. Johnson compared the view from Interstate Highway 95 with what she had seen as they had moved down Highway 1. On the Interstate, "which has a broad right-of-way and complete control of access," she noted what had been accomplished "by selective cutting, by skillfully maintaining the best native trees and shrubbery, by planting the banks for erosion control, by preserving the vistas." The highway, "a beautiful drive," was "a model of what can be done, and the median strip is a great plus."[44]

Highway 1 offered a less-rosy picture. "A narrow right-of-way with uncontrolled access," the state road impressed her as "a tunnel of filling stations, billboards, neon signs, and dilapidated little buildings." As she dictated her thoughts for her diary, she raised issues that echoed the comments that J. B. Jackson had applied to the natural-beauty program: "And yet these enterprises are conveniences for people, and this is private enterprise. What is the answer? Some control by government and some raising of taste levels?" She concluded that "the contrast of frenetic billboards on one road and only nature on the other was a significant lesson."[45]

At the dedication of a wayside shelter in Dumfries, Virginia, Mrs. Johnson said to her audience: "No one can drive this scenic highway without feeling a deep sense of gratitude for such a lush, green land, and a rush of pride in man's increasing determination to keep it within eyesight of the motorist." The group went on to Monticello, where she "took movies and wandered around the grounds." That evening they saw a performance of *Julius Caesar* at the Barter Theater in Abingdon, where the First Lady presented an award to Roger L. Stevens, a theatrical producer who was then a presidential assistant for cultural affairs. On the second day of the tour she visited a handicraft exhibit in the Blue Ridge Mountains before returning to Washington in the afternoon.[46]

The trip proved that beautification outings offered a means to publicize the campaign in settings that attracted press coverage and national attention. Mrs. Johnson realized that the celebrity aspects of her position offered the chance to turn popular fascination with the activities of the First Lady into an asset for her programmatic objectives. She became increasingly adroit in offering to the media occasions when the positive qualities of her beautification work might be seen in newsworthy settings.

As the date for the White House Conference on Natural Beauty approached, the rhythm of events related to the subject accelerated. The ABC-TV network was beginning preparations for a special on Washington, D.C., and the First Lady for airing in the fall. She hoped that it would "speak to the whole country and sow some seeds of interest in nationwide beautification." Some of her shyness about public appearances now returned. "I have never been more scared of anything or felt less confident or competent to undertake it." At this time the Johnsons were also initiating a quiet effort to assist in persuading Joseph Hirshhorn to donate his collection of modern art to the Smithsonian Institution. After wooing the prospective donor, she observed in her diary: "What a situation I find myself in! A First Lady should be a showman and a salesman, a clothes horse and a publicity sounding board, with a good heart and a real interest in the folks in 'Rising Star' and 'Rosebud,' as well as Newport and whatever the other fancy places are. Well, the last—real interest—I do have."[47]

The last meeting that the First Lady's Committee held before the White House Conference was on 19 May 1965. The members gathered on the USS *Sequoia* for a cruise on the Potomac. During the day, Mrs. Johnson had presented beautification certificates to two Washington-area businesses for work they had done in supplying plants and landscaping assistance to schools and community centers in the city. At the dock the chairman of the Citizens Council for a Clean Potomac gave her a litter bag, like the ones that would be used on Sunday, 23 May, during Potomac Pick-up Day. The committee then embarked on a four-hour journey on the river, on which Secretary Udall and others talked about its history and current pollution problems. There followed the customary reports. Nash Castro described the flowers received from Mary Lasker, the *Reader's Digest* forum of late April was reviewed, and a citywide beautification plan that the National Park Service was developing was outlined.[48]

Mrs. Johnson also announced the formation of a private fund-raising organization, the Society for a More Beautiful National Capital. Mary Lasker would serve as president, and there would be six trustees, including

Carolyn Agger Fortas, the wife of Abe Fortas, as treasurer. Lasker knew that governmental funds could not be used for many of the projects that the committee envisioned, and she wanted to tap the resources of those who were, as she later put it, "rich and possibly sympathetic." Creating the private committee and securing its tax-exempt status took time, so it did not become fully functioning until 1966. Nonetheless, it represented not only a further elaboration of Mrs. Johnson's program but also one that would raise substantial amounts of money.[49]

The climax of the opening phase of the natural-beauty initiative came when the White House Conference began on May 24. The process of pulling the meeting together had been laborious ever since the Task Force on Natural Beauty had first suggested the idea in November 1964. Udall wrote the president in mid January 1965 to argue that "this conference will be meaningful to the American people if it inspires new action— and produces *new ideas* and *new solutions* to our conservation problems." The secretary added that the administration should "try to involve the best minds in the country," and he suggested that Laurance Rockefeller serve as the coordinator of the conference. By early February, Rockefeller had been so designated, and that led to the conversation that he and his wife had with Mrs. Johnson on February 3 about the conference and about conservation in general.[50]

Laurance Rockefeller would turn fifty-five the day after the White House Conference concluded. He had emerged as an important figure in American conservation during the 1950s, after a career in the aerospace industry and other high-technology ventures. Long interested in his family's holdings in such projects as the Jackson Hole Preserve in Wyoming and elsewhere, he had participated in evaluations of the nation's resources that looked to conservation for defense purposes. He also linked resort projects in Wyoming and the Virgin Islands with land donations to the National Park Service. Nathaniel Owings called him "a collector of exotic Shangri-las to be found in rare and beautiful locations where virgin powdered beaches and sparkling oceans met." In 1958, President Eisenhower had named Rockefeller to chair the Outdoor Recreation Resources and Review Commission (ORRRC), which was to report back in three years on the state of the country's recreational resources and their anticipated use in the years ahead.[51]

The ORRRC's report, *Outdoor Recreation for America*, went to President Kennedy in January 1962. It predicted that outdoor recreation would triple by the year 2000 and said that new approaches to the issue were imperative. One solution was recreation areas nearer to the cities, because "the need is far more urgent close to home." The commission also recommended that a Bureau of Outdoor Recreation be established within the Interior Department. Rockefeller worked through the American Conservation Association, which he funded, to spread the message of the ORRRC during the early 1960s. Expenditures from the association eventually totaled almost $800,000 for this publicity campaign. Kennedy then named Rockefeller to direct the Advisory Council on Recreation, and it was natural that he should also be a member of the Task Force on Natural Beauty in 1964.[52]

The extent of Rockefeller's commitment to conservation principles would come into question by the end of the Johnson presidency. Unfriendly biographers have suggested that he lacked a genuine understanding of the ecological spirit of the 1960s and 1970s. One former colleague said, "It's helpful to his image to have a do-gooder approach, but let's face it—the environmental problems facing the country aren't a very zealous concern of his." This harsh judgment was probably unfair to the Laurance Rockefeller of 1964/65, who believed that the beautification impulse and the business sector were not necessarily in conflict. "Business should not regard this awakening of an appetite for natural beauty as unexpected or something novel or temporary," he told the Congress of American Industry in December 1965. Natural beauty "will turn out in the end to be just plain good business." This attitude mirrored many of the views held by the president and Mrs. Johnson in the same years, and it was logical that a working collaboration evolved.[53]

Rockefeller began to organize the conference in February 1965 under the assumption that the delegates should focus "on case histories of 'how to do it,'" taking examples of successful community action to promote natural beauty and learning from them. One problem that especially concerned him was "effective intergovernmental relations," by which he seems to have meant placing more authority in the Recreation Advisory Council for coordinating the federal government's activities on natural beauty. In mid March, Rockefeller met with the president in what a White House staff member dubbed a "really good On the Record" appointment that would command favorable news coverage for the announcement of the conference. The Johnsons both talked with Rockefeller during his visit, and the First Lady agreed to open the conference itself. The closing ceremonies would be at the White House, which Rockefeller believed would "lift this conference out of the ordinary and help it claim the public attention we seek."[54]

Throughout April and March, requests to attend the conference flowed into the White House. Rockefeller said that in choosing panelists, he and his associate Henry L. Diamond had emphasized "the individual, not the office." They had sought a "cross section of varying points of view," a goal that required the careful selection of the fifteen panels of eight participants each. There were three thousand nominations or applications to attend the conference. Because the meeting would be held in the auditoriums of the State Department and the Civil Service Commission, the number of those who could attend was limited to eight hundred. From that group, Diamond and Rockefeller settled on the 120 people who would actually participate in the panels themselves.[55]

Panelists were instructed that they were taking part in a "hard" conference that sought "concrete, specific proposals for action, visionary or immediate." They were also asked to provide two-page summaries of their anticipated remarks. Initial submissions proved to be too vague and philosophical, and the organizers had to insist on more focused presentations. On Sunday, 23 May, closed sessions of the panelists provided more direction and created what was later called "a constructive tension."[56]

Lady Bird Johnson opened the conference the next day. "In the catalogue of ills which afflicts mankind," she said, "ugliness and the decay of our cities and countryside are high on America's agenda." She asked the panelists and the delegates: "Can a great democratic society generate the concerted drive to plan, and having planned, to execute great projects of beauty?" Laurance Rockefeller followed her with remarks that identified "the city, the countryside, and the highways as the broad topics for scrutiny, and he urged his listeners to present "new, practical ideas for solving specific problems." They would not "solve all the problems of creating a beautiful America" in the thirty-six hours of the conference, but they could "take a big step—perhaps many steps—in that direction."[57]

The proceedings of the White House Conference eventually totaled more than seven hundred pages of text to cover the deliberations that followed in the next day and a half. Mrs. Johnson moved from panel to panel, taking "copious" notes in her own shorthand as the discussions went forward. Occasionally the panelists noticed that the First Lady was in their audience.[58] There was much for her to hear. From the "Federal-State-Local Partnership" through the use of "Citizen Action," the panelists experienced "a whole college course in the American environment in two days." Some sessions proved controversial. The "Roadside Control" panel revealed the sharp differences that separated advocates of billboard regulation from representatives of the outdoor advertising industry. Ian McHarg of the University of Pennsylvania warned the "Landscape Action Program" panel: "We cannot indulge the despoiler any longer. He must be identified for what he is, as one who destroys the inheritance of living and unborn Americans, an uglifier who is unworthy of the right to look his fellows in the eye—be he who he is—industrialist, merchant, developer, Christian, Jew or agnostic." There was also, as landscape architect Lawrence Halprin noted, "throughout

Lady Bird Johnson addresses the White House Conference on Natural Beauty, 24 May 1965.

the conference the continuing dichotomy between the feeling that beauty must be equated with natural beauty and that manmade events are inherently ugly."[59]

On the afternoon of May 25 the panel chairmen made their recommendations to the conference delegates. Then everyone assembled on the White House lawn, on what Henry Diamond recalled as "a hot, humid May afternoon." Rain washed out the plans to have the president hear some of the reports there near the south portico. Instead, Lyndon Johnson beckoned to everyone: "You all come inside." In the East Room, with most of the delegates sitting on the floor, the chairs of four panels gave brief digests of the reports to the president. "Natural beauty, as you and I conceive it," Lyndon Johnson responded, "is the world we live in. It is the environment in which we were born, and grow to maturity, and live our lives." In his rambling remarks, which referred to his responsibilities in Vietnam and the Dominican Republic, Lyndon Johnson added that he was sometimes awakened from his afternoon naps "by Lady Bird and Laurance Rockefeller and others in the next room, talking about flowers, roadsides and so forth." That afternoon, as he awoke, he heard conversations and said: 'My! Am I dreaming? Is Laurance Rockefeller back in town again?' And I got up and went out and pulled the curtain and peeped behind it and looked, and there was not only Laurance Rockefeller and Lady Bird and the 60 that started out with them but a thousand more that joined them."[60]

On a more substantive note he promised that his next State of the Union message would contain beautification recommendations. He would call local and regional conferences on natural beauty, and he would send the conference's proposals for state and local action to appropriate officials at those levels. He also announced that on the next day, Congress would receive a package of four bills dealing with the beautification of the nation's highways. "I thought that you would be glad to know that we have not been idle while you have been working," he told them.[61]

The Johnsons were proud of the Natural Beauty Conference and its work. The First Lady called it "an occasion of inspiration and brilliance," and she believed that "all of us who attended feel renewed in our dedication to the enhancement of the cities and communities in which we live." Writing for an architectural journal, one observer called the conference "well organized and well run" and labeled it "on the whole a great success. It came forth with no new great solutions; many platitudes were passed around; an occasional bright and shining new idea came through." *National Wildlife* reported that Lady Bird Johnson was becoming "an unofficial 'secretary of the exterior.' "[62]

While the general verdict was favorable, in one aspect the conference received low marks. The way in which the issue of highway beauty and billboard control was handled left some of the participants grumbling that the White House had yielded too much to the outdoor advertising industry. Complaints then spilled over to the conference as a whole. "It was a kind of shambles," one delegate said to a magazine reporter, and the upshot was that members of garden clubs and roadside councils among the delegates were angry when they went away from the conference. The fight over billboard regulation was so complex that it requires separate treatment later to put events at the White House Conference in proper perspective. The unhappiness over highway beauty did diminish the impact of the conference among some potential allies of beautification, but the controversy did not mean that the rest of the gathering lacked importance.[63]

The White House Conference marked an early climax of Mrs. Johnson's beautification drive. As Henry Diamond said nineteen years later, "the word went out from the White House that the President and the First Lady cared." For Diamond, the meeting itself represented "a major transition—a bridge from the traditional conservation to the new environmentalism, and the start of something grand." Allowing for Diamond's own role in the conference, he reached a fair evaluation. The White House Conference did serve as a constructive catalytic event that provided a national impetus to the conservation and beautification policies of the Johnson years. In the two decades that followed, Mrs. Johnson often encountered people who told her, "with a sense of comrades in arms, 'I was at the White House Conference on Natural Beauty.' "[64]

The conference also occurred around the time when the Johnson presidency was moving away from the euphoric optimism of the 1964 election and the early months of 1965, when legislative progress toward the Great Society seemed inevitable. At the Conference on Natural Beauty there were no protests about Vietnam and almost no sense of the social turmoil that was soon to envelop Johnson's administration. Within three weeks, at the White House Festival of the Arts in mid June, protests from some of the guests about the war signaled that a new and more difficult phase was beginning for the Johnsons and the nation.[65]

For Mrs. Johnson the first half of 1965 had seen the beautification campaign launched to a highly positive public response. National legislation to improve highway beauty went to Congress on 26 May 1965, with reasonable prospects of success, in the White House's view. The First Lady's committee had captured the imagination of many in Washington; volunteers and contributions were still flowing in. It now remained for her to implement her programs in the capital city, where she would have to balance the desires of those who wished to beautify the monumental and tourist areas of Washington with the ideas of those who believed that beauty should also be conveyed to the residents of the inner-city ghetto.

5

Beautifying
Monumental Washington

Lady Bird Johnson's beautification effort in Washington, D.C., developed along two complementary lines between 1965 and 1969. These contrasting tendencies were not in conflict with each other, and in some instances they became reinforcing. For the most part, however, they operated independently and deserve separate attention. The first, associated with Mary Lasker and Nash Castro, looked to improvements in the appearance of the city in areas where tourists were most prevalent and the buildings most monumental. To some extent their work overlapped with Nathaniel Owings's campaign to revive and improve Pennsylvania Avenue. Mrs. Johnson also devoted her energies to securing an art museum for Washington through her work to persuade Joseph Hirshhorn to donate his collection of paintings and sculpture to the nation.

The second approach grew out of the commitment of Walter Washington and Polly Shackleton to the inner city. They believed that beautification should make an active appeal to the sympathies of the black population. Katie Louchheim styled the Lasker-Castro group as the "daffodil and dogwood" set, in contrast to Walter Washington's ghetto-oriented concern with schools, playgrounds, and housing projects. Such a neat division has simplistic elements in it that are unfair to both groups, but it offers a convenient starting point to describe the evolution of the First Lady's campaign in Washington.[1]

Mrs. Johnson understood from the outset of her work that success in the nation's capital would depend on her ability to achieve favorable publicity for what she was trying to do. Her background in journalism and television made her aware of the extent to which First Ladies were celebrities whose fame attracted attention more than the substance of what they accomplished. To achieve changes in the way that Washington looked, she had to capitalize on the natural curiosity about presidents' wives, and she had to link that popular interest to beautification. Her emphasis on how to make monumental Washington look better was a

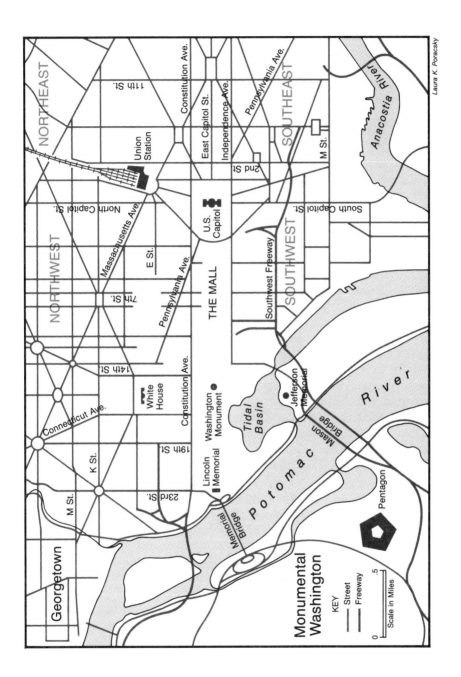

Monumental Washington

KEY

— Street
— Freeway

0 .5

Scale in Miles

Laura K. Poracsky

first step toward addressing the whole issue of enhancing the city's appearance in less glamorous areas.

The First Lady encouraged such media events as the coverage in 1967 of the government of Mexico's donation of sixteen sets of Mexican playground devices to the children of Washington. The Johnsons had traveled to Mexico in 1966, and in return the wife of Mexico's president sent the equipment. There was a ceremony at Hains Point on 8 March 1967: a plaque was installed, and a small White House reception occurred. In her acceptance remarks, Mrs. Johnson called play "one of the universal languages that brings a smile to the face of mankind everywhere." For four years the First Lady adroitly used such occasions to reinforce her linkage of beautification with the ceremonial duties of her position in a way that brought her maximum press attention.[2]

Lady Bird Johnson also had as her volunteer associate in Washington a woman whose influence on the nation's health and environmental policies attested to her mastery of the instruments of publicity and the less visible levers of executive and legislative power. Mary Lasker put money, time, and hard work at Mrs. Johnson's disposal from 1965 onward, and she became the most important single force in the floral and monumental aspect of beautification in Washington. Lasker's concern for the environment was genuine, but having such a close relationship with the First Lady also helped Lasker's other crusade—health care. Mrs. Johnson understood her friend's priorities, and the two women forged a mutually beneficial alliance.

Mrs. Albert D. Lasker came naturally to the beautification campaign in 1964/65. Upgrading the look of cities stood second only to the nation's health as a claim on Mary Lasker's energy and philanthropy. Born Mary Woodward in Watertown, Wisconsin, in November 1900, she later had studied art history at the University of Wisconsin, then at Radcliffe, where she graduated in 1923, and finally at Oxford. After seven years as an art dealer, she decided that she "wanted to sell masses of things to masses of people," so she opened Hollywood Patterns, a company that sold dress patterns to women who did their own sewing. She married Paul Reinhardt in 1926 but their marriage ended eight years later.[3]

In 1939 she met the advertising executive Albert D. Lasker, who had already retired from his firm of Lord and Thomas in order to pursue philanthropy in medical research. In his advertising career, Lasker had worked for the Republican party in 1920, and his campaign techniques had featured the extensive use of billboards to promote the claims of Warren G. Harding. Albert Lasker and Mary Woodward found an immediate joint interest in medical research. "You will need *federal* money," Lasker told her; "what's more, I'll show you how to get it." They were married in June 1940. Over the next dozen years, the Laskers funded the Albert and Mary Lasker Foundation, which underwrote research on major diseases through a program of annual awards to doctors and scientists. They revitalized the American Cancer Society in the mid 1940s and sought, for other medical charities, to learn "what is wrong, then helping people who try to clean up the mess."[4]

Albert Lasker died of abdominal cancer in 1952, and his widow carried on his work during the ensuing years. Throughout the 1950s she argued that more federal money should be devoted to medical research. "What did the major voluntary health agencies allocate for cancer research in 1955? Under $8 million," she said in 1957. "What did the American people spend for chewing gum that year? $282,360,000." As an advocate of health research, Lasker combined philanthropy with a highly refined political sense. Her personal fortune made her a natural campaign contributor, and she placed her donations with the committee chairmen and rising politicians who could serve her needs in the future. She operated through surrogates and committees; she rarely stepped into the limelight to claim credit for her achievements. Representatives and senators received a never-ending flow of clippings and letters from her, reminding them about how much money medical research required. By the late 1950s, Lasker had what amounted to a personally financed health lobby on Capitol Hill.[5]

Natural beauty claimed another part of Lasker's relentless energies. She was "an avid lover of flowers and greenery" from her Wisconsin youth, and her marriage enabled her to use seeds from her husband's estate in greenhouses and plantings in New York City during the 1940s. In the next decade she concluded that the streets of Manhattan needed flowers as well as trees along the sidewalks. "Flowers in a city are like lipstick on a woman," she informed New York officials. "You *have* to have some color." Over the objections of those who argued that automobile fumes would kill the plants, she began with four blocks on Park Avenue in 1956. The experiment worked, and she had planted an additional twenty-two blocks by a year later. "It's important in dollars and cents for a city to establish a pleasant image of itself," she said in 1960.[6]

Health issues remained Lasker's main concern, however. She told an interviewer from the *New Yorker* in 1957: "The flowers are just a side issue with me. . . . I just hope that I am spark-plugging a movement that the city will carry on. What I am most interested in is the expansion of medical research."[7] Her priorities were the same in the mid 1960s. She understood that her commitment to health and beautification gave her a natural and reinforcing access to the president and the First Lady in the Johnson administration. By pursuing both projects simultaneously, she could ensure that her views would be heard on the medical issues that mattered to her. Mary Lasker's concern for natural beauty in cities was sincere and of long-standing. Her work with Lady Bird Johnson was more than simple benevolence. It was also a central component in the lobbying of an unsurpassed mover of the levers of power and influence in Washington.

When Lyndon Johnson became president, the family's connections with Mary Lasker went back over more than a decade and a half to campaign contributions that she and her husband had made in the 1948 senatorial race. In 1960 she told Eleanor Roosevelt that Lyndon Johnson was "a secret liberal who will push hard for Mary's bill." Two and a half years later, in November 1962, Lady Bird Johnson presented the Lasker Medical Research Awards in New York City. By 1963 the two women were exchanging warm letters and were on a "Dear Mary" and "Dear Lady Bird" basis. "It means a lot to us to know we are in your hearts," the First Lady wrote to Lasker on 29 November 1963. She added that "these are difficult days for all of us, but when a quiet time comes, if ever (it must! for I need to ask your help on so much) I want to have a visit with you."[8]

Lasker was a good friend to have. Her New York apartment was a showplace of French Impressionist and other modern paintings; there was a Picasso in the elevator. She sent gifts to those who helped her: French stamps to Richard Goodwin when he was a White House aide, pictures and rugs for the mansion itself, and the use of her apartment for Lynda and Luci, and other bounties that her ample fortune sustained. She was, Mrs. Johnson observed in her diary, "vivacious, competent, attractive," with "that rare quality of making suggestions that, somehow or other, winds up by getting them done."[9]

To some degree, Lasker used the First Lady for her own benevolent purposes. The endless gestures of thoughtfulness and kindness were the price of ready access to the White House to plead the case for medical funding. There was no insincerity in Lasker's concern for beauty, but there was no innocence either. Yet, influence and use did not run in a single direction. Mrs. Johnson gained as much from Mary Lasker as she gave to her. The money and the time that Lasker spent on beautification, which ran into hundreds of thousands of dollars, was largely responsible for the breadth of the beautification campaign in Washington. There would not have been a Society for a More Beautiful National Capital without Lasker. Considered only as a political exchange, and leaving out the real affection that the two women shared, the balance in the Lasker-Johnson transaction tilted heavily to the First Lady's side.

Mrs. Johnson's interest in the public places and the tourist areas of

Washington brought to her assistance the National Park Service, which had charge of the development and maintenance of its sites within the National Capital Region. In 1965 the assistant regional director for administration was Nash Castro. An Arizona native, the forty-five-year-old Castro had joined the Park Service in 1939 and had risen by 1961 to become the assistant superintendent of National Capital Parks, where "one of my responsibilities was that of fielding the White House." Castro was a consummate public servant. He had the capacity to carry out efficiently the wishes of a First Lady when the resources of the National Park Service were needed, and he did so with discretion and good humor. Mrs. Johnson soon came to regard him as "indispensable." Castro, in turn, identified with the conservation side of the beautification campaign and developed a high regard for her abilities. "I continue to marvel at the depth of the First Lady's interest in the great work she has begun," Castro told his superiors in January 1966. The square-faced, wiry-haired official became a familiar part of Lady Bird Johnson's journeys around Washington, and his exertions helped to produce the successes that beautification achieved in recasting the look of the Federal District.[10]

The National Park Service and Mary Lasker were natural allies. They shared the conviction that money and manpower were best devoted to those parts of Washington that tourists visited and that governmental officials traveled through. As Lasker put it, her goal was to "plant masses of flowers where the masses pass," and she looked to a general improvement of what Sharon Francis called "the monumental and tourist parts of the city." Lasker also believed that it would be easier to persuade wealthy donors to provide funds for parks and gardens than for projects in the city's black districts. The Park Service emphasized the same set of implicit priorities. What it managed could be kept clean and tidy. What ghetto residents operated tended, in Castro's view, to deteriorate over time. Lasker and Castro did much for Washington and for Lady Bird Johnson. If their social vision had limits, it was only on how best to involve the black community in the beautification cause. Their contribution to the overall appearance of Washington was substantial, and they provided a dedication in planning and execution that produced tangible results for the First Lady.[11]

The pattern of activity that Mrs. Johnson, Mrs. Lasker, and Castro followed for the next four years was set in mid March 1965. On March 17, the same day that the First Lady met with her beautification staff to explore the direction of her campaign, she spent the morning with Castro, his associate Kathryn Simons, Liz Carpenter, and Mary Lasker in a ride along Pennsylvania Avenue to inspect sites that the Park Service had selected for plantings. Mrs. Johnson spotted "scraggly areas of grass" along the avenue, and she suggested that climbing roses be planted on the fences of the tennis court near Sixth Street. Lasker offered to donate 200,000 daffodils for Rock Creek Park, in one of the benevolent acts that she regularly revealed when she was with the First Lady. Castro came away from the journey with a list of items for action that he then passed on to Sutton Jett, the regional director, before executing the First Lady's requests himself. "All in all," Castro predicted, "I am convinced that Mrs. Johnson's attention on beautification will now focus primarily on Pennsylvania Avenue."[12]

Throughout the rest of 1965, Castro learned that Lady Bird Johnson had a wider vision of what her program should do. At their next meeting on May 19 she told Lasker and Castro that she wanted her committee's work to reach into parts of the city that few tourists saw. "We must earnestly give attention to the development of tot lots and playgrounds, particularly in the poorer sections of town." At the same time she knew that beautification could not depend on the resources of the Park Service alone. Their discussion thus centered on the mailings that would go out to potential donors to the newly formed Society for a More Beautiful National Capital. "The brochure should be prepared in such a way that it will cover big and small things," the First Lady remarked. "It should suit every variety of donor. It must be attractive, eye-catching, and appealing." Above all, it needed to be available "as fast as possible."[13]

This sense of urgency revealed itself in large and small ways. When the firm of S. Klein and Company adopted a traffic triangle near the White House and agreed to keep it planted year-round, Mrs. Johnson called it "a truly significant contribution to our beautification program" as part of her effort to involve Washington's business community in her campaign. At her request, Castro drafted a letter from her to District Commissioner Walter Tobriner, asking him to place additional welcome signs at the entrances of the city. After a visit to the National Airport, which revealed shabby spots in the roads and grounds, she told the administrator of the Federal Aviation Agency that there were a number of places near the facility "that might be improved in their appearance merely by the introduction of a few plantings of shrubs and flowering plants." Otis Singletary of the Job Corps was informed that "there is a shortage of trained gardeners in the Washington, D.C. area," and she inquired whether the corps might add gardening to "its admirable training program."[14]

Each trip that Mrs. Johnson took around the city with Castro and Lasker during the second half of 1965 revealed more places where beautification needed to occur. "Attritioning dogwoods" on a triangle at Third Street and Maryland Avenue were noticed and replaced; other dogwoods were added at the Gravelly Point area; weeping cherries went in on the South Grounds of the White House. Throughout these activities the First Lady cautioned her associates to "remember we are using public funds to carry out these beautification projects" and to be "sure to use them wisely and well." The American people, Castro decided, were fortunate "to have in the White House a First Lady of Mrs. Johnson's makeup, who so deeply loves her fellow human beings as to strive as assiduously as she does to enlarge the quality of their lives through the upgrading of the environment." In the end, Castro believed, "the upgrading of our environment will inevitably upgrade the American character."[15]

The national character could only be improved if the American people knew about what Lady Bird Johnson was doing, and she continually stressed the need to pay attention to the publicity aspect of beautification. She warned Castro to be sure "to take plentiful 'before' and 'after' pictures of all park sites we undertake to beautify with floral plantings." In November the acceptance of the gift of cherry trees from the Japanese government received extensive newspaper coverage. A week later, on November 25, the American Broadcasting Company aired a one-hour television special: "A Visit to Washington with Mrs. Lyndon B. Johnson on Behalf of a More Beautiful Capital." Produced by John Secondari, the program looked at the splendor of the District of Columbia but also pointed to its accumulating environmental problems of pollution and decay. "Other generations have left us these monuments, this beauty which we admire," she said in her concluding statement. "What will we leave to those who come after us?" Stewart Udall wrote to her enthusiastically after the program: "What a radiant film—and a radiant narrator! Who knows, maybe your ripple will become a wave?"[16]

Private funding was central to the flexibility of her program, and Mary Lasker pushed ahead in 1965 with the organization of the Society for a More Beautiful National Capital. By midsummer the group had accumulated $25,000, and Mrs. Johnson decided that it was time for the money to be used. Her suggestion was to allocate $10,000 for the improvement of the approach to the city along its Southwest Freeway. In late September the fund-raising brochure, *For a More Beautiful Capital,* was made public. Its distribution brought in an additional $11,000 through the end of the calendar year. The society's treasurer, Carolyn Agger Fortas, pursued the necessary tax-exempt status through the Internal Revenue Service, and Nash Castro agreed to serve as executive director for the group.[17]

Mary Lasker was the main monetary resource of the society during this initial stage of its life. In early January 1966 she showed Mrs. Johnson a check for $70,000 toward the planting of cherry trees at Hains Point.

To this donation, Lasker added $70,000 of her own funds toward the rest of the project's cost of $140,000. With characteristic energy, she arranged for a landscaping service to commence locating Yoshino cherry trees that were ten to twelve feet high. By this time Lasker had already donated almost 100,000 daffodil bulbs for planting along the Rock Creek and Potomac Parkways, as well as 175 dogwoods in the area of the Key Bridge.[18]

Lasker stepped up her courting of the First Lady with gifts and policy proposals during the waning months of 1965 and into the winter of 1966. At Christmas she sent Mrs. Johnson a book on gardens in England, a decorated antique plate, and a camera. The New Yorker also secured assurances from both the District's government and the Park Service that the plant materials that had been donated for beautification would be properly maintained. Others of Lasker's letters to the White House conveyed information about a state beauty conference in California and contained an autographed letter of Thomas Jefferson that spoke to Mrs. Johnson's desire for historic memorabilia for the White House. In these diverse ways Lasker enhanced her usefulness at the Johnson White House.[19]

A few weeks later, Lasker introduced Lady Bird Johnson to the work of the English landscape architect and gardening writer Russell Page. First came a copy of Page's book *The Education of a Gardener,* duly inscribed to the First Lady. Then she received "splendid landscaping suggestions for Hains Point and other locations." Page met Mrs. Johnson at the White House on 13 April 1966 and discussed his plans for a new landscape design for the Ellipse, for the redoing of the park area between E Street and Constitution Avenue, and for the creation of a national horticultural school. These ambitious proposals faced the imposing obstacle course of the District's and the Park Service's bureaucracy before implementation could occur, and Mrs. Johnson was properly noncommittal about what she could do personally to advance Page's ideas.[20]

As it happened, the future of the Ellipse itself related to the recommendations that Nathaniel Owings was making with regard to the future of Pennsylvania Avenue, the Mall, and the White House area generally. Page's proposals regarding E Street and Constitution Avenue, which involved a park site, enjoyed more chance of success, because a Washington donor became interested, through Mary Lasker and others, in putting up from $75,000 to $100,000 for the project. By the autumn of 1966, Rose Zalles had pledged the necessary money for the park, which constituted part of the area near the White House called the President's Park. Newspaper renderings of the project envisioned flowers, walks, and fountains for the site when completed. Mrs. Johnson told Castro that

Laurance Rockefeller, Mary Lasker, Lady Bird Johnson, and Secretary of the Interior Stewart Udall at the White House on 13 April 1966 for a meeting of the First Lady's Committee for a More Beautiful Capital.

the Park Service should "do our best to save the trees" in the area when actual construction started. A fountain for the park became the preferred solution as planning for the use of Mrs. Zalles's gift went forward.[21]

The evidence of Lasker's contribution to Lady Bird Johnson's beautification work was abundant as 1966 came to an end. Castro reported to the First Lady in November that the Park Service intended to put in 543,390 bulbs and spring flowering plants in sixty-four park sites around the District before winter arrived. Lasker's one hundred thousand bulbs

Katie Louchheim helps a Washington student plant geraniums, 16 June 1966.

had already been planted. A year earlier the total had been about 438,000 bulbs and plants throughout the city. An exultant Castro wrote to the White House that "spring 1967 promises to be mighty beautiful in Washington!"[22]

At the meeting of the First Lady's Committee on 30 November 1966, Stewart Udall told his colleagues that "the most dramatic change" in Washington's appearance was occurring in "the monumental part of our city." He cited Lasker's cherry trees along Hains Point and the 500,000 bulbs that would blossom in the spring. "We can give a cheer or two that 25,000 new trees have been planted in Washington," he went on. "This is a city of trees." Udall added that "Mrs. Johnson's program is showing the Nation that we do not have to wait for the millennium or the construction of new, clean cut cities, but that here and now, in the 1960s, we can renew the old cities, and have new dimensions of beauty and delight."[23]

In her opening remarks to the committee the First Lady linked their work to the trip that she and the president had made to Asia in late October and early November. She had gone to see "what much of the world is doing in beautification. The Problem of town planning is as old as the industrial revolution but it has become more acute as the population explodes." She returned after having seen "things to admire and to thrill to" and holding the conviction that "the instinct for beauty is an instinct deep in the heart of everyone." The Australian capital, Canberra, was "an interesting example of a planned city," where the society had "enlisted the real working hands of all the citizens, everybody who has a house." She was equally impressed with the Parliament Building in Kuala Lumpur, the Malaysian National Museum, and the city's mosque; she also spoke warmly about the botanical and rose gardens in New Zealand's capital. As Udall noted after she had finished, linking her work to the "New Conservation," beautification was not "the cherry trees, or daffodils, or more trash cans, or great architecture. But it is the bringing together of all of these things into an urban fabric that can be handsome and can be inviting."[24]

By early 1967, however, the financial and political constraints arising from the Vietnam War and the fact that Congress was in an economy mood began to impinge on the beautification of Washington. Mary Lasker was as energetic as ever during these first months of the New Year. She had sent Mrs. Johnson a truckload of weeping cherry trees just before Christmas 1966, which she followed up with suggestions to Liz Carpenter for "good people" for the Fine Arts Commission. One of her choices was her brother-in-law. Lasker's staff also coordinated the lobbying for highway beautification at this time. Her most ambitious initiative was the lengthy report that she sent to Douglass Cater at the White House on 30 January 1967. In it, she sought to make the case for increased funding for beautification at all levels.[25]

Lasker contended that the program "had captured the Nation's interest and imagination unlike anything I know." The 1960s "will be known to historians as the decade of the conservationist and the beautifier, the years when Americans decided to improve their environment," she predicted. *"President Johnson has done more for the American environment than any President before him."* She then urged Cater to recommend additional money for the Park Service's budget, for highway beautification, and for urban-beautification projects. To make the program more visible, President Johnson should visit some park sites and urban centers in 1967 to see what had been beautified. Lasker's idea came at a time when the president found travel around the nation more difficult because of the rising tempo of Vietnam War protests; her call for higher appropriations was also badly timed, given the administration's difficulties with Capitol Hill.[26]

Mrs. Johnson reiterated her own emphasis on maintenance and upkeep as part of the overall appearance of Washington as funds became tighter. After she had driven down New York Avenue in early February 1967, she wrote to William Walton of the Fine Arts Commission that "there was not a single waste basket in the expanse of three or so blocks and there was a good deal of trash." At a meeting with her on March 1, Nash Castro reported concern "over our ability to maintain improvements" because "maintenance funds are not keeping pace with development commitments." He was able to tell Lady Bird Johnson that the issue of litter on New York Avenue had been addressed through the action of both the Park Service and the local government, which had "doubled their maintenance in this area."[27]

As spring arrived in 1967, the effects of the 1966 plantings became evident. When Mrs. Johnson drove with Castro and Lasker in the early days of April, the First Lady saw the several hundred thousand daffodil bulbs that were flowering along the Rock Creek and Potomac Parkway because of her friend's benevolence. Down Connecticut Avenue they passed a landscaped area that a $20,000 grant from the society had paid for. Later, at the Washington Monument, they looked at the cherry trees in bloom, and they witnessed a similar spectacle at the tip of Hains Point. After reviewing prospective dogwood-planting sites on Columbia Island, Lasker pledged that her foundation would contribute $65,000 toward the cost of installing one million daffodils on the island. For Castro it was a triumphant afternoon. "Everything looked fine and this was reflected in their general approbation and enthusiasm."[28]

Two months later, when the committee assembled on 6 June 1967, its members suggested that the coming year in Washington be called the "Year of the Shade Tree—Bench—and Trashcan." Lady Bird Johnson wanted "to see us do something effective" about providing more shade trees in the District, as well as increasing the number and distribution of attractive benches and trash cans. As always, the problem of cost arose. Nash Castro reported back to Sharon Francis that the most urgent deficiency was private money to step up the tree-planting program. With nine thousand vacant spaces for street trees in Washington, the $100 required to buy and plant each tree meant that $900,000 was the minimum amount required to accomplish the First Lady's goal for shade trees. That was more than double the District's budget for planting trees. Benches cost $125 each, and again, Castro said, private money would be the fastest way to pay for their installation.[29]

Mrs. Johnson also requested a general report on the beautification projects, and Castro told Francis that the Park Service had made "reasonable progress." They had already landscaped eighty-two sites and by the end of the 1967 fiscal year "will have completed just about 100." Because maintenance costs rose with the growth in projects, "we are at a point where we are seriously considering a retrenchment of further capitol improvements until we catch up with our maintenance funding." For Castro, his "biggest disappointment" in the beautification work had been "the almost complete lack of support and interest on the part of the Washington business community." They were, he concluded ruefully, "among the greatest benefactors of our work and the ones who least support it."[30]

Governmental money was then the ultimate resource for the success of beautification. In mid March, Mary Lasker went before a subcommittee of the House Appropriations Committee, which was chaired by Congresswoman Julia Butler Hansen (D, Wash.) on behalf of the Society for a More Beautiful National Capital. In requesting "proper maintenance funds for the Park Service," she informed the committee that the service "simply cannot stretch the budget to do the kind of job needed to be done." She sought an additional $2.5 million in the maintenance appropriation. In early July, Lasker met with Charles L. Schultze, director of the Bureau of the Budget, to make the same plea for greater resources. Her intercession had succeeded, Nash Castro told Lady Bird Johnson, in securing an administration endorsement for more money for the Park Service.[31]

This accomplishment proved timely, because later in the summer, unexpected congressional resistance against money for beautification appeared. Congresswoman Hansen issued a statement in mid August that she would "not authorize funds for beautification projects when money is urgently needed for essential programs." Hansen said that she could not approve a request from the Interior Department to beautify Walt Whitman Park in the District because the $340,000 could be better spent on projects "which will provide badly needed housing, jobs, and playground facilities."[32]

Hansen's edict, if carried out, "seriously compromises our beautification objectives," Castro and Liz Carpenter told the First Lady on 29 August 1967. The Park Service would have to decline a gift from Lasker of trees worth $200,000 because funds would not be available for planting them. In the case of the Walt Whitman Park project, $163,000 from the Associated General Contractors would also have to be turned down. To the congresswoman's point about funds for the ghetto, the memo countered that $1,127,000 had been spent "in depressed neighborhoods" over the preceding three years, as compared with $845,300 in other areas of Washington.[33]

The Park Service began negotiations with Hansen that looked to having the beautification funds reprogrammed so that the gifts could be accepted. Lady Bird Johnson tried to help matters along as well. When she made a trip through the Middle West in September 1967, she commented positively on the virtues of small-town America. Her remarks led Hansen to write the president, praising the First Lady and making the case for breaking up "our ghettos in the cities and redistribute some of our population into the rural areas of America." Hansen did not think that all governmental installations should be located in large cities, and she noted the advantages of having a federal hospital in her district. The White House staff passed the letter on to Mrs. Johnson, who in turn wrote to Hansen about her beautification experiences. The letter grouped the congresswoman with "far sighted leaders" who could "keep the whole effort moving." As 1967 ended, it remained to be seen whether the Park Service could retain the funds for the projects that it wished to pursue for beautification purposes.[34]

The First Lady's Committee held two meetings in late 1967. At the October 18 session the members heard about plans for the landscaping of Columbia Island from architect Edward Stone, Jr., and learned about the pledge from an "anonymous donor"—who was, of course, Mary Lasker—to give 800,000 daffodil bulbs. Secretary Udall reported on the Potomac River Task Force and its recommendation about how to overcome the absence of effective zoning regulations in the District. After the meeting had concluded, the First Lady went to the Yellow Oval Room on the second floor to talk over other beautification questions with Castro, Lasker, Elizabeth Rowe, and William Walton.[35]

The discussion focused on two projects that Mary Lasker had proposed. On the south side of the Ellipse, she wanted to have two fountains installed that would "frame the Jefferson Memorial from the White House." She needed to have a tentative go-ahead from Rowe's Planning Commission and Walton's Fine Arts Commission before she could approach her prospective donor. Castro warned Sutton Jett, however, that locating the fountains might necessitate moving sidewalks and thus sacrificing some trees, "which is out of the question." Lasker's second idea concerned a favorite area of hers in Washington, Hains Point. She wanted to have "a jet of water rising about 100-150 feet in the air," which would resemble a similar jet on Lake Geneva. The projected cost for the "watermark" was put at $300,000. Lasker's fountain ideas would occupy much time and energy of the beautification program in the year that remained for Mrs. Johnson in Washington.[36]

The committee met again on December 18. Sutton Jett was stepping down as the regional director of the Park Service; Nash Castro succeeded him and became a member of the committee as well. The end of the year saw a flurry of donations and announcements at this gathering. The

Hains Point jet project, launched with a gift of $160,000 from Lasker, was discussed, along with a contribution for the two fountains on the Ellipse. There would be flowering dogwoods and other trees on Columbia Island, paid for by funds from the usual "anonymous donor" and the society. The Inaugural Committee, using money that remained from the 1965 ceremonies, gave $40,000 to landscape a circle at the west end of the Memorial Bridge. Mrs. Johnson also announced that the work of the committee had benefited from $322,000 in donations and pledges.[37]

The shade-tree theme that was developed in 1967 continued as a keynote of the committee into 1968. A gift of $10,000 from Marjorie Merriweather Post for the acquisition of trees gave the opportunity to improve a specific area of the city and served as a means of securing other gifts from the city's wealthy philanthropists. The committee wanted to join the District's own Arbor Day festivities on April 26. At its 17 January 1968 meeting, Elizabeth Rowe noted that there were still 6,700 empty tree boxes around Washington. "Every neighborhood," Rowe suggested, "should have an Arbor Day sometime in the spring." Sharon Francis, Cynthia Wilson, Libby Rowe, and others met a week later to coordinate publicity and to persuade local newspapers "to give this Arbor Day appeal some strong coverage." They agreed that an exchange of letters between Mary Lasker and the First Lady would secure the most visibility for the campaign.[38]

Lasker's letter, dated 26 February 1968, asserted that "as you have pointed out so often, one of the glories of Washington is the shady trees that grace its avenues and parks." Because of the high mortality rate among urban trees, "too many neighborhoods are still lacking the refreshing shade they need and want." With Mrs. Post's gift, however, the society had the chance to raise more money to plant additional shade trees. Lasker noted the District's Arbor Day celebration, which the society's fund raising would supplement, and she said that her group hoped that generous Washingtonians "will all want to add to the enjoyment of the city by giving or providing a spot of shade or beauty for future generations to enjoy." In her response of 29 February 1968, Lady Bird Johnson praised the "wonderful news" of the society's campaign: "School-grounds, housing projects, barren neighborhood streets and long avenues all would benefit from this effort."[39]

To ensure that the Post gift did not mean more shade trees only in the affluent parts of the city, Mrs. Johnson asked Castro to see whether the society might match the donation to "attract more attention to the shortage of shade trees" in some poorer areas of Washington. She mentioned in particular the Shaw urban-renewal area, which she had recently visited. Castro reported back to her at the end of March that half of the Post funds should be sent to the Redevelopment Land Agency of the District to serve as "a community activator." Because the agency could obtain governmental funds on a two-to-one basis for matching purposes, the positive impact of the donation would be further enhanced. By late April the shade-tree campaign had brought in a total of $14,500, of which Shaw was allocated $9,000.[40]

It is not clear, however, whether the society itself made any donation. In April the group sought to give $2,600 for flowering trees in Georgetown, to the dismay of Polly Shackleton, who was on the City Council as well as the committee. Such money, she believed, should go to neighborhoods that lacked Georgetown's resources. Elizabeth Rowe also raised objections to the money that was to be spent on the various fountains that Mary Lasker so much wanted around the city. "These monies should be diverted instead to projects in the ghetto," Rowe contended. In responding to this criticism, Lasker told Lady Bird Johnson "that the prospective donors would very likely not wish to divert their money" as Rowe wished, and she asked the First Lady "to talk to Libby in respect to this." What Mrs. Johnson may have said to Libby is not recorded, but the monetary clout that Lasker and her fellow donors exercised made it unlikely that their gifts would be diverted to the ghetto, even in the troubled spring of 1968. That problem had to be addressed in other ways, and Lady Bird Johnson did just that.[41]

This issue also arose in a related manner in Congresswoman Hansen's subcommittee, where it became obvious that the Park Service had not succeeded in persuading her either to restore funds for Walt Whitman Park or to back off her edict of the summer of 1967 about how money for beautification should be used. When the director of the Park Service, George B. Hartzog, Jr., testified before her subcommittee on 7 March 1968, she pressed him on whether the service's request for money to do District landscaping had bowed to her wishes. "You don't have Walt Whitman Park in this, have you?" she asked. Hartzog replied: "No, I don't have it in there. I got the message." Hansen's insistence that fewer funds should go for such projects, coupled with the need to honor her social priorities as a powerful chairperson of an influential committee, limited what the Park Service could accomplish in 1968.[42]

Even Hansen had to concede, however, that the service had had an impact on the District in achieving beautification. Hartzog laid out for the record the eighty park sites, the thirty-nine public schools, and the eight playgrounds that had been landscaped. The number of flowers and bulbs that had been planted under Castro and Lasker's aegis ran into the millions. Hansen acknowledged that the appearance of Washington had "improved a thousand percent within the 8 years I have been here," and she noted that it was particularly true when "you have the chrysanthemums and azaleas in bloom." Hartzog responded that "the leadership that the First Lady has given to this program and that her committee has given and the support we have received in the Congress is going to be something that people will be proud of for years and years to come."[43]

Lady Bird Johnson had her own chance to feel pride in what she had accomplished in the floral aspect of her beautification work before the dramatic events of the spring of 1968 overshadowed everything. On Saturday, 30 March, the day before her husband's surprise announcement that he would not be a presidential candidate, she went with Castro, Liz Carpenter, and a few reporters on an extended tour of the city's parks. They began at Rawlins Park, where she posed for pictures and talked with tourists. Then they moved on to West Potomac Park, for more picture taking and chatting with the visitors. At Hains Point, amidst Mary Lasker's cherry trees, Mrs. Johnson held a picnic lunch, where members of the group "enjoyed our hamburgers and visited about the beautification program as a whole." The entourage then stopped at Pennsylvania Avenue to see the *Magnolia soulangeana* "at their peak of bloom." Visits to Pershing Square and the site of Walt Whitman Park preceded a final stop at the end of Constitution Avenue. "Seeing so many people enjoying the beauty of the parks, which have been so enhanced by the plantings she inspired," Castro remembered, Mrs. Johnson turned to him and said: "It makes it all worthwhile, doesn't it Nash?"[44]

On the next evening, after the president's televised speech, Mary Lasker called the White House, "and it sounded as if she were crying," to say "I know it must be the right thing to do, since the President did it." After the murder of Martin Luther King, Jr., on April 4 and the subsequent rioting in Washington that the assassination had sparked, the Arbor Day activities on April 26 were somewhat muted. Lady Bird Johnson did take part in a planting ceremony of a fern-leaf beech tree on the White House grounds with schoolchildren from the District. She announced then that some of the money from the Post gift would go for shade trees in the Shaw neighborhood, where the violence had been heavy. She wished the residents "long-term happiness from the new trees that will grow along their streets." The trees would be planted under the supervision of the beautification committee of the Model Inner City Community Organization. In the ensuing weeks, the emphasis of what Mrs. Johnson and her associates did fell on the programs for the inner city that ran parallel with her work with flowers and monuments.[45]

As the end of her husband's presidency neared, Lady Bird Johnson

Lady Bird Johnson and Nash Castro, 30 March 1968.

pressed Castro and the Park Service to launch some of the programs that she most wanted before she had to leave Washington. In July she and Lasker saw a District fireboat simulate what the proposed jet of water would look like at Hains Point, and "the First Lady was elated at the prospect of having the jet in operation by early fall." She also wanted construction to begin at Walt Whitman Park. In addition to the funds that Congresswoman Hansen's subcommittee had blocked, promises of Park Service and private money had fallen $100,000 short. Money was also lacking in the service's budget for the fountain at the circle of the west end of Memorial Bridge, and Mary Lasker undertook to raise some of the needed cash.[46]

On the positive side, the appearance of the National Airport had been improved, and the progress of Mrs. Johnson's two-year campaign was evident by the summer of 1968. Both the First Lady and Lasker hoped that such unfinished endeavors as the fountains for Constitution Avenue and the fountains on the Ellipse could be brought to fruition by the end of the year in time for projected meetings of the committee during the last three months of 1968.[47]

Early in September, at another of his regular meetings with the First Lady, Castro suggested that a report be prepared on the beautification results that the committee had achieved. Mrs. Johnson liked the idea, but she broadened the concept into a report to the president for submission to the December meeting. Sharon Francis had already begun to assemble a chronological record of the committee's work for her own use, employing the services of summer interns. That document was ready in mid September. Using it as a base, Francis and Castro then collaborated on the more formal report that Mrs. Johnson wanted for the president. They talked to Henry Diamond, Laurance Rockefeller's associate, about covering the costs of printing and distributing the final product.[48]

Lady Bird Johnson's impact on the monumental features of Washington, which these reports sought to record, extended beyond the work that she had pursued with Castro and Lasker in planting and landscaping. She had played an important role as well in the acquisition of the Joseph Hirshhorn art collection and the creation of the Hirshhorn Museum. Her contribution had been even more significant in the efforts by Nathaniel Owings to rehabilitate Pennsylvania Avenue as part of the city's culture and commerce.

Joseph Hirshhorn had begun to look for a museum to house his huge collection of modern art and sculpture during the early 1960s. Negotiations with groups in Los Angeles, London, New York City, and the state of New York had fallen through or had reached an impasse before S. Dillon Ripley, secretary of the Smithsonian Institution, approached Hirshhorn in the summer of 1964. By early 1965 Ripley had proposed that a Hirshhorn Museum be built on the Mall in Washington as a place for the entire collection. To woo Hirshhorn, Ripley needed presidential influence. He decided, as one avenue of his campaign, to work through the First Lady. Mrs. Johnson hoped to obtain a painting by Thomas Eakins for the White House collection, and Ripley told Liz Carpenter that Hirshhorn possessed thirty-two works by Eakins. Ripley also let his potential donor know about the White House's interest. "Mrs. Johnson is herself keenly aware of the importance of your collection to the nation," Ripley told Hirshhorn in a letter in which he arranged a luncheon for the collector and one of his legal advisors in May 1965. The letter from Mrs. Johnson assured Hirshhorn that they would have "a little time to ourselves just to see the paintings of the White House" before the other luncheon guests arrived.[49]

The occasion was partially successful. Mrs. Johnson showed her guests the White House art, and over the meal, they talked about the nature of the proposed museum. Then the president entered and said: "Joe, you don't need a contract. Just turn the collection over to the Smithsonian and I'll take care of the rest." It wasn't to be that simple. Hirshhorn and his party hedged away from an immediate commitment, though the general foundation for an ultimate agreement had been created. "The Hirshhorn gift may open a great chapter," said the First Lady in her diary; "we will see."[50]

Hirshhorn had written to President Johnson on 17 May 1965, four days before their meeting, to lay out the conditions for making his gift. There would be a museum on the Mall, operated by a board of trustees and the Smithsonian, and Hirshhorn would contribute $1 million to collect more art. The museum must also, Hirshhorn specified, "bear my name in perpetuity." Legislative action would be necessary from Congress to have the museum built, but first the Johnsons had to persuade Hirshhorn to agree to donate his art. Delays during the summer of 1965, some caused by newspaper publicity about the ongoing talks, threatened to stall matters and to turn the mercurial Hirshhorn's attentions elsewhere.[51]

Lady Bird Johnson became a central means of reassurance. Arrangements were made to have her see the collection at the Hirshhorn home in Greenwich, Connecticut. In late July she and the president sent the Hirshhorns some unpublished photographs that they had "personally selected," and when she was in New York on a shopping trip in early August, the Hirshhorns invited her and Lynda to visit their home. The First Lady said to Hirshhorn as she arrived: "I really know nothing about art. I'm prepared to learn." Her comments, which downplayed the real extent of her knowledge, suitably impressed her host. "That was honest," he told his biographer, "and I respected her." Mrs. Johnson had not lost her understanding, gained first in East Texas, that men became uncomfortable with women whose intelligence and learning equaled or exceeded their own.[52]

As the group walked around the grounds, Hirshhorn, "all of five feet two and bouncy," showed them the sculpture and paintings. "I was delighted to encounter the French Impressionists' works in sculpture," the First Lady wrote about the afternoon, "(I'd only known their paintings)—Matisse, Degas, many Daumiers." Bess Abell kept saying: "If we are going to catch that plane, we have to leave," but Mrs. Johnson "kept on walking, none of us willing, least of all me, to stop and thing about planes or drinks." She saw the Eakins portraits, and then it was time to go. The First Lady revisited the Hirshhorn home again in a few years and demonstrated her retentive memory and her eye for art. To her host's surprise, "She remembered a lot of things I had told her. I couldn't get over it."[53]

The pace of negotiations accelerated during the rest of 1965 and into early 1966. Ripley found a potential site for the museum where the Armed Forces Medical Museum stood at Independence and Seventh Avenue. The Defense Department agreed to move this facility, but Congress would also have to concur. When Hirshhorn suffered a heart attack in September, President Johnson sent him a sympathy note that also said how Mrs. Johnson had "stirred a very considerable interest" in the collection in the president's mind. Hirshhorn responded that the First Lady was the "most perfect wife a President could have—and, as you know, she has become interested in modern art." The warm relationship thus established moved the discussion forward during the first half of 1966. By mid May, Hirshhorn had agreed to donate his collection to the United States. The administration, through Harry McPherson, began to prepare congressional leaders for the necessary legislation. In these conversations, Ripley told the lawmakers that "Mrs. Johnson was the decisive factor. Hirshhorn is crazy about her and the President."[54]

The official announcement of the Hirshhorn gift came on 17 May 1966. President Johnson reported that the First Lady had returned from her visit to the Hirshhorns "filled with awe and admiration for the great works that were collected there." In his comments, Hirshhorn gave President Johnson and "his darling and charming wife" most of the credit for influencing him to give his collection to the nation. Now, said the president, "we must begin to build a museum that is worthy of the collection and worthy of our highest aspirations for this beautiful city, the Capital of our country." In late 1966, Mrs. Johnson also received her Eakins for the White House, a 1903 portrait of Ruth Harding. "I am aglow with pride," she wrote the Hirshhorns, "that you have given it to the White House while we are here."[55]

The legislative route to the passage of the Hirshhorn bill was not smooth in 1966. Neither was the location and construction of the museum during the late 1960s and early 1970s. Lady Bird Johnson received criticism about the quality of the Hirshhorn collection from Sherman Lee, director of the Cleveland Museum of Art, and the project was attacked by friends of the Armed Forces Medical Museum. Still the bill cleared Congress in the fall of 1966. After further controversy about the site, groundbreaking ceremonies occurred on 9 January 1969, just before the Johnsons left Washington. The museum was dedicated more than five years later, and Mrs. Johnson then told reporters, "The fact of its being in the nation's capital is very special to me." She had reason to be proud of what she and President Johnson had done to bring Hirshhorn, his collection, and his museum to Washington.[56]

The First Lady's involvement in the campaign to revitalize Pennsylvania Avenue and to develop the Mall as a setting for "national memorials and buildings" was more extensive and prolonged than were her contributions to the creation of the Hirshhorn Museum. She worked closely with Stewart Udall and architect Nathaniel Owings to bring these two endeavors to completion, and her influence with her husband and Congress, her "charm and serenity," were exercised at decisive points to shape the projects in ways she deemed appropriate. She had told the First Lady's Committee at its initial meeting in February 1965 that the Mall should become "a showcase of beauty" that would represent a "magnificent national landscape worthy of the American people." She also urged the committee to "lend strong support to the broad concept of such splendid projects" as President Kennedy's plan for Pennsylvania Avenue. From then on, what Owings called the First Lady's "gentle urgency" was behind both aspects of the effort to improve the monumental center of the city.[57]

The initial impetus to address the future of Pennsylvania Avenue came from President John F. Kennedy. His inaugural parade in 1961 down that avenue passed such a shabby array of rundown shops and unimpressive federal buildings that he had instructed Secretary of Labor Arthur J. Goldberg to prepare plans to refurbish the area. In 1962 the President's Council on Pennsylvania Avenue was created through the work of Goldberg and his young assistant secretary, Daniel Patrick Moynihan. The noted architect Nathaniel Alexander Owings, of Skidmore, Owings and Merrill, was named chairman of the council on 1 June 1962, and he proceeded to try to provide for "the nation's ceremonial way" something of "a special character." By the time President Kennedy was shot, a plan was ready to be presented to Congress, but the transition to the new administration stalled the momentum for the avenue plan.[58]

As Nathaniel Owings recalled in his memoirs, it was during this interval before the Johnson administration became fully interested in Pennsylvania Avenue that the First Lady invited him to come to the White House along with his report on Pennsylvania Avenue. Liz Carpenter stressed that the meeting was tentative and unofficial; Mrs. Johnson and Owings "discussed open spaces and flower beds," all of which "tied in with the Pennsylvania Avenue plan." Owings's account is not precise about dates, but the first conversations with Mrs. Johnson probably took place after his council had delivered its report to the president in late May of 1964. At a press conference on June 3, President Johnson called what the council had proposed a "bold and creative plan," and he gave it other endorsements during the rest of that election year. The public response to the plan itself was favorable.[59]

In late March 1965, President Johnson set up the Temporary Commission on Pennsylvania Avenue by executive order. Owings chaired that body and also became the architect to design plans for the Mall. By that time the First Lady had assembled her committee, and Stewart Udall had suggested Owings for membership on it. The architect soon became an active participant in the early gatherings of the committee. The group visited the Mall in March 1965 for its second meeting, and Mrs. Johnson told Owings that she "particularly" hoped to "familiarize myself with your sketch of the Mall before the meeting." Over the next several months she did so in some detail. She made her feelings known to Owings about such specific aspects of the Mall's design as the proposed location of the Hirshhorn Museum, the possibility of a parking garage beneath the Mall, and the potential destruction of trees in the course of any construction. On one occasion, she, Owings, and Udall were "sitting on the floor of Lady Bird's sitting room studying a great long drawing rolled across the carpet, Stewart squatting at one end, I [Owings] at the other, and Lady Bird in the middle." At that point, President Johnson walked in and said, "What in hell, Udall, are you doing down there on the floor with my wife?"[60]

Owings presented his overall plan for the Mall at the meeting of the First Lady's Committee on 24 September 1965. He showed it to Mrs. Johnson on the day before the presentation, and she immediately focused on how trees would fare as the Mall was changed. She asked him "if the plans mean cutting down any of the nice stand of trees now growing, particularly opposite the Smithsonian Building," and also whether he envisioned "clipped European trees" where others were to be planted. As she told Marjorie Merriweather Post, who had also noticed the way trees were handled when Owings's plan was announced, "I registered my objection to the 'clipped trees' for whatever it was worth."[61]

On the next day, Owings publicly unveiled his Mall plan for the first time before the committee. "This central area of Washington should be the image of our country in the tradition of America," he told them, and the Mall "should become a welcome, open park for the love of life and the enjoyment of living for every single citizen in Washington, regardless of where they live." He then outlined at some length what would happen to cars, where he hoped to put a reflecting pool, and how freeways would be rerouted underground or away from the Mall itself. Mrs. Johnson made a point of asking him how, if cars were kept at a distance, tourists would get to what they wanted to see. "It is very marvelous to have that dignified view of the Lincoln Monument without the cars in front," she said, "but we are surely going to have to change the addiction of folks to going everywhere in a car." After Owings had finished, the First Lady added that her main hope was to see "some little gem completed within two or three years because it would give evidence to the public, and make them want to see the long completion of it."[62]

President Johnson took the next step toward the completion of Pennsylvania Avenue when he asked Congress on 30 September 1965 to declare it a national historic site and to create a Permanent Commission on Pennsylvania Avenue. On that same day, Udall designated much of the avenue as a historic site under authority he possessed over federal property in the area. The issue then went to Capitol Hill as a joint resolution to establish the council. There it encountered difficulty in the spring of 1966.[63]

The Senate approved the joint resolution, but the House balked. Congressmen criticized the structure of the proposed commission, its relation to other planning agencies in the District, and the size of its budget. Owings's plan for a National Square at the White House end of the Avenue drew heavy attacks from Elizabeth Rowe's National Capital Planning Commission. The avenue proposal also became entangled with planning for the John F. Kennedy Center for the Performing Arts. One congressman in particular, John Saylor (R, Pa.), the ranking minority member of the House Committee on Interior and Insular Affairs, disliked the commission as proposed. He called it a duplication of other agencies, which was "nothing more than icing on the cake." The resolution came out of the Interior Committee in mid 1966, but it failed to reach the House floor before Congress adjourned.[64]

During this period, Owings and Udall sought to solidify the First Lady's connection with the plans for the Mall and for Pennsylvania Avenue as they emerged. Udall told Liz Carpenter in March 1966 that "the First Lady should be personally identified with the master plan for the Great Central Mall" which Owings had developed for Interior. Mrs. Johnson, Udall went on, "could endorse the broad concept without being committed to any of the specific details." Owings wrote to Mrs. Johnson in early May that a new model of the Mall and the Avenue was available and could be used at a meeting of the committee in the summer. The model, Owings informed Liz Carpenter, would "lay at rest" many of the existing public concerns about how freeways would be handled in the plan, while it would also help to "clarify the White House's position" without "committing them to any specific feature." By mid 1966, Mrs. Johnson's approval of a Washington project represented a public asset that men such as Owings and Udall coveted.[65]

As discussions about the summer meeting proceeded, Owings had to reassure the First Lady about her persistent concern regarding trees in the areas where the architect was working. In May 1966 he felt compelled to transmit "a word of explanation" about the "present disappointing appearance of the cherry tree clusters at the Washington Monument." The trees were not too closely spaced, and their "regimented" look was illusory. Still, he agreed to replant some of the trees to "break up the visual impact of the regimented lines of stalks." She thanked him for "keeping me informed on all your plans and projects," but she added that "from time to time I will go by and see the effect of the changes."[66]

On 28 June 1966, Owings reported to the committee about his plans. There were other events that afternoon, and the architect, who could be long-winded, followed Liz Carpenter's injunction to "make it shorter." In his presentation, Owings mentioned informal recreation areas where his planners had "gone back to a rather informal America." The First Lady commented, "I do like that." She was, however, still having problems with the amount of trees: "To me, it is so full of trees there is no room below for people."[67]

In the fall of 1966, as the end of the congressional session approached, Owings and Moynihan sought to obtain tangible expressions of support from the president and the First Lady for the Pennsylvania Avenue resolution. Owings spoke to Lady Bird Johnson personally, and she agreed to "push" the measure. He thanked her in mid October for "taking out the time and helping on the Pennsylvania Avenue problem." Apparently President Johnson was less inclined to assist. In any case, Congressman Saylor's opposition and his procedural understanding with the committee chairman, Wayne Aspinall (D, Colo.) prevented action on the resolution in 1966.[68]

The resolution began its course through Congress again in 1967, and the Senate, as before, passed it easily. The problem remained in the House, where Saylor was still opposed and Aspinall told Owings he was "not sure that there is any interest anymore in the administration." Stewart Udall tried in the spring "to move it, without success," and Owings asked presidential aide Harry McPherson for help in July. Moynihan also sought McPherson's assistance. "To rebuild the center of Washington at this time, and in this manner, could have vast influence on the future of urban living," Moynihan argued, but the president would have to act. In late July, McPherson drafted a letter for Johnson to send to Aspinall, which said that Mrs. Johnson and the president were "extremely interested" in seeing the Pennsylvania Avenue measure passed.[69]

These remarks were certainly true of the First Lady. Owings went to see Lady Bird Johnson in August 1967 to press his case. "I tried to ex-plain to Mr. Owings," she observed to Sharon Francis, "that just because we stand behind something or just because we work for it does not mean the Congress is going to give us just what we want." But in this instance, she concluded, "I think we do want to work for the Pennsylvania Avenue Commission." She also continued to monitor plans for the National Square, and White House staff members, such as McPherson, complained to the First Lady when the proposed FBI Building failed to give the same space for pedestrian sidewalks as other buildings on the avenue did. As 1967 came to an end, Mrs. Johnson once again said that she "thought we should support" the Pennsylvania Avenue resolution.[70]

The president's commitment to the avenue and its commission seems to have been less intense, in part because he appears to have regarded Moynihan as a member of the "Kennedy underground" and also because of more pressing obligations during the waning years of his presidency. Johnson was still debating whether to make "a few phone calls" to congressmen about the measure at the end of January 1968. By early May, Udall and the White House had "reluctantly" agreed to meet some of Saylor's demands in an effort to get a bill he favored through the House. That did not succeed while Lyndon Johnson was in the White House. Only in October 1972, under Richard Nixon, did a Pennsylvania Avenue bill finally emerge from Congress in a form acceptable to Owings. Four years earlier, Mrs. Johnson concluded her immediate connection with the project by sending out a statement, drafted by Sharon Francis, that said about his work, "America's foremost ceremonial street has benefited vastly from Nathaniel Owings's creative vision."[71]

Mrs. Johnson and Owings had collaborated effectively because of his capacity, which rivaled Nash Castro's, to get things done. In 1967 the committee received $160,000 from the publisher of *Seventeen Magazine*, Enid Haupt, toward the construction of the two fountains on the Ellipse that Lasker had envisioned to frame the White House and the Jefferson Memorial. Owings was named the architect for the fountains, and he soon found that the Haupt donation "hardly covered the overhead." He decided to "beg and borrow the necessary ingredients," and he persuaded the owner of a granite quarry in Minnesota to send two "samples" of stone that were two feet thick and twenty feet square. Once out of the ground, the huge blocks of granite took two weeks and seven different railroads to reach Washington. The stones were installed and survived the student demonstrations of the late 1960s and early 1970s. They seemed, Owings concluded, "to belong there."[72]

So the First Lady and Nathaniel Owings helped Pennsylvania Avenue pass through the difficult first phase of what became a two-decade process of revitalization. The architect later wrote about Lady Bird Johnson that she "provided the leadership that changed the political climate in Washington to being favorable to aesthetic considerations, through her personal participation in a positive program."[73] Her role for Pennsylvania Avenue underscored Owings's point. She gave him a forum in which to show his plans to influential Washingtonians at her committee meetings, and her public appearances with him as they looked at drawings and models legitimized his endeavors. President Johnson regarded the avenue project as one more demand on his time that had roots in the Kennedy years. Lady Bird Johnson grasped the cultural significance of what the avenue could represent as a model for other cities in the same way that Moynihan did, and she made a decisive contribution to the ultimate success of the project.

The report that Sharon Francis and her beautification colleagues assembled in the autumn of 1968 well reflected the dimensions of what Mrs. Johnson and her committee had accomplished when it was presented to the president at the last formal meeting on 17 December 1968. The Society for a More Beautiful National Capital had raised in excess of $2.5 million for its work, and one hundred separate park-landscaping projects had been done. Hundreds of thousands of bulbs, trees, and plants had been added to the landscape. In terms of Washington's monuments, the report proudly noted what had been accomplished on the Mall, along Pennsylvania Avenue, on Columbia Island, at Hains Point, and at numerous other locations in the city. At the meeting itself, formal dedications took place of the proposed Zalles fountains on the Northwest Ellipse, the Haupt fountains on Constitution Avenue, and Mary Lasker's fountain jet at Hains Point.[74]

For Nash Castro it was a poignant moment. "I realize that this is probably the last time I will visit with Mrs. Johnson in the Yellow Oval Room." He felt "a keen sense of nostalgia" as he thought of "the fervor and dedication that this very special First Lady has demonstrated." Castro and Mary Lasker had reason to be proud of what they had accomplished with Mrs. Johnson. Not all their endeavors succeeded, but most of the bulbs that they planted and the flowers that they nurtured did bloom over the years, and the look of monumental Washington was the better for it.[75]

The driving force of their success was, of course, the First Lady. She supplied the enthusiasm and the energy that enabled Lasker, Castro, Owings, and the others who helped them to draw on her influence and support. As she said to her committee in April 1968, "My criteria of a project is that it receive the fullest human use—that it be well cared for—and a third ingredient—that the desire for it emanate from the neighborhood and the users." Gently, quietly, but with tenacious persistence, she reminded her co-workers that these principles had to be embodied in the parks and monuments that the tourists and residents saw and experienced.[76]

Two decades later her influence on the city's appearance was still visible. When Congress awarded her a gold medal in 1984, the letters in support of the idea from her Washington friends sounded a unified theme. "Through her and her committee's work," wrote Elizabeth Rowe, "Washington bloomed as it never had before. And it is still blooming." Robert Lederer of the American Association of Nurserymen commented that "each spring we are greeted with flowering plants and trees which would never have been a part of our daily lives without Mrs. Johnson and her National Beautification Program." Across all of Washington, as the cherry trees blossom on Hains Point and the flowers appear in the parks and along the roadways, the collective thought in Washington is "Thank God for Lady Bird Johnson."[77]

Had the First Lady's efforts in Washington, D.C., been restricted to the monumental areas of the capital, her beautification work, as valuable as it might have been, would have remained flawed and incomplete. From the outset of her committee's campaign, however, she recognized that the inner city and its black neighborhoods had to be an essential part of her priorities. Through Walter Washington, Polly Shackleton, and others, Mrs. Johnson took beautification into the ghetto and, as Washington put it, "went to the heart of filling the gap and beginning to work with the alienation" of the city's black residents. That aspect of her career as First Lady was as important and as central as her work with Nash Castro and Mary Lasker.[78]

6

A Pattern of Quality
for Washington's Neighborhoods

From the formation of the First Lady's Committee for a More Beautiful Capital in late 1964 and early 1965, there was a consensus among the people involved that a beautification strategy directed only at the Washington, D.C., which the tourists saw, would be politically vulnerable and substantively incomplete. "It is not enough to have a showcase, even the most beautifully designed and landscaped cultural center," wrote Antonia Chayes in December 1964: "these human expressions must be made relevant to everyone, or they are as inaccessible as if they were miles away." Talking with Katie Louchheim at about the same time, Mrs. Johnson said that one goal of a beautification effort might be to make "the people who live in the public housing area aware of what they, themselves, can do—put out their own packet of seed, etc." When the announcement of the establishment of the committee was made in early February 1965, news reports emphasized that "a major effort" would "probably be directed towards finding ways of beautifying the areas few tourists ever visit." The group, wrote Wolf Von Eckardt in the *Washington Post*, would supply leadership for neighborhoods, especially "low income neighborhoods," that would seek to "help people to help themselves to self respect as well as to mere cosmetic beauty."[1]

The question, of course, was how to accomplish these goals in a manner that would have a positive impact on the black neighborhoods of Washington itself. The committee would need to have at least one black member to provide links with the inner city. In early 1965 there were only a few blacks whose careers had given them enough visibility to come to the attention of the First Lady and her advisors. Secretary Udall's initial list of potential members contained the name of Robert C. Weaver, who later became the first secretary of the Department of Housing and Urban Development of the Johnson Cabinet. To Udall's suggestions was added, under the category of "public housing," Walter Washington, who had been the executive director of the National Capital Housing Author-

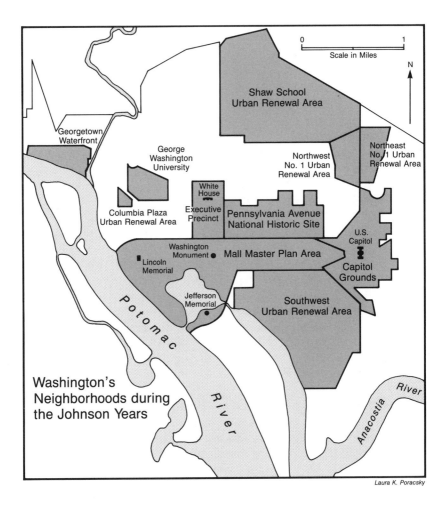

Washington's
Neighborhoods during
the Johnson Years

Laura K. Poracsky

ity since 1961. He attended the first meeting on 11 February 1965 and was named to the Subcommittee on Neighborhoods and Special Projects. This was the beginning of a long and fruitful working relationship with Lady Bird Johnson.[2]

Walter Washington was approaching his fiftieth birthday in the spring of 1965. Born in Georgia, his mother's home state, he had grown up in Jamestown, New York. He received a B.A. from Howard University in Washington in 1938 and did graduate work at American University over the next three years. In December 1941 he married Bennetta Bullock, the daughter of a prominent Washington clergyman; and his marriage made him part of the network of influential black families in the city. Mrs. Washington's work in the District's school system and her commitment to racial equality added to her husband's political appeal. By this time, Walter Washington had started to work with the Alley Dwelling Authority, the agency that dealt with public housing in the District. It became the National Capital Housing Authority in 1943, and he steadily rose within it over the next two decades. In 1948 he earned a law degree from Howard. One of his black associates at the time called him "a smooth briefcase operator who had learned the white man's game and was excellent at it."[3]

Mrs. Johnson's committee gave Walter Washington a way to improve the situation of some of the city's black residents, and he proceeded with his customary efficiency and persistence to take advantage of the chance. "I like to be judged on performance, and not on what somebody believes," he later said, and the First Lady discovered that his sensitivity and ingenuity also produced positive results. He urged her, during the early days of her work, to include a public-housing area in the tour of the city that occurred in conjunction with the second meeting of the committee on 9 March 1965. She went to the Greenleaf Gardens Project "where a small crowd of the neighborhood folks were gathered to greet us." The First Lady believed that "all of our efforts will fail unless people in these neighborhoods can see the challenge and do the work on their own front yards."[4]

With Washington as her guide, Mrs. Johnson went out into the black neighborhoods in the spring of 1965, "where the conditions are gray and dismal," to see what her committee might accomplish. Two decades later he recalled that she rarely missed any key details, and he knew that he had to be ready to respond to the items she noticed as they walked along and talked. Her readiness to plunge into even the most grim surroundings and her ease with the crowds that gathered also left an enduring impression on him. At the third committee meeting on 8 April 1965, Washington read a letter that Mrs. Johnson had received from a young black man who lived on Fiftieth Street, Northeast. John Hatcher wrote to her: "I would like for my yard to look more beautiful. If you would please send me azaleas, I will plant them. Then you would not have to come all the way out to 50th Street to plant them for me." For Walter Washington, the letter illustrated "the depth to which the program under Mrs. Johnson's leadership has come."[5]

Addressing the committee, Washington outlined plans for the spring and summer ahead. In an area such as the Second Precinct, he proposed "a rather massive cleanup campaign" for the Forty-ninth Census Tract. He wanted to plant trees and shrubs around twenty-one local schools and other recreation centers. The effort's main focus, as he later wrote, "was an attempt to motivate the children, youth, adults, and family units in a long-range program of self-involvement for enhancing the physical appearance of the community." Washington understood, however, that his long-term goals required immediate publicity, and he used the First Lady and John Hatcher's letter to create news that would stimulate other beautification activity.[6]

Mrs. Johnson replied to John Hatcher that "we can keep our properties and school grounds neat, we can pick up litter, but there are few things we can do that will bring more joy than the planting of fine flowers." Walter Washington also ensured that the delivery of an azalea bush to Hatcher's home was well covered in the local press. Washington garnered more favorable news for the First Lady when he followed up promptly on an inquiry to the committee from a small donor in the District. The woman had called the White House at the suggestion of a *Washington Post* columnist to test how the First Lady's staff would react. The quick response from Liz Carpenter and Washington turned a potentially negative report into a positive press notice.[7]

By the time the committee met on May 19, Washington had pulled together his summer agenda. Working with the District's school system, he had identified Kelly Miller Junior High, Richardson Elementary, and Jefferson Junior High as schools to undergo pilot beautification plantings. Money from the S. Klein Company and the Hechinger Company funded the installation of plants and trees through the work of neighborhood children and adult residents. Both companies received beautification certificates from Mrs. Johnson at a White House ceremony on 16 May 1965. Meanwhile, Walter Washington had already begun working with Lynda Johnson in selecting a school where she might sponsor a beautification project.[8]

During the summer, Walter Washington pushed forward in the Forty-ninth Census Tract with his "clean-up," "fix-up," "paint-up," and "plant-up" campaign, including an effort to control rats in the area. He drew

Lady Bird Johnson and students at Jefferson High School in Washington, D.C., on 19 May 1965.

on the Community Service Project, an organization of Howard University students, faculty, and other community volunteers, for weekly cleanup drives, and he secured tools and plants from local businesses. In late August the Health Department hauled away sixty-five truckloads of trash from a single block, and on August 28, one thousand people swept, planted, and painted in the neighborhood. As he reported to Mrs. Johnson in a memorandum of 24 September 1965, he wanted to take similar programs to the southeast, in the vicinity of the Kentucky Courts housing project and the Buchanan School.[9]

Mrs. Johnson seconded Walter Washington's campaign in the summer when she told the superintendent of recreation for the District about a visit that she had made to the John F. Kennedy Playground. She was convinced, she wrote to Milo F. Christiansen, "that we would be well advised to provide more playgrounds of this type in the District of Columbia, including possibly one for each quadrant of the city." She also informed him that the playgrounds "would be made aesthetically more pleasing, I believe, if trees, shrubs and other plant materials could be

Lady Bird Johnson and Walter Washington engage in an animated conversation at the White House on 3 November 1967.

selectively planted in and around them." She asked him for a priority list of playgrounds because "Who knows, someone might step forward with funds?"[10]

Walter Washington's activities went on vigorously as the fall of 1965 approached. In mid September, after touring the city with him, Lynda Johnson selected the John F. Cook School at 30 P Street, Northeast, and donated $1,500 of her own funds for its beautification. Her check was presented at a ceremony on September 16, when plans were also disclosed to beautify the Slater-Langston Schools across the street from Cook. In a separate endeavor, Walter Washington talked with District officials about an Urban Beautification Program for the city, under the provisions of the recently enacted Housing and Urban Development Act of 1965. His proposal looked to a committee, made up of city agencies involved with beautification projects, that would "develop a unified beautification program for the District involving all interested elements, both public and private."[11]

The impulse to centralize and coordinate the work of beautification in the District also showed up within the First Lady's committee itself in September 1965. Katharine Graham of the *Washington Post* had William

Walton, Wolf Von Eckardt, Walter Washington, and Katie Louchheim to lunch in what Graham described as an attempt "to try and pool our efforts, and perhaps even establish a series of priorities, in order to give more effective service to your cause." They told Mrs. Johnson, through a letter from Graham, that they wanted "to be certain we are all moving in coordinated directions," and they suggested that the First Lady might appoint "a steering committee composed of members of your over-all committee, a central clearing house so to speak." In that way, Graham concluded, "we would be within nearer reach of common goals and might also avoid the mistakes of undirected action."[12]

It is not altogether clear what motivated Graham's initiative to the First Lady, though it may have reflected a sense that what Mrs. Johnson had done up to that point spoke more to the needs of Washington tourists and the white community than to the residents of the inner city. Walter Washington lacked the staff resources and support that Mary Lasker could call upon from Nash Castro and the Park Service, and he talked with Graham and Louchheim in these months about finding additional personnel. At a luncheon with Louchheim on 6 October 1965, she and Washington spoke about the "urgent need . . . to harness or coordinate activities under direction of local citizens who understand the dangers implicit in some of the more depressed areas. It is imperative that beautification take place where it can bring 'hope' and accompanying recognition of the other problems in the area." To the contention that the need for schoolbooks outweighed the need for plants and trees, Washington and Louchheim countered that such thinking missed the intent of what the First Lady was seeking to do. "It is the care and appreciation of plants that welds the PTA, the school principal and the children into one group and not the gift of books."[13]

Lady Bird Johnson did not reject what Graham, Louchheim, and Walter Washington had put forward, but neither did she accord it her immediate endorsement. Writing to Graham on October 11, she said that it might be mid November "before I can really sit down and give such a meeting the uninterrupted thought it deserves." She acknowledged that beautification had "grown a little like Topsy, but I do see results, and I'll be calling you so we can talk about how to get more of them." The First Lady no doubt understood that allocating influence to a committee of the type that Graham and the others had in mind would reduce her own capacity to pursue beautification in the manner that suited her.[14]

At the same time there was a need to intensify her commitment to the local schools, on which Walter Washington was focusing his attention. She had him obtain a list of the schools that were slated for beautification, and he told Liz Carpenter which of the facilities would benefit from these improvements. In mid November, after accepting the gift of cherry trees from the Japanese government, the First Lady went with Washington, Carpenter, and Nash Castro to look at Terrell Junior High and the Walker-Jones High School in the area of First Street in Northwest Washington. Outside of Terrell, students from the nearby Perry School spotted Mrs. Johnson in her car. As they waved, "she lowered her car window and motioned them over. She shook hands with many of them and asked them all to be sure and tend the plants and otherwise look after them, to keep litter away from the area, and to protect the new windowpanes that have been installed at the Terrell School."[15]

As they drove through these neighborhoods, Washington invited Mrs. Johnson to see the Walker-Jones School, which the firm of J. H. Burton and Sons of Hyattsville, Maryland, had recently landscaped. Students at the school had prepared some beautification exhibits that Washington wanted the First Lady to inspect. She spent ten minutes in the school's lobby and, Nash Castro noted in his report, was "so pleased" with what the students had accomplished "that she took a card out of her purse and wrote a note to the children." Castro pinned the note to one of the exhibits, and then they departed. Later in the drive, when the party passed Buchanan School, she commented "that it is urgently in need of landscaping." Walter Washington agreed to do something to upgrade the appearance of Buchanan. Mrs. Johnson added a public endorsement of what she had seen at these schools when she dedicated their landscape projects at formal ceremonies on 6 December 1965.[16]

In addition to his work with schools, Washington, along with Katharine Graham and Wolf Von Eckardt, was still attempting to fund beautification projects from the money that the 1965 Housing Act was providing. He wanted contributions to the Society for a More Beautiful National Capital to be funneled through the District government so that these donations would become eligible for matching federal money. A related benefit would be that "money would go for the beautification of neighborhoods, schools and public housing, thereby avoiding the criticism that some of the beautification efforts are merely cosmetic and superficial." Such a process would involve a reduction in Mary Lasker's influence and a change in the emphasis of her beautification commitment, and it was unlikely that she would sympathize with what Walter Washington had in mind.[17]

In early December 1965, Walter Washington and Commissioner Walter Tobriner passed along to Lady Bird Johnson the news that the Inter-Agency Committee on Beautification Programs had been formed in the District. Walter Washington became vice-chairman of the panel, and the First Lady responded with a letter of congratulations to Tobriner: "Everyone is well aware in a program of this magnitude that often the right hand does not know what the left is doing. This Inter-Agency Committee is a practical step in preventing duplication and cutting red tape." Reflecting Walter Washington's impact and perhaps even his own language, she concluded: "Beautification is no final solution to the problems that plague our mushrooming urban areas, but it is an important step." The District of Columbia's government was so fragmented and internally divided, so inchoate in the face of congressional oversight, that the Inter-Agency Committee represented the possibility of constructive action, but no more than that, unless Washington and his allies could impose coordination upon it.[18]

Early in 1966, Brooke Astor enlisted in the First Lady's and Walter Washington's campaign for the beautification of the District's school facilities. As president of the Vincent Astor Foundation, named after her husband who had died in 1960, she had used the foundation's resources to install parks in New York housing projects, along the lines of what was being contemplated for the District. On January 12, Lady Bird Johnson, Mary Lasker, Liz Carpenter, and Walter Washington joined Astor and her architect, Simon Breines, on a tour of schools and housing projects. Astor tentatively decided, after looking around the city, to concentrate on facilities in the Southwest area. Later Astor and Washington also toured the Buchanan School grounds again. Mrs. Johnson recalled in 1968 that Astor "decided right then that Buchanan School should become a place of variety and delight." Though that firm a commitment was made at the outset of 1966, it took most of the rest of the year to work out the details of Astor's financial donation to the First Lady's school-beautification program. Astor's generosity, however, gave this aspect of Mrs. Johnson's work in the District of Columbia a momentum that it could not otherwise have achieved from what was available to Walter Washington in personnel and funds.[19]

The difficulties that confronted Walter Washington's labors on neighborhoods and schools mounted during the winter of 1966. He had received some assistance from S. Klein Company in 1965 in temporary personnel, but that loan of individuals was ending. He still lacked money and staff for all the projects he hoped to sponsor. Moreover, he did not have effective help from within the First Lady's Committee itself. Commissioner Tobriner lacked force, and Antonia Chayes had gone overseas with her husband on his service for the State Department. The presidential aide for the District, Charles Horsky, was reaching the end of his White House tenure. Katie Louchheim, among others, suggested that the Neighborhoods and Special Projects Subcommittee be reconstituted with four women who could help to evoke "a continu-

Polly Shackleton at the White House on 13 October 1967.

ing citizen interest for beautification projects in schools, in playgrounds, etc."[20]

One of the names that Louchheim submitted was that of Polly Shackleton, who had been on the First Lady's Committee since its inception. A District resident since 1939, Mrs. Robert W. Shackleton was fifty-five years old and had worked in a staff capacity for the American Institute of Architects in Washington for a decade and a half. She had also been a member of the Democratic Central Committee for the District from the mid 1950s and had become Democratic national committeewoman in 1961. She brought organizational ability, a commitment to the inner city, and a good deal of political insight to her manifold beautification activities. She wanted to use what the First Lady had already done as a means of expanding job training for ghetto youths, and she wrote to Lady Bird Johnson in January 1966 about what more she, Shackleton, wanted to see accomplished. "While I know a new W.P.A., if called that, would be political murder," Shackleton argued, "perhaps it would be possible to launch some useful work-training programs in cleaning-up and beautification for the 'hard core unemployables.'" She believed that an Operation Pride project could address the many alleys and streets in the city that were "full of litter and trash," and she sought the First Lady's blessing to "try and come up with some suggestions and recommendations."[21]

Lady Bird Johnson told Shackleton that "nothing would please me more than to see" the list of job-training projects in the District expanded. "Beautification is not only for people, it is by people too," the First Lady said, and "without the willing hands and hearts of many trained workmen, the goals of the Committee for a More Beautiful Capital would only be faintly realized." Shackleton should "continue to emphasize this activity in the various programs that come to your attention, and do all you can to strengthen them."[22]

A month later, Shackleton reported on her efforts in the Second Precinct and a vocational-training program for six black high-school seniors at the National Arboretum. Mrs. Johnson praised her as "a can-do woman" and knew "if we put the second precinct beautification in your hands, you would find some angels for it." The First Lady added that if she could "help by writing activists, I will be glad to."[23]

Shackleton and Walter Washington wanted to go beyond these relatively small operations and to establish a more comprehensive program of employment opportunities for young black men in the summer of 1966. At a meeting in the spring at Katie Louchheim's office, they decided to build on what Walter Washington had accomplished in the Forty-ninth Census Tract with the Community Service project from Howard a year earlier. Working again with District officials, they drew up a proposal for Project Pride, which the Society for a More Beautiful National Capital agreed to fund with a grant of $7,000 in May. The Project Pride Committee was formed, staff help came from the National Capital Housing Authority, and headquarters opened at 913 P Street, Northwest. Twenty Howard University students were employed through a Department of Health, Education and Welfare grant, and eighty high-school students worked on the project through the Neighborhood Youth Corps.[24]

The launching of Project Pride occurred in mid July 1966 in the Shaw

School urban-renewal area. The press release quoted Mrs. Johnson as being "delighted that the people in the Shaw area have taken the in- itiative in Project Pride and that private and governmental agencies are cooperating to make this demonstration project a success." The program announced that it would be concentrating on rat control with a follow- up on trash collection. Subsequent work would focus on cleaning up vacant lots and saving endangered street trees.[25]

Within a month the work had begun to show results. Liz Carpenter told the First Lady that "rat baiting, painting-up, etc.," was "going full force" and represented "just the kind of thing needed to offset long, hot summer situations." Sharon Francis and Nash Castro visited the proj- ect with Mrs. Tracy Barnes of Shackleton's committee a few days later and reported that the rat baiting had gone well and a "huge amount of rubble has been removed from the area." There were three projects that Mrs. Johnson could easily see—a vacant lot that had become a neighborhood garden, another that was now a play area, and a summer education project at the Rising Mount Zion Baptist Church. Francis suggested that the First Lady might want to see what Project Pride had accomplished, with a view to having Shackleton report to the October 5 meeting of the committee. "I'd like very much to do this," Mrs. Johnson wrote on Francis's memorandum, and she inspected the achievements in the Second Precinct on September 29.[26]

When the committee met, Polly Shackleton provided a detailed review of what Project Pride had accomplished. The aim of the program had been to "show the public that beautification is a very basic concept with many facets including eradication of rats and vermin, litter and trash removal, and clean-up and paint-up, as well as the planting and main- tenance of trees, grass, shrubs and flowers." They had selected the Shaw neighborhood as "one of the most deprived areas in the city," and they had witnessed rat baiting in eighty-six blocks, the removal of 1,304 cubic yards of trash and 600 abandoned cars, and home repairs, vacant-lot clean- ing, and care. In the end, 250 children took part in some aspect of Proj- ect Pride, and Shackleton quoted some comments from Shaw-area residents. "Makes you feel better to walk around and see something so pretty," said one; and another remarked, "I sure hope you get bigger next year so you can clean-up the whole city."[27]

Having done that much in one summer, Shackleton wanted to con- tinue her efforts into 1967 and to provide a resounding negative answer to the *Washington Post*'s headline that asked "Will Pride Go before the Fall?" She asked Carolyn Fortas of the society if they might allow her to retain the services of a retired soil conservationist to advise school custodians on how best to maintain what had been planted during the summer. She also worked with private and quasi-public groups in the District to expand programs in 1967 for the city's youth. Because of substantial cutbacks in the District's budget for beautification-related projects in the spring of 1967, Shackleton had to look to private funding agencies to carry out the projects that local residents had created for the Shaw area, the Capitol East neighborhood, and the Benning Park region, located in Far Northeast Washington.[28]

To underwrite her idea, Shackleton approached Laurance Rockefeller, who agreed to make a $50,000 gift to the society for a summer project, to be called Project Trail Blazers, which would enlist "low income young people living in areas east of the Anacostia River in Washington in efforts to enhance the environment of their neighborhoods." The project eventually enrolled 110 youths, 95 boys and 15 girls, aged thirteen to fifteen, many of whom came "out of a background of extreme deprivation which often makes its mark physically and emotionally." Their work included the reshaping of a shuttered movie theater into the Anacostia Neighborhood Museum, as well as the creation of play spaces near the Frederick Douglass home. In late August 1967, Mrs. Johnson toured the project with Henry Diamond of Rockefeller's staff. "It was just great," Shackleton noted, "for the youngsters, the staff and the Anacostia population in general to have her go out there."[29]

Once the summer of 1967 had ended, however, the familiar question would arise of how to carry the Trail Blazers program through the ensuing autumn and winter. Laurance Rockefeller agreed that "we must not look upon these projects as summer palliatives to be dropped as soon as the cool weather comes." At Shackleton's request, he gave an additional $25,000 to the society in order to sustain Trail Blazers on Saturdays throughout the winter months. Rockefeller warned Shackleton, however, that "programs of this kind cannot be indefinitely carried by private sources," and it would soon become necessary for the city or the federal government to keep Trail Blazers alive.[30]

The program continued to function into early 1968. In February the Board of Education approved its operation through the remainder of the school year. Lady Bird Johnson applauded this administrative action, because in her meetings with the members of Trail Blazers in 1967 she had concluded that many had "made a good transition from dreary and unfulfilled lives to an enriching pattern of constructive activity." By September 1968, however, after President Johnson's withdrawal and the spring rioting that followed the death of Martin Luther King, Jr., Trail Blazers had been suspended because of the lack of money. Sharon Francis wrote to Walter Washington, who was now the city's mayor, of her regret about how the program had fared. She cited "the investment of

Lady Bird Johnson visits Project Trail Blazers at the Anacostia Museum on 17 August 1967.

know-how and money already in this project, the 85 boys who have benefitted from it, and its future potential in improving schools and combatting vandalism." During the waning days of the administration, with such black-oriented youth programs already out of fashion, the desire to revive a project such as Trail Blazers no longer existed among either private or public sources of funding.[31]

The shift in political mood did not invalidate what Polly Shackleton, Walter Washington, and the First Lady had tried to do in Project Pride and Project Trail Blazers. Within the modest means that the Society for a More Beautiful National Capital could command in absolute terms, Mrs. Johnson and her associates had done what they could to make beautification relevant to the inner city. They had endeavored to involve the residents themselves and not to dictate from above what should be done. These small-scale projects did not strike at the roots of Washington's racism, poverty, and urban decay; but neither did they adopt the easy view that until one could improve everything, the best course was to do nothing. Walter Washington said to a *National Geographic* writer in the fall of 1966: "When this program started, there were some, I suppose, who regarded it as Marie Antoinette's piece of cake. I mean, out in east Washington, how many rats can you kill with a tulip? But it hasn't been that way at all. We started with mass plantings, then we moved on to Project Pride, and now we are here."[32]

When Walter Washington made this remark, his life was about to experience a highly public change. His last significant contribution to Mrs. Johnson's work during this first phase of her activities came in October 1966, when Brooke Astor decided to make the Buchanan School area the beneficiary of a $300,000 grant. Her tours of the neighborhood with Walter Washington, as well as her own studies, persuaded Mrs. Astor to support the building of an outdoor community center on a one-acre tract just east of the school itself, at Thirteenth and D Streets, Southeast. Lady Bird Johnson had seen a model of the center in May 1966 on a trip to New York, and then plans for the structure were assembled over the summer. Actual work began in early 1967, and Mrs. Johnson looked forward to opening the center in September, "when construction is done and the children have their playland." The play areas that Astor funded in New York and Washington, the First Lady said to her, "are setting a standard of imagination and usefulness." As she had done with Mary Lasker, Lady Bird Johnson gave her new friend just enough of herself to keep the bonds of philanthropy strong. Liz Carpenter drafted a letter to Astor in April 1967 that needed, Mrs. Johnson wrote, "more of a personal touch." An additional sentence asked: "I wonder if anyone enjoys the beauty of this city as much as I do?" Another phrase evoked "the autumn plaid of trees." Lady Bird Johnson's ability to get her aides to shape letters that used such ideas and images was an indispensable part of her effectiveness as a leader.[33]

Walter Washington was drawn away from the First Lady's influence and that of her husband by the end of 1966. In an effort to revitalize the District government after the failure to achieve home rule for the city in 1965, President Johnson tried, during the summer of 1966, to persuade Walter Washington to become one of the three commissioners for the District. The sticking point was whether Washington would become president of the Board of Commissioners, replacing Walter Tobriner. If he assumed that post, he would exercise responsibility over the city's police. In 1966, President Johnson, still attuned to southern sensibilities in Congress, did not want a black man in charge of the police force. In June the White House offered Washington the place of second commissioner, which was then held by another black official. No promises were forthcoming about an eventual promotion to the presidency of the board, so Washington declined the appointment. The episode left some tension at the White House regarding Walter Washington and probably contributed to his decision to accept Mayor John Lindsay's offer to be housing commissioner for New York City in November 1966.[34]

While Walter Washington was serving in New York, the Johnson administration made another attempt to reorganize the District's government. The president sent Congress his plan in the late spring of 1967. It called for a single commissioner, or mayor, and a city council of nine presidential appointees. The measure cleared Congress in August, and now the issue became who would hold the mayor's position. The president looked first to some white politicians of recognized national standing, but they either lacked interest or declined. Johnson then explored the idea of a District black other than Walter Washington. Mrs. Johnson, however, kept coming back to Walter Washington as the logical choice, and the president finally decided to appoint him.[35]

The word of Washington's selection leaked out, much to Lyndon Johnson's anger. Harry McPherson reminded the president that dumping Washington at this point in the process would be "a costly mistake." To turn him down just because "someone blew it to the papers" would be an action that Johnson should not take "when you are at a low in the polls." President Johnson agreed and sent Washington's nomination, along with that of a white deputy mayor, to Congress on 6 September 1967. Mrs. Johnson's part in the selection had been central. When the president telephoned Walter Washington to talk about the appointment, he said: "A good friend of yours is sitting here beside me, and she and I think there's important work for you [to] do down here." Just before the announcement of the nomination, President Johnson told Washington "those gals who work for Bird in the East Wing sure like you, Walter." The nomination, which met with broad approval in the District and across the country, exemplified the personal credibility that Washington had enhanced during his collaboration with the First Lady.[36]

Mrs. Johnson's encouragement of Walter Washington and Polly Shackleton on their inner-city projects and her work with Brooke Astor on the Buchanan playground did not conclude her involvement in efforts to transform Washington, D.C., as an urban center in the mid 1960s. Beginning in the second half of 1966, she sponsored an ambitious project to refurbish and rehabilitate the Capitol Hill area and other parts of the city under the auspices of her committee and the Society for a More Beautiful National Capital. What she tried to achieve with landscape architect Lawrence Halprin did not, for the most part, get beyond the stage of planning and design. Reduced governmental budgets and bureaucratic inertia stalled the program even before Mrs. Johnson had left the city. For an evaluation of the purposes of her beautification campaign and a comprehension of the range of her goals for Washington, D.C., a closer review of what she sought to do with Halprin is appropriate.

The initial impetus for a more sweeping approach to the city's design came from an urban philanthropist and supporter of the civil-rights movement, Stephen Currier. Married to a member of the Mellon family, Currier used the resources of his Taconic Foundation to support a number of different organizations that pursued social change in the cities. He was president of Urban America, which styled itself "a non-profit organization to improve man's surroundings" and which sought "to help make our cities more liveable, more workable and more beautiful for all their people." In December 1965 Currier proposed to the president that a conference be held in May 1966, on the anniversary of the Natural Beauty Conference, to look at issues of urban beauty. The Johnson administration responded positively, and Harry McPherson was delegated to be a link with Urban America. The date for the conference was moved back to September 1966, and Currier asked Mrs. Johnson to take an active role as hostess for the meeting itself.[37]

By midsummer, Mrs. Johnson had agreed to hold a reception for the delegates to the conference and to make a formal speech at the occasion. As Currier collaborated with Nash Castro and Sharon Francis, they initiated discussions about underwriting the services of an additional staff member for the First Lady's beautification campaign. They gave some thought to an archivist for the growing body of documents that Mrs. Johnson's work had already generated. Another idea was a "Business community contact," who could approach the city's businessmen about the aesthetic aspects of commercial activity. The possibility of an assistant for Polly Shackleton and her inner-city work was also touched upon. As the date of the conference neared, Currier's ideas became more specific. He wanted to support fund raising for the committee with the infusion of professional advice and to seek in general "someone who could make the Committee's work more productive." Once again, there was a sense in Currier's commitment that male ideas would make a campaign that women had begun more relevant and more publicly appealing.[38]

In the mid 1960s, Lady Bird Johnson had few choices other than to turn to a sympathetic male donor such as Currier. Had she conceived of what two decades later would be called networking, she would have encountered obstacles to a woman-oriented approach to her campaign. Despite the highly visible presence of Mary Lasker and Brooke Astor, there were not enough female philanthropists available to make wealthy women the sole resource for her cause. More important, such a strategy would have run up against the attitudes of her husband and other men at the White House that policy matters were appropriately a preeminently male preserve.

The Urban America conference on "Our People and Their Cities" took place over three days in mid September 1966. Midway through the proceedings, Mrs. Johnson invited the eight hundred delegates to the White House, where she endorsed the purpose of Currier's project. "The challenge to American cities," she said, "is how to govern their growth boom with beauty and with compassion for every life and its fulfillment." While the conference went on, Sharon Francis continued her talks with Currier and his aides about how he could best promote beautification in Washington. In late September she informed Liz Carpenter that "we have come up with an approach which I think would be outstanding, if you and Mrs. Johnson approve."[39]

The proposal was that Currier would arrange for a "top ranking landscape architect" to come to Washington to devise a series of plans for the city that might encompass vest-pocket parks or the entire Anacostia waterfront. Currier and Francis also selected an architect as the leading candidate for the commission. Lawrence Halprin of San Francisco had done Ghirardelli Square in that city, and "any number of award-winning parks, shopping malls, plazas, fountains, playgrounds, etc." Francis approached Halprin about the Currier initiative and reported to Carpenter that "he would be honored and happy to work on this, if Mrs. Johnson wishes."[40]

By the time she sent this memorandum to Carpenter on September 27, Francis had already brought Halprin and his work to the First Lady's attention. In September, Lady Bird Johnson made a three-day trip to California to dedicate Point Reyes as a National Seashore and then to Glen Canyon Dam in Arizona. To assist Governor Edmund G. ("Pat") Brown, who was in a difficult reelection race with Ronald Reagan, she also agreed to dedicate the state's first official scenic highway, the Big Sur Coast Highway at Carmel. On Wednesday, 21 September, she had an extra hour in San Francisco before her plane left for the Monterey peninsula to meet Brown and state senator Fred Farr. "What should we do? Is there anything I should see?" she asked Sharon Francis and Liz Carpenter.[41]

Francis took them to Ghirardelli Square. "She was just as enchanted, and Liz was, " Francis remembered. As they drove away, Lady Bird Johnson heard about Halprin and said "it would be an honor to work with someone like that." The First Lady asked her aide to call Currier when they returned to Washington to see if Halprin would be acceptable. If that is what happened in California, it is not clear why Francis had to go into such detail in her memorandum to Carpenter. In any case, on Carpenter's note transmitting Francis's memo, Mrs. Johnson wrote, "Fine—let's proceed!" and plans went forward rapidly for Halprin's visit to the city in mid October 1966.[42]

Raised in Brooklyn, Lawrence Halprin was fifty years old in 1966 and had operated his own architectural firm since 1949. In addition to Ghirardelli Square, he had attracted national attention for such projects as the Sea Ranch vacation community in California, had worked on the design of the Bay Area Rapid Transit system, and had written about urban freeways and their proper relationship to the cities through which they ran. He was an energetic, lively man with a quick mind and an ability to present his ideas in rapid sentences or deft, vivid sketches. "What we need to do at the moment," he said in 1966 before he had met Lady Bird Johnson, "is to plan environments that let people live on the land without destroying it." The bearded Halprin had been a participant at the National Beauty Conference, and it is possible that Mrs. Johnson had seen or heard him during her visits to sessions and her careful note-taking. She noted that she wanted to see Halprin "whenever I can" in his initial stay in Washington as a potential collaborator with Stephen Currier. As always with this First Lady, it is not easy to be sure how much she was being moved in one direction by events or how much she was allowing herself to be taken toward a goal that she wished to achieve in the first place.[43]

Halprin toured the city on October 13 with Nash Castro, Polly Shackleton, and Walter Washington. The issue soon arose about where the architect's work should be directed in the city. He told them, after Nash Castro left, that the Park Service could handle flower beds. "If we wanted to get into more serious problems, he would feel challenged by doing so." As Halprin, Washington, and the others drove around the inner city for the next two days, he asked his hosts: "Are you trying to tell me it's boring over here?" Walter Washington replied: "Now you're getting it. Yes!" There were, they concluded, "just miles of not particularly beat up, but monotonous housing and nothing to do." Halprin and Washington worked together during these last weeks of Washington's service in the District, before his New York job was to begin, pulling together ideas to present to the First Lady's Committee.[44]

Lady Bird Johnson also spent time with Halprin as they looked at vacant lots, school grounds, and potential recreation sites. He asked the First Lady for her thoughts, and she answered with her customary attention to maintenance costs: "Well, I'm no expert in these fields. You experts who know how to do the things must make the judgments. All I would say is that any area this committee undertakes should be usable by lots and lots of people. It should be fun, and its maintenance should be easy because any project we sponsor will be a stepchild of the city." She also made a point of asking Halprin how long Ghirardelli Square had taken to design. When he said eighteen months, Sharon Francis noted for her journal: "I think in the back of her head Mrs. Johnson was thinking that she had only two years left.[45]

After Halprin's tour, negotiations with Stephen Currier led to a pledge to underwrite Halprin's fees up to $100,000 and to make available the services of an aide, Victor Weingarten, to help with the fund raising for the First Lady's Committee. In late October it looked as if Mrs. Johnson and her organization would have secure and committed private financial resources for the rest of her husband's presidency. At a time when Walter Washington was leaving for New York and congressional appropriations were shrinking, the Currier-Halprin initiative gave promise of beautification achievements that otherwise might not have occurred.[46]

During November and December 1966, Halprin's ideas for Washington, D.C., acquired a more precise focus. He planned to move on two levels. For specific neighborhoods in the East Capitol area, he would concentrate on block interiors to be developed as play spaces, vest-pocket parks, school playgrounds, and community recreation areas. All would be examples "of how beautification elements can interweave, and ultimately upgrade an entire neighborhood." In the same East Capitol locale, however, he also had in mind projects that had a larger application. There was an old carbarn between Fourteenth and Fifteenth streets that could become "a gay and attractive activity center." Halprin also had ideas about how a projected freeway along the Anacostia River could be redesigned to reflect aesthetic values, and he saw important possibilities in Kingman Island, in the river itself, which could support a park and recreational complex.[47]

While Halprin was shaping his plans, Sharon Francis was trying to prepare the way for later implementation with the District and with the federal government's bureaucracy. If the District of Columbia gave the beautification program sufficient priority, the Department of Housing and Urban Development (HUD), in its turn, might make available some funds from its urban-beautification program. In addition to what Halprin had in mind, Francis discussed with HUD the beautification of the Capper Housing Project which had emerged from ideas offered by Simon Breines, Brooke Astor's architect. In the early days of January 1967, Francis reported to the First Lady on the state of Halprin's anticipated presentation to the full committee on January 12. "There is strong interest in Mr. Halprin's work," Francis argued, "and I believe we will have full public cooperation in carrying it out." The first step, she said, was Mrs. Johnson's "response to these suggestions, and your interest in carrying them out." A showing of Halprin's presentation was scheduled for the First Lady a day or so before the committee would see it.[48]

Lady Bird Johnson's reaction was positive, and press accounts, based

Lawrence Halprin addressing the First Lady's Committee about his plans for Washington, D.C., on 12 January 1967.

on interviews with Halprin and data from Francis, promised the public "an entirely new direction" for the First Lady's beautification work in her collaboration with the West Coast architect. "What people really want in an environment is what's going to solve their needs," Halprin told Roberta Hornig of the *Star*; "if living problems are solved, the chances are the environment will end up being beautiful." Hornig wrote that Mrs. Johnson was seeking ways "to improve Washington's neighborhood environment, particularly in the neglected Northeast and Southeast."[49]

When the committee convened at the White House on Thursday, 12 January 1967, at 2:30 P.M., Mrs. Johnson announced that they had "an exciting presentation for today; one that some of us have had a preview on and I am very anxious for everybody to see it thoroughly and consider all it could mean to the future of the city. You must examine it very earnestly." Introducing Halprin, Stewart Udall noted the initial "reservations" that some within the committee had had about "whether we were going to be interested in learning superficial things—in the cosmetics as it were." Halprin's presentation, he said, would demonstrate "just how deeply into the very core of urban problems we can go if we are resourceful."[50]

Halprin then said that what was being done in monumental Washington was "all to the good" and that what the committee and Nathaniel Owings had accomplished "could not be better." What he wanted to do was to treat Washington "as the prototype of the rest of the country," because it exhibited "some of the growing pains that all cities of the United States have." Cities could become "once again, the great centers they should be" if they provided "for their citizens not only places to work" but also "for living, residential homes which will have dignity and quality, which any human being ought to have."[51]

Specifically, Halprin concentrated his presentation on the East Capitol area, because it possessed "a high degree of stability in the community" and could, "from a series of demonstrations, uplift the neighborhood, which is not so far downhill." He wanted to use the triangles in the vicinity for functional purposes, and he wanted to turn vacant lots into vest-pocket parks. Washington had numerous alleys which might find their spaces transformed into swimming-pool areas, parking lots, or small playgrounds. On a larger scale, he spoke about developing "small plazas and small community center activities" on each of four corners of a block, while creating arcades and shops within the interior of a block. For schools, there could be a joining of recreational areas and playgrounds to make them a "focus for community activities of all kinds." The old carbarn on East Capitol Avenue, which belonged to the D.C. Transit system, could be transformed from an empty structure into something on the model of Ghirardelli Square. Finally, he mentioned the freeway along the Anacostia River and the recreational park that would sit on Kingman Island in the middle of the river. When his slide presentation ended, Halprin said that the committee, "by expressing an interest and by acting as a catalyst," could "generate all kinds of solutions which other people might take." In so doing they might stimulate "action in this community which might not otherwise be able to happen."[52]

Halprin's remarks set off a lively discussion within the committee. Victor Gruen, who had wanted an ambitious social agenda for the group from its inception, made an impassioned plea that what they had heard would "inject urban values and urban virtues into people who have not known what they are. And they are in the end effect, beautiful." If the committee would follow up on Halprin's ideas, Gruen concluded, "we can prove that beautification is not a luxury. Beautification is the very heart of the health of this country." Out of the ensuing interchange came the formation of a smaller committee to implement what Lady Bird Johnson called "an imaginative, exciting program with great potential." In the *Washington Post*, Wolf Von Eckardt wrote that what Halprin had outlined were "not luxuries." Instead he had "shattered the myth" that there was no space for community facilities by showing that there was ample room "on an unused island, in messy vacant lots, and in rat-infested alleys." Halprin's "functional beautification," Von Eckardt believed, "goes deeper than sprinkling daffodils around and yet saves us the agonies of conventional 'urban renewal.' "[53]

The enthusiasm that Halprin's report evoked at the committee meeting reflected to some extent the passion of that moment. There were still those on the panel, such as Mary Lasker, who viewed Halprin's emphasis on neighborhood beautification with skepticism. The idea for an amusement and cultural park on Kingman Island also aroused the opposition of Elizabeth Rowe, who believed that the black population of the city would dominate the proposed facility. She told Francis that "at this day and age in Washington the city just wasn't ready to integrate, and it would be too hard to get support on the Hill for the kind of money that would be needed to develop such a park." The Park Service had its doubts about Halprin's ideas for changes in the Anacostia freeway.[54]

The Halprin initiative also had to compete for the available beautification money that had been allocated to the District with the Capper Housing Project idea of Brooke Astor. Housing and Urban Development had a program that provided 90 percent funding for demonstration projects. Only about a million dollars of that money, however, would be available for all of Washington, D.C. That amount would only take care of part of the Capper project; it would do several of the interior blocks that Halprin had discussed. Mary Lasker pushed for the Capper idea with HUD, but nothing had been decided by 17 January 1967. Sharon Francis conceded, in retrospect, that "we were all in a bind of having too many expensive recommendations before us to be able to cope with."[55]

Currier's generosity remained the linchpin of Halprin's program, but it ceased on 17 January. The Curriers were lost at sea when their plane vanished on a flight from Puerto Rico to the Virgin Islands. "Our thoughts are with you these important hours," Mrs. Johnson wired Mrs. Currier's mother, and the First Lady saw to it that the navy made a search for survivors. The news was bad, and no trace of the Curriers was found. In mid February, Mrs. Johnson attended the memorial service for the couple in New York City.[56]

Whatever momentum the Halprin proposals had acquired slowed when the Curriers died. The affairs of the Taconic Foundation passed into other hands, and the commitment that Currier had made to the First Lady was put into limbo. To keep Halprin at work and to sustain what he had proposed, Mrs. Johnson and Sharon Francis had to persuade the directors of the Taconic Foundation all over again about the merits of what the landscape architect wanted to accomplish. That process took time, and in the interval the initial enthusiasm for the Halprin projects encountered bureaucratic and political delays, with an attendant ebbing of interest in the affected neighborhoods.[57]

In the beginning, prospects for the Halprin project seemed promising. Sharon Francis went before the citizens groups of Capitol Hill on February 9. Despite a two-day postponement because of a heavy snowfall, several hundred residents turned out. Francis handled a difficult situation well. The majority of the audience was in favor of the Halprin report, but as Polly Shackleton reported to the First Lady's Committee, "there was a small but very noisy conservative element which consistently has opposed new schools and recreational facilities" that would threaten their property values. Francis stressed that the support of residents was essential and that nothing would be done unilaterally. The proposal to develop the carbarn, as well as the projected refurbishing of the interior blocks, the vest-pocket parks, and the local triangles, secured more support as the discussion continued. In the wake of the gathering, Sharon Francis said to the president of the Capitol Hill Restoration Society: "Mrs. Johnson's Committee now looks to the community itself for firm proposals of which sites need attention and help."[58]

Ideas from the public, while welcome, were not enough in themselves, and Francis noted on 1 April 1967, in a progress report on the Halprin proposals, that with two exceptions, the initiative was "presently at a standstill." The absence of funding from the Curriers for Halprin meant that the architect could not go ahead with planning for budget estimates and grant requests. The Department of Housing and Urban Development's urban-beautification funds, which they estimated to be around $500,000, could be used for the Capitol East project. Unfortunately, Francis added, "we need Halprin's services, however, to make the initial sketches and budget application to H.U.D." In two cases, the picture was brighter. The National Park Service had contracted with Halprin about the Anacostia River Parkland, and the District Highway Department had made a similar arrangement regarding the eastern leg of the proposed freeway. Halprin also had begun to work with the District's Land Redevelopment Agency on playgrounds for the schools in the Shaw area. Otherwise, for the carbarn, the other schools, and Capitol East, progress had stalled.[59]

Francis looked for funding for Capitol East from the Rockefeller Foundation and from the Taconic Foundation. She asked Stewart Udall for help with the Taconic people to get "the seed money that would permit Larry to plan a few of these and do the initial sketches for the HUD application." She worried that if the Taconic board did not act in time to make the July 1 deadline for applying to HUD, the whole project might fail. Francis was receiving encouraging reports about the department's attitude through April 1967. Assistant Secretary Charles Haar, who had served on the Natural Beauty Task Force three years earlier, wrote that his agency was "especially enthusiastic about the possibility of the development of several interior blocks in the East Capitol Area as an urban beautification demonstration." HUD might provide an "involvement" of around $400,000. Haar warned, however, that Francis and Lady Bird Johnson would have to choose among the Capper Plaza, the Halprin proposals, and the regular District beautification program, because the department could not allocate more than $1 million for the fiscal year 1967/68 to the city.[60]

During May, prospects for success brightened. Mrs. Johnson invited the New York attorney Lloyd K. Garrison, of the Taconic Foundation, to a beautification luncheon at the White House in late April, and Sharon Francis followed up with information on Halprin's report and how it owed its existence "to the keen foresight of Stephen Currier and the imagination of Lawrence Halprin." By May 12, Francis had told Lady Bird Johnson that "progress is underway on a number of phases of the Halprin report," and she especially cited Haar's enthusiasm and the prospect of the $400,000 in urban-beautification funds. The key to that commitment was that HUD could supply 90 percent of the funding. While Haar and his associates had agreed in principle to the idea, no formal application to the urban-demonstration program had yet been made by mid May 1967. In fact, planning for the preparation of the application was not far advanced.[61]

In late May, to the surprise of Francis and the White House, the House Appropriations Committee acted to change the beautification program in HUD on which the Halprin project depended. Responding to criticism of the Johnson administration's housing program and to the cost-cutting spirit that the Vietnam War had aroused, the committee trimmed the department's overall request for beautification money from $125 million to $75 million. More important, the panel rewrote the terms under which beautification projects could be funded. The new language stipulated that "funds from this appropriation cannot pay more than 50% of the cost of any project."[62]

Sharon Francis sought help from Liz Carpenter on 23 May 1967 in regard to these changes. The fund cutback was "bearable," but the new restrictive terms "could wreck our Capitol East program here in Washington." Would it be possible to have the offending phrase eliminated by the Senate Appropriations Committee and its chairman, Warren Magnuson (D, Wash.)? "This item might get overlooked," Francis contended, "unless Mrs. Johnson's staff speaks up for it." Carpenter sent the memo on to Douglass Cater, who in turn alerted the White House staff member who was in contact with the Senate.[63]

The problem was that the changes that the House made effectively slowed the grant-making process until Congress had finished with the legislation. Sharon Francis found this turn of events particularly frustrating, because the money would have been available if HUD had acted more promptly in preparing the application. Francis and a departmental staff member volunteered to do the work on the application themselves. Instead, regular procedures were observed, and a draft application, still based on the 90 percent standard, was not ready until August 1967. The delays in the federal bureaucracy became even more irritating in July, when the Taconic Foundation decided to make a grant of $10,000 to the Society for a More Beautiful National Capital to enable Halprin to start design work on the Capitol East proposal. "This designing money," Francis told Mrs. Johnson, "will enable the District to make an application to HUD for a demonstration grant." It could not be used to pay Halprin, apparently, until HUD approved the actual grant.[64]

Matters dragged along throughout the fall of 1967. In late August the District put in a grant request to HUD for $521,000. Conferences on the application were held in the office of the assistant secretary for renewal and housing assistance in mid September. Then, in October, the Senate-House conferees on the HUD appropriations bill took out the 90 percent demonstration program. HUD officials elected to recast the proposal to seek funds only where their department would supply 50 percent of the funds needed. This meant that the District would have to rewrite its entire application to meet the different standards of the 50 percent program. Finally, in January 1968, a draft application from the District government, now headed by Walter Washington, went to HUD on the 50 percent basis.[65]

For two months the Halprin project became ensnared in the federal bureaucracy. In early March 1968, Sharon Francis spoke with Don Hummel, the assistant secretary for renewal and housing assistance, about the status of the application. He replied that he was "painfully aware" that the proposal "has been jockeyed between programs for an inordinate period of time." Hummel sent Francis a copy of a letter that he had sent to Walter Washington, specifying where the application, as the department saw it, fell short. Many of the things that the larger Halprin project proposed to do, including youth- and adult-education programs about beautification in the affected neighborhoods, fell outside the scope of what HUD could fund. Other parts of the renovation work conflicted with language in the law that prohibited the use of funds to pay for ordinary governmental expenses. HUD also questioned allocating public money to improve private property and worried about the wages that Project Pride workers might receive. Assurances of friendliness and support in principle could not outweigh the generally discouraging tone of the letter itself.[66]

The available records do not indicate how the grant proposal for Capitol East fared after March 1968. When Sharon Francis was interviewed for the Oral History program of the Johnson Library in May 1969, she ruefully remarked that "the District government has yet to figure out how it can pay 50 percent of the funds to do these small neighborhood parks and interior blocks." This feature of Halprin's program failed to get past even the preliminary stage during Mrs. Johnson's years in Washington, primarily because of the bureaucratic obstacles to mobilizing the energies of either the District government or the Department of Housing and Urban Development.[67]

Other parts of the package that Halprin had presented in January 1967 also remained uncompleted by 1968. After discussions with the National Park Service in August 1967 about the Anacostia River Park Plan, Halprin agreed with the service's director, George B. Hartzog, Jr., to develop "a staging diagram" for a park centered on Kingman Lake. The maps were prepared but were not reviewed with Hartzog. In December 1967, matters had reached a "standstill," Halprin wrote, and accomplishing anything in the year that remained "becomes less and less feasible as time drifts on."[68]

Francis returned to the subject in the spring of 1968. She tried to persuade the Bureau of the Budget to find some money to underwrite a study of the Kingman Lake proposal. With the city in turmoil after the death of Martin Luther King, Jr., there was for a time in the bureaucracy a desire to respond to requests from the White House. The First Lady was to hold a beautification luncheon for her committee on April 17. On the day before, Francis called Phillip S. Hughes at the Budget Bureau to say that "Mrs. Johnson might want to announce a Kingman Lake study" on that occasion.[69]

While Hughes was looking for the money, Francis. Halprin, and representatives of the Park Service met in Stewart Udall's office on the morning of April 17 about the project. Udall gave his approval and provided the "trigger" that the Park Service required in order to go ahead. Francis immediately called Hughes, who reported that the funds could be found. "Tell her to say it," he informed Francis. "We'll find the money." Lady Bird Johnson announced at the meeting that the study would proceed, and she cited Anacostia Park and Kingman Lake as meeting her criteria that the desire for a project "emanate from the neighborhood and the users."[70]

As happened in the case of so much else that was connected with
Halprin and his plans, the announcement did not truly foreshadow further effective action on Kingman Lake and the Anacostia River Park
design. First, the use of the money, which came from funds authorized
in 1961 for parking near the District stadium, had to be cleared with
Julia Hansen and the Interior Committee. Then, in the late summer
of 1968, the federal-aid highway act contained a provision that required
the eastern leg of the freeway along the Anacostia River to conform to
the plans of the D.C. Highway Department. Their proposal did not include a park for Kingman Lake. Instead, the freeway would fill it in,
as Sharon Francis told the First Lady, "and forever preclude the swim-
ming lake there, as well as the entire park complex in that area of the
city." President Johnson signed the bill for other reasons, and the crippling language remained. When Lady Bird Johnson left Washington,
the Anacostia Park and the Kingman Lake project were still only ideas.[71]

Could the Currier-Halprin proposals ever have worked? Given sufficient time and a greater degree of commitment from Congress and the
bureaucracy, they could have had a chance for success. Some around
Lady Bird Johnson, including Cynthia Wilson and Liz Carpenter, found
Halprin impractical and his ideas difficult to sell. His proposals represented
some fresh thinking about the District's problems, and his ideas could
have had a positive impact as demonstration projects. Once the initial
impetus of the Currier gift had disappeared, however, the Halprin concepts collided with the interests of the affected residents, the opposition of the Park Service and the highway interests, and the growing popular disillusionment with the Johnson administration and all of its policies.
Nonetheless, Lady Bird Johnson's willingness to encourage and promote
Halprin and his plans revealed how ambitious her definition of urban
beautification was and how far she was willing to see it proceed.

For many reasons, the spring of 1968 was a painful and awkward time
for Mrs. Johnson and the Washington she had lived in for so long. After
the murder of Martin Luther King, Jr., on 4 April 1968, the black residents
of the city poured into the streets and began to burn businesses, loot other
stores, and riot throughout the heart of the ghetto. Mrs. Johnson was at
the White House when the news of the assassination came, and for her
"the evening assumed a nightmare quality." The next day, at the suggestion
of her husband, the First Lady continued a scheduled trip to "Discover
America," which took her to Texas to dedicate the Padre Island National
Seashore and to visit the Hemisfair exposition at San Antonio. On the flight
to Texas, she told the forty European editors, Stewart Udall, and the others in
the party: "The greatest tribute we could pay to Dr. King is to bring forth
from this cruel tragedy some good action on our problems."[72]

Lady Bird Johnson returned to Washington on April 10. During the trip, Bess Abell had told her about "the incessant barrage of TV coverage . . . of looting and fires." It had been, she wrote in her diary, "as though I were talking to an inhabitant of another planet." Over the next week, with a trip back to Texas thrown in, the First Lady and her staff prepared for the meeting of her committee on April 17, the Arbor Day ceremonies on April 26, and the dedication of the plaza at Buchanan School on May 7. As she surveyed the damage across the city, Lady Bird Johnson was gratified that many of the places she had sought to beautify had been spared in the rioting. "One would like to assume that these beautiful spots meant so much that people didn't want to harm them," Sharon Francis recalled, "and that can be at least in part true." But she also decided that "those places hadn't hurt the people of the neighborhoods," and hence were spared from destruction.[73]

At the committee meeting on April 17, the main event was a one-hour bus tour for more than two hundred guests to see the projects that the group had sponsored. They visited Buchanan Plaza and the Capper Housing Project, saw the plantings that Lasker and Castro had achieved, and then returned to the White House for lunch. In her remarks, Lady Bird Johnson praised what the committee had accomplished in such endeavors as the Anacostia Neighborhood Museum and the work of Project Trail Blazers. These disclosed "a pattern of quality that we want to see everywhere." The Kingman Lake project also possessed these attributes. She observed: "This has been one of the most lovely springs I can remember in Washington's history. It has also been one of the most poignant and grave. That fact underscores the urgency of improving our environment for all people." Summing up what they had done together, she said to them: "If we have changed this city just one iota, it has also changed all of us . . . to the catalyst for a better neighborhood, a better city, a better America."[74]

Walter Washington then responded to Mrs. Johnson's introduction with a moving address that looked back on the committee's record and her part in it. It was, Sharon Francis said, "his charismatic kind of performance where he started out with tears coming down his face." The committee members had "traveled through this city; we have been in the alleys, we have been in the byways and side streets." They had gone there because they had decided that "there was a big job to do and that this job had to be done in the sense of identifying an individual with his environment." To those who labeled beautification as "cosmetic," the mayor replied: "You cannot tell me that the neighborhood in Greenleaf Housing Project in Southwest, when hundreds of people came out, painted, fixed up their neighborhoods and said 'we would like to be part of this' that this is cosmetic." In Mrs. Johnson's work, despite the riots and the damage of the preceding days, "we had here the signs and the beginnings of something that really went to the heart of filling the gap and beginning to work with the alienation." So, Washington said in closing, "the greatest thing that we can do for the greatest First Lady I have ever known is to dedicate ourselves to continue with her this great work." Lady Bird Johnson sat there as the mayor said "so many kind, warm, generous things about me that I began to shrink down and look at my plate." Still it was for her "a great climax to three years of hard work together."[75]

Her beautification work for Washington was winding down now that the end of Lyndon Johnson's presidency was in sight. Some moments of achievement remained. In early May, Buchanan Plaza was dedicated. The First Lady praised Brooke Astor, Walter Washington, and Julia Hansen for their contributions to the plaza. It had been built "out of the belief that children will respond affirmatively to improvements they can see, and touch, and take part in." Many years before, she had said: "I married a school teacher. And one of the many things he has taught me is that children grow best with the best facilities and the best instruction." Buchanan Plaza, a "round-the-clock community playground," was "a new and constructive answer to the urban problem." When the ceremonies were over, the fountains were turned on, and the children responded. "It was just a flamboyant moment of 'Ah,' " Sharon Francis said, "when they saw this great amount of water spraying up into the air."[76]

Events during the rest of 1968 took Lady Bird Johnson away from other examples of her commitment to the aspects of beautification that spoke to Washington's urban difficulties. She had reason to be content that spring with her feeling of a "job well done" for the Capital City. Her labors with the Shaw neighborhood, for Anacostia, and for Trail Blazers had not, of course, affected the intrinsic ills of the city and its black ghetto. The forces that had shaped that network of racism, economic impoverishment, and despair were so intractable that even the larger policies of the Great Society made only a partial impression. The riots that broke out in April 1968 underlined how much white America had failed in dealing with the plight of black citizens.[77]

Nonetheless, Lady Bird Johnson had addressed these issues with the means available to her. She had no dependable source of funds and no formal staff apparatus beyond what she could pull together on her own. Working through the First Lady's Committee, relying on the efforts of Walter Washington, Polly Shackleton, Lawrence Halprin, and countless others, she created demonstration projects and pilot initiatives that took beautification into the community. Two decades later, Walter Washington expressed the belief that the First Lady's work had made some difference, as did Lawrence Halprin. It was, in their judgment, less important that they had fallen short than that, in cooperation with Mrs. Johnson, they had tried to do something tangible about the city's problems.[78]

Walter Washington had been right on 17 April 1968, when he had harked back to John Hatcher's first letter to Mrs. Johnson in 1965. "The First Lady sent a plant out there. The result was that a little boy would be reborn; a neighborhood and a school was electrified and the community moved into action." Her willingness and readiness to respond to the John Hatchers of the 1960s in Washington reflected Lady Bird Johnson's commitment to a broad definition of beautification that had room for Mary Lasker *and* Polly Shackleton, for Nash Castro *and* Walter Washington. And she made the city better. It is difficult to see how Mrs. Johnson could have done more for Washington, D.C., than she did, and it is a measure of her impact that the Society for a More Beautiful National Capital did not flourish after she left Washington. By the mid 1970s it had become defunct.[79]

A male-centered history often demands of women in public life that their accomplishments be measured against daunting standards of achievement and action that their masculine counterparts themselves rarely attain. If a man had beautified the monumental areas of a major American city and had simultaneously addressed the thorny problems of inner-city life, no one would have called his work trivial or cosmetic. In the history of Washington, D.C., Lady Bird Johnson deserves to be seen as a significant figure who did more than any man during the 1960s to change the appearance and the tone of that metropolis. Her record becomes even more impressive when it is placed in the context of another separate and distinct campaign that she conducted contemporaneously—the effort to beautify the nation's highways and the landscape through which they ran. Her sponsorship and implementation of the Highway Beautification Act of 1965 was another aspect of Lady Bird Johnson's years as First Lady that discloses her ambitious agenda during her husband's presidency.

7

The Highway
Beautification Act of 1965

The Highway Beautification Act of 1965 was the most tangible legislative result of Mrs. Johnson's national campaign for beautification, and it continues to be a subject of both historical and contemporary controversy. Environmental advocates and proponents of the regulation of outdoor advertising now regard it as a flawed measure. A spokesman for the Coalition for Scenic Beauty wrote in January 1985 that "the act created the illusion that the Federal Government was doing something while in fact it was giving the billboard companies custody of America the Beautiful."[1] Like other Great Society legislation, the Highway Beautification Act is now seen as an example of good intentions gone wrong because of the inadequate drafting of the law and an insufficient commitment to its successful implementation.

These charges have some merit, but they generally overlook the difficulties that confronted any type of national billboard-regulation law. It is not surprising that the 1965 act was only a partial measure; it is noteworthy that any law was passed at all. Had it not been for the energy and commitment of both of the Johnsons in 1965, billboard control would not have been adopted. To the legislative process, Lady Bird Johnson brought a personal commitment to roadside beauty. Her activities were instrumental in the law's initial conception, its progress through Congress, and its final enactment in October 1965.

The question of highway beauty and billboard regulation became an issue of national scope during the 1950s, when legislation creating a system of interstate highways moved through Congress. Controversies over the control of outdoor advertising, however, had gone on at the local and state levels since the end of the nineteenth century, and the emergence of the problem nationally during Lady Bird Johnson's time was the culmination of a long history of discord between the proponents of a billboard-free landscape and the operators of billboards and signs in cities and along American highways.

136

The initial phase of the effort to control billboards was part of the City Beautiful campaigns of the Progressive Era. By 1908, one industry source estimated that there were 8.5 million linear feet of billboards across the whole nation. At a time before modern roads had been constructed, most of the outdoor advertising was in the cities. Drawing on English precedents, the proponents of billboard control attacked the rapid proliferation of advertising signs in urban areas. They assembled a variety of arguments to demonstrate that urban signs should be controlled or, preferably, eliminated. Billboards desecrated the scenery, they encouraged littering behind them, and they intruded on the attention of passers-by. Civic leagues, local art associations, and architectural groups sought to use the police power or the zoning laws of towns and cities to bring billboards under restrictions. During the era of the City Beautiful, these reformers established the principle that outdoor advertising in the city could be regulated. Most often, however, the criteria for control were not purely aesthetic; they also embraced such issues as cleanliness, decency, and safety.[2]

During the four decades after the City Beautiful movement and the billboard regulation that it spurred had ebbed away, the billboard industry prospered as automobiles and the roads they used became fixtures in American life. "Outdoor was the one means of communicating with this moving market" was the way an industry spokesman later put it. Billboard owners organized into trade associations such as the Outdoor Advertising Association of America, created in 1925 by the merger of the Poster Advertising Association and the Painted Outdoor Advertising Association. Six years later the industry set up Outdoor Advertising Incorporated to promote national sales, and in 1933 the Traffic Audit Bureau was born to provide "authenticated outdoor advertising circulation data." The organization of these groups also gave the billboard industry potent lobbying mechanisms in city councils, county governments, and state legislatures.[3]

Up to the mid 1950s there were periodic skirmishes between the billboard forces and their critics over the extent to which advertising should be allowed along the roadway. In 1913, Hawaii began a campaign to ban all billboards from roads on the islands. After fourteen years of "hard, uphill work," the Outdoor Circle, a women's group dedicated to Hawaii's beauty, bought out the local billboard company in 1927. Thereafter billboards in Hawaii were tightly regulated and generally limited to on-premise signs for businesses. Elsewhere the results were mixed. In New York State the power of Parks Commissioner Robert Moses helped to hold down the number of billboards on the new parkways of the 1920s and 1930s, but even Moses had to wage a long battle against billboards along the New York State Thruway. Other states used zoning laws, scenic easements, and the police power to regulate signs. Enemies of billboards sought to establish the principle that a state could order the removal of a billboard, give the owner several years to amortize the costs, and then expect to see the sign taken down. They also tried to convince the state courts, where billboard-control laws were challenged, that aesthetic considerations could come under the scope of the police power. By the 1960s, several state courts had accepted that argument.[4]

The likelihood of billboards' being constructed along the thousands of miles of projected interstate highways aroused opponents of outdoor advertising to a national campaign in the 1950s. Senator Richard L. Neuberger (D, Oreg.) introduced first an amendment in 1955 and then more elaborate proposals in 1957 to encourage states to acquire land along interstate highways and to prohibit billboards within five hundred feet of these federal roads. The Eisenhower administration adopted, in response to Neuberger, an approach that would have penalized states that did not regulate billboards. These states would have had to pay 15 percent of the cost of highway projects in their states, instead of the 10 percent that complying states would contribute.[5]

In mid April 1957, President Eisenhower expressed public reservations about what his Department of Commerce had offered, and he questioned whether the federal government should try to oversee billboard advertising. In Congress, the penalty method was cast aside, and the lawmakers decided to grant states that controlled billboards an extra 0.5 percent of federal-aid highway funds. This bonus amendment, as it came to be called, went through the Senate committees on a series of very close votes and ultimately achieved passage in the upper house by a vote of 47 to 41. The House concurred, because the language was attached to a broader highway bill, and Eisenhower signed the measure in April 1958.[6]

The political alignment on this first national proposal to regulate billboards revealed the opposing sides, which never significantly altered during the next thirty years. The public supported the general idea of billboard control by decisive majorities in public-opinion polls. Garden clubs, roadside councils in individual states, and newspapers that competed with billboards spoke out in favor of limitations on the ability of outdoor advertisers to change the landscape that the motorists saw. A garden organization in Montana told Congressman Lee Metcalf that "modern highway construction, in order to insure safe and pleasurable travel, includes control of the environment of the highways, including outdoor advertising." Similar sentiments were sent to other members of Congress.[7]

In the campaigns against billboards, women had constituted a major element of the opposition to outdoor advertising for more than fifty years. Elizabeth Lawton of New York had assembled a network of local and state roadside councils during the 1920s and 1930s. Hilda Fox and Helen Reynolds carried on the fight during the postwar years. As Fox noted in 1965, these state and local bodies lacked a central clearing house for information in the years after Lawton's death in 1954, and the billboard industry easily labeled them as self-appointed advocates of parochial and impractical "women's" attitudes in public controversies. "We are not just a group of starry-eyed billboard fighters," Fox said at the Natural Beauty Conference; "we are just volunteers trying to fight for the beauty of our country." These women were a potential political resource of real value, but they lacked the visible muscle of the billboard lobby. Their importance would be easy to overlook.[8]

The opposition to highway beautification through billboard removal or restriction possessed great political power. Though united against regulation, the billboard industry was not a monolith. The Outdoor Advertising Association of America spoke for the owners and operators in the urban and developed areas of the nation. Other organizations, such as the Roadside Business Association, represented the interests of rural sign owners. Allied with the industry forces were the businesses that depended on traveling motorists for their livelihood: these included motels, service stations, and tourist attractions, such as caves or parks. Organized labor made up an additional element of the probillboard coalition. Those who constructed, painted, and maintained the signs joined with union members who worked in motels, restaurants, and other businesses to add the backing of the AFL-CIO (the American Federation of Labor and the Congress of Industrial Organizations) for the billboard cause.

The billboard industry enjoyed great influence on Capitol Hill. All politicians knew that billboards were an important aspect of modern campaigning. Opposition from local operators could imperil a reelection. Businesses throughout a congressional district or a state used signs of all kinds. An effort to regulate outdoor advertising could have an immediate adverse financial impact across his constituency that a legislator would hear about at once. The billboard lobby was attentive to lawmakers who might be helpful against regulatory legislation and watchful for bills directed against it. Proponents of regulation could not match this array of political power. They could only summon the intangible benefits of a billboard-free scenery for the traveler. The constituency for natural beauty at the roadside was large, diffuse, and hard to mobilize. As a result, only carefully drawn, limited, and cautious proposals in regard to billboards had a chance of surviving the hazards of the legislative process.[9]

As a senator, Lyndon Johnson did not devote much attention to the billboard issue, but the available evidence indicates his sensitivity to the clout of the industry. He opposed the bonus bill in 1958, and a year later he joined with Senator Robert S. Kerr (D, Okla.) in supporting legislation that exempted from federal control all areas that had been zoned for business use before the bonus act went into effect. The Outdoor Advertising Association of Texas praised Johnson for having been "most helpful in the passage of this Act" and applauded him for having "consistently opposed this trampling of the people's rights," which billboard control represented in their minds. The billboard industry regarded Johnson as a friendly senator at the end of the 1950s.[10]

During the Kennedy administration the major focus of the billboard question was on the renewal of the billboard bonus bill at two-year intervals. In 1961, in a message to Congress, President Kennedy said that the Interstate Highway System "was not intended to provide a large and unreimbursed measure of benefits to the billboard industry, whose structures tend to detract from both the beauty and safety of the routes they line."[11] In 1961 and again in 1963, Senator Maurine Neuberger (D, Oreg.), who had succeeded to her husband's seat after his death in 1960, and the other proponents of billboard control were able to have the act renewed.[12]

By the early 1960s, opinions differed about the merits of the bonus law. Its critics said that the states were moving slowly to take advantage of the bonus provisions. At the time of the second renewal, in October 1963, fewer than twenty states had agreed to participate; by 1965 the number stood at twenty-three. Even its advocates agreed that the law had other serious flaws. All states were not included, certain areas of the highway system were exempted from control, and setting the control area 660 feet from the roadway encouraged the creation of "jumbo" billboards. Most important, fewer than two hundred miles of highway had been affected. In 1965 the secretary of commerce, John T. Connor, summed up this position when he told a House panel that "the present law had definitely proved to be ineffective in obtaining adequate control of billboards along our highways."[13]

Despite these apparent flaws, the Bonus Act of 1958 had its defenders among the antibillboard groups. The law provided clear national standards for compliance, and its language also specified a date after which the states could not designate new commercial and industrial zones wherein billboards could be located. The states that participated were in the Northeast, on the Pacific Coast, and in the Middle West; they were "all heavy traffic corridors where billboards and roadside business were attracted." As a proponent of the act later put it, "by getting agreements in those 23 states, the future construction of the major traffic corridors of the times was protected." The law allowed these states to use any legal means to regulate billboards. Three states employed eminent domain alone, another seven combined the police power and eminent domain, and fifteen used the police power alone. Though relatively few miles were covered by 1965, it was also true that only a relatively small number of miles of Interstate highway had been built in areas where billboards were likely to be built. There was not, in the minds of those who supported the Bonus Act, a clear distinction between "the largely preventive protection" of that law and the remedial approach that the Highway Beautification Act of 1965 adopted.[14]

During the early 1960s, popular interest in billboard control once again surfaced; at that same time the Task Force on the Preservation of Natural Beauty added outdoor advertising to its recommendations. Then Lady Bird Johnson added her influence on behalf of more beautiful highways at the end of 1964. A book by Peter Blake, *God's Own Junkyard*, recorded public concern about the deterioration of the landscape and made a powerful indictment of billboards as being dangerous to motorists and a sore on the environment. "There are presently some 800,000 miles of federally aided highways in the United States," Blake wrote, "and the billboard lobby is permitted to deface every blessed mile of them." *Reader's Digest* and other periodicals also called for strengthening the laws beyond the Bonus Act and the steps that had been taken during the 1950s.[15]

The Natural Beauty Task Force saw billboard regulation and highway beauty as part of its responsibilities. In a draft paper on "Natural Beauty and the Public Interest," a task-force writer noted that a citizen could not "look away when an outdoor billboard confronts him while he drives along a highway." Reporting to the president in late November 1964, the task force advocated stringent controls on billboards, such as the coverage of primary and secondary roads that were receiving federal aid; raising the bonus to the states to 2 percent; and the creation of scenic areas along the Interstate system where no billboards would be allowed.[16]

The most significant addition to the highway-beauty coalition was Lady Bird Johnson. According to a contemporary newspaper story, she became interested in the state of highways and the junkyards along them in late 1963 or early 1964. Later she recalled that as she drove from Texas to Washington or as she campaigned across her own state, she noticed the junkyards of abandoned automobiles. That experience for her was the catalyst that led to her being concerned about highway beautification. A few days after the 1964 election, the president called then Secretary of Commerce Luther Hodges and said: "Lady Bird wants to know what you're going to do about all those junkyards along the highways." He also indicated that he wanted the Commerce Department to come up with a program for highway beautification. The First Lady's interest galvanized the president, whose heightened sensitivity, in turn, aroused the bureaucracy in the White House and in the Department of Commerce.[17]

The Bureau of Public Roads made a hasty estimate and reported that there were over 16,000 junkyards along the nation's highways, with 1,602 in Texas, the most of any state. The Commerce Department also began to work on a program of action for 1965. The staff concluded that the government had the resources to do much of what President Johnson and his wife wanted "without additional legislation." In 1940, Congress had said that states might use 3 percent of their federal highway funds for the improvement of scenic corridors. Nothing had happened with this program for a quarter-century, because the states preferred to use the money for construction, and the federal government did not promote scenic easements at all. Now the Bureau of Public Roads said that it would push the states to act. Other initiatives included federal studies of scenic roads, the use of the Job Corps in beautification programs, and various advisory and clearing-house functions.[18]

The most crucial decision regarding new legislation centered on junkyards and billboards. On 16 December 1964, Luther Hodges wrote that a "key item for attention and action by the Federal Government is the matter of control of billboard advertising along the Interstate System and new segments of the Primary System built on new locations." The secretary further recommended that junkyards and billboards be treated together. As to specific legislation, the Commerce Department proposed that the 1958 Outdoor Advertising Control Law be extended until 1972, that it include junkyards, and, most important, that it be mandatory for states to control outdoor advertising and junkyards, or they would lose federal highway-aid funds. Hodges noted that this program would be controversial. More than that, if followed, it would commit the Johnson administration to a difficult political fight with an entrenched and powerful lobby on Capitol Hill.[19]

To have a chance to prevail in the legislative battle over billboard regulation, the Johnson administration adopted a strategy aimed at enlisting part of the outdoor advertising industry on its side. This approach established a context within which the Highway Beautification Act developed, and it accounted for much of the controversy that has plagued the law since its passage. The decision to follow this line in seeking billboard control grew out of earlier negotiations between the industry and the Department of Commerce. It also probably embodied Lyndon Johnson's conclusion that a direct assault on the billboard lobby would certainly fail in Congress. He knew the political strength of the billboard and highway-construction coalition, both of which would be targets of laws that devoted money to removing billboards, cleaning up junkyards, and improving roadside landscapes. The president had made the call that his wife had asked him to place to Secretary Hodges. In shaping the necessary laws, he and his men would determine the strategy that would be pursued to implement her desire.

During the latter part of the Kennedy presidency, the Department of Commerce, wherein the Bureau of Public Roads was then located, opened negotiations with the Outdoor Advertising Association of America (OAAA) about billboard control "to agree upon an amended law which would be satisfactory to both the Government and the Industry."[20] These talks reflected the contrasting aspirations of both sides. The OAAA, whose members operated "within incorporated municipalities and areas zoned or used for business," wanted the "Kerr Amendment" of 1959 altered to change language that had frozen zoned areas to those in place on 21 September 1959. Outside of the zoned areas, billboard advertising would be limited "in rural business areas to a 600 foot frontage where businesses of other nature are actually being conducted." The OAAA representatives also agreed to restrict informational advertising along the Interstate System to one sign per mile within five miles of an intersection. As their major "concession," the OAAA spokesmen agreed that all segments of the highway system, even portions built before July 1956, would be subject to federal control. In accordance with the association's long-standing policy, none of these changes would be mandatory, and the control of billboards would remain with the individual states.[21]

The negotiator for the Bureau of Public Roads, Lowell K. Bridwell, reached what a billboard representative styled a "tentative agreement" on these issues and said that he would refer it to the secretary of commerce. The Commerce Department, however, concluded that the OAAA proposals "would really not take care of the billboard problem, and would in fact result in more and bigger billboards than we have under our present weak regulation." Commerce pointed out that the OAAA's initiative about "informational advertising" would result in federally sanctioned "off-premise" advertising that would benefit property owners who were under the association's regulations and would harm those outside. Moreover, the opposition to a mandatory federal law would leave real control with the states, where, as a Commerce spokesman delicately put it, the billboard forces did not "have to be concerned about stringent state legislative action against billboards."[22]

The strategy that the Bureau of Public Roads and the Commerce Department followed of negotiating with the major billboard lobbying group for owners in urban and municipal areas grew out of the realistic political calculation that legislation directed against all billboards had little chance of gaining congressional approval. If the support of the OAAA could be secured in advance, a winning coalition on Capitol Hill might be possible. The problem was that such an approach would, when it became known, probably alienate the antibillboard forces who wanted more restrictive legislation. In addition, the agenda of the OAAA did not at all harmonize with the goals of the Bureau of Public Roads. The billboard people wanted a franchise that had federal endorsement and an explicit recognition of their right to do business with a minimum of regulation. They pretended to acquiesce in the goals of billboard reduction while they were actually seeking governmental protection for their interests.[23]

Bill Moyers became the White House staff member in charge of working with representatives of the billboard industry and the Bureau of Public Roads in framing legislation. He was thirty years old at this time, and had come back to President Johnson's employ after a stint as an executive with the Peace Corps under Kennedy. He had no particular expertise in either billboard regulation or conservation matters, and had to rely on the Department of Commerce for most of his knowledge about this complex and technical problem. Working closely with the industry's agents during the first half of 1965, Moyers directed his energies toward obtaining a bill that would command their support and embrace the commitments that Commerce had made. If he did, in fact, reach out to the proponents of billboard control, evidence of such contacts does not remain in the files. After leaving the White House, Moyers distanced himself from his connection with the billboard organizations and particularly the president of the OAAA, Phillip Tocker.[24]

Tocker was a Texas lawyer who became the president of the OAAA in the Johnson years. Articulate and informed, he performed skillfully on Capitol Hill with those lawmakers whom his organization had carefully cultivated over the years. The OAAA had gone one step better, hiring the Austin law firm of Clark, Thomas, Harris, Denius and Winters to represent its interests with the White House. Donald S. Thomas of that firm was the personal attorney and a long-time friend of President and Mrs. Johnson's. He had ready access to Moyers, and Thomas helped to provide Tocker with an entree to Moyers and to the president's staff in general. Other industry spokesmen conveyed similar information to Jack J. Valenti, also then a Johnson aide. At this stage in the shaping of the Highway Beautification Act, the billboard industry had much better ability to influence policy than had any of the antibillboard groups that would have to support the legislation later.[25]

After Secretary Hodges met with the president at the LBJ Ranch on 21 December 1964 to make the final decisions on the highway-beauty program, the public campaign for the new policy was launched in January 1965. In his State of the Union message on January 4, Johnson said that "a new and substantial effort must be made to landscape highways to provide places of relaxation and recreation wherever our roads run." On the next day the Department of Commerce announced the administrative steps that it would take to promote more beautiful highways. On January 8 the White House staff completed work on a presidential letter to the secretary of commerce, setting out what Johnson thought should occur on highway beauty. Released to the public on 21 January 1965, the letter did not mention billboards. Johnson asked that landscaping be made a part of highway projects. The states should be encouraged to provide easements for highway rights of way that would preserve beauty along the roadsides, use wild flowers on public roads, and provide additional rest areas. "It is my hope," he added, "that high priority will be given to landscape projects for screening junkyards, excavation scars, and other unsightly areas adjacent to highway rights-of-way." Finally, he sought additional legislative proposals as needed.[26]

Lyndon Johnson's thought processes are not usually discernible amidst the masses of documents in his presidential library. Other people drafted most of his letters, speeches, and public statements. Often there are few clues as to what he believed, other than a check mark by a "Yes" or "No" on the memoranda that his staff had sent to him. It is a valid measure of Lady Bird Johnson's influence in the area of beautification that the president added six lines in his own handwriting at the bottom of the original letter to Secretary John T. Connor, who by then had replaced Luther Hodges:

> Jack. All industry, labor and public service organizations quartered here should be enlisted. Touch base with these organizations and get their help. Talk to Udall (get his cooperation on the proposed conference)—also check out appropriate Congressional Chairman and ranking members. Let's get all garden clubs working—with Mary [Lasker] and Lady Bird giving them encouragement by appearances. Get back to [Horace] Busby on the National Conference and when we should announce it and call it. L.

During the winter and spring of 1965 the president kept the pressure on his administration to do something about highway beauty and billboards. On February 5 he sent Secretary Connor a newspaper story about highways, with these comments: "I can't emphasize too much the importance of this particular program to all of us. I hope you will follow through on it seeing that it not only gets off the ground but gathers steam as it goes along." Three days later, in his message on natural beauty, Johnson reviewed his program for highway beautification and linked it to his "New Conservation." He sent Connor another editorial about billboards in early March and a letter in April, praising the Bureau of Public Roads for having acted against unauthorized road signs in Alabama.[27]

Throughout the controversy over billboards during his administration, Lyndon Johnson sought to involve his wife in the process of making decisions on the issue. Other men in the White House would, in their memoranda to each other, express disparaging opinions of the women around the First Lady and indicate a sense that highway beautification was not worth the political trouble it was causing. When a member of the Joint Center for Urban Studies at MIT and Harvard sent an article on "highway ugliness" to Lee White, a member of the White House staff, in April 1965, White responded that he had sent the essay along to "our 'beauty queen.' " Whatever his private reservations may have been about the feasibility of billboard regulation, Lyndon Johnson consistently gave his wife support until the end of his presidency.[28]

During the early months of 1965, Lady Bird Johnson did not identify herself with the specifics of a highway-beautification law, but she did make clear, in public and in private, her commitment to the principle of improving the appearance of the nation's highways. In a *U.S. News* interview, she contended that "public feeling is going to bring about regulation, so that you don't have a solid diet of billboards on all the roads." The OAAA made an approach to her through Liz Carpenter, stressing the organization's ostensible public commitment to the natural-beauty program. Carpenter sent them a polite letter of acknowledgment. On the other hand, the First Lady's letters to the proponents of billboard regulation who wrote to her struck a more positive note. "Preservation of this land's scenic heritage is of great importance to me," she wrote; and she promised to pay careful attention to their concern for "the elimination of unsightly billboards." During this period, Lady Bird Johnson was also informing the Bureau of Public Roads about her correspondence from the public about the issue of highway location and construction. The bureau certainly had good reason to be aware of Lady Bird Johnson's commitment to highway beauty during the first half of 1965.[29]

Responding to President Johnson's prodding and to the expressed interest of his wife, the Commerce Department and the Bureau of the

Budget began to pull together a legislative program on highway beauty in March. There would be four bills. One would deal with junkyards along highways. The second and third would seek the improvement of the appearance of highways through the reallocation of money from the Highway Trust Fund for landscaping and scenic purposes. These measures seemed relatively uncontroversial, though there were already protests from junkyard owners. More important, congressional opposition might be anticipated to any shifts in Highway Trust Fund away from its traditional purpose of paying for road construction.[30]

Billboards constituted the difficult problem, and the questions that were to plague this phase of highway beautification came up at once. Should the administration's bill include signs along primary roads as well as the Interstate Highway System? Should billboards be allowed in areas zoned for commercial use, and what should be the status of areas that were being used for commercial and industrial purposes but had not yet been zoned to that effect? On the question of including the primary roads, the president decided to put them under the bill's coverage in response to a memorandum from Moyers dated March 26. Plans then went forward to send the package of bills to Congress in early April.[31]

The Outdoor Advertising Association, which was well informed about the discussions within the White House, intensified its efforts to sway the administration through its access to Bill Moyers. In a letter to Johnson of March 28, Donald Thomas argued that the OAAA's earlier discussions with the Bureau of Public Roads and Commerce had produced a workable compromise, which would allow billboards in areas zoned for business within cities or in areas used for business purposes in rural counties. The OAAA sought the right to have these areas expand as cities grew, and it wanted authority to place "informational" signs within five miles of a motel or restaurant at a spacing of one per mile. "We cannot believe that you would advocate any more stringent controls than these," Thomas pleaded. He added, however, that the OAAA would oppose any kind of mandatory law. If the states were encouraged to do so, they could be relied on, he asserted, to adopt the law in the form that the OAAA wanted.[32]

Thomas's argument went too far even for a Commerce Department that was normally friendly to outdoor advertising. In its response, the department noted that the states in which the industry possessed great influence were hardly likely to have signs removed in a stringent and effective way. Nor did Commerce approve of the OAAA's proposed "compromise" about informational "off-premise" signs. Such language, if included, would actually increase the number of signs allowed along a highway. Writing for the department, Robert E. Giles, its general counsel, said that the acceptance of what Thomas had proposed "would in fact result in more and bigger billboards that we have under our present weak regulation."[33]

By the middle of April the Johnson administration was ready to show its highway-beautification package to Congress. Emissaries from the Commerce Department, when they briefed the legislators who would have charge of the bills, encountered a cool reception, which foreshadowed how billboard control would fare on Capitol Hill for the next four years. Senator Patrick McNamara (D, Mich.), chairman of the Senate Committee on Public Works, did not like the plan to pay for beautification projects out of the Highway Trust Fund, and he was lukewarm on billboard control. "I'm not bothered by billboards," he said. Jennings Randolph (D, W. Va.), chairman of the Senate Subcommittee on Public Roads, indicated that his hearings would be lengthy. In the House, George H. Fallon (D, Md.) was friendly, but the prospects generally were questionable. As one White House aide put it, "The billboard thing would be tough but not impossible."[34]

Subsequent critics of the Highway Beautification Act would say that the Johnson administration either should have sought a stronger measure for highway beautification in 1965 or it should have waited until popular sentiment for billboard control grew in later years. The initial congressional reaction to the cautious package of bills that was presented in April 1965 suggests that no proposals that were more restrictive would have had a chance on Capitol Hill. As the White House viewed the situation during the spring of 1965, some accommodation with at least a segment of the billboard industry was in order if any law was to be passed at that time.

Through Bill Moyers, the administration now sought to win the endorsement of the OAAA for the beautification program. Fearing more restrictive laws, but also sensing an opportunity the leaders of the industry group saw a chance for an agreement with the administration. An excited Tocker told Thomas on April 14 that he "had an idea for a new approach to the whole problem that would completely satisfy everybody, except the extremists who want no regulations, or those who want total abolition." What Tocker advanced was that the White House accept a law "which will have the effect of prohibiting all signs, regardless of size or placement, on the Interstate System, excluding from the operation of the law only the unrestricted right to place signs on commercially zones [sic] or commercially used areas inside or outside of cities. The effect of this amendment will be to permit signs only where other business is being actively conducted or permitted." At this time the OAAA accepted that any signs that were removed would be taken down under the government's "police power," which would require the billboard owner to amortize the cost, usually over a five-year period.[35]

The billboard group was offering less than it seemed on the surface. The exception for areas that were zoned commercial or were used commercially meant that billboard companies could persuade states or localities to change zoning laws to allow outdoor advertising structures. Billboard interests had substantial influence on these political units. Tocker also knew that his proposal would give the OAAA members what amounted to a government-sanctioned franchise to carry on their business. Even on the issue of the police power, he had later plans to dilute or eliminate the provision. Up to this point he had already obtained Moyers's agreement that the primary-road system would not be covered by the bill.[36]

In return for the administration's concession on this last point, Moyers expected the OAAA either to adopt a position supporting the White House or, at worst, to take a stance of "benevolent neutrality." When Tocker took his work to the OAAA membership informally, he found intense resistance among those billboard operators who wanted no regulation whatsoever. As a further inducement to them, he suggested that instead of relying on the police power and amortization, billboard owners should receive monetary compensation from federal funds for taking down their signs. Tocker also saw Vice-President Hubert Humphrey, who added his voice to the pressures on Moyers. As a senator from Minnesota, Humphrey had long been solicitous of the interests of the 3M Corporation, which had extensive interests in road signs.[37]

During the first week of May, an understanding was reached that reflected a shift on both sides. Tocker said that he would put before the board of directors of the Outdoor Advertising Association a recommendation that they endorse a bill to control billboards along the Interstate and primary systems, "excluding from such control measure, however, areas zoned or used for business or commercial purposes." The definition of business use would be the one agreed upon with the Bureau of Public Roads. The date when all affected billboards had to come down would be early in 1968.[38]

Again, Tocker encountered resistance from his board when it met on May 11. Its members demanded that a specific date for the bill's impact on commercial areas be deleted, that a more precise definition of "business areas" be made, and that monetary compensation occur when signs were taken down. The administration acceded to the first two requests. On the question of compensation, the clause relating to the police power was modified to allow for the payment of governmental money when a state was "unable to secure effective control" through the police power.

There remained those in the OAAA who wanted no regulation at all. It took the efforts of Tocker to secure the acceptance of the White House program. Mark Evans, vice-president of Metromedia, a company that had major billboard holdings, also pledged his support. By May 21 he was promising to use five thousand billboards to spread Johnson's beautification message and to "tell the story so dear to your heart." In a more formal letter from Tocker of May 24, the OAAA pledged to back "President Johnson's beautification program" because "it is entirely consistent to preserve this important medium of commercial communication and at the same time to develop a more beautiful America." How these things were to be done simultaneously Tocker's letter carefully did not say. The key phrase was the OAAA's promise to "restrict our outdoor advertising structures to those areas zoned for business and industry or predominantly used for business and industry."[39]

The talks between the OAAA and the administration had now continued up to the date when the White House Conference on Natural Beauty was to open. How much did Lady Bird Johnson know about the Moyers-Tocker negotiations on the eve of this conference? The entries in her published diary for May are sporadic, with none for the White House meeting at all, and there is at this point no way of learning what the unpublished entries and their supporting documents might contain. There are a few clues, however. In 1968, Liz Carpenter mentioned to Sharon Francis "that we had too weak a bill to start with, and that Bill Moyers and Phil Tocker of the outdoor advertisers had drafted our administration bill over the telephone and it had the wrong name, beautification." These remarks were made after several years of disillusionment about highway beautification on the part of Carpenter and Lady Bird Johnson, but they suggest that the First Lady had probably been aware of what Moyers was doing. Whether she approved of the strategy of courting the OAAA is not known, but she probably did, for the same reasons that motivated her husband.[40]

A related issue is why the proponents of billboard regulation were not given the same degree of access to the White House that Tocker and the OAAA enjoyed. Senator Maurine Neuberger, who was carrying on her late husband's antibillboard struggle, did meet with "White House representatives" in February about billboard control, but she apparently had little contact with the administration thereafter. Such visible advocates of regulation as Helen Reynolds of the California Roadside Council and Hilda Fox of the Pennsylvania Roadside Council received warm replies when they wrote to Lady Bird Johnson, but they did not take part in shaping the legislation.[41]

The failure to consult conservation representatives such as Fox and

Reynolds and the groups that they led was a major mistake in the Johnsons' campaign for highway beautification. It may have occurred because Lyndon Johnson and his wife believed that the billboard opponents had no alternative but to support what the White House ultimately proposed. The OAAA had clout in Congress; roadside councils did not. The predominance of women in these groups also played a part. Rex Whitton of the Bureau of Public Roads had been quoted earlier in the year to the effect that women who were beautifying the roadside might pose a safety hazard for motorists. The condescension that Whitton reflected was widespread in the administration in regard to highway beautification. The result was that Lady Bird Johnson's approach to billboard regulation lacked any strong champions among the existing conservation organizations in 1965.[42]

Hilda Fox and Maurine Neuberger were both slated to be members of the panel on "Roadside Control" at the Natural Beauty Conference. The two women wrote to each other about the strategy they might follow when their panel met, and they were suspicious when Tocker's name was added to the slate for the "Roadside Control" session. "The billboard story has been told all over the landscape," Fox wrote, "and I can see no reason for giving them a chance to cite their 'philanthropies,' etc. Do you? Tocker openly boasted around Washington that there would be no danger of control laws,—'we're in the White House.' " The resultant tension was evident when the panel convened on Tuesday morning, May 25. Tocker read the substance of the OAAA's letter to the president. In the ensuing discussion, one panelist questioned why Tocker was there at all. "Why is it," inquired the president of the Arizona Roadside Council, "that there is a representative of the outdoor advertising industry sitting on this panel, considering the defamation of scenic views. They are one of the most destructive elements of beauty in this country, and I am talking about all kinds of signs, all types, including billboards." Tocker did not get a chance to answer, and no one at the conference yet knew how closely he had been working with the White House.[43]

The extent of that association emerged later in the day, when the Roadside Control panel considered its recommendations to the conference at large. With only Tocker recorded in the negative, they "voted to recommend that no off-premise advertising be permitted in any areas adjacent to the primary system and the interstate system." Senator Neuberger and Lowell K. Bridwell were not present, but their statements for the record indicated that they now knew what the White House would propose. They said that they would have allowed exceptions for business areas.[44]

Having decided to urge President Johnson to support the strictest kind of billboard regulation, the panel members were shocked when the president said on the afternoon of May 25 that he was sending four bills to Congress the next day to "help make our Nation's highways sources of pleasure and sources of recreation." The most startling remark was Johnson's assertion that the bills on junkyards and billboards would operate "except in those areas of commercial and industrial use." The proregulation participants at the Conference would have been further outraged had they known that as the president was speaking, Phillip Tocker was sitting in Bill Moyers's office, listening to the speech.[45]

What the advocates of control had heard the president say was enough to arouse their anger and dismay. "This is terrible," one member of the Washington Roadside Council said to Helen Reynolds. "Believe you were seriously misadvised in statement to White House conference regarding billboards," read one telegram to the president, which warned that "already opposition growing in groups needed to lead natural beauty followup." Another correspondent, an attorney in Seattle, Washington, wrote that "the President has tied into a buzz saw when he took the industry position." The general reaction of the roadside councils and other proregulation forces was one of indifference to the fate of highway-beautification legislation for the rest of its course on Capitol Hill. If the Johnson administration had acted on the premise that the roadside councils would have no option but to support the billboard package, they had miscalculated about the impact of disinterest from the antibillboard side.[46]

The support of the Outdoor Advertising Association and its members was highly visible during the summer of 1965. The OAAA placed large advertisements in trade journals, which proclaimed the virtues of the administration's program. Its endorsement, however, did not carry with it all of the billboard industry. Smaller billboard operators protested vigorously. One asked Lady Bird Johnson: "Why do you want to destroy my job?" The leading lobbying force behind the opposition was the Roadside Business Association, of which the Minnesota Mining and Manufacturing Company (3M) was "a principal member," because "one of its subsidiaries is a predominant manufacturer and supplier of outdoor advertising and sign materials." The White House had not avoided a difficult fight over billboards through its pact with the OAAA, but it had purchased the support of some of the industry at the cost of endorsement from any substantial part of the antibillboard camp.[47]

The arena for the battle over highway beautification now became Congress, and Lady Bird Johnson was drawn into the legislative struggle directly during the late summer and early autumn of 1965. The billboard, junkyard, and scenic-highway proposals that the Johnson administration offered had acquired the popular label "Lady Bird's bill." She followed the progress of these measures through the House and Senate committees, participated in strategy conferences, and both coordinated lobbying and did some herself. The result was a unique degree of involvement for a First Lady in the legislative process.

Before the summer of 1965, Lady Bird Johnson's interactions with Congress were the social occasions when she and the president had entertained lawmakers at the White House. These events had an obviously political dimension, and the guest lists were compiled with a nice sense of how the president's purposes would be advanced. Bess Abell received lists from presidential aides that suggested congressmen and senators who might be invited, along with such comments as "he can always be counted on to support the Administration when the chips are down" or "above av. support on Repub. side." The First Lady herself knew which senators and congressmen had recently been to the White House and which had not, and she made an effort during the later years of her entertaining to see that those who had not been to a presidential social event did get to come. The direct lobbying that was implicit in such occasions she left to her husband.[48]

In the case of highway beautification, however, circumstances required that she become a more direct part of the campaign to enact the laws that the administration had developed. The highway-beautification package went to the House, accompanied by a presidential message, on 26 May 1965. Senator Randolph submitted similar bills to the Senate on June 3. There was no great rush to act on these measures in the midst of a busy summer, and there was no great surge of popularity for them on Capitol Hill. The House Subcommittee on Roads scheduled its hearings in mid July. Senator McNamara took his time about assembling his colleagues, to the point that Secretary Connor said to the president, "McNamara is dragging his feet on highway legislation." In response, Johnson ordered his aides to approach Walter P. Reuther, president of the United Automobile Workers, about pressuring McNamara "*muy pronto.*" The senator scheduled hearings to begin on August 10.[49]

The issue that initially troubled the highway-beautification effort during the summer of 1965 was not billboards; it was how to pay for all the aspects of what the administration wanted to do. One major difficulty on the White House side was its vagueness about the exact price tag for the beautification campaign. The Bureau of the Budget's estimate was $780 million, while the Department of Commerce's was $1.175 billion. The figure for billboard control was set at $180 million, but that referred to the acquisition of advertising rights along the affected highways. If the cost of removing existing billboards through monetary compensation were added in, the figure would rise dramatically, especially in the absence of any reliable inventory of the number of billboards along the highways in question. The Commerce Department advised Secretary Connor on 30 August 1965 that it was "unable to furnish an accurate estimate of the cost of billboard legislation."[50]

From the beginning of the antibillboard campaign, the Johnson administration expected that beautification would be financed out of the Highway Trust Fund. Oil and gas revenues flowed into this fund to pay for construction that was supposed to complete the Interstate Highway System by 1972. In 1965, however, estimates showed that the fund would need an additional $3 to $5 billion to meet its projected completion date. There was an elaborate linkage of interests on Capitol Hill that supported the Highway Trust Fund—state and local officials, highway contractors, construction unions, and the congressmen and senators whose constituents prospered from highway money. Any money that might be diverted from the fund and then used for beautification would ripple through the highway business empire in a directly adverse way. The fund, as Lawrence O'Brien told Lady Bird Johnson, was almost sacred in Congress. If billboards affected lawmakers directly, issues of highway funding were even more politically sensitive.[51]

To find money for beautification that might go into the Highway Fund, the administration looked to the revenues generated by excise taxes on automobiles. In mid May, President Johnson sent Congress a package of reductions in excise taxes, which included lowering the manufacturers' excise tax on cars from 10 to 7 percent. Working with Senator Paul H. Douglas (D, Ill.), the White House succeeded for a time in having one percentage point of the tax on automobiles that remained, estimated at $190 million, allocated for beautification purposes. "I can honestly tell you," wrote Joseph Barr, undersecretary of the Treasury, to the First Lady, "that had it not been for your insistence on beauty in our countryside, it would have probably been impossible for us to retain this $190 million a year." The conference on the tax bill, however, did not agree to put the money into a special fund for beautification until the program had been authorized. What the administration had in the end was the Senate's agreement in principle to use the excise-tax money for future beautification purposes. This achievement helped somewhat, but the cost of beautification remained a vexing question.[52]

When hearings opened on July 21 before the House Subcommittee on Roads of the Public Works Committee, the financial problem provided the major source of opposition, aside from the predictable outcry from the representatives of the billboard lobby who were not part of the OAAA. Attention centered on one bill that would have allocated one-third of federal highway funds, ordinarily apportioned to the states for use on secondary highways, to the new purpose of scenic roads and landscaping projects. Another bill would have compelled the states to use 3 percent of federal-aid funds to preserve scenic beauty near federal-aid highways. The president of the American Association of State Highway Officials said that speeding up the construction of the Interstate System would save lives, "which I think is more important than trying to do much about beautification at the present time." The National Association of Counties joined in criticizing any diversion of secondary-road-fund money. Reporting on the hearings to the Speaker of the House, Congressman Fallon contended that the total cost of the program was a major problem. "It is quite evident," he continued, "that before any final resolution can be made of this legislation a great deal of additional work must be done in revising these bills as they are now pending before the Committee." Diversion of money from the Highway Trust Fund, Fallon implied, would cause serious political problems with his colleagues.[53]

Senator McNamara was making similar arguments on the other side of the Capitol. He wanted "infusions" of money from general revenues for the Highway Fund to pay for beautification, and he regarded the bills that the administration was pushing as "in effect open-end commitments to spend untold money on beautification." As these talks with McNamara got under way, Lady Bird Johnson began to inform herself about the difficult legislative situation. Mike Manatos, the White House aide who was handling beautification in Congress, reported to Liz Carpenter on August 5, at the First Lady's request, that there was "stalemate" on the funding issue. "It is not realistic to believe we can go all the way on these four bills," Manatos warned. If the question of financing could be settled, he thought "a good start" might be made on the bills. On billboards, "if we can get a substantial piece" of the proposed billboard law, "we may have to settle for it." Further compromises on the language of the legislation in favor of the billboard interests was the clear thrust of what Manatos was telling Lady Bird Johnson.[54]

The hearings in the Senate Subcommittee on Public Roads from August 10 to 13 paralleled the earlier hearings in the House. The primary public issue continued to be the financial arrangements. By August 14, McNamara had abandoned his proposal to take money from general revenues for beautification and had agreed to have $200 million added to the Trust Fund, to be used for the control of junkyards, the regulation of billboards, and the construction of scenic stops along the highways. He would not accept the scenic-highway bill that involved money for secondary roads, and he balked at having an extra $200 million from the Trust Fund used for additional beautification work. O'Brien, the chief White House supervisor of legislation, brought Lady Bird Johnson up to date on these negotiations on August 16; he told her that agreement on the bills was possible if they could be funded without drawing on the Trust Fund directly. O'Brien suggested that Mrs. Johnson might invite McNamara, Randolph, Fallon, and other lawmakers, along with their wives, for a luncheon or dinner at the White House to discuss the beautification bills. Either because of scheduling conflicts or because of a desire not to commit the First Lady to the process at this stage, that social event did not occur.[55]

By mid August the bill to use secondary-road money for scenic roads was clearly dead, and on August 17 Mrs. Johnson acknowledged that it could not be revived. The officials from the Commerce Department who also met with her admitted that "*we could not spend effectively more than* $200 million per year" on all three remaining beautification proposals. At this point the Commerce Department was not inclined to press for an overly restrictive billboard law. As Assistant Secretary Alan Boyd told Connor on August 6, they would probably have to agree to compensation and a loose definition of what constituted an unzoned business area to get the bill through. Boyd thought that this would be a "completely reasonable solution" to the beautification problem, and he wanted to "clear up the highway beautification program this session if at all possible," so as to clear the way for other legislation that the department wanted to push in 1966.[56]

The administration now recognized that beautification money would have to come out of general revenues or increased taxes that would go into the highway fund. The Bureau of the Budget devised a two-pronged strategy to either seek, first, in 1966 to use either 1 percent of the excise tax on cars or other taxes for beautification purposes. Second, they suggested that $200 million of general revenues from the 1966 budget be allocated to a fund for beautification. By early September the White House had settled on the first alternative: "The funding would come from the Trust Fund after action on a tax bill to transfer the 1 percent excise tax into the Trust Fund." This result would be achieved by amending a bill to implement a Canadian-American agreement governing trade in automobile products, which the Senate was to consider shortly. Apparently, the precise nature of this process was not mentioned to any of the Senate leaders who were handling the beautification program.[57]

As the date for action by the Senate subcommittee neared, Senator Randolph's personal opposition to beautification further complicated an already-snarled legislative agenda. Never an admirer of the program, he complained about his relations with Commerce and their alleged slowness in responding to his inquiries. The White House believed that the senator preferred to see beautification passed in 1966, when it would help his reelection chances. "Senator Randolph's nose obviously is out of joint," Mike Manatos wrote on August 23, "and he is of a mood to drag his feet on Highway Beautification" when the full Public Works Committee would meet on the next day. In fact, there was no subcommittee report on the bill, now titled S.2084, until 1 September 1965.[58]

The dubious prospects for Senate action roused the White House to more intense lobbying as August ended, and they brought Lady Bird Johnson into a more visible role as an advocate of beautification and of billboard control. Tocker and the OAAA had already sent out letters to every lawmaker, outlining their support of the president's package as part of the deal that was still in place. Lady Bird Johnson now met with Walter Reuther, who told her that he regarded bills for beautification and for home rule for Washington, D.C., as "of the highest priority." He promised to assemble a broad coalition from organized labor and civil-rights groups to push these bills. Mrs. Johnson said to him: "We'll keep our fingers crossed about the beautification legislation. I've lived through enough last days of congressional sessions to know that anything can happen. We'll hope for the best!"[59]

Around Washington at the end of August 1965 the word was that the Johnsons were doing more than relying on hope. The White House was saying "that the highway beauty bill was one of the ones the President wanted this year, that he had to have this one, it was reported, 'for Lady Bird.' " A participant in one of the strategy sessions in October 1965 recalled, in a slide presentation for the LBJ Library, that Lyndon Johnson said to his cabinet and staff: "You know I love that woman and she wants that Highway Beautification Act" and "By God, we're going to get it for her."[60]

When the Roads Subcommittee of the Public Works Committee unanimously reported out S.2084 to the full committee on September 3, the result underlined just how much work Lyndon and Lady Bird Johnson had had to do in order to achieve highway beautification. Several key changes on billboards had watered down the enforcement thrust of the bill. The administration wanted signs to be banned to a distance of one thousand feet from the road. The senators specified 660 feet from the right of way. What constituted a zoned industrial or commercial area would be left to the state legislatures, not to the secretary of commerce. The effective enforcement date had been changed from 1 July 1970 to 1 July 1972. Most important, the provisions using the police power to remove signs had been dropped, and language had been added requiring "just compensation" to all billboard operators or property owners that the act covered. Finally, for billboard removal, the panel had allocated $40 million from general revenues. Two other titles on junkyard control and landscaping had come though reasonably well, but the section on scenic roads had disappeared. The upshot was a draft bill that in the judgment of the White House, markedly decreased the amount of highway beautification obtained while increasing the cost to the federal government of achieving an improved landscape. Compensation meant that in the estimation of antibillboard groups, the people who polluted the highways with their billboards would now be paid not to pollute. That was the political price of getting any measure through Congress in the autumn of 1965.[61]

The Johnsons now began an effort to restore some of the teeth to the Senate bill when the full committee reported. By September 8 this pressure had produced some results, as the White House worked through Senator McNamara. His committee moved the effective date of the bill back to 1970, and the payment of compensation was prorated between the states and the federal government. The authority of the states to determine what were commercially or industrially zoned areas remained intact; funding levels for both Title I and Title II were trimmed to $20 million yearly. The financing was still to come out of general revenues, but the White House hoped that a change to the Trust Fund could occur on the Senate floor. There was enough improvement to encourage the president and his men about the bill's chances.[62]

Lady Bird Johnson was in Jackson Hole, Wyoming, when the committee acted on September 8. She was attending a meeting of the American Forestry Association and the National Council of State Garden Clubs. Along with Laurance Rockefeller, his wife, and other leading conservationists, Mrs. Johnson enjoyed the scenery and spoke to the two groups about beautification. "It is far easier," she told them, "to devastate a flowering countryside than to make it bloom again." In this congenial atmosphere, she received a call from her husband to inform her about what the Senate committee had done. "I'm very glad," she said to her aides. "It's one more step in the right direction. I was delighted to learn that the bill has been strengthened." The call indicated how closely she was following the legislative process, and she was about to become even more centrally involved after her return to Washington.[63]

While the Senate committee had done its work, the House Subcommittee on Roads had reconvened for additional hearings on September 3 and 7. Now the members were preparing to write a report on highway beautification on Monday, 13 September. The panel's chairman, John C. Kluczynski (D, Ill.), was as lukewarm toward what Mrs. Johnson wanted as were the rest of his colleagues. The White House learned before the weekend of September 11-12 had begun that the outcome of the subcommittee's deliberations would be a bill no stronger than what the Senate committee had approved. There was a good chance it would be even weaker. When Lady Bird Johnson returned from Wyoming on Saturday, 11 September, she joined conferences aimed at turning opinions and votes in the House subcommittee toward what the White House desired.[64]

The proposed alterations sought to change the definition of what constituted an "unzoned business area" to allow the secretary of commerce to establish the criteria or, at worst, to give the secretary the final approval of state action on the issue. The secretary would also receive authority to regulate the size and spacing of permitted billboards. Other less significant changes included inducing states that had accepted the billboard bonus to meet the highest applicable standards, and corrections in the language of the junkyard title. Mike Manatos correctly noted that any change in the billboard provision "will be met with all-out opposition from the outdoor advertising groups."[65]

To move minds and votes on Capitol Hill, a working group met with President Johnson on Saturday afternoon. Lady Bird Johnson joined Lawrence O'Brien, Horace Busby, Douglass Cater, and ten other men as specific lobbying decisions were worked out. Participation in a substantive gathering of this kind was a departure for the wife of a president. Not even Eleanor Roosevelt had sat in on legislative strategy sessions, nor had she been given assignments to woo votes in Congress. Lady Bird Johnson was stretching the boundaries of what first ladies could do.

She was assigned four House Members to call personally, including Kluczynski. The congressman owned a restaurant, and the president suggested that the call might find him "slapping mayonnaise" on bread. Lady Bird Johnson reached Kluczynski that afternoon, and a White House aide reported that "obviously Mrs. Johnson's call has had its effect and the Congressman is all for anything we want."[66]

When the subcommittee assembled on Monday morning to write the bill, White House aides, including Bill Moyers, and representatives from the Commerce Department were outside the room, suggesting changes and sending in "scraps of paper" with administration amendments. Moyers had become the press secretary to the president in mid July, but he remained a key participant in the billboard fight. During the ensuing week, a bill that was acceptable to the administration was worked out. By this time, Tocker and the OAAA believed that the White House was abandoning the agreement made in the spring. After a bitter confrontation with Moyers, Tocker took his organization back into the probillboard camp.[67]

The Senate took up S.2084 on Tuesday, 14 September, with Senator Randolph managing the bill. Before the measure went to the floor, the administration asked Randolph and McNamara to accept amendments to strengthen the bill. This put the West Virginia Democrat especially in the awkward position of seeking to make changes in a bill that his committee had reported unanimously. The central amendment in the Senate debate, which Randolph offered, changed the language in Title I, section e, to specify that billboards could be located either within areas zoned for commercial and industrial purposes or in unzoned commercial and industrial areas, "as may be determined by agreement between the several states and the Secretary." The final wording was changed several times, which further contributed to Senator Randolph's predicament and the sense that the White House representatives were not well informed on the issue. Randolph told his colleagues that the states and the secretary of commerce would be on an equal footing, and the latter would not have dictatorial authority on the zoning question. After lengthy debate, the amendment narrowly passed, by a vote of 44 to 40. Few senators at the time thought that they were voting to give the secretary of commerce the final and decisive right to determine where billboards could be located.[68]

On 16 September 1965, the highway-beautification bill cleared the Senate. The vote was 63 to 14, with 23 senators not voting. The bill retained the "just compensation" clause and would have failed if that language had been removed. Speaking about the billboard owners who would be affected by the law, Senator John Sherman Cooper (R, Ky.) said: "The committee felt that as a matter of justice they ought to be paid." Funding for all titles of the bill was to come from general revenues. In pursuing highway beautification, Lady Bird Johnson and the White House had passed an important marker in the legislative process, but the political price had been high. Mike Manatos told O'Brien that "some of our best friends are shaking their heads in disbelief that we have made ourselves look so inept." The real problem was that the Johnson administration now sought a billboard-control bill that was stronger than Congress would accept, and it had become necessary to make substantive concessions to get any measure through on Capitol Hill.[69]

O'Brien warned President Johnson about "our confusion, about our unnecessary harassment of friendly members, and about irritations which can prove damaging with other bills." He noted that ineptness in regard to the question of financing had resulted in failure to have the necessary language about the Trust Fund put into the Senate bill, "and realistically no effort should be made to put it in the House bill." Most important, indecision in the administration and some mixed signals from

Johnson himself about whether to ask the House to take the Senate bill exactly as written had resulted in delays in getting the measure to the lower house in time for prompt action as adjournment in mid October neared.[70]

The House Public Works Committee reported out S.2084 with amendments on September 21. The Republican minority, in its views on the bill, described it as a "poorly thought out proposal which was brutally forced upon the Committee on Public Works by spokesmen for the administration who wielded the power and influence of the White House to an extent which we have never before seen." The bill itself was not all that members of the administration wanted, but it was now all that they could get. "There is not evident at this point," wrote Alan Boyd, "any broad, enthusiastic support for the bill." Fallon and Kluczynski were apathetic, and the attitude of the committee staff verged on open hostility. By this time in 1965, Congress was showing the strain of the session that had enacted the Great Society legislation, and as Lyndon Johnson had foreseen, the large Democratic majorities that the election of 1964 had produced were growing weary and restive.[71]

Alan Boyd warned that when the House bill reached the floor in early October, the White House would need its "best effort" in order to prevent further amendments or outright defeat. In late September the Johnson White House launched its campaign to see that the House would approve S.2084. It was a fight in which the advantages lay with the billboard lobby. Mail on Capitol Hill was running four to one against highway beautification, as the industry and its friends mounted a letter-writing campaign. The administration was also confronting the lingering coolness from the garden clubs and roadside councils, especially as the bill had become weaker.[72]

Despite these obstacles, the White House sought support from such groups as the Izaak Walton League, the National Wildlife Federation, the National Consumers League, and the American Society of Landscape Architects. Liz Carpenter joined administration aides and representatives of the Democratic National Committee in mobilizing conservation groups and Democratic women's clubs to call potential voters on the Hill. Lady Bird Johnson sent out letters to those citizens who wrote to her on behalf of the bill. "I know that the people of this country will be disappointed—as I will—if a bill on highway improvement is not enacted before Congress adjourns."[73]

Despite the First Lady's endorsement, highway beautification encountered "a brick wall of opposition" when it reached the House Rules Committee on September 29. Congressman Thomas P. O'Neill (D, Mass.) said that some billboards "are more beautiful than old buildings."

The Rules Committee sent the bill forward by a 7 to 6 vote, reflecting the lack of congressional ardor for a bill "that the President—and Mrs. Johnson—want badly." In the face of this narrow success and its portent of more trouble on the House floor, Lady Bird Johnson decided to step up her public involvement in the legislative battle. She had Liz Carpenter go to the House to see lawmakers in person. Carpenter "put on my best Joy perfume and tightest girdle" and visited undecided Texas lawmakers. George H. Mahon (D, Texas), an influential member, summarized the state of affairs in Congress: "No one in the Texas delegation likes the bill, but no one wants to vote against Lady Bird."[74]

Carpenter reported back that Phillip Tocker and the OAAA were actively trying to defeat the bill. At the First Lady's behest, Carpenter coordinated lobbying through conservation organizations and elicited favorable newspaper editorials. Meanwhile, Lady Bird Johnson was trying to assuage the apprehensions of the antibillboard forces about the overall merits of the bill. "The use of compensation, rather than police power," she told Helen Reynolds, "is one of those facets of the bill that falls short of our ultimate wishes." Nevertheless, the bill represented "reasonable regulation, and thus is a major stride toward achieving the goal of beauty along our highways to which we all aspire."[75]

With adjournment nearing, the most important issue that the Johnsons faced was when to bring the bill up. On October 6, Carpenter informed the president that it would be better to go with the bill the next day, Thursday the seventh, "because the members want to go home and are tired of hearing about the bill." Faced with what one newspaper called the prospect of an "ungallant rejection of Mrs. Johnson's special project," House leaders were "counting noses and twisting arms to beat the band on this one."[76]

As the vote was set for October 7, the interplay between Lyndon Johnson, Lady Bird Johnson, and Congress became still more intricate. The president was suffering from an ailing gall bladder; he planned to enter Bethesda Naval Hospital on Thursday evening for surgery the next day. Before that had come up, the Johnsons had scheduled a gala "Salute to Congress," with entertainment by Frederic March, Anita Bryant, Gordon and Sheila MacRae, and the Ned Odum Boys, among others. Senate and House members were supposed to meet at the White House, have a drink, and then be bused to the State Department for the entertainment. The schedule depended on the House's concluding its business by late afternoon on Thursday.

The beautification bill was not brought up for debate until late in the afternoon. As talk ran into the evening, House members heard that Lyndon Johnson had told some Democrats that "he would rather have the bill for which his wife had campaigned zealously, than to go ahead with the Salute." Republicans charged that they would not be welcome at the festivities without the beautification bill. The Salute went on late, with senators, their wives, and the wives of congressmen listening to what proved to be rousing music and dramatic readings. As the evening ended, President Johnson said good night to his audience. He was sorry that the House members could not be there, but "they saw their duty and I hope they're doing it (applause), and I believe they are."[77]

On the House floor, "duty" was a burden for the legislators that evening, and they vented their resentment on both of the Johnsons. One congressman called S.2084 "the President's wife's bill," while Melvin R. Laird (R, Wis.) complained about press reports that "we must pass this bill tonight so that it can be delivered to the lovely First Lady as a present or package at the White House party." If the bill passed, said H. R. Gross (R, Iowa), he hoped that "the President will pull up a chair and sign it in the shade of the big billboard down on Route 290 outside of Austin, Tex., advertising KTBC, the television and radio station owned and operated by the Johnson family." Robert Dole (R, Kans.) offered an amendment to delete "Secretary of Commerce" wherever it appeared in the bill and to substitute the words "Lady Bird." The amendment lost on a voice vote. Other amendments carried the debate on past midnight. It was nearly one A.M. before the House voted.[78]

The central amendment in this extended discussion came from a Florida Democrat named Russell Tuten, who acted at the urging of Tocker and the industry. Tuten's language further diminished the authority of the secretary of commerce to make rulings about the size, lighting, and spacing of billboards. The secretary would have to defer to and respect "customary use" in affected areas. Second, the states would have "full authority" to zone "for commercial and industrial purposes and the actions of the States in this regard will be accepted for the purposes of this act." Tuten's amendment tracked what Secretary Connor had already declared in a letter to Kluczynski, and the amendment to the bill made it mandatory to adhere to standards what would otherwise have been left up to the secretary's discretion. The Tuten amendment passed, 122 to 112. Finally after a motion to recommit the bill was defeated by a vote of 230 to 153, with 49 not voting, the Highway Beautification Bill passed, 245 to 138, with 49 not voting.[79]

The White House now had to decide whether to seek a House-Senate conference about the amendments, particularly Tuten's, that the House had added. The problem was that going to a conference committee might raise the possibility of further erosion in the bill's substance at a time when Congress was still bitter about the events of October 7. Making a fight over the part of the Tuten amendment that dealt with size, lighting, and spacing would be highly risky. An aide reported: "Everything I get out of the House indicates major defections in New England and the South" if changes were proposed on this subject. The Johnson administration would have to be ready to "apply the necessary muscle to roll over" men such as Tuten and others who believed as he did. To a large extent, the Johnson presidency no longer had that kind of muscle by mid October 1965 as Congress was growing tired of Great Society programs and as the Vietnam War was eroding the Democratic grip on power. On October 13 the Senate concurred in the bill as the House had passed it, and S.2084 went to President Johnson for his signature.[80]

The Johnsons held a ceremony in the East Room of the White House for the signing of the Highway Beautification Act on 22 October 1965. "The atmosphere was very pleasant and relaxed," Paul Southwick of the Commerce Department reported, and the president and his wife "mingled with us during the serving of coffee, punch, etc." The informal setting allowed House members such as Kluczynski the chance to chat with the Johnsons, and "relations were thereby considerably improved all around." The law, Lyndon Johnson said in his remarks, "will bring the wonders of nature back into our daily lives." He conceded that it did not "represent everything that we wanted," but it was "a first step and there will be other steps." After the signing was over, the president asked Southwick "to make sure the Department [Commerce] followed up strongly on billboard control" and that "the billboard industry does what it is supposed to do."[81]

Lady Bird Johnson did not speak at the bill-signing ceremony, but photographs showed her pleased expression as her husband gave her one of the pens. In the letters that she sent out that autumn, she noted: "Isn't it wonderful that Congress has made highway beautification the law of the land?" The immediate reaction to the passage of the law was that the First Lady had secured a notable triumph. "Lady Bird Wins on Billboards" said an editorial in the *Washington Star*, and a cartoonist depicted her with a sword, jousting at a monster on a billboard under the title "Beauty and the Beast." She had performed in "a new 'First Lady' role" in securing the bill's passage, wrote the editors of the *Christian Science Monitor*.[82]

For Lady Bird Johnson, however, public visibility also meant political criticism. "This legislation is a WHIM of Mrs. Johnson," the owner of the Dallas Outdoor Advertising Company wrote to the president, "and you are backing it to the hilt to please her with no regard to the effect it will have on thousands and thousands of people in the Outdoor Advertising Business." When his colleagues in the House criticized Robert Dole

President and Mrs. Johnson at the signing of the Highway Beautification Act on 22 October 1965.

for his "Lady Bird" amendment, he noted her "active interest" in the legislation and added that "when one chooses to step down from the pedestal of the dutiful preoccupied wife of the President, or other public official, and to wade into the turbulent stream of public controversy, one must expect to, at least, get her feet wet." In Montana a billboard appeared briefly, calling for "Impeachment of Lady Bird," which led cartoonist Bill Mauldin to depict a motorist crossing a landscape festooned with billboards, one of which read "Impeach Lady Bird."[83]

Lady Bird Johnson's reaction to Mauldin's cartoon was "Imagine me keeping company with Chief Justice Warren!" Her response to being an object of public controversy herself was more guarded. Her associates recall that she decided to be more careful and less visible but no less active in her advocacy of beautification measures involving highways and billboards. She knew that publicity was the most powerful weapon that a First Lady could wield but that it had to be used in unifying and non-partisan ways to be most effective. As Dole's comments indicated, there were limits that a male-dominated society still imposed on the wife of a president when she openly moved from being a celebrity to being a political leader of substance.[84]

The initial reaction among the conservation and antibillboard community to the bill was cautiously positive. Hilda Fox wrote Maurine Neuberger: "I still gag over the 'compensation' provision, excepting junkyards, perhaps, but at least the pot will be kept boiling, as it were, and Lady Bird scored a notable victory." The reaction of other proponents of a stronger law ran along these lines. Then, in the December 1965 *Atlantic Monthly*, Elizabeth Drew wrote a critique of "Lady Bird's Beauty Bill" that emphasized the weaknesses in the law, the administration's negotiations with Tocker and the billboard industry, and the rough treatment that Lady Bird Johnson and the White House had received on Capitol Hill. "Not until there had been considerable bloodletting, and the full commitment of the powers of the White House, did a bill of only wan beauty finally reach the President's desk," Drew contended.[85]

The Highway Beautification Act did have many of the weaknesses that Drew and subsequent critics have identified. There was the change in public policy that "just compensation" represented, along with the amendments that limited the power of the government to enforce the measure. Other problems would emerge as the law was interpreted and as the billboard industry sought to water it down even more. To what extent might these lapses have been avoided in the drafting, presentation, and passage of the bill? Sharon Francis believed that a better law might have been passed had Lady Bird Johnson and the president mobilized conservation support, written a better law, and made the campaign for enactment in 1966. Conservation critics of the law have echoed that charge. The political problem with that strategy, however, was the pervasive lack of enthusiasm for any billboard control in Congress at any time during the 1960s. By 1966 the ascendancy of Lyndon Johnson on Capitol Hill was over. It is doubtful that he and his wife could have put together then the fragile coalition that prevailed in October 1965.[86]

A more fundamental problem lay with the failure of the White House staff to master the details and nuances of the outdoor advertising industry as a target of regulation. Lyndon Johnson preferred to have generalists on his staff, rather than experts. This approach made sense in dealing with the ever-changing array of problems that came to the presidency. When a complex and technical issue such as billboard control was involved, however, the intelligence of a Bill Moyers was not the equal of the expertise of a Phillip Tocker. As Elizabeth Drew noted, the president and his men believed that the OAAA shared the broad goals of billboard regulation and that the details of implementation and enforcement could be worked out. The "consensus" was bogus. The OAAA had its priorities, including federal recognition of the industry, and the Johnson administration had its aims. They were not reconcilable through negotiations, no matter how intense and prolonged they might be.[87]

Why did the Johnson administration not reach out to roadside councils and conservationist groups for help? In 1965 there was no environmentalist coalition as such. Roadside councils lacked a national clearing house or governing body, and thus they had no means of mobilizing the opinion of their members on a national issue. In the Department of Commerce, on Capitol Hill, and to some degree even within the Johnson White House itself, there was the pervasive sense that such groups, in which women dominated, somehow lacked the practicality and the political sense that men possessed. So chauvinism prevailed. Phillip Tocker and Donald Thomas could get in touch with Bill Moyers directly. Hilda Fox, Helen Reynolds, and the California Roadside Council were as likely to have their letters routed to the Department of Commerce, where answers would be prepared. Even the intercession of Sharon Francis and Liz Carpenter was treated with an elaborate courtesy and gestures of respect that masked a good deal of masculine condescension.[88]

For all the problems that plagued highway beautification in 1965, a bill finally did become a law. That result would not have occurred without the impetus that Lady Bird Johnson supplied to her husband in November and December 1964. The momentum that she imparted sustained the campaign through the White House Conference on Natural Beauty and into the summer of 1965. When Congress began committee consideration, her intervention kept the bill alive in the House. She supplied overall direction to the lobbying campaign once the measure had reached the stage of floor action. She did play a new role as First Lady by serving as a legislative aide and lobbyist.[89] Without her commitment the bill would not have passed. Lyndon Johnson also deserves much credit for his strong support of the bill, but it was his wife who had channeled his energies in the way that she desired.

Like the president, she deemed the bill a promising start. The money that was set aside to beautify highways was a constructive step, as was the title relating to junkyards. The outcome of billboard regulation would depend on how the law was administered. Though she did so with less publicity, Lady Bird Johnson expended as much energy in overseeing the implementation of the Highway Beautification Act from October 1965 through January 1969 as she had put forth in sponsoring the law originally.

8

Protecting Highway Beauty,
1966–69

While the signing of the Highway Beautification Act on 22 October 1965 reflected a legislative victory for Mrs. Johnson and the billboard opponents on Capitol Hill and in the White House, it did not change the existing political alignments on the issue itself. The billboard industry remained intent on defeating the new law in its administrative phase or, at worst, on transforming it into legislation that would work to the advantage of the outdoor advertising business. Advocates of billboard control outside of the administration had strong doubts about the effectiveness of the new law; they were waiting to see how strongly it would be implemented. If the First Lady did not take as much interest in how the law worked in practice as she had shown in its passage through Congress, the Highway Beautification Act would be a program without friends in a political world of abundant and resourceful enemies.

After President Johnson had indicated to Department of Commerce officials at the bill-signing ceremony that he expected prompt action to put the highway-beautification program into operation, Rex Whitton took the hint. Invitations went out to state highway officials who were responsible for beautification to attend a conference in Washington on November 2. The day after that briefing, regional engineers from the Bureau of Public Roads came to town, and the National Advisory Committee on Highway Beautification gathered on November 4. Meetings were also scheduled with probillboard groups on December 1 and with the friends of highway beautification on December 9. "We are endeavoring to put the 'hard sell' on the Act," Lawrence Jones, the deputy highway administrator, told Liz Carpenter on November 23, though he noted that roadside councils and enemies of billboards tended "to feel that we didn't get enough in the present bill."[1]

Putting the law into operation was a cumbersome and protracted process. The Department of Commerce had to appoint a highway beauty coordinator and had to create beautification units within its existing offices. From the outset the department encountered difficulty in locating someone to take on the coordinator's post. An inventory of billboards and junkyards was launched in January 1966. By the middle of the same month, some 141 projects were under scrutiny as part of the act's implementation, including 1 for "screening a junkyard, 15 for safety rest areas, 12 for landscaping, and 3 for acquisition of scenic strips." The most elaborate set of requirements had to do with billboard control. Public hearings had to be held in each state on such topics as the definition of zoned and unzoned commercial and industrial areas and other contemplated standards for billboards.[2]

Lady Bird Johnson kept her eye on this set of activities. Talking with Secretary of Commerce Connor at the White House over dinner, she asked for a progress report, which he sent to her on January 19. After reading a memorandum from Alan Boyd, she replied that "it seems most valuable to have strong administrative procedures at the outset," and she expressed her pleasure at "the important steps that are being taken to further this program which can have such a positive impact on the roadsides of America." On 28 January 1966, the department made public in the *Federal Register* the draft standards for billboard regulation, which would form the basis for discussion at the hearings in the fifty states.[3]

In its announcement the department specified carefully that the standards and guidelines "do not represent any conclusions, or even tentative conclusions on the part of the Secretary of Commerce." However, the substance of the draft standards took positions that favored more stringent regulation of billboards than the industry had anticipated or that Congress had had in mind. The suggested language would have barred signs that moved or were animated, and the department defined an unzoned area in a precise and unequivocal way. The size of the permitted signs was smaller than what the industry normally used, a 150-foot distance from the roadway was established, and signs on roofs would be drastically curtailed. Lights that flashed, blinked, or moved would also be prohibited, and the draft regulations outlawed signs within 2,000 feet of an interchange or intersection on a freeway or primary road and within 250 feet of an intersection on a standard street.[4]

The publication of the draft standards triggered a prompt and overwhelmingly negative response from the billboard interests and on Capitol Hill. A Louisiana congressman called the standards "a serious misinterpretation of the intent of Congress in passing the Highway Beautification Act," which would "seriously jeopardize, perhaps almost destroy, the outdoor advertising industry." In the Senate, Jennings Randolph denounced the standards, and Senator Edmund Muskie (D, Me.) warned that the law "may be unnecessarily jeopardized by an overzealous inter-

pretation in the Department of Commerce of one section of the act."
Phillip Tocker and the Outdoor Advertising Association of America circulated critical comments on the draft standards among friendly
lawmakers; and the president of the Brotherhood of Painters, Decorators,
and Paperhangers wired Secretary Connor that "in my judgment the standards you propose are in outright conflict with the intent of Congress
and the Highway Act as passed in 1965."[5]

The Department of Commerce had an impossible task in early 1966.
No matter what tentative language it proposed, one side in the billboard
struggle would have been angered. The Highway Beautification Act of
1965 had contained the kind of deliberate obscurity that sometimes ac-
companies disputed legislation. The Johnson administration believed that
in October 1965 it had preserved the authority of the secretary of commerce to have the final word on billboard regulations. Both Congress
and the industry thought that they had prevented such a role for the
government. Now the struggle would begin again over the draft standards and the actual rules that came out of the hearing process.

The issue of funding the beautification program, which had hampered
the legislation during the summer and fall of 1965, arose again in 1966.
In March the Johnson administration proposed a Highway Safety program when the president told Congress that "the carnage on the highways
must be arrested." The Traffic Safety Act would be financed by transfer-
ring to the Highway Trust Fund amounts equivalent to 1 percent of
the excise tax on passenger cars. That tax had been reduced at the beginning of 1966, and the Budget Message asked that the levy be reinstated
and that other scheduled reductions be postponed to help offset the
rising costs of the Vietnam War. As the administration envisioned it,
highway-beautification money would go into the same trust fund and
come from the same source. With dedicated revenues, beautification
would be outside the vagaries of the congressional appropriations process. The 1965 act had provided funds for the 1966 and 1967 fiscal years.
Because the act would have to be renewed in 1967, the funding question would be settled before the law came under legislative scrutiny.[6]

The initial responses to the administration's funding scheme were not
encouraging. In February an irate constituent of Senator Everett M.
Dirksen's (R, Ill.) asked, "Is it more important to satisfy the *Whim of
Mrs. Johnson* or use the money he wants appropriated for saving our
youth in Viet Nam?" When the Senate held hearings in May on the
Federal-Aid Highway Act of 1966, representatives of the American Road
Builders Association and the American Association of State Highway
Officials expressed reservations about having any money from the
Highway Trust Fund allocated away from construction purposes. By the

end of June the administration was confronting problems "in securing a commitment from Wilbur Mills for early action by the Ways and Means Committee" on the highway safety and beautification trust fund.[7]

Another issue growing out of billboard regulation troubled the Commerce Department in mid 1966. The Highway Beautification Law specified that a state would lose 10 percent of its federal-aid highway funds if it had not effectively controlled outdoor advertising on the Interstate and primary-roads systems within its borders. The law also mandated that billboard owners must receive compensation when their signs were taken down. Were the states required to pay compensation and would they lose their federal highway funds if they chose instead to reduce the number of billboards through the use of the police power? Since this approach was the preferred method in such an antibillboard state as Washington, federal insistence on compensation and the penalty of lost federal funds would work against those localities in which effective regulation was already taking place. To resolve this issue the Department of Commerce decided in July 1966 to seek an opinion from the attorney general. "May Congress constitutionally force a state to choose between an otherwise lawful exercise of its police power and the State's full share of highway construction funds?" was how the department posed the question. The Justice Department did not respond promptly, and Rex Whitton told Helen Reynolds of the California Roadside Councils on 10 November 1966 that the department was still waiting for an opinion from the attorney general that would have "a significant impact on the cost of implementing the Act, both on the Federal and State levels."[8]

While these related issues were developing on the sidelines, the hearings process to develop standards for billboard regulation went forward across the country. The OAAA participated extensively in the process of reshaping the proposed rules in a direction that would be more favorable to the industry, and Tocker's lobbying had an effect. In July 1966 the Bureau of Public Roads circulated revised guidelines for billboards that moved closer to what outdoor advertisers wanted. In negotiating with the states, the secretary of commerce would have definitions at hand for what constituted an unzoned commercial or industrial area and specific criteria for the size, lighting, and spacing for signs in zoned commercial or industrial areas. The Bureau of Public Roads allowed a maximum size for billboards of 750 square feet and also said that there could be as many as ten billboards per mile. In the January proposals the maximum size had been 300 square feet within 150 feet of the highway and 400 square feet at any greater distance. The number of signs allowed in the January rules had been six per mile.[9]

These changes caused Sharon Francis to ask Rex Whitton of the bureau "if anything could be done to decrease the size of the huge 750 foot signs in the BPR regulations." Whitton countered that these larger signs would be used only in commercial areas. When Francis complained that these billboards did not reflect "customary" usage "as defined in the Act, but an extraordinary and 'new' usage," Whitton asked her "whether this meant we wanted the size decreased, and I [Francis] said 'definitely.' He did not seem happy, but said he would talk it over with his 'boys.' " Francis also drafted, but did not send, a letter to Lawrence Jones about billboards. Given the delicate situation in Congress over the administration's highway proposals, an assertion of the First Lady's influence at that point probably did not seem wise.[10]

In July and August the Johnson administration was retreating on several topics relating to beautification in the highway program. Lowell Bridwell and Paul Sitton of the Commerce Department asked the staff of the Senate Public Works Committee not to include additional funds for beautification until "a reasonably firm cost estimate" for the program was submitted in January 1967. As it happened, such a request might have been turned down in any case. Efforts to create a trust fund for safety and highway beautification also were bogged down in the Ways and Means Committee. When the full House took up the Federal Aid Highway Bill on 11 August 1966, the bill contained, despite the administration's wishes, an authorization of $243 million for highway beautification in fiscal 1968 and $250 million for fiscal 1969. Each year, $80 million was allocated to control outdoor advertising. The money was included in this way to underline that beautification appropriations had to come from general revenues. To underscore that point, the House measure also contained explicit language to prevent the White House from diverting funds from the Highway Trust Fund for beautification purposes.[11]

In the House debate, Republicans endeavored to have all authorizations for beautification removed from the bill. One lawmaker said: "There is considerable uncertainty about the beautification program, about its implications, its costs and how it is going to work out. To force ourselves to review this program next year makes eminent good sense." Democrats responded that the amendment "would simply do away with the Beautification Act entirely." This position was weakened because the Johnson administration itself had not asked for the authorization at a time when the president was publicly criticizing Congress for excessive spending. The amendment failed by a vote of 48 to 65. After approving what the Public Works Committee had proposed as the Committee of the Whole, the House then considered the measure as a bill. Gerald R. Ford (R, Mich.) offered a motion to recommit the bill to the Public Works Committee with instructions to report the bill back stripped of all beautification authorization. The recommital vote narrowly failed, 173 to 175, with 84 members not voting. Enthusiasm for beautification in the House was diminishing during the summer of 1966, and the response to the program indicates that a bill stronger than the one passed in 1965 would have had almost no chance.[12]

When the highway bill went to a House-Senate conference, the administration met more trouble. The conferees agreed to keep the House language that barred any use of the Highway Trust Fund for beautification. The Senate also insisted that the $493 million for all highway beautification be deleted, a loss that the White House could more readily accept in light of its decision to concentrate on a push for funding in 1967. The House debated the conference report on 31 August 1966 and readily agreed with the Senate's insistence on cutting beautification. "This is a program," said William Harsha (R, Ohio), "that could well be held in abeyance while the administration attempts to get its fiscal house in order." Two days after the report had gone through by a vote of 359 to 1, Congressman Bob Wilson (R, Calif.) said that it was a "dramatic way for the Chamber of Congress closest to the people to show the White House how Americans feel about nonessential spending, however desirable, in this wartime economy."[13]

After the legislative setback, the prospects for highway beautification became even gloomier. In early October 1966, Liz Carpenter and Sharon Francis warned the First Lady "about an obvious all-out effort" by the "billboard lobby" to shape the way the Highway Beautification Act was being implemented. The OAAA had hired a crack Washington attorney to press for the least-stringent standards possible, and the Bureau of Public Roads had already backed away from the tough January proposals in the revised language of July. Mrs. Johnson should call Rex Whitton, Alan Boyd, or John Connor "and tell them that we do not want their regulations to make us a laughing stock." In 1967, they went on, strengthening amendments should be added to the law to make it "a more positive tool."[14]

The record is unclear about whether the First Lady made a call to these officials, but she did engage in an effort to enhance the enforcement of the law by locating a candidate for the still-vacant position of coordinator of highway beautification. Lady Bird Johnson had first met Fred Farr, a California state senator, on her trip into Virginia in May 1965. In September 1966, on her visit to the West Coast, he had been with her when she had dedicated the Point Reyes national seashore. Meanwhile, Public Roads had been unsuccessful in persuading anyone to take the beautification post. After the 1966 elections, Mrs. Johnson had Liz Carpenter suggest Farr's name to the Department of Commerce. Lowell

Bridwell wrote to him on November 21 about beautification, adding that "we are not yet at the place where we have great confidence that this program is moving forward as well as we had expected." By December, Farr had shown interest in the appointment, and in early January 1967 he agreed to accept the post. His selection, which came at Lady Bird Johnson's instigation, was designed to put an official who was sympathetic to beautification into the Bureau of Public Roads to offset its perceived tilt toward the outdoor advertising industry.[15]

As the White House and the industry prepared to respond to the guidelines on billboards that would be made public on 10 January 1967, the new Department of Transportation, which had been created by Congress in 1966, began to take over from the Department of Commerce the responsibilities for beautification. The head of the Department of Transportation would be Alan Boyd, who was moving over from the Department of Commerce, where he had dealt with billboards in 1965 and 1966. He had generally supported Lady Bird Johnson's program, but once in office, he would confront the inescapable reality of beautification's unpopularity on Capitol Hill.[16]

Boyd reviewed the status of highway beautification in a memorandum that he sent to Mrs. Johnson on 4 January 1967. He projected a five-to-ten-year effort that would have an estimated cost in the $200 to $300 million range, and he told her about the administration's plans for a safety-and-beautification trust fund. Boyd asserted that in economic terms, "highway beautification provides an overall gain to the Nation's economy." He predicted that industry representatives would have a different view during the next session of Congress. The controversies arising from beautification, he wrote, resembled "parallel issues which arise in the fields of resource conservation, air pollution, highway safety improvement and general aesthetic, historical and cultural preservation, when the interests of powerful and articulate segments of our society and economy are prescribed." The program would be an "interesting test" of the relative political impact of contrasting attitudes "which grow from the phenomena of adjusting overall social and aesthetic aspirations of an affluent society to conventional economic attitudes in a free enterprise system where private interests are adversely affected by broader social objectives."[17]

When the standards became public knowledge on January 10, the reaction of Congress and the industry disclosed that the secretary's prediction of an "interesting test" of contrasting attitudes was a mild understatement. On several points, the Bureau of Public Roads had moved away from the relaxed language of the July 1966 provisions and had gone back to the more restrictive January 1966 guidelines. The definition of what constituted an unzoned commercial or industrial area said that there had to be at least two separate and distinct business activities in actual use on one side of the highway. The other side of the road would be excluded from the definition. The billboard forces and the motel industry maintained that an unzoned commercial area was where advertising would be appropriate even if actual use was not taking place.[18]

On the size of billboards, the new standards represented a further departure from what outdoor advertisers had advocated. The 750-square-foot maximum of July 1966 was cut back to 550 square feet. Both figures were well below the 1,200-square-foot size that the industry said reflected "customary use." As to spacing, a minimum standard of 500 feet was to be established, which the billboard companies contended was inflexible and a departure from customary use. The regulations also prohibited signs within 2,000 feet of an intersection on the Interstate or primary system, largely on grounds of safety. In regard to all of these points of regulation, the billboard lobby charged that the federal government lacked the power to issue national standards and instead was required to reach a mutual agreement with each individual state. Boyd countered that the billboard industry "appears to be asserting to some degree an absolute and inherent right to invade the highways with their advertising devices without regard to national objectives."[19]

Boyd's arguments on behalf of these standards embodied the Johnson administration's view that the 1965 act had been designed to control and reduce outdoor advertising and that the secretary of commerce and now the secretary of transportation had the authority to seek "minimum compliance with the overall purpose of the Act." Congress had intended, Boyd stated, to establish "minimum standards," and the secretary had been "given responsibility for establishing a floor to assure consistency with the national objectives of the Act" and the means to do it by withholding highway funds. It remained to be seen whether Congress had passed the Highway Beautification Act with this set of assumptions in mind. The debates in 1965 suggested that the aim of the lawmakers had been to limit the power of the national government to set billboard standards, not to increase it in the way that Boyd and the Bureau of Public Roads had done.[20]

Initial reaction from Capitol Hill was not encouraging to the administration's position. After receiving the January 10 report, Senator Jennings Randolph wrote to Boyd to warn him that "these standards and criteria are not to be used as a statement of the Department's final position to which the States must agree if they are to avoid imposition of the 10% penalty." Within two weeks, the White House had learned that the billboard industry wanted Congress to hold extensive hearings on the proposed standards. At the same time the announced price tag of $2.7 billion for the beautification program ran into the economy mood in Congress as the Vietnam War escalated.[21]

Conservationists were already pushing for a stronger beautification law in early 1967. Congressmen from Washington State, which had strong billboard-control laws that the 1965 act might actually weaken, introduced measures to remove the mandatory compensation feature and to limit the application of a revised law to the Interstate Highway System and to scenic roads, rather than to the 220,000 miles of the primary-roads system. The pressure from this side of the issue was still not as forceful as it might have been. The Conservation Foundation, with which Sharon Francis had been talking, assured its members that the Bureau of Public Roads had "done a fair and conscientious job of administering the Highway Beautification Act to date," but the issue that remained, in their view, was "whether the billboard control program is administratively workable." With the conservation groups still skeptical about the law, the administration had to defend Mrs. Johnson's program against the mounting anger on Capitol Hill.[22]

President Johnson endeavored to use his influence to deflect congressional opposition to beautification in late January. He suggested to the First Lady that she should get "the women organized" for highway beauty and "give some awards" for successful examples of beautification. Liz Carpenter set about arranging a ceremony to honor "outstanding examples of highway beautification"; this would take place before any hearings occurred in Congress. At the same time the president told congressional leaders of both parties that if they made "any attempt to cut back funds," Mrs. Johnson would "come to the Capitol to lobby for such funds."[23]

Despite these White House responses, pressure from the billboard industry reached such an intense level by the first week of February 1967 that Congressman John Kluczynski prepared to call hearings on the revision of the 1965 law. The Democrats on the Public Works Committee feared that if they did nothing, the Republicans, especially William Cramer of Florida, would "take the initiative and force such hearings anyways." Alan Boyd told the president that the Senate was in the same angry posture, and he recommended that the administration accept "a moratorium on urban billboards," which would leave the rest of the program intact. The secretary opened negotiations with the staff of the House Public Works Committee to seek a compromise by February 22. Boyd made some important concessions, which would have allowed "billboard regulation in zoned commercial and industrial areas to be handled by local zoning authorities." With this signal that the administration might give ground, the congressional side pushed for more concessions, and the talks stalled in mid February.[24]

On February 16, Mrs. Johnson held her reception to honor the Citizens Advisory Committee on Recreation and Natural Beauty, the main purpose of which was to put Congress in a more receptive mood toward the beautification program. The First Lady worried that the event "might lose us some Congressional support," but Sharon Francis said that it would be "a rallying point—to set the vision of the future, not the Congressional Act of the moment." The event went on as planned, and eight awards for highway beautification were also presented. Mrs. Johnson told the guests that "our challenge is to see that these highways are not only superbly functional, but also in harmony with our landscape and a pleasant asset to our lives." It was a nice occasion, but it changed few minds in Congress, where attitudes on billboards had become solid and unbending.[25]

As evidence of this situation, Kluczynski went ahead in early March with his plan for public hearings and for congressional resistance to the administration. He wrote to each governor on March 3 that "mutually acceptable revisions in the proposed regulations under the Highway Beautification Act" had not been worked out, and he assured them that no penalty would be invoked against any state that had failed to take legislative action to be in compliance with the law by 1 January 1968. Then, on March 20, Kluczynski and Cramer announced that hearings would be held in early April.[26] Boyd informed President Johnson that the demands for "a softening of our billboard control regulations" had been intensifying; he now believed that it was "impossible to avoid a public confrontation on legislation." He did not emphasize how far the administration had perceptibly weakened its stance on billboards to conciliate the lawmakers. Under the Transportation Department's concessions, the states could "delegate control of urban outdoor advertising to local zoning authorities" as long as some regulation or land-use planning existed. In rural areas, only one commercial activity would have to be present to justify the existence of a billboard. Boyd hoped to retain flexibility on how much highway frontage billboards might cover.[27]

Boyd's memorandum about the beautification situation went to White House aide Douglass Cater and from there to the president. The secretary asked that Cater meet with conservation lobbyists, and President Johnson agreed, adding in his own handwriting: "See Liz & Mrs. J about this also." The meeting took place at the White House on 3 April 1967, two days before Kluczynski's hearings were scheduled to begin. Boyd told Sharon Francis, Mary Lasker, Spencer Smith, and others in attendance that "there was no way to avoid public hearings." The White House should accept no changes in the 1965 law. "We may be blooded in the House committee, but we hope we can hold fast in the Senate."[28]

The conservationists pointed out that their members liked the bill sponsored by Thomas Pelly (D, Wash.), which would give the states a choice between compensation and the police power in regulating billboards on the primary-roads system. Boyd told them that there was no chance of removing the compensation provision. An opinion of the attorney general had indicated in November 1966 that a state did have to pay compensation to avoid losing 10 percent of its federal-aid funds, and there was no likelihood that the lawmakers would vote to abandon what they had insisted on in 1965. "The discussion produced general recognition among the beauty groups that the situation is very grim," Cater told the president.[29]

As the House hearings opened, a columnist wrote: "Highway beautification is the President's baby. Will he do anything about this orphan?"[30] The White House and the First Lady were still caught between conservation organizations that wanted a tough billboard law and Congress, which would accept only the weakest kind of billboard control. The testy mood of the House Public Works Subcommittee was apparent when the hearings convened. Kluczynski's opening statement asserted that "the present law and its proposed implementation are satisfactory to almost no one." Cramer was equally critical in his remarks: "To make the highway beautification program workable it may require substantial changes in the law." The ostensible purpose of the hearings was to examine the administration's bill to create a trust fund for highway safety and beautification, but it rapidly became evident that the real goal was to assail the 1965 law and Secretary Boyd. Jim Wright (D, Texas) reported that the White House had "frustrated the intent of Congress on customary usage," and another observer said to Sharon Francis, who sat in on the hearings the first day: "We do have real trouble. They are determined to weaken—not regulations but the statute."[31]

The witnesses that paraded by the committee during the rest of April and into May vied with each other in condemning the 1965 measure and the interpretation that the Johnson administration had given it. The president of the Foster and Kleiser division of Metromedia asked that the committee persuade the Transportation Department "to rescind these unreasonable criteria" or make clear in the committee report "that they are unfair and unworkable and in no way reflect the intent of the Congress." The labor counsel for the National Restaurant Association said that the draft standards represented "a return to the belief that killing billboards can produce beauty." When Helen Reynolds testified in favor of billboard control, Congressman Jim Wright asked her, "Do you not see a danger in the over exercise of what the majority might think is or is not pretty?"[32]

Alan Boyd appeared before the subcommittee, along with Lowell Bridwell, on 2 May 1967, and he correctly reported to the president that he found the lawmakers "generally hostile." Jim Wright told the secretary that "Congress feels or members of the committee feel that you fellows are trying to do things within these commercial industrial areas, for one thing, that were not contemplated in the act." Cramer inquired at one point: "Why is this before us during the Vietnam crisis?" Toward the end of Boyd's testimony, Kluczynski said about the 1965 law, "I believe we enacted a can of worms," and he promised, "I am going to try to untangle that." As Boyd concluded, the "consensus was that the law is not working as Congress intended; it will cost too much; it must be changed." After Boyd had testified, White House aide Henry Wilson told Postmaster General Lawrence O'Brien that "the reaction from the committee is just terrible." He then added, in a sentence that reflected the male assumptions about the beautification program in general, "But I can appreciate Alan's problems what with Liz Carpenter, etc."[33]

After the House hearings had ended in early May, the two sides in the billboard dispute began negotiations to see if any compromise could be reached. As these talks progressed, Lady Bird Johnson and Carpenter tried to mobilize the probeauty forces in Congress. Carpenter met with one of the few friendly members on the Public Works Committee, Richard McCarthy, a New York Democrat, and began to form the "bill bards," who would seek "to save the Highway Beautification Act of 1965." He urged that "we should try to get a beauty lobbyist in bed with every member of Congress." The campaign to arouse support on the Hill resulted in some positive speeches in the *Congressional Record,* which Carpenter and the others in the White House drafted for lawmakers to deliver or insert. Still, the balance of forces in Congress remained averse to Mrs. Johnson's position, as Secretary Boyd's discussions with the Democrats on the House committee soon revealed.[34]

Boyd met with these lawmakers in late May and reported to the White House that their discussion had been "as harmonious and as productive as any I have been involved in with the Congress on Beautification." The good feeling probably arose because Boyd had yielded to most of the demands that the Democrats had made upon him in regard to billboard control. He agreed to send a letter to the chairman of the full committee, promising to leave the regulation of billboards "to local zoning authorities" and to relax the definition of an unzoned commercial area. Boyd conceded that this meant the removal of "less billboards along the rural stretches of highway," but he assured the White House that "nevertheless, we will still have a sound billboard control program." He also told the committee members that he would not impose penalties on states that failed to reach enforcement agreements with the federal government in 1967 or 1968.[35] Joseph A. Califano, Jr., informed President Johnson that "this is not a bad deal, and we will be fortunate if we can hold it." The Republican leader in the House, Gerald R. Ford of Michigan, had announced that he would seek to have the entire highway-beautification program dropped, "and our main fight on the floor will be on that basis."[36]

These developments left the supporters of billboard regulation who were outside the Johnson administration at a loss regarding what congressional position they should endorse. The House subcommittee was not going to report out the Pelly bill, which the roadside councils preferred to the 1965 law, and yet the "just compensation" feature of the law threatened to stymie state action against billboards. "We have to be ready to take a position as soon as the Kluczynski monstrosity appears, hiding under the cloak of the Highway Beautification terminology," Helen Reynolds told Spencer Smith. The upshot of these comments was that Lady Bird Johnson and the White House still lacked any semblance of the enthusiastic backing of the conservationist forces for her approach to billboard regulation.[37]

Equally vexing to Lady Bird Johnson and those around her were the persistent charges that she and her husband had selfish motives in seeking highway beautification and also that the federal government itself frequently used billboards to advertise its programs to the public. From the outset of the billboard controversy, there had been gossip that the Johnsons wanted to restrict outdoor advertising because of their television holdings. In early 1966 it was reported to the White House, as a widespread rumor in Minnesota, Arizona, and North Dakota, that "the reason the Johnsons want to do away with highway signs, is that they have television interests and that way, TV will get all the advertising. Hence the campaign by Lady Bird Johnson to beautify the highways to cut down on advertising signs." Complaints were also made to the First Lady that the LBJ Ranch had a sign along the highway that violated beautification principles. Liz Carpenter wrote to the president of the Colorado Motel Association, who had made the protest, and Mrs. Johnson remarked privately: "First of all the sign has come down. Secondly, she doubts that any answer would satisfy them." While she was probably aware of how billboard advertising related to their media holdings in a general way, Lady Bird Johnson did not base her views about outdoor advertising on how her personal financial interests or television-station holdings would be affected. As for her husband, if he was for billboard regulation because she wanted it, it is hard to see how he could also have had a hidden financial agenda in mind at the same time.[38]

The problem of persuading all component parts of the government to limit the use of billboard advertising was a continuing irritant to Lady Bird Johnson and her staff. In October 1966 a woman in Texas sent her pictures of signs that the Defense Department used to promote recruiting. Bess Abell fired off a memorandum to the secretary of defense: "Because of Mrs. Johnson's known identification with the Federal Highway Beautification Act, we hope that posters advertising government activities are not in violation of provisions of the Act." The answer was sympathetic in tone, but it noted that the military services agreed that "billboard advertising does have some effective results." The billboard industry also shrewdly exploited opportunities to undercut the White House. In the spring of 1967 the Internal Revenue Service was offered free advertising space on billboards that were not being used. Cynthia Wilson spoke with the IRS information office "and told them how embarrassing their billboards were to us." The first answer that Wilson received was, "We've been afraid someone from the White House would call."[39]

A few weeks later, in April 1967, a "Discover America" campaign began with great publicity, launched by Discover America, Inc., a nonprofit corporation that Vice-President Hubert Humphrey had inspired to promote tourism. The campaign slogan "Discover America—It's 3,000 Smiles Wide" was to appear on forty-five hundred billboards in space that outdoor advertisers had once again donated. "Don't you think that the above use of billboards is ill-advised?" a New Jersey woman asked Mrs. Johnson, and a Connecticut man wondered, "How we will ever be rid of billboards if the Government sets a poor example, by using them to advertise, for instance, the army and the Peace Corps?" Liz Carpenter told Douglass Cater that the use of billboards by the Discover America campaign "makes us look pretty foolish."[40]

At a cabinet meeting on 31 May 1967, President Johnson asked for information about how federal departments and agencies were using outdoor advertising. The Department of Transportation said that it rented billboards in only two places. The General Services Administration (GSA) asserted that it used no outdoor advertising at all. Then, in July, Senator John J. Williams (R, Del.) charged that the government was becoming "one of the worst violators" of the highway-beautification program. The senator, a persistent and effective critic of the administration, said that the Transportation Department and GSA had spent $4.5 million to build seventy thousand signs. "The sole purpose of these billboards is to make sure the voters in the next election understand that the building projects or the road improvements are a result of the benevolence of one of the Great Society programs." It turned out that, in fact, "construction identification signs" were included in the number and at the cost that Williams had specified. If outdoor advertising were defined to include such signs as well as billboards, Alan Boyd conceded, "there is a certain validity to Senator Williams's accusation of 'Federal double-talking.'" The senator's point, of course, did not address the issue of commercial signs, but it well reflected the Republican offensive against the highway policy of the Johnson administration.[41]

On 30 August 1967, Lady Bird Johnson met with Liz Carpenter, Sharon Francis, Cynthia Wilson, and others involved with beautification to talk about signs and billboards that the government itself used. "We would like to see a strong policy of No billboards (Join the Army, etc.) used to advertise federal programs," Carpenter told Cater in her report on the meeting. "Until the Federal agencies set an example, the Administration is going to be subject to valid criticism of not practicing what we preach." Identifying signs on highway projects were mandated by law, but the First Lady's staff sought at least to have smaller and more attractive signs.[42]

This effort persisted into 1968, when Liz Carpenter was still complaining about how to persuade "our friends to quit being a party to the billboard lobby with our own programs." The letters and snapshots that poured into the White House and to Lady Bird Johnson caused "a setback every time the legislation comes up. I can't tell you how many people love to make pictures of these billboards and send them to the First Lady!" This sense of continuing division and ambiguity within the Johnson administration over billboards themselves as advertising devices represented a further obstacle to renewed funding and support for Mrs. Johnson's program in Congress during the summer and fall of 1967.[43]

After the House subcommittee hearings ended in May, the Senate Subcommittee on Roads of the Public Works Committee opened hearings in late June on the highway-beautification and highway-safety trust fund. In his statement, Alan Boyd stressed the agreement that he had reached in May with Kluczynski over the enforcement of the law, emphasized the administration's complete acceptance of the principle of just compensation, and came out against any attempt to amend the law to exclude billboards from scenic areas. The ensuing statements from other witnesses duplicated what had been said in the House hearings. Under friendly questioning, Phillip Tocker told the senators that "the Federal Government under the act of 1965 has no authority to promulgate standards" about the size, lighting, or spacing of billboards. Regulations for billboards, said the representative of the Roadside Business Association, "should not be left to Federal-State agreements." Mrs. Thomas M. Waller, president of the Garden Clubs of America, praised Lady Bird Johnson for "the outstanding job" she had done "in arousing public enthusiasm for uncluttered natural beauty," but she asked that the lawmakers delete mandatory compensation and provide for federal enforcement standards. The senators showed minimal interest in her position.[44]

In August 1967 the Senate subcommittee voted out an authorization for the appropriation of $85 million in beautification funds for fiscal year 1968 only. The White House had sought $160 million for 1968 and $220 million for 1969. The full Public Works Committee ratified the subcommittee's action on August 22. The Department of Transportation, which always tended to put the best face on bad news, told Cynthia Wilson that it was "a victory to get any money at all without 'a change in the ground rules.' " Because negotiations with the states over billboard standards were moving slowly anyway—only four states were in compliance—the department had concluded that "the money should be adequate for now." The full Senate then endorsed the bill on a voice vote.[45]

The crucial fight over the authorization bill was going to come in the House, where William Cramer was winning Republican converts to his probillboard position. Lady Bird Johnson had Sharon Francis rally the conservation groups for an intensive lobbying effort in the autumn of 1967. At her meeting about beautification on August 30, the First Lady discussed, as Liz Carpenter put it, "how the Beauty act can be pried loose from the Roads Subcommittee." By early September it looked as if the public pressure for beauty might be building. Francis reported that the mail reaching the House Public Works Committee was running four to one in favor of Mrs. Johnson's position. Drew Pearson warned his readers that "a skillful lobbying drive against Lady Bird Johnson's beautification program appears to be bearing fruit." His column singled out Cramer for particular attention and noted that the "billboard moguls" had placed signs "featuring the Mona Lisa and Gainsborough's Blue Boy" in Senator Randolph's home state of West Virginia. Sharon Francis hoped that the increased public support for the highway program would "coincide with full House consideration."[46]

None of the efforts that Lady Bird Johnson and her staff had expended had made any difference on Capitol Hill, as the House soon demonstrated. On September 21 the Public Works Committee reported out the highway-beautification measure by a straight party vote of 18 to 14. The House's money figures stood at precisely the same levels that the Senate had adopted. The Republican minority came out strongly against the bill. "At a time when the Nation is facing a huge deficit even if the

President's tax increases are enacted and is confronted with a war and critical domestic difficulties," their report stated, "it is a peculiar kind of priority which would provide $85 million for an ineffective highway beautification program."[47]

The immediate assumption at the White House was that the beautification bill would come to the floor of the House in late October. Mrs. Johnson asked H. Barefoot Sanders, the aide who was now handling the legislation, for a list of congressmen to whom she could send information about her program when the bill was being debated. Then the administration realized that prospects for the program were bleak. Lowell Bridwell predicted that if the House were to turn down the legislation to authorize funding, it would be impossible to secure any additional agreements with the states on billboard control. On the other hand, Bridwell argued, waiting until 1968 to ask for authorization legislation would give additional time to conclude agreements with the states. "If we can sign up enough states, it will present Congress with a fait accompli and lessen the opposition to the continuation of the program." With the 1968 appropriation, the implementation of beautification could move along to finish projects that had already been started and to plan for the future.[48]

Barefoot Sanders had equally gloomy news after his soundings on the Hill. Neither Kluczynski nor the House Democratic leadership wanted to bring the bill to the floor. "The fact is that we do not have the votes in hand or in sight to pass the bill," Sanders told Lyndon Johnson. "We cannot count on any Republican support. We are so far away from having a majority that considering the economy mood of the House and the increasing pressure for adjournment we would lose the bill on the floor." President Johnson showed Sanders's memo to his wife and said to her, "I think that is right—we ought to wait until next year then get all the members down here." That decision, which she accepted, meant that the trust-fund measure languished in the Rules Committee until Congress adjourned, went home for the year, and came back in 1968.[49]

When Congress reconvened, the predicament over highway beautification had not changed in any fundamental way. The trust-fund proposal still had no chance of emerging from the Rules Committee. President Johnson set up a meeting in late February "to discuss Highway Beautification, whether and when to run with it, possibilities of compromise, etc." Sharon Francis, Liz Carpenter, and Cynthia Wilson took part in the meeting, and a decision seems to have been made to have Carpenter touch base with the congressmen whom she had seen about highway beauty in 1965. In mid March she spent an hour with George Mahon, who advised her to "forget '68 and struggle along with what we've got."

For the succeeding two years the administration should "have a reasonable item for beauty in the overall highway authorization act. Word it in the most palatable way." Mahon added: "Mrs. Johnson's program has waked up a lot of people to start thinking about it. When Helen and I drive through the country, those junkyards and billboards really are eyesores much more. I have learned the difference in how great it is to drive in from Dulles with no billboards and drive on many of our roadways." Finally, Carpenter reported that Mahon thought "the billboard bills are not as tough as they once were and he feels they think they have something they can live with." Mahon's language reflected a shrewd assessment of the political climate about billboards that the Johnson administration was facing in 1968. It also underscored how little real support for billboard control the First Lady could expect.[50]

To the men in Congress and in the White House for whom highway beautification was only a nagging issue and not a cause, fighting for the program had less appeal than seeking a compromise resolution. At about the time that Carpenter was making plans to see Mahon, Congressman Carl B. Albert, an Oklahoma Democrat, was asking Barefoot Sanders "to come up with the minimum possible figure on which Highway Beautification could exist—not live, but just exist." In instructing an associate to find an answer to Albert's question, Sanders said: "I would prefer that you ascertain this without going to Liz Carpenter and her group." What this review revealed is not known, but there is some evidence that Sanders and his aides concluded that they could get along with a much-lower figure than the $85 million that was before Congress. In any case, the House was likely to trim the figure, especially if Cramer and his allies had their way. This action demonstrated once again that when Lady Bird Johnson looked beyond her husband for support on highway beautification, she could count on few men in the White House to give her enthusiastic backing.[51]

The prospects for Lady Bird Johnson's program dimmed further when the conservationists' criticism of the 1965 law increased. In April 1968 the Washington State Roadside Council labeled the act "a fraud on the public expectations" and said that it was "moribund and of little positive value." In early June the California Roadside Council, "after some real agony," decided to join its Washington counterpart in seeking the repeal of the mandatory-compensation provision even if it meant the defeat of the whole program. "We all continue to be deeply grateful to Mrs. Johnson for the impetus she gave to this movement," Helen Reynolds said to Sharon Francis; "it will go foward eventually and on the national level she was the pioneer."[52] The White House once again confronted solid opposition on Capitol Hill but with no help from its potential allies on the environmental side of the issue.

The trust-fund measure remained stalled in committee, and the future of highway beautification was contained in the Federal-Aid Highway Act of 1968, in which the administration got very little of what it wanted. At Cramer's behest in mid June, the Roads Subcommittee authorized only $1.25 million a year for the next three years. States were prohibited from setting higher standards for billboard control than were applied at the federal level. The subcommittee also removed the authority that had been granted to the secretary of transportation two years earlier to consider alternative routes for freeways that threatened parks, wildlife areas, or historic sites. The full committee restored the beautification funds the next day, but the $8.5 million that they authorized was only 10 percent of what the White House had sought. "The situation is fluid," Sharon Francis told Lady Bird Johnson, but assured her that "all possible effort is being made."[53]

The full House prepared to debate the bill on July 1. The aide who was handling Congress reported to Barefoot Sanders that Cramer was going to offer an amendment to eliminate all funding for beautification beyond the $1.25 million that would cover administrative costs. The White House would be fortunate to defeat Cramer; there was little chance of increasing the authorization. Sanders told Lady Bird Johnson on June 29 that he was "pessimistic about our chances of beating the Cramer amendment" in the House. The best hope was the conference committee and Senator Randolph. The idea was tested of giving Randolph what he wanted on a bridge in West Virginia in return for placing highway beautification on the priority list in the House-Senate conference. This trade-off would imperil a section of the bill involving increased construction on the Interstate Highway System in Cramer's district, which was "of life and death importance to him."[54]

First, the House had to act, and the debate on the highway bill spanned the first three days of July 1968. Cramer offered his amendment on July 3. He would leave in the money for administrative expenses and would require the Department of Transportation to report on beautification by January 1969. Otherwise, all funding would be dropped, along with the 10 percent penalty for states that were not in compliance. "No one would claim that beautification is a high priority item," Cramer said; "certainly we will not accomplish beautification by this means." The only defense of the program came from Jim Wright of Texas. He noted that the full committee had made a 90 percent cut in the money authorized. "The Committee asks 'How much more blood do you demand?' And the opposition replies 'We want it all.' "[55]

Wright noted that beautification had been labeled a "frivolous frill and a woman's whim. Facetious comment has referred to it as 'Lady Bird's bill.' " Wright then asserted, on the First Lady's behalf, that she "has never coveted a personal spotlight. She has not sought the glitter and glamor of public applause. She has not presumed to set new styles either in the world of fashion or in political ideology." Accordingly, Wright concluded, her legacy should be preserved. "Let us not snuff the very life from this laudable effort by hasty action." Despite Wright's pleas, the House adopted Cramer's amendments by a recorded vote of 92 to 54 and then reaffirmed its decision on a roll-call vote of 211 to 145.[56]

"As you know, Cramer scuttled the Highway Beauty bill," Francis and Carpenter reported to Lady Bird Johnson, "and our best hope is to get the conferees to stick close to the Senate version." To that end, they asked her to "give encouraging pep talks to" Boyd and Randolph. Fred Farr also sought her help to delete the language that eliminated the 10 percent penalty and allowed states to define what constituted an unzoned commercial area.[57]

Two other issues that complicated the fate of the highway measure had a direct connection to the legislative prospects of the section on beautification. In the 1966 law that created the Department of Transportation, section 4.f of the law had instructed the secretary not to approve projects that required the use of land in any park, recreation area, wildlife or waterfowl refuge, or historic site unless there was "no feasible or prudent alternative to the use of such land" and unless efforts to find alternatives had been unsuccessful. In the 1968 federal-aid bill, the House had added language to restrict the authority of the secretary to a consideration of alternatives and to planning to minimize the effects of harm to sites where road construction was to occur. Boyd was regarded as "antihighway" because he invoked section 4.f to question projects that members of Congress favored. The House included an amendment, which Cramer offered, to confine the secretary's authority to federal parklands alone.[58]

The other hot issue had to do with a controversial project in Washington, D.C., itself. The Three Sisters are small islands in the Potomac River where Georgetown and Virginia meet. The District of Columbia Highway Department and the Virginia Highway Department wanted to build a bridge across the Potomac at that point to link traffic from Washington with freeways in Virginia. The proposed bridge had been a source of public dispute since it had first been offered as part of the District's freeway system in the 1950s. Passions surrounding the

Three Sisters had intensified by the middle of the 1960s. The bridge would be built across parkland on both sides of the Potomac, and the highways that ran from it would move through the heavily black areas of Washington. By 1968 the bridge had become a symbol of the argument between the proponents of freeways and an opposition that emphasized aesthetic and environmental issues as well as the social consequences that highways had on neighborhoods and inner-city communities.[59]

Secretary Boyd opposed the Three Sisters Bridge during 1966 and 1967, thereby incurring the anger of Kluczynski and Cramer, as well as the majority of the Public Works Committee in the House. Cramer denounced "the master planners, who feel you can force the vast majority of commuters out of their automobiles and onto the mass transit." Boyd countered that the Washington freeway routes would interrupt commercial activity and would increase traffic through the city's core. "The net effect of these two factors," he told the committee in December 1967, "makes it unwise at this time to construct the Three Sisters Bridge at its planned location." During the first half of 1968, despite growing citizen opposition in the District, the House members worked on a bill to compel the construction of the Three Sisters Bridge. Rather than reporting the measure out as a separate item, however, the project was attached to the larger federal-aid bill, which would be much harder to defeat in a presidential-election year.[60]

The more complex issue of locating freeway routes and how they would be designed, which the Three Sisters Bridge represented, had been one that Lady Bird Johnson had encountered with growing frequency as her beautification campaign had developed. In April 1965, Sharon Francis told Liz Carpenter about the letters that the First Lady was receiving "from citizens who are disturbed and shocked by proposed route locations that are destroying irreplaceable parks and spots of natural beauty." Carpenter sent copies of the letters to Rex Whitton of the Bureau of Public Roads. He assured her "that we are keenly aware of and give careful attention to each of the kinds of problems" that were raised. But Whitton also contended that freeways were the best means of moving large numbers of people in the affected areas. Lady Bird Johnson could not openly challenge an agency of her husband's administration, and the responses that she had sent out to members of the public in 1965 and 1966 reflected her endeavor to be sympathetic to the concern about freeway construction without criticizing the politically powerful highway establishment.[61]

This awkward balancing act sometimes brought embarrassment to Lady Bird Johnson. When residents of Mount Kisco, New York, wrote to her to complain about the proposed route of Interstate 87, she sent back a general letter that spoke of the hope, which she and the president shared, "that America's highways can enhance the beauty of our landscapes and can be planned with full and sensitive consideration of all natural values." When her letter was read aloud at a meeting of local citizens in early January 1966, the audience laughed derisively. "It was a slap in the face" to the concerned residents. Elizabeth Rowe sent Mrs. Johnson a clipping from the *New York Times* about the incident and cautioned her friend not to let the beautification program "become the apologist for freeways." Rowe cited the Three Sisters Bridge as a case in point of a controversial project.[62]

The effect of this experience with the New Yorkers showed up a week later at the 19 January 1966 meeting of the First Lady's Committee, when she discussed the selection of highway routes with landscape architect Ian McHarg. She arranged appointments for McHarg with Rex Whitton and Alan Boyd to look at possible routes for Highway 95 on the East Coast, as well as the larger dimensions of the problem. Her talks with McHarg and others, their conversations with Sharon Francis, and the ideas of Fred Farr—all helped to shape the speech that Mrs. Johnson gave to the national convention of the American Road Builders in Denver on 23 February 1966. She praised their accomplishments in constructing the Interstate Highway System, but she told them that "we must also weigh in the social and esthetic values of the routing" of highways. "What a tragedy it will be if we do not make our highways instruments of beauty as well as convenience in the vast construction program which lies ahead of us."[63]

The highway-location issue continued to call forth large amounts of mail to the First Lady over the next several years. Residents of New Orleans, San Antonio, and numerous other cities in which freeways were being built wrote to seek her assistance. She tried to prod the Bureau of Roads to a greater awareness of the issue by supporting Congress's efforts in 1966 to have parks and historic sites spared in Interstate-highway construction. "Changing the course of history—or of a bureaucracy—is something akin to nudging a steamship in midocean," Sharon Francis wrote in early 1967. Mrs. Johnson and her husband knew that Alan Boyd, the incoming secretary of transportation, would place a greater emphasis, in his decisions, on aesthetic issues than had been true for past policy makers. Flying over the New Jersey highway system in 1967, Lady Bird Johnson commented that "freeways are efficient, they get you where you are going in a hurry. But we are just now beginning to do something about the esthetic values of highways."[64]

Sharon Francis alerted the First Lady to the nature of the Three Sisters battle even before the federal-aid highway bill had reached the stage of

Lady Bird Johnson talks with Senator Jennings Randolph (left) and Louis W. Prentiss (right) at the meeting of the American Road Builders Association in Denver, Colorado, on 23 February 1966.

congressional floor action in the spring and summer of 1968. A decision to build the bridge, she told Mrs. Johnson in February 1968, "could materially undo much of the good you have done in your efforts to add amenity to the parks and open spaces of the city, and generally improve the urban environment." The issue, Francis wrote, had become "a national test case" on both sides of the highway question. That situation had not changed by the summer of 1968, as the question of the attitude of the White House toward these interrelated aspects of the highway bill became central to the outcome on Capitol Hill.[65]

The administration had to be unyielding on the issue of section 4.f to retain conservationist support, and it had to endorse Alan Boyd's position on Three Sisters for the same reason. If there were faltering on either matter, then any prospect of help from the probeauty groups on the billboard issue would vanish. "Our best position is really to stand firm with the Senate enactment," Francis and Carpenter informed the First Lady on 10 July 1968. The Senate had passed its version by the time the House acted, and the two versions would be before a conference committee during the rest of July. For lobbying purposes, Lady Bird Johnson obtained a list of how the House vote had gone on the Cramer amendment. Changing minds would not be easy. As Republican Senator John Sherman Cooper of Kentucky told his colleagues, the bill that the House presented to the conference "was more anticonservationist than any other bill I have seen come before this body."[66]

The antibeautification attitudes of the House members shaped the negotiations over the conference report. On July 24, House conferees submitted a package to their Senate counterparts. Billboard control would get $2 million, junkyard control would receive $3 million, and the improvement of scenic highways would be allocated $20 million. That was a distinct improvement over the $8.5 million that the House Public Works Committee had originally recommended and, of course, was far better than Cramer's killer amendment. It was still $60 million less than the administration had sought at first. In place of the 10 percent penalty for not removing billboards, states would receive a bonus for compliance. The amendment limiting the power of the secretary of transportation over parkland would be dropped. The proposal represented some slight change in the House position, but it was still not as acceptable to the White House as the Senate version was.[67]

Lady Bird Johnson was as much involved in the 1968 struggle as she had been during the autumn of 1965. Ed Edmondson, an Oklahoma Democrat, informed her about the nature of the House package, and she passed on the news to her husband. Lyndon Johnson and Jim Wright talked on July 24 and agreed that the House would accept the retention of the 10 percent penalty clause and would also give in on the parkland amendment. The Senate would yield to the House language about what would be considered "customary use" in the size, lighting, and spacing of billboards. Wright and President Johnson also worked out that the Senate would vote first, "so that the House will be faced with an up or down vote on the entire Conference Report." If the House were to vote first, the Republicans could move to recommit the bill with instructions that the beautification provisions be removed. As Barefoot Sanders admitted, "We would lose in the House a separate vote on beautification."[68]

They almost lost it anyway. The House debated the conference report on 26 July 1968, before the Senate had acted. Samuel Stratton of New York, a Democrat, moved to recommit the bill, with instructions to delete all the beautification funding that the conference report contained. "Sam came out of nowhere on this one," Barefoot Sanders told Lyndon Johnson, and the Speaker and Carl Albert had to change "votes in the well after the rollcall was finished" in order to defeat Stratton's motion. The vote was 166 in favor and 167 opposed. The House then adopted the conference report, and the Senate took similar action three days later, by a vote of 60 to 6.[69]

As passed, the Federal-Aid Highway Act crippled the authority of the secretary of transportation over parklands in the building of highways, the billboard-control program was "virtually extinguished," and the Three Sisters Bridge and other District of Columbia highway projects were mandated to begin within thirty days. It was, said Senator Joseph Clark of Pennsylvania, "a significant victory for the uglifiers." Stewart Udall added bitterly that "most Congressmen don't give a damn about conservation values."[70]

The question now became whether President Johnson should sign the bill, veto it, or let it fail through a pocket veto if Congress adjourned. In a presidential-election year, a veto would have an obvious negative impact on the fortunes of Democratic congressional candidates. The Three Sisters Bridge was a critical element in the deliberations, as opposition to it intensified within the District. Yet, on the other side, there was the money that the beautification section contained, as well as the scant prospect that Congress would appropriate funds for the program under any other circumstances. Stewart Udall recommended, in a stinging memorandum, that the bill be vetoed. It was "an arrogant, calculated effort to undermine critical conservation victories achieved during your Administration," and he asked, "Why should we accept a further weakening of billboard control?"[71]

Liz Carpenter countered that since both of the Johnsons had asked House members, and particularly Jim Wright, to support the bill, it would be politically difficult to justify a veto. Lady Bird Johnson was undecided in her own mind about the merits of stopping the bill. On August 1 she called the measure "a mother hubbard, with many things thrown in. The beautification advantages may not be worth the disadvantages. We are weighing. . . ." Later she remarked: "Politics be damned, we don't owe anybody anything." Her political compass then balanced itself, and she asked, given the overwhelming Senate vote, whether a veto could even be sustained.[72]

Jennings Randolph made a particular effort to have the bill signed. He wrote to President Johnson on July 31 that the measure was "the most socially progressive highway legislation we have enacted during my tenure in the Senate." Three weeks later, with the issue still not resolved, Randolph called the White House just before he left for the Democratic National Convention. Urging that the bill be accepted, he warned "that if the Highway Bill is vetoed, there will never again be another beautification program." Randolph was confident, however, that he could "keep beautification alive in the years to come." On August 22 he called Mrs. Johnson, and he had a "pleasant and understanding conversation" about the bill and its prospects with the president.[73]

In a letter that followed up their talk, Randolph claimed that he "presumed" to counsel with her because of their shared and "very genuine concern" about "responsible and necessary highway legislation at this time." The bill contained "the desirable beautification program to which you have given stimulating and effective leadership," and the program would continue "intact and without damaging modification because you had earlier made the importance of this program clear to me." Having evoked his responsibility for having preserved her interest in the bill, Randolph then outlined the reasons why he believed the bill should be signed. He cited the provisions for relocating those whom highways displaced, the equal-employment-opportunity section, additional aid for cities, and the inclusion of highway construction workers under the Davis-Bacon Act. He also stressed his approval of the language relating to parklands and the District of Columbia. Randolph ended his letter with the claim that the highway bill was "a real contribution to the improvement of the environment in which our people live and work."[74]

In the end, Lyndon Johnson decided to sign the bill. His aide Joseph Califano convinced Johnson that he could approve the bill and still frustrate Congress's effort to compel the immediate construction of the Three Sisters Bridge and other highway projects in the District. In his statement about his decision to sign, Johnson stressed the language in the law that mandated public hearings before construction could occur. He instructed Secretary Boyd to assemble the interested parties and to develop a comprehensive highway plan for the Washington area. He also noted that the bill diluted billboard control and reduced the protection of parklands. Lady Bird Johnson later told Sharon Francis that she, "while not trying to make the decision for him, had been sympathetic toward those people who were urging him to veto it until this legalism was found that she and he both felt got around the biggest problem, which was the District of Columbia problem." Mrs. Johnson's comments suggest that she accepted implicitly Senator Randolph's contention regarding the likelihood that highway beautification would not survive a veto.[75]

Despite the congressional directives in the 1968 Highway Act, the Three Sisters Bridge was never built. When construction began in 1969, demonstrators battled police amid shouts of "Smash the bridge" and "Free D.C." Ten more years passed before the Potomac project was abandoned and plans for Three Sisters were scrapped. In July 1985 a private developer began the demolition of the six-block elevated roadway that was the only part of the proposed freeway that was ever finished.[76]

After the signing of the 1968 Highway Act, Lady Bird Johnson's formal involvement, as First Lady, with highway beautification and billboard control came to an end. In the four and a half months that remained to her in the White House, the issue did not again become a public one. When she resumed her interest in highways in Texas later in 1969, she decided to sponsor an annual series of beautification awards to members of the Texas Highway Department. Given each fall at the LBJ State Park, the awards recognize the use of wild flowers, roadside parks, and the maintenance of roadside plants and shrubs that were installed as part of the scenic enhancement of the 1965 law. Looking back on the awards program in 1980, she hoped that it had "helped to make preservation and propagation of our natural assets an ongoing aim—happening naturally in the course of a day's work." The spirit of these occasions—relaxed, informal, and good-humored—suggested that she had accomplished much of her aim in establishing the awards.[77]

The record of the Highway Beautification Act itself during the two decades since 1969 is a less inspiring story. The landscaping and scenic-improvement section was not intrinsically controversial, so it went forward with reasonable progress except as it related to billboard control. The effort to screen junkyards achieved more modest results. In 1979 the Department of Transportation reported that 2,345 nonconforming junkyards had either been removed or screened and that 1,055 illegal junkyards had been removed. Still, the department estimated that as many as 10,608 nonconforming junkyards still required governmental action.[78]

Billboard control evoked the most controversy. By the 1980s, however, the ideological positions on the subject had been reversed. The outdoor-advertising industry was defending the Highway Beautification Act, and environmentalists were opposing it as being ineffective and weighted toward the business it was supposed to regulate. Senator Robert Stafford, a Republican from Vermont, said in early 1985 that "with the stranglehold the billboard industry has on the Highway Beautification

Act, we would be better off without it." From 1969 to 1978, the money
that was allocated to the billboard-control program had gradually increased after the cutbacks of the late 1960s, reaching a high of
$26,694,000 in 1976. In 1971 the first billboard, located in Maine, was
removed after compensation had been paid. By 1978, 30 percent of all
nonconforming signs had been removed at a total expenditure of $107.5
million. Estimates of the amount needed to complete the program varied
between $500 million and $800 million. Critics contended that levels
of available funding would bring an end to the program in more than
one hundred years.[79]

In addition to the slow progress in removing billboards, the environmentalists argued that the law was further crippled because of continuing loopholes in defining what constituted commercial and industrial
areas and because of weaknesses in the regulatory process itself. Those
billboards that did not conform to federal guidelines did not lose their
value over time. They were repaired and upgraded in a way that made
the payment of compensation a heavier, rather than a decreasing, cost.
In some states, such as Georgia, billboard owners were authorized to
cut down trees along the highways if the trees blocked the billboards
from view. Mandatory compensation remained the most debilitating
feature of the law, and in 1978, Congress, as friendly to billboards as
ever, amended the provision to require compensations payments for signs
that were removed under local ordinances or laws. "The effect of the
act," said one leading proponent of billboard control, "has been to halt
sign removal programs which local governments wish to undertake."[80]

After 1978, funding for the billboard program declined in response
to the budgetary stringencies of the Carter and Reagan era. "Of course
I regret the omission of highway beautification funds from the budget,"
Lady Bird Johnson said in 1979, "but I do understand the urgency of
curtailing all possible spending in order to hold down inflation." In her
experience, she added: "There are troughs and crests in the establishment of many programs. If the majority of citizens want the beauty of
landscaped highways where scenery is not obscured by billboards or blight,
I firmly believe we can continue toward that goal although we may be
delayed in its realization." The question, in fact, was whether citizens
were any longer enough concerned with billboard control, as an aspect
of highway beautification, to overcome the power of the outdoor-
advertising industry. In 1979, a former staff aide to Senator Stafford concluded: "It is not something that captures the imagination of the
American public."[81]

That seemed to be the verdict as far as federal legislation was concerned
by the mid 1980s. Such groups as the Coalition for Scenic Beauty as-

sailed the 1965 law as a failure, and the Outdoor Advertising Association labeled it a law that the industry could live with. In cities around the nation, however, there were indications of renewed local campaigns against outdoor advertising. Segments of the business sector found that billboard-lined avenues put off prospective corporate executives as they rode from airports to interviews. Municipal laws placed restrictions on the number of signs that could be displayed within the city limits and sought the removal of notable offenders. The next phase of the billboard battle, environmentalists asserted, was likely to be fought in individual cities in separate campaigns, while the 1965 Highway Beautification Act was either being ignored or criticized. Billboard control had come full circle, back to the City Beautiful impulse of the turn of the century.[82]

Events in 1986 and 1987 seemed to confirm that action against billboards would have to come at the local level if it came at all. A strong effort was made in the Federal Aid Highway Act of 1986 to change the just-compensation provision of the 1965 law and to remove the 1978 amendment affecting local signs. Advocates of the proposal received a telegram from Lady Bird Johnson and Laurance Rockefeller in September 1986, seconding their efforts. "We encourage your support of this reform," the wire said, "which is needed to restore the scenic beauty of our Nation's highways." When the amendment came to the floor of the Senate on 3 February 1987, the president of the OAAA was watching from the members' gallery. His organization had contributed $350,000 in campaign funds and honoraria to members of Congress between 1983 and 1985. The amendment was soundly beaten by a vote of 57 to 40. The alignment of probillboard forces that Lady Bird Johnson had confronted in the 1960s remained intact and powerful.[83]

How much responsibility did Lady Bird Johnson and Lyndon Johnson bear for the troubled early years of highway beautification? Would a different approach to the issue between 1965 and 1968 have been more productive? The key problem was the "just compensation" section of the 1965 law, and the most enthusiastic advocates of billboard control recognized during the Johnson years that the repeal of that provision had no hope for success in Congress. The choice was either no regulation at all or the enforcment of the 1965 law. From 1966 to 20 January 1969, Lady Bird Johnson sustained the highway-beautification program with her personal commitment and influence. No one in the government who was in a position of authority cared as much about it as she did, and no one with power gave it as much backing as she gave it. Her efforts, as well as her influence on her husband, prevented the program from disappearing in a Congress that was angry over the Vietnam War and was determined to cut back on social programs. Lady Bird Johnson was the essential element, the catalyst, that kept highway beautification alive as an administration program during the 1960s.

Had she done nothing about highway beautification as First Lady, the issue would probably have sputtered along in the rear of environmental questions. Instead, the Highway Beautification Act of 1965 made the problem a matter of continuing public debate. For all the faults of the law that was associated with her name, Lady Bird Johnson deserves credit for her part as a catalyst and stimulant in making highway beauty and billboard control enduring aspects of the effort to improve the national landscape.

9

Natural Beauty
for the Nation

Beautifying Washington, D.C., and pursuing billboard regulation and its enforcement in Congress represented formidable demands on Lady Bird Johnson's time as First Lady. While they were two primary goals of her White House tenure, she carried on other activities on behalf of the environment between 1965 and 1969. She preached the gospel of beautification in a series of speeches during these years, and she made highly visible tours to wilderness or threatened areas to draw attention to the attractions of the American landscape. At the same time, she sought to involve the business community in the cause of beautification, because of her conviction that environmental sensitivity would be good for the corporations concerned. Her campaign here achieved less than impressive results, because her message evoked only modest support from those at whom it was aimed.

Within the federal government itself, the First Lady supported the official bodies that had a commitment to natural beauty. The President's Council on Recreation and Natural Beauty enjoyed her particular endorsement, and she used her influence with her husband to obtain appointments for those who were sympathetic to her point of view. She was also involved directly and indirectly in two of the major environmental controversies of the Johnson presidency—the fate of the Grand Canyon and of the California redwoods.

The public thought of her as an advocate for an improved environment, for the wilderness and nature, and citizens wrote to her in the belief that she herself could change policy. That assumption granted her too much influence, but she did have an impact on Lyndon Johnson and Stewart Udall in the broad implementation of the New Conservation policies of the 1960s. Her endeavors to place beautification in a larger interpretive setting caused her to emphasize quality-of-life issues in a way that anticipated ecological concerns. In December 1967 a *Sports Illustrated* article on the environment and the Johnson record accused the administration, as Matthew Nimetz of the White House put it, of concentrating "too much on 'natural beauty' and too little on more fundamental problems." Such a judgment, despite its implicit male bias, indicated how much effect the First Lady had in setting the agenda for the Johnson administration and in determining the nature of its environmental priorities.[1]

This accomplishment was not easily achieved. Not all the men around the president helped the First Lady become an advocate for beautification and conservation. She had to overcome both institutional obstacles and derisive male jabs at the term *beautification* in making her personal record on environmental issues. One persistent problem was persuading the White House Staff of the legitimacy of her need for support and personnel as the demands on her time increased. There was no First Lady's office as such during this period, and Lady Bird Johnson's operation had to borrow from the Interior Department, as in the case of Sharon Francis, or use talented individuals, such as Cynthia Wilson, who were originally brought in to work on correspondence in general. Finding enough office space in the White House was a perennial dilemma. So, too, was funding for trips during a presidency in which financial savings within the executive were always pursued.[2]

In the late summer of 1965, Liz Carpenter sought to have her trip to Jackson Hole, Wyoming, with the First Lady paid for out of White House funds. When she put in a request for travel money, W. Marvin Watson, the aide who handled such questions, returned it to her unsigned. "Is the East Wing always to be considered 'second class citizens'?" Carpenter asked in a forceful memorandum. The trip should be paid for out of the White House Staff Travel Fund, she argued, because she worked "for the White House staff just like Marvin Watson, Dick Goodwin, or anyone else." Whether it was a trip of Mrs. Johnson's or of her daughters', Carpenter thought that the staff was "working for the entire Johnson Administration—the entire White House, the President's best interests." Nonetheless, Watson returned her requests unsigned, and the money had to be found from the First Lady's own funds. In evaluating Mrs. Johnson's performance, these limitations on her resources and her staff are important considerations. She did much to institutionalize the role of the president's wife in the government, but that result came through much improvisation, and it was done on a skimpy financial base.[3]

Once her beautification program had been announced in 1965, Lady Bird Johnson began to receive numerous invitations to address groups that were interested in her work. She used her staff in the preparation of most of her public remarks, but she also reached out on occasion

Lady Bird Johnson with Cynthia Wilson at the White House on 13 April 1966.

to other sources of information and talent. In the actual writing of the speeches, Sharon Francis would usually prepare a first draft in consultation with Liz Carpenter, though sometimes when several speeches were needed, members of the White House staff added their thoughts. Francis "found it ever so much easier for me to write for her than it had ever been for Udall," because the two women shared "a practical and yet cheerful and constructive approach." They would confer over sandwiches in the First Lady's bedroom. Lady Bird Johnson would read the drafts aloud and make comments, such as "but we haven't yet mentioned this and this, and shouldn't we add them?" Once the speech had been agreed upon the First Lady would not see it again until it was "on little speech cards ready for her to give." Francis later recalled that none of Mrs. Johnson's beautification speeches had to be cleared with the president's staff in the West Wing.[4]

For speeches to particular groups, Mrs. Johnson would go outside the White House for ideas. She spoke to the Associated Press Managing Editors in October 1965 about how news regarding beautification might be covered. Wolf Von Eckardt, the *Washington Post*'s architectural critic and reporter, sent in comments that the First Lady might consider. "Newspapers are the yeast which, by analyzing the causes of ugliness and encouraging efforts of beauty," he wrote, can foster the emergence of beautiful cities. Mrs. Johnson carried the yeast image over into the speech as she delivered it on 1 October 1965. This eclectic approach to her public speaking enabled Mrs. Johnson to infuse her appearances with a broad range of ideas about beautification and the environment.[5]

The general thrust of her speeches stressed the positive aspects that beautification would have for American society. "Beauty cannot be set aside for vacations or special occasions," she told the National Council of State Garden Clubs and the American Forestry Association in September 1965. "It cannot be the occasional privilege of those who came long distance to visit nature. It cannot be reserved 'For nice neighborhoods ONLY." The nation was facing, she said at Williams College in the fall of 1967, "one of the most fateful questions of the time: whether the physical setting of American life will be pleasant or squalid."[6]

She tried to impart to her audiences a sense of the larger issues and dilemmas that the word beautification did not always convey. In so doing, she addressed concerns that would emerge with more force during the early 1970s as part of the ecological impulse: "How can we bring order rather than chaos out of our highways and transit systems? How can we provide parks and open spaces to let our cities breathe and our people relax? How can we control the waste we pour into our air and water?" Beautification meant for Lady Bird Johnson "our total concern for the physical and human quality of the world we pass on to our children." The comments that she made to the Yale Political Union in 1967 illustrate the transitional nature of Lady Bird Johnson's contribution to the environmental consciousness that followed her husband's administration: "Can a great democratic society generate the energy to plan and build projects of order and beauty? Or does democracy, after all, mean the lowest common denominator?"[7]

In her numerous public appearances, Lady Bird Johnson did not single out the federal government as the primary agent for the promotion of a more beautiful country: "We have learned that we cannot protect and enhance the beauty of this Nation solely through federal action, or just through citizens groups, or simply through academic institutions. All of these are necessary, plus a strong national will. Today, the crying need is for a partnership of thinking, planning, and action on the part of all groups." Mrs. Johnson believed that a potential consensus on the protection of the environment existed and could be called forth if enough citizens would join together in constructive action. She continued to be a proponent of consensus long after political reverses had led her husband to abandon the concept.[8]

To stimulate that kind of communal effort, the First Lady toured the nation to visit local beautification projects and to see wilderness areas in their natural state. The purpose of these trips went beyond an obvious political dimension, and her appearances had more significance than her male critics realized. It was important that citizens who were engaged in the improvement of their communities should gain recognition and attention through the presence of the wife of the president. And if she could attract media coverage of the environment and its problems, she would be sending a message about the priorities that she and her husband had for the nation. When Lady Bird Johnson visited the redwoods in California, dedicated a seashore at Padre Island, or rode down the Rio Grande on a raft, she was using her fame and public standing in a manner that put conservation issues before the nation. As Stewart Udall recognized, the willingness of the First Lady to pursue a "wilderness experience" encouraged other Americans to emulate her example.[9]

Mrs. Johnson's beautification trips were natural lures for the section of the Washington press corps, still predominantly female, that regularly tracked her activities. "Newspaperwomen want an activist First Lady," Liz Carpenter noted, both because of pride and because it "improved their beat." Mrs. Johnson wanted each trip to have an identifiable theme, and she expected thorough advance work from her staff and meticulous preparation from herself. The success of her campaign in attracting public support for beautification in 1965 meant that enough reporters wanted to accompany her to make chartering a plane for the whole entourage economically feasible. The First Lady could not use governmental airplanes as a matter of routine. Lady Bird Johnson rode in the plane with the press corps, said Carpenter, "because there were no funds except out of her own pocket to pay her way."[10]

On the tours themselves, a rapport developed between Mrs. Johnson and the reporters. "On trips she will talk to reporters and give them an opportunity to talk with her," said Marie Smith of the *Washington Post*. "It's a first-hand relationship and when somebody is that nice to you, it's hard to write a bad story." In 1968, on one of the last journeys, the women with Mrs. Johnson produced an affectionate parody of Bob Hope's trademark theme: "Thanks for the memories / Of Big Bend rattlesnakes / Of barbecues and steaks / Of conservation / Restoration / And New England lobster bakes . . . We thank you so much."[11]

The visit to the Big Bend of Texas in the spring of 1966 became one of the most celebrated of the First Lady's excursions during her White House years, and it illustrated her style in promoting the environment and beautification. It began in Presidio, Texas, on April 2 with a party that included Mrs. Johnson, Liz Carpenter, Stewart Udall, Secret Service men, Park Service representatives, and seventy reporters—about one hundred people in all. The "wilderness experience" also became a media event. The group hiked through the park, with Udall, Mrs. Johnson, and a naturalist identifying birds, wildlife, and local plants. In the evening they camped on a mesa and watched what Mrs. Johnson described as "the unceasing play of lights and shadows and the nuances of colors in the sky and on the sides of the mountains."[12]

On the next day, after Palm Sunday services and the planting of a piñon tree, they drove to the Rio Grande to board their rafts. Twenty-four rafts, with five to six people to a raft, set off on a five-hour eleven-mile ride down the river. One lady reporter sported a red umbrella and red pants during the entire voyage; another wore "a black-and-white polka-dot bikini, with a figure to suit it." Mrs. Johnson observed the country closely from her vantage point on the raft. It was "marked with great soaring cliffs that rose up on each side like great pipe organs or cathedral spires, battlements of some long-ago civilization, or the vast escarpments of another world in which the dinosaurs might still be living." At the conclusion of the ride, an exhausted Liz Carpenter commented that she liked "the parks where all the concessions are run by the Rockefellers." After the reporters described the First Lady's activities, attendance at the Big Bend Park rose during the ensuing weeks. "You have had a wilderness experience," Udall told her; "I think you will look back five, ten, or twenty years from now and remember this as spectacular."[13]

Not all the trips were as scenic and rewarding as the Big Bend expedition had been, but the number of outright successes in the forty-seven journeys that Mrs. Johnson made was quite high. Liz Carpenter estimated that the First Lady traveled two hundred thousand miles for beautification and the other causes she endorsed. Among the significant tours were the visit to the California redwoods and the Pacific Coast in 1966, the two New England trips in 1967, and the swing through Texas with the foreign editors in April 1968. On most occasions, Mrs. Johnson commanded responsive audiences for her beautification messages, and she had become a seasoned public advocate of her environmental priorities.[14]

Lady Bird Johnson and Secretary of the Interior Stewart Udall in the Big Bend Park, Texas, on 3 April 1966.

She could not escape the passions over the Vietnam War that consumed her husband's presidency. They began to manifest themselves in public protests in 1966 as she traveled, but the climax came in the autumn of 1967. In October she went to Williams College and to Yale University to deliver speeches on the environment. At Williams she was to be awarded an honorary degree and to recognize the opening of the college's new Center for Environmental Studies and Planning. The Yale Political Union also asked her to talk about the environment. The union's president said to her: "We really want to know more about what we, as students and young men who will be going out in the world, can do about the natural environment." Mrs. Johnson and her associates spent a large amount of time on both speeches. They did not seek extensive press coverage, because, as Liz Carpenter later said, "we thought it was quite possible that there would be some trouble" with Vietnam War protesters.[15]

At both institutions the demonstrations overshadowed the First Lady's remarks. Mrs. Johnson had anticipated her visit to Williams "with a rising ripple of apprehension just below the surface," and the day that she spent there involved a "sheer battering of emotions" that was "pretty wearing." As she was introduced, part of the graduating class walked out. The audience then gave her a standing round of applause. Her speech was well received, though she concluded that her appearance was "probably a mistake on balance" because it provided the demonstrators with the opportunity "to get inches in the paper and minutes on the television screen that they would not have gotten without me." That night she had a phone call from the president, who said, "I just hate for you to have to take that sort of thing."[16]

She went on to New Haven the next day for her afternoon address. Her greeting from Yale's president, Kingman Brewster, Jr., was correct and cordial, but Mrs. Johnson felt "that my presence here was really an imposition on him." Liz Carpenter found Brewster "a soft-headed, academic type" who exemplified what was "wrong with American colleges." Outside the hall where Mrs. Johnson was to speak, there were twelve hundred students in silent protest. Inside, the eight hundred members of the Yale Political Union received her warmly, and she spoke to "a very quiet, very attentive audience." She had "never tried harder in my life—not even at Williams the day before." The environment, she told them, "is where we all meet; where we all have a mutual interest; it is one thing that all of us share. It is not only a mirror of ourselves, but a focusing lens on what we can become." Other societies, more autocratic than the United States, had built great cities. "Our wealth surpasses theirs combined. Will our taste and intelligence and foresight be as great? The answer we give will reveal our quality as a civilization. A better answer will unfold, I think, in the next two decades—and they are yours." She was given another standing ovation when she finished.[17]

After returning to Washington, Mrs. Johnson appeared "very, very disheartened and upset" to Sharon Francis. Perhaps, the First Lady observed, "she just couldn't go on campuses any more." By the time she prepared her diary entry a few days later, Mrs. Johnson had decided: "I must not live only in the White House, insulated against life. I want to know what's going on—even if to know is to suffer." Most of the public comment on her speeches and on the protests praised her performance. She had been subjected, said Senator Birch Bayh (D, Ind.) "to the kind of rudeness that seems to be commonplace nowadays among irresponsible elements on our campuses." By the time that Mrs. Johnson made beautification tours again in 1968, her husband had withdrawn from the presidential race, and the edge went off protests against his policies insofar as they affected her activities.[18]

The initial public interest that beautification stirred in 1965 was so marked that Mrs. Johnson received many more requests for speaking engagements than she could possibly fill by herself. To meet the demand for talks on beautification, a Speakers Bureau, made up of cabinet and Senate wives, was created in March 1965. The leading participants were Lee Udall and Jane Freeman, who worked with Sharon Francis on a speaker's kit for those who filled appointments on behalf of the First Lady. When Mary Connor, wife of the secretary of commerce, delivered a beautification speech in Minneapolis in the summer of 1965, she received the report of the White House Conference on Natural Beauty, a pamphlet on community action for beautification, and copies of letters to the First Lady and a recent speech as background material for her remarks. Mrs. Johnson also kept track of how the bureau members performed. After Trudye Fowler, the wife of the secretary of the Treasury, spoke in Syracuse, New York, in early 1966, the First Lady wrote to her: "I hear you were GREAT! If Syracuse becomes a far, far better place than it has been before, it will be thanks to you and your words about beautification."[19]

By the end of 1965, Mrs. Johnson's mail was bringing about seventy-five speaking offers each week, a third of which related to beautification. The White House staff offered alternative speakers to about twenty-five of the inquiries it received, and about ten of these replies asked for someone from the Speakers Bureau to be sent. The work of the bureau continued unabated into the first part of 1966 with workshops and with briefing papers from Sharon Francis and Cynthia Wilson flowing out to its members. By February 1967, however, Francis, Nash Castro, and

Henry Diamond reported to Mrs. Johnson that the bureau was "no longer being inundated with speech requests, although a few possible ones come in every month." The program, they recommended, needed to be reactivated if it was to address the concern Mrs. Johnson had about putting the natural-beauty message before mayors and governors. As it happened, the major substantive suggestion was to add governmental officials to the bureau, all of whom were men, who would be "specialists in various federal programs." Little came of this proposal, and those speaking engagements that Mrs. Johnson could not fill during her last two years either were handled by Sharon Francis or were not met at all. The fate of the Speakers Bureau raised the issue of the extent to which the beautification campaign had to rely on the popularity and celebrity status of the First Lady and could not be transferred to or sustained by surrogates.[20]

Another area in which Lady Bird Johnson attempted to reach out with her message about conservation and the quality of life was in her attempts to include the business community directly in the work of beautification. Environmental change, she believed, could not occur simply through the traditional agencies of the conservation movement. These groups, which were well intentioned and earnest, lacked clout and were often seen as being impractical and as being dominated by women. To some degree, she shared the assumption that hard-headed and realistic businessmen would bring a degree of experience that supporters of beautification did not possess. Coming from a business background herself, the First Lady thought that others in the community would see, as she did, the cost benefits and potential profits in a cleaner and more beautiful society. As Liz Carpenter put it, "she was trying to preach the fact that it was good business and that it did pay off in dollars and cents."[21]

Like the overtures to the billboard industry, her initiatives with business produced ambiguous results. Some companies cooperated; others seemed to; many did not. It is now impossible to say with confidence whether the energies that she devoted to wooing business would have been better spent in strengthening her ties with roadside councils, conservation lobbying groups, and women who were disposed to help her cause. Lady Bird Johnson tried to establish a network with the men who managed corporate America on behalf of beautification. As a result, other potential sources of support and influence for the environment were left underdeveloped.

Mrs. Johnson's overtures to business dated from the formation of her Washington committee. Adam Rumoshosky, the marketing director for the American Petroleum Institute, was an original member of the panel.

At their first meeting, he commented: "In my judgment businessmen were beginning to understand the literal definition of the word attractiveness," and he mentioned that service-station operators were trying to improve the way their facilities fit into the landscape. His remarks aroused Mrs. Johnson's interest, as did a letter from the chairman of Texaco, who expressed "a growing concern about inadequate and poorly designed facilities, the spread of blight over so many miles of our nation's highways and in general, the lack of a constructive program to retain the beauty of our countryside." He said that Texaco would commence a "Service Station Beautification Program" by upgrading stations in the District of Columbia, training personnel, and creating model service stations across the country.[22]

Despite these glowing assurances, the oil company did little in the way of actual follow-up on its program in 1965. In December, Mrs. Johnson told Nash Castro and Mary Lasker "that the petroleum industry does not appear to have done much to give thrust to the beautification program." Castro mentioned the letter from Texaco that, as he recalled it, had promised "to take the lead in beautifying their service stations throughout the Nation." Mrs. Johnson asked him to draft a letter to send Texaco as a reminder of their commitment.[23]

Her instructions led to a February 1966 meeting in the White House with petroleum marketing executives about the appearance of service stations. A news account before the gathering predicted that "oil officials will argue that ugly stations are being replaced gradually and that it would be uneconomic to speed up the process." The executives confined their remarks to the First Lady to what the industry had done voluntarily; they made no commitment to any sustained program of action.[24]

So Mrs. Johnson had to rely on the quiet encouragement of the industry's sporadic beautification efforts, especially in the Washington, D.C., area. By the spring of 1967, Rumoshosky reported that filling stations in the District area were spending $1.5 million on beautification improvements that year and forecast that " 'landscaping' will follow 'clean rest rooms' as a service station appeal." In all, it was not much of a follow-through on the assurances that the oil industry had made originally. As Rumoshosky said, "It is a constant battle" to overcome the impact of independent salesmen and companies who marketed unsightly banners and pennants to service-station dealers. In 1968, Mrs. Johnson and her committee recognized such oil-industry examples as Carl's Sinclair Coach House in Washington, which was redone in a colonial style to fit the nearby Georgetown architecture. The First Lady and her staff were also pleased that 150 stations in the District had been landscaped and another

20 had been remodeled. In the aggregate, however, beautification in the service-station business came slowly during the 1960s.[25]

Undaunted, Mrs. Johnson responded positively to other beautification overtures from business. When the Reliance Insurance Company of Philadelphia observed its one hundred and fiftieth anniversary, its executives asked Sharon Francis how they might mark the occasion with a beautification project. They decided to plant trees near low-income schools in 100 to 150 cities, an effort that the First Lady's staff encouraged. "The business-establishment audience is one we need to reach with personal contact," Francis told Liz Carpenter in presenting a request from Reliance that the First Lady also attend their birthday ceremonies. That proved impossible for scheduling reasons, but otherwise the connection with Reliance had been productive.[26]

The working relationship with Giant Food in Washington brought more enduring results. After an initial meeting with the First Lady, the grocery chain in the District agreed to accept her suggestion to emphasize "the beautification of parking lots and shopping centers." They selected a store located in the Cardozo neighborhood of the city's ghetto, which opened in mid August 1966 with "a vest pocket park, trees, flowers and shrubbery." Company representatives met with members of the local community about the store, appointed a black manager, and drew employees from the local community. A youth gardening club was created to care for the park. The store received a beautification award from Mrs. Johnson's Committee in 1967. When the riots came to Washington in April 1968, the Giant outlets "were spared destruction, although they were located in the midst of the devastated areas." The chain was convinced that the work it had done for beautification and with the black community generally had played some part in that positive outcome.[27]

At various other points in her beautification campaign, Mrs. Johnson received overtures from beer companies, highway paving concerns, electrical companies, and glass-container manufacturers about cooperating with her. The National Coal Association ran an advertisement in the form of an "Open Letter to the First Lady," which proclaimed agreement with her goals and said that in strip mining, "the industry for many years has been actively encouraging proper restoration of mined land." Stewart Udall sent her the ad, and her letter of reply, drafted by Sharon Francis, responded: "It is wonderful to see how far the natural beauty message is spreading . . . and even more wonderful to know that some of these strip mined scars may disappear." Always realistic about the extent of the industry's real compliance with its professed aims, the First Lady added in her own hand that she had recently flown over West

Virginia and had seen "the results of strip mines that had not been reclaimed in any way—so the need is very fresh in my mind."[28]

Mrs. Johnson's links with business never proved to be as rewarding as she had hoped they might become. Laurance Rockefeller told the Seventieth Annual Congress of American Industry in December 1965 that "this concept of beauty as good business can and should be extended to the full range of corporate activity." Rockefeller was more a solitary voice than a sign of change within the business community during the 1960s, and even some of his business dealings aroused criticism from environmentalists about his lack of sensitivity to the impact of his actions. The people around Mrs. Johnson felt the absence of cooperation from business. In Washington, D.C., for example, Nash Castro told Sharon Francis in June 1967 that his "biggest disappointment" in the beautification enterprise had been "the almost complete lack of support and interest on the part of the Washington business community." That result was characteristic of the response of business in general to Mrs. Johnson's program.[29]

Within the federal government itself, Mrs. Johnson did not confront a visible sluggishness about the merits of beautification akin to the apathy of the corporate world. Few bureaucrats or agencies wanted to be seen as being in direct opposition to the president's wife. The problem was more subtle than that. She had to struggle against the perception that what she sought to do was worthwhile in an abstract sense but should not outweigh the more practical and realistic needs of busy men in the White House or the executive branch. Nonetheless, the First Lady sought to use her influence to promote public occasions at which the federal government could stress beautification, to strengthen those agencies with a role in protecting the environment, and to push forward candidates for governmental positions who shared her views on conservation.

One thing the First Lady could do was to build on the example of the White House Conference on Natural Beauty and to encourage similar meetings, "conferences of continuity" as the president called them, on a smaller scale within the states and at colleges and universities. Many states, including California and Arizona, held natural-beauty meetings in 1965 and 1966. When the president of the Texas Landscape Association suggested that Governor John Connally of Texas call such a conference "in line with the wishes of President Johnson's overall program for the beautification of the entire country," Lady Bird Johnson wrote Connally, to pass on her personal endorsement. "There is a lot Texas can brag about beauty-wise," she informed him, and beautification would complement his own emphasis on tourism.[30]

Connally became a cosponsor of the Texas Conference on Our Environmental Crisis, which was held at the University of Texas at Austin in November 1965. The speakers included Philip Johnson, J. B. Jackson, and Senator Gaylord A. Nelson (D, Wis.). Jackson told the audience that beautification would "get nowhere until we overcome this tendency to see the landscape in esthetic, tourist terms." Most of the other participants did not echo Jackson's critical note. Henry Diamond said that President Johnson "has energized the federal bureaucracy and his First Lady has rallied citizens across the land." Mrs. Johnson later wrote to Professor Patrick Horsbrugh of the School of Architecture, the coordinator of the gathering, that she had "been bragging about the experts and talent which Texas has on this whole project," and she praised his "remarkably catalytic role in putting it together." She hoped that the Texas example would serve as a model for other states.[31]

In an effort to involve the nation's young people in beautification, Mrs. Johnson lent her support to the National Youth Conference on Natural Beauty and Conservation in the summer of 1966. The organizing spirit for this Conference was Diana MacArthur, the First Lady's niece. The meeting brought together five hundred teenagers from ten national youth organizations, such as the Boy Scouts, the Girl Scouts, 4-H Clubs, and the Camp Fire Girls, for four days of deliberations from June 26 through June 29. Mrs. Johnson regarded the conference as "one of the more meaningful things that has been done since the beginning of the beautification program," and she welcomed the participants on the South Lawn of the White House on June 27. "You will not have reached maturity until you have tackled a hopeless, idealistic cause," she told them, and "you may be surprised to find it was not so hopeless after all." On the next day her Beautification Committee met to hear what Nathaniel Owings had done about the Mall, and then she made beautification awards to local winners from the District. It was a day of important work, of decisions on Vietnam, and of religious feelings by the president who prayed in a Catholic Church. As she was writing her diary entry, she thought about her beautification campaign: "Using the White House as a podium—hopefully—to thank, to applaud, to advertise, to rally citizens to action in improving our environment, gives me joy."[32]

The young people at the Conference heard addresses by Secretary Udall, Jane Freeman of the Speakers Bureau, and the president of the Conservation Foundation, Russell E. Train. They discussed air pollution, roadside control, city beautification, litter control, and other environmental topics. When their talks had concluded, they reported back to the First Lady with a pledge to take further action in their home communities. Diana MacArthur was named to coordinate a year of follow-up activities, and she received grants from the Ford Foundation of $75,000 to sustain the campaign. The cochairs of the conference wired to President Johnson on June 30, asking him to declare 1967 a "Youth Natural Beauty and Conservation Year."[33]

Action on the latter proposal went forward slowly during the rest of 1966. First it lingered for five weeks in the White House before Harry McPherson referred it to the President's Council on Recreation and Natural Beauty, to be coordinated with other beautification programs that that panel had under review. Secretary of Commerce John T. Connor chaired the council in the autumn of 1966, and he asked its executive director, Edward C. Crafts, to examine the suggested presidential proclamation. Crafts, who was also the director of the Bureau of Outdoor Recreation in the Interior Department, responded that the proclamation would show the president's interest in youth and his "keen interest in enhancing and conserving the environment where we work, live and play." On balance, Crafts concluded, "The costs would be minimal; the probable gains are high."[34]

Connor sent this endorsement forward, but that was not the end of the deliberative process about the proclamation. The idea then had to make the rounds of the council members themselves. Their affirmative answers to the proclamation were ready on November 25. Liz Carpenter then told the president and Mrs. Johnson that the proclamation offered an "excellent between Christmas–New Year news possibility" for December 28. The two cochairs of the Youth Conference, one of whom was a black Girl Scout, could be there at the LBJ Ranch, along with representatives from the other youth groups. The proclamation, Carpenter contended, "costs nothing and involves 20 million young people in eleven national youth organizations." Showing them around the Ranch would be "good for pictures with youth." For an administration that was encountering problems with college protests about policy in regard to Vietnam, the chance to show the president and the First Lady in a positive setting with teenagers who favored a White House policy was an opportunity that should be welcomed and used.[35]

On 28 December 1966 the Johnsons spoke to the press at the Ranch, with the young people in attendance. The presence of the youths, Lyndon Johnson said, "will be extremely helpful to all of us who want to see not only a better America but a more beautiful land." Mrs. Johnson added: "It is not too much to hope that it can be a time of great change in our national attitudes toward our environment, in our appreciation and enjoyment of the beautiful things of this blessed land and our resentment and determination to change those things that have marred it." She singled out a campaign by young people in Pawtucket, Rhode Island, to clean the Old Slater Mill, and a Youth Cleanup Day in New Mexico, which had improved the appearance of that state's highways. After the ceremony itself, Diana MacArthur sought to have the Youth Natural Beauty Program mentioned in the State of the Union message in January 1967 and otherwise to have it publicized more widely. The speech reference did not occur, but the Youth Natural Beauty program did have other constructive results. Young people around the nation sponsored beautification projects, including the restoration of a run-down park in Mellen, Wisconsin, by members of a 4-H Club and the improvement of a park site in New Bedford, Massachusetts, as a joint project of the local YWCA and the Girl Scouts. In July 1968 the leaders of the National Youth Conference on Natural Beauty and Conservation presented the First Lady with an evaluation of the accomplishments of the 1967 campaign, along with recommendations about how "youth power" could aid in conservation and beautification in the future. Lady Bird Johnson had taken maximum advantage of this quasi-governmental program to publicize her priorities and to identify beautification with the volunteer efforts of youth organizations.[36]

She also lent her public support to the National Trust for Historic Preservation. She had prepared a foreword to its 1966 report, *With Heritage So Rich,* in which she said that "preservation does not mean merely the setting aside of thousands of buildings as museum pieces"; it also involved "retaining the culturally valuable structures as useful objects." She placed her own beautification work "within the sturdy American tradition which seeks the beautiful which is also useful." She was part of the favorable climate for preservation and its support by the national government that led to the National Historic Preservation Act in October 1966, as the Trust recognized when it made an award to her during her "Discover America" tour in the spring of 1968.[37]

Lady Bird Johnson paid equally close attention to more-formal governmental agencies that could promote the cause of the environment. The White House Conference on Natural Beauty had recommended to the president that the existing Recreation Advisory Council be broadened into a National Council on Natural Beauty. Participants also urged him to name a Citizens' Advisory Committee on Recreation and Natural Beauty. Laurance Rockefeller hoped that the expanded council would become "the central point for follow-up" on the White House Conference and that it would give him the important role in resource policy that he had long sought. On 5 May 1966 a presidential executive order established the President's Council on Recreation and Natural Beauty and simultaneously set up the Citizens' Advisory Committee on Recreation and Natural Beauty. The federal government, said the president, "must pursue a course that will enhance and protect" natural beauty, and to accomplish that end, "its own house must be in order."[38]

Mrs. Johnson and her staff monitored the activities of the President's Council in 1966 as it dealt with such issues as the follow-up to the White House Conference on Natural Beauty, the creation of "a national program for scenic roads and parkways," and the difficult question of where highways should be located in relation to parks and open spaces. Differences between the departments of Commerce and the Interior over jurisdiction for these highway matters, as well as the fate of the legislation to create the Department of Transportation, limited the council's effectiveness during this period.[39]

Then, in the spring of 1967, after some questioning of the value of the council and the advisory committee, the Interior Subcommittee of the House Appropriations Committee disallowed a request for an increase of $100,000 that Interior had sought for both panels. With the Citizens' Advisory Committee in "a precarious position," Douglass Cater told Michael Manatos of the White House that "this Committee works closely with Mrs. Johnson," and he hoped that the funding might be restored in the Senate. The Senate Interior Appropriations Subcommittee put back $60,000 of the original $100,000 request, and the issue then turned on the House-Senate Conference in May 1967. The conferees agreed to fund the council and to accept the Senate version.[40]

With its appropriation assured, the members of the council and of the advisory committee returned to the issues of the effectiveness of the two bodies as lobbying forces for natural beauty within the government. They also recommended greater sensitivity in the selection of highway routes and the promotion of scenic highways. Mrs. Johnson saw to it that her associates were present whenever possible at the meetings of the citizens committee. When the body assembled on 29 June 1967, Liz Carpenter and Sharon Francis were there. Carpenter told the committee members that they could "serve as a catalyst to the Federal Departments" in the context of the positive public response to Mrs. Johnson's beautification campaign. The two groups spent the rest of 1967 pulling together a report on the environment, to be sent to the president in 1968 with various recommendations on urban problems, rural needs, and issues of transportation policy. The work moved slowly, and the proposals were not likely to be ready before autumn.[41]

In the spring of 1968 it became necessary to make more appointments to the Citizens' Advisory Committee when the two-year terms of its original members expired on May 4. The committee was scheduled to meet in Washington on 29 March 1968, and then it planned to meet again on May 4, "to finalize its concluding report to the President."

Edward Crafts warned Douglass Cater that "policy guidance is needed, and there is not too much time left." Cater in turn alerted John W. Macy, Jr., who had charge of presidential appointments to governmental service, that "we don't want to let The President's Council on Recreation and Natural Beauty lapse."[42]

At the same time, Liz Carpenter had suggested to President Johnson that since the First Lady would be meeting with the Citizens' Advisory Committee on March 29, the occasion could be used to publicize the appointment of Vice-President Hubert Humphrey as chairman of the President's Council on Recreation and Natural Beauty. Johnson's response was "let's make this a real production," which they did. In the East Room on the twenty-ninth, Mrs. Johnson told a gathering of officials and citizens that "the really gratifying thing about the whole business of improving the environment is that it encompasses tasks for everyone from children in an anti-litter campaign to adults working on zoning legislation or building community centers in the ghetto." With the usual male deprecation of beautification, President Johnson spoke about "flower power," but then conceded that "flower power, architectural power, urban planning power—all these powers are shaping a better country."[43]

The president and the First Lady also worked together on the appointments to be made to the Citizens' Advisory Committee, once an executive order reestablishing it had been issued in May 1968. On March 22, Macy, the director of the appointments process for the Johnson administration, sent Mrs. Johnson a summary of the prospective appointees for the panel. "Knowing of your keen interest in this," Macy said, he wanted to let her consider which of the current members should be retained and what new selections should occur. By mid May, the Johnsons had "mutually agreed" on a list of selections to the committee, including Texans such as John Ben Shepperd of the Texas Historical Survey Committee and Dewitt C. Greer, the state highway engineer. Mrs. Johnson's participation in this process continued throughout the summer and fall of 1968. Macy sent her the names of others being considered, and she helped to secure the selection of Marvin B. Durning, a Seattle attorney who had helped her with beautification, and she pushed for the designation of Fred Farr to the committee as well. By the last year of her husband's presidency, Mrs. Johnson was directly involved in the selection of individuals to this advisory body and was accorded a role in the process of recommendation and nomination.[44]

In the suggestions that she made about appointments to the Citizens' Advisory Committee and in other instances, Lady Bird Johnson recommended a number of women for the available positions, but those proposed were very much in the minority compared to the number of men that the president and the First Lady suggested. Mrs. Johnson and her aides did stress to their male colleagues the practical value of women in promoting natural beauty. Liz Carpenter recommended to the President's Council on Recreation and Natural Beauty in June 1967 "that women be used on the committees and task forces that are established for they have both the time and the interest, and can supplement experts who know about a particular subject." These arguments were not couched in feminist terms, nor was the case made that including more women was right and just. Instead, Lady Bird Johnson put forward a smattering of women for the available openings. Within an administration that was not receptive to the idea of equity for women, this was probably all that she could have done without seeming to become an advocate for a cause that did not command the support in her husband's White House.[45]

The President's Council on Recreation and Natural Beauty concluded its work in the Johnson administration with the issuance of its report "From Sea to Shining Sea" in the autumn of 1968. Vice-President Humphrey said in his letter of transmittal that he hoped the document "will generally advance the efforts made by you and by Mrs. Johnson to improve the quality of the physical environment for the benefit of the people." Humphrey also hoped that the release of the report would buttress his environmental credentials in his presidential campaign against Richard M. Nixon. The wide-ranging report praised the First Lady's efforts in Washington and attributed to her committee "an important catalyzing role in overcoming the inertia which often greets new programs." The council itself had been a useful instrument through which the Johnsons had spread their conservation message; it involved like-minded citizens in the goals of the administration.[46]

Mrs. Johnson's beautification campaign led many individuals and groups to try to secure her endorsement of their cause or to gain her public approval for their position in a particular environmental controversy. For the most part, her staff was able, through sympathetic but noncommittal form responses, to deflect these inquiries to the proper federal agency or to turn the writer away without rancor. On two of the major conservation issues of the period, however, she had to adopt a more public position. Her role in the dispute over the Grand Canyon and the California redwoods illustrates, in these instances, how the public had come to regard her as a voice within the White House that spoke for the environment.

During the mid 1960s the Bureau of Reclamation in the Department of the Interior proposed to construct two dams in the Grand Canyon as part of the effort to bring additional water to the desert areas of Arizona. The Sierra Club and other conservationists began a prolonged fight to block the dams and to preserve the Canyon in its unspoiled state. "If there is anything you can do to save our Grand Canyon," wrote a disabled veteran from Tucson, "do it if you can. Help buy a little time." In this case, Secretary Udall, himself an Arizonan, and the administration were for the dams and against the conservationist position. Mrs. Johnson had to tread carefully lest she appear to be in direct opposition to her husband's policies. When mail came in protesting the dams, her answers were carefully phrased. "I am certain," the letters said in the spring of 1966, "that the legislators will give full attention to any realistic alternatives for meeting the water needs of the thirsty Southwest before they enact any measures that would in any way diminish the wild beauties of the Grand Canyon."[47]

Sharon Francis had some part in drafting this language, which to a degree diverged from the prodam position of Udall and the Interior Department. The secretary's associates regarded Francis with great suspicion in the Grand Canyon battle. She was, as they saw it, "about as 100 per cent a preservationist as they come," and her "influence" with Mrs. Johnson was regretted. In fact, the First Lady was advancing her own views on the controversy. Asked whether her staff should answer the mail on the Grand Canyon or simply refer it to Interior, she read a week's incoming protest letters and said "that they were the highest calibre letters that had ever come to her on any subject." She decided that the staff in the White House should continue to respond to this correspondence, because "she could not afford to preach natural beauty and ignore what was happening to the greatest beauty of them all—Grand Canyon."[48]

Some of the letters that went out from Mrs. Johnson's office inevitably reached the public. One of them was reprinted in the *Congressional Record* by Congressman Henry Reuss (D, Wis.), who interpreted the key phrase in the letter from the First Lady's office to mean that she believed "that the Southwest can have needed water and America can continue to have the Grand Canyon as nature made it." Mrs. Johnson's actions during the spring and summer of 1966 were not as decisive as was the advertising campaign of the Sierra Club against the dams. Nonetheless, her willingness to act as a conduit for mail opposing the dams and the extent to which she made protest legitimate on the issue underscored her contribution as a catalyst for sentiment to preserve the Grand Canyon.[49]

Something of the same process took place with regard to the California redwoods and the effort to create a national park for the trees that remained in that state. In September 1964 the National Park Service recommended that a national park be established on Redwood Creek, and for the next year the Johnson administration and Secretary Udall tried to work out the specifics of a park proposal that would satisfy Californians, the lumber industry, the Sierra Club, and the Save the Redwoods League. Mrs. Johnson answered the mail that she received on the redwoods issue during these months with general language. "Certainly these stately old trees should be preserved," she told Susan Frey of Newhall, California, "and I hope a national park will be established to protect them." By early 1966, however, Udall and the administration sent to Congress a scaled-down proposal for a national park that reflected the influence of Laurance Rockefeller, the Save-the-Redwoods League, and California lumbering interests. The Sierra Club was strongly opposed to the White House plan.[50]

When Mrs. Johnson made her visit to the California coast in the fall of 1966, the legislation to create a redwoods park was bogged down in Congress, and the Johnson administration was still caught between the Sierra Club's desire for a larger park and the resistance of Californians, both in and out of the state government, to what the White House wanted. The First Lady did not visit the true redwoods on the trip, but was impressed with some one-hundred-year-old redwoods that she saw at Big Sur. In the remarks that she made at Point Reyes she did not mention the trees. She praised efforts to protect the coastal region, and she said that "we have misused our resources, but we haven't destroyed them." When she returned to Washington, she assured a Californian who had written to her that she hoped to be back in the state one day "and visit a redwoods national park."[51]

The situation of the redwoods legislation remained stalemated in Congress in 1967 as the administration tried to work out a compromise with California and its new governor, Ronald Reagan, through the good offices of Laurance Rockefeller. For its part, the Sierra Club attempted to use the First Lady to make its case for a larger national park than either the state or the Johnson administration would accept. Martin Litton,who served as travel editor of *Sunset* magazine, called Sharon Francis in April 1967 to urge Mrs. Johnson to visit the redwoods herself. He said: "Only Mrs. Johnson can save us, and I have been delegated to call you and plead with her to come out. People are badly demoralized out here, and if she could only see the redwoods she would understand the difference between the larger area we are advocating and the much smaller area that many members of Congress are now beginning to support."[52]

When it became obvious that Mrs. Johnson could not make the trip, Litton asked Francis to come out and prepare "an eyewitness report." After discussing the proposal for a week with Mrs. Johnson, Liz Carpenter, and Edward Crafts of the Interior Department, Francis was authorized to go. "The park's supporters needed to have their morale boosted" was the consensus as Francis remembered it, and "such a trip on my part would be advantageous." She was "very impressed" with how few redwoods remained and thought that as many as possible should be preserved "because future generations will judge the Johnson administration by the size and integrity of the park we leave." She returned to Washington with the conviction "that if the larger unit could be afforded it offered a better ecological whole."[53]

Francis believed that these impressions, which she conveyed to Udall and others in the administration about her trip, "helped tip the scales toward spending and getting more for our money, which eventually we did." The most careful student of the redwoods battle assigns Mrs. Johnson and her staff "little role" in the creation of the park, and it would be wrong to overstate the impact of Francis's visit or her personal influence as evidence of Mrs. Johnson's involvement with the issue. The letters that Francis wrote about the matter in 1967 and 1968 suggest, however, that she was accurate when she told an oral-history interviewer in 1969: "Mrs. Johnson kept in close touch with these matters as well. Again, she didn't try to touch the purse or the pocketbook, but it was certainly known and felt throughout the administration that she was supporting as much as we could do."[54]

When Lyndon Johnson signed the compromise Redwoods National Park bill into law on 2 October 1968, Mrs. Johnson had one of the pens that he used in signing the measure sent to the Save-the-Redwoods League. She told another citizen who had written to her that "I am so glad to know you share my happiness that the Redwood National Park will be preserved for future generations to enjoy." So it was appropriate that Lady Bird Johnson was present on 27 August 1969, when the Lady Bird Johnson Grove was dedicated in the new Redwood National Park.[55]

By the end of her husband's presidency the First Lady had established in the popular mind her identification with the environment, and she had transformed the term *beautification* into a word that connoted respect rather than triviality. The process of gaining credibility for her campaign had been a slow one, but it had also been persistent and had suffered few reverses. Press coverage of her activities gradually recognized that she was more serious about the environment than reporters had originally understood. The tone of news stories about her became increasingly favorable as the White House years progressed.

In July 1965, writing in the *Reporter*, Meg Greenfield observed that Mrs. Johnson had integrated "the traditionally frivolous and routine aspects of East Wing life into the overall purposes of the administration" and had also enlisted "the peculiar assets of First Ladyhood itself in the administration's behalf." Greenfield reviewed Mrs. Johnson's campaign work and looked at her sponsorship of Head Start. Beautification was mentioned toward the end of the article, with the observation that Mrs. Johnson would "need every bit of the sensitivity and shrewdness she had displayed in the past in her current project, known by the deceptively sweet and simple-sounding name of 'beautification.' Who could be against beautification?" As Greenfield noted, however, the White House Conference on Natural Beauty showed that reconciling the diverse constituencies that beautification affected would not be an easy undertaking. The tone of polite skepticism about Mrs. Johnson's work was still present.[56]

By the fall of 1965, *Time* was referring to the First Lady as "Claudia the Beautician." Despite the condescending label, the report itself asserted that the pace of her activities showed that she was "in dead earnest about her beautification program." In the summer of 1966, writing on the presidency for *Life*, columnist Hugh Sidey said beautification might be "the single most successful Great Society venture so far" and noted that White House mail to the First Lady was running more than two hundred letters a week about highway location and other beautification issues. Sidey quoted the president as having said, "with gruff delight," that his wife was "going to beautify us right out of existence." When Mrs. Johnson made her trip to California in September 1966, *Time* reported that "from business and mayors to garden-clubbers and old-time conservationists, she is receiving a rousing chorus of 'America the Beautiful'—or, more precisely, 'America Must Be More Beautiful.' "[57]

Conservation groups increasingly sought to identify themselves with Lady Bird Johnson's initiatives. "Mrs. Johnson has become a gallant figure," said James Craig in the November 1966 issue of *American Forest;* "her great contribution has been that she has made us feel needed." The American Institute of Architects cited her in the same year for "her determination to restore beauty where it has been forgotten; to preserve beauty where it exists and to protect our natural resources." In 1967 the American Forestry Association gave her its Distinguished Service Award, "to this nation's foremost tree planter and missionary for the beautification of our environment."[58] While Lady Bird Johnson never enjoyed the international fame of Jacqueline Kennedy or the high visibility of Eleanor Roosevelt, she had attained an impressive level of public credibility for her work on the environment as her husband's presidency entered its last year.

10

Her Space in the World

The most elusive issue in Lady Bird Johnson's campaign for the environment is the precise extent of her impact on Lyndon B. Johnson himself. How closely the Johnsons worked together on matters involving beautification and natural resources may not be known until the remaining full text of the First Lady's diaries is published and her private papers are opened. Because so much of their collaboration has left no record, the substance of what they did may not be recoverable. The degree of familiarity that they both displayed with highway-beautification legislation and the readiness that Lady Bird Johnson showed in asking for White House staff help with Congress on such issues as Pennsylvania Avenue, the Citizens' Advisory Committee on Recreation and Natural Beauty, and several other matters indicate that theirs was a working partnership.[1]

As far as policy was concerned, Lyndon Johnson provided constant support to his wife's endeavors and to the causes of beautification in general. In 1965, cabinet officers and heads of governmental agencies received reminders of the president's "desire that all Federal buildings be beautified through the planting of trees, shrubs, and flowers." After the White House Conference on Natural Beauty, Lyndon Johnson's White House sent out a summary of the proceedings and recommendations to members of Congress, governors, mayors, and county officials. In the cover letter that accompanied the document, Johnson expressed his hope "that these recommendations will be studied and put to work to build a more beautiful America." By early September 1965 the president was asking for "a thorough report" from his administration on what had been done about natural beauty to show that "the Johnson administration has made beauty into a national issue and national cause."[1]

President Johnson added his public backing to his wife's campaign during the latter half of the same year. In August he spoke at the site of a future park in Johnson City, which *Life* magazine had donated to further the First Lady's beautification effort. "In case you have not heard it yet," he told the crowd, Lady Bird Johnson "is rather interested in beautification. And it appears that she not only wants people to say it with flowers, she wants them also to say it with trees." Nothing, said the president, could make him more pleased on his birthday. At the signing of the Highway Beautification Act in October, he proclaimed that "Beauty belongs to all the people." While he was in office, "what has been divinely given by nature will not be taken recklessly away by man."[2]

The level of presidential support for beautification remained high throughout 1966. In February he asked Congress for legislation to preserve the nation's natural resources so as to avoid "a barren America, bereft of its beauty, and shorn of its sustenance." The year 1966 should be, he concluded, "the year of the new conservation, when farsighted men took farsighted steps to preserve the beauty that is the heritage of our Republic." On the occasion when the President's Council and Citizens' Advisory Committee on Recreation and Natural Beauty was established, Lyndon Johnson jokingly remarked that "for all my personal interest in beautification, some people, including some very close to me and on the platform this morning, seem to think that I am not quite interested enough. Sometimes she has to prod me a little bit. Sometimes I would actually swear she is shoving." It would please her, he said, that he could "carry out her suggestion and ask you to come here and redouble our efforts to try to beautify our land."[3]

When he spoke at the National Youth Conference on Natural Beauty and Conservation in June 1966, the president was gratified that at a time of "so many critical problems" there were those such as "Secretary Udall and Mrs. Johnson and Mrs. [Robert C.] Weaver and Mrs. [Orville L.] Freeman and others who are excited about conserving this Nation, and who are dedicated to making it a more beautiful country."[4]

The Johnsons held a joint press conference at the LBJ Ranch on 27 August 1966, the day of Lyndon Johnson's fifty-eighth birthday. Reporters asked the First Lady, toward the end of the session, what her job had been "as a political wife over the past 30 years." She responded that it had been "sharing all of my husband's experiences and learning about our country." They had visited Idaho, Colorado, and Oklahoma on the preceding day, and Lady Bird Johnson had taken the opportunity to address her environmental concerns. The West, she said, needed water, as Idaho demonstrated, while a nuclear-testing plant in the same state caused her to reflect on the possibilities for power that the facility represented. As they drove through Denver, she noted "several big boulevards with their gorgeous green median strips, bordered by great trees, and with brilliant flowers—all so well kept." Denver had achieved this beauty because "somebody loved this town and gave it a long lead time in planning." Now, as she and her husband agreed, "what happens to our cities is at the top of our list of problems."[5]

In the autumn of 1966 the president, the First Lady, and Lawrence O'Brien unveiled a postage stamp that urged Americans to "Plant for a More Beautiful America." Lyndon Johnson recalled that "Lady Bird and I have been working together on what is now called 'beautification' for more than thirty years." Harking back to their work on roadside parks in Texas during the 1930s, he added: "Mrs. Johnson had as much influence with me then as she does now. I think that you can see the results of that influence every time you ride through Texas and every time you see the National Capital." He praised Mary Lasker and Laurance Rockefeller for their work on Washington's appearance and concluded that he was "especially pleased to have the chance to work with Mrs. Johnson."[6]

In the following week the president spoke to members of the National Recreation and Park Association. In these remarks and in other appearances, Lyndon Johnson fell into a bantering style about his wife's commitment to natural beauty. "Mrs. Johnson not only talks about conservation and recreation, but she occasionally has some observations to make about beautification." The president was adopting a jocular tone that men from his state and region frequently used about their wives and women in general. Employing a slight edge of sarcasm in public references to a spouse was preferable to an outright declaration of love and respect, which might seem too sentimental and less manly. The style reflected no lack of affection between the president and the First Lady; in fact, the exact opposite was the case. Presidential teasing, however, did embody an implicit masculine uneasiness with natural beauty as a cultural value.[7]

The Johnsons' partnership on beautification continued into 1967. In his State of the Union address on January 10, he restated his administration's commitment to natural beauty: "We should continue to carry to every corner of the Nation our campaign for a beautiful America." When he spoke on the subject, Lady Bird Johnson wrote in her diary, "he raised his eyes to the Gallery, hunting me, and I smiled back." Two weeks later, forty-six mayors visited Mrs. Johnson at the White House to talk about conservation and beautification. The urban leaders told her that "a good many of them were finding out" that beautification "is good business and good politics." Lyndon Johnson came in, listened to the discussion, and then said to the mayors: "If your constituencies want model cities, they must express themselves." His wife noted proudly in her record

President and Mrs. Johnson and Postmaster General Larry O'Brien at the unveiling of the beautification stamp on 5 October 1966.

of the day: "What had started out to be 'tea and thank you' by a timid First Lady had turned out to be a fairly substantive meeting."[8]

The Johnsons' partnership continued throughout the turbulent months of Vietnam protests, the marriage of their daughter Lynda, and the discussions that led to the decision in 1967 not to seek reelection in 1968. President Johnson pushed for such occasions as the reception for the Citizens' Advisory Committee on Recreation and Natural Beauty in February 1967, in order to advance billboard regulation in Congress, and he used cabinet meetings to address the issue of having federal agencies use outdoor advertising in ways that undercut the First Lady's program. Lady Bird Johnson's support of Walter Washington's candidacy for mayor of Washington, D.C., derived from their beautification work together and proved to be important in persuading her husband to make the appointment. When a private citizen wrote to Mrs. Johnson to protest the money that was being spent on highway beautification, Douglass Cater's answer linked the president and the First Lady in their commitment to the environment. "The effort of the President and Mrs. Johnson," Cater said, "to beautify our nation is aimed not only at improving the material but the spiritual well-being of our people."[9]

By the time 1967 had ended, the Johnsons had already concluded that sometime in early 1968 the president would announce that he would not be a candidate for reelection. Lady Bird Johnson had worried about her husband's health all during the second term, as his periodic ailments,

Champions of the New Conservation: President and Mrs. Johnson with Secretary of the Interior Stewart Udall at the White House on 13 October 1967.

which reflected the uncertain state of his health, came and went. In September 1965, at the onset of his gall-bladder problem, her thoughts were on the heart attack ten years earlier. "For a long time—months, years—I have been keenly aware how lucky we have been." As she left for her Wyoming trip then, she saw him on the bed "with the wires of an electrocardiogram machine attached to his body. I am glad I am a controlled person, and I do not believe there was a flicker on my face of what was going on in my mind" as she talked with others about her travel plans.[10]

As the months passed, Lady Bird Johnson dropped occasional hints that she and her husband might not be in Washington after January 1969. Sharon Francis caught one of these indications in October 1966, when she sensed that the First Lady was thinking in terms of only two more years in the White House. In May 1967, Mrs. Johnson entered in her diary her feelings regarding another four years. "I do not know whether we can endure another four-year term in the Presidency," and she contemplated another presidential campaign "like an open-ended stay in a concentration camp." She had believed that Lyndon "was of the same mind," but now she was not sure. So she talked about the matter with

Abe Fortas, and asked him about her sense that Lyndon Johnson, like Harry Truman in 1952, should announce his withdrawal from the presidential race in March 1968. Fortas said that a withdrawal should occur only if the war in Vietnam had improved by that date. After weighing the alternatives yet again, Mrs. Johnson wrote: "I cannot control the outcome, though I will have some effect on it. And it will not, I hope, be decided until next March."[11]

The pace of the decision making about withdrawal soon quickened, and in the summer of 1967 the Johnsons made their joint judgment not to run again. They then "convinced" John Connally of their intention. In early September the president and the First Lady met with Connally and Jake Pickle to discuss the exact timing of the announcement. Connally argued that it should come at an early date, even perhaps in the following month. As the three men talked, Mrs. Johnson, "in little sausages" (curlers), voiced her fear that "if Lyndon were back in office for a four-year stretch—beginning when he was sixty years old—bad health might overtake him, an attack, though something not completely incapacitating, and he might find himself straining to be the sort of a President he wanted to be—to put in the eighteen hours a day—and unable to draw enough vitality from the once bottomless well of his energy. A physical or mental incapacitation would be unbearably painful for him to recognize, and for me to watch."[12]

They decided, later in September, not to make the announcement at a Democratic dinner in October. Lady Bird Johnson spoke with Dr. Willis Hurst, a cardiologist who had treated the president. He informed her that Lyndon Johnson was "running on marginal energy—that he was bone tired." That evening, 4/5 October 1967, she and her husband went to bed late, arose early, and then went over the possible timing of an announcement again. "Our mood was bleak and dispirited, and no answers came."[13]

During the remaining months of 1967 the First Lady made her speeches at Williams and Yale that drew the attention of anti-Vietnam demonstrators. In the middle of October she talked with another doctor, James Cain, about whether her husband could survive another term. She did not know if she "could endure having Lyndon face the sort of trial that President Wilson did—that is, to be in office, to be incapacitated, or reduced to half his mental and physical abilities while still being President. I think that would be the most unbearable tragedy that could happen to him." Cain agreed that President Johnson had aged, but could not say that he would not survive another term.[14]

The question of withdrawal remained in her mind and yet was not fully resolved as the end of 1967 approached. On December 5 she had

tea with Stewart Udall, and they talked about conservation and beautification. Udall said to her: "We have raised our sights. We have set our national goals to have a clean country." Much remained to be done, and
the Committee for a More Beautiful Capital would face reduced federal
funds to support its work. Four days later, Lynda Johnson married Charles
Robb in a White House ceremony. The next day, Sunday, 10 October,
the First Lady stayed in her room and read the letters that Lyndon
Johnson had written to her in 1934. Early the next morning she went
over the letters that she had sent to him during the same period. "I
felt that I was slipping back in time to the fall of 1934," and she recalled
"the excitement of Lyndon mounting with every letter." The journey
to Washington that she had begun in November 1934 was now nearing
its end.[15]

In early January the Johnsons talked again with the John Connallys
about the decision to withdraw. Connally himself had already announced
that he would not run again for governor of Texas in 1968. He informed
Lyndon Johnson that "you ought to run only if you look forward to
being President again—only if you *want* to do it." The questions that
had been dogging Lady Bird Johnson, mindful of her husband's uncertain health, surfaced again in her mind. "Suppose he runs and wins?
Would he be able to carry the load in a way that he would be proud
of and that the country deserves?" The discussion ended indecisively.
"Who knows, who knows," she wrote, "and so we went round and
round on the same hot griddle, finding no cool oasis, no definite time
for an acceptable exit."[16]

They had talked about the wisdom of making the announcement when
the president delivered the State of the Union message on January 17.
If he decided to do that, the statement would come at the end of his
remarks. During that cold afternoon, Lady Bird Johnson went with
Sharon Francis, Laurance Rockefeller, and Brooke Astor to visit Buchanan
School, and then her committee assembled in the Red Room of the
White House for its first meeting of the year. They talked about
maintenance, money, and trees for the city. Later the First Lady had
a moment with her husband. "Well, what do you think?" he asked;
"What shall I do?" She replied that their daughters were divided; as for
herself, she said: "Me—I don't know. I have said it all before. I can't
tell you what to do." In part because an announcement would have
undercut his legislative program, President Johnson did not use the statement and the withdrawal moment was again deferred.[17]

On the following day, Lady Bird Johnson had scheduled the first
Women Doers Luncheon of 1968 on the general topic of crime in the
streets. She had been thinking about the subject for some time, and the

Lady Bird Johnson with Sharon Francis, Brooke Astor, Laurance Rockefeller, and two local residents at Buchanan School construction in Washington, D.C., 17 January 1968.

occasion brought together about fifty women who were active in anti-crime causes in their home areas. One of the guests was the black actress and singer Eartha Kitt, who had been recommended to Liz Carpenter by an Illinois congressman and to Sharon Francis by the Department of Justice. Kitt's popularity had waned since her theatrical debut in the early 1950s and a series of hit records including "Santa Baby" and "C'est si bon." She had, however, testified on behalf of the administration's anticrime bill. According to the checks that Liz Carpenter had made, Kitt was also not identified with any anti-Vietnam protest.[18]

After the First Lady made her prepared remarks, several women spoke to the group about what they had done to curb crime. Midway through the meeting, Lyndon Johnson came in. As he left, he and Kitt exchanged comments about crime, day care, and Social Security. Alert now to Kitt's mood, Mrs. Johnson watched as "she smoldered and smoked." Liz Carpenter later believed that the actress did not eat anything but may have had something to drink. When the question period began, Kitt was one of those who were recognized, and she started with remarks that lasted for about five minutes, as Sharon Francis recalled. Kitt began: "We send the best of this country off to be shot and maimed. They rebel in the streets. They take pot and they will get high. They don't want to go to school, because they are going to be snatched from their mothers to be shot in Vietnam."[19]

Lady Bird Johnson kept her eyes on Eartha Kitt, matching her "stare for stare." The actress repeated herself several times, and then came to her conclusion: "You are a mother, too, although you have had daughters and not sons. I am a mother and I know the feeling of having a baby come out of my guts. I have a baby and then you send him off to war. No wonder the kids rebel and take pot. And, Mrs. Johnson, in case you don't understand the lingo that's marijuana!"

As she heard Kitt's impassioned remarks, the First Lady experienced what she remembered as a "surge of adrenalin into the blood, knowing that you are going to answer, that you've *got* to answer, that you *want* to answer, and at the same time somewhere in the back of your mind a voice that says, 'Be calm, be dignified.' " Lady Bird Johnson recalled that when Kitt paused for a moment, Mrs. Richard Hughes, wife of the governor of New Jersey, spoke out in defense of the war and assailed Kitt's message. The First Lady then said, in a trembling voice but without the tears in her eyes that the press reported: "Because there is a war on . . . and I pray that there will be a just and honest peace—that still doesn't give us a free ticket not to try to work for better things—against crime in the streets, and for better education and better health for our people." Eartha Kitt's memory had Mrs. Johnson saying only: "Miss Kitt, just because there's a war going on doesn't mean that we cannot be civilized." The First Lady's diary indicates that she concluded by saying: "I cannot identify as much as I should. I have not lived the background that you have, nor can I speak as passionately or as well, but we must keep our eyes and our hearts and our energies fixed on constructive areas and try to do something that will make this a happier, better-educated land."[20]

The room was filled with applause as Mrs. Johnson finished. By late afternoon the episode with Kitt was on the national news services. The singer told *Newsweek* that "if Mrs. Johnson was embarrassed, that's her problem." Kitt's career declined over the next ten years because, she believed, of governmental probes into her actions. President Johnson was sent a file that the CIA had assembled on her in the 1950s, but there was no other official response to the incident. The White House received some thirty-five thousand letters about the confrontation, and Liz Carpenter later concluded that "perhaps Miss Kitt's behavior was a blessing in disguise," because it attracted public attention to the First Lady's concerns about crime. The case also revealed the degree to which Vietnam had polarized the nation in the winter of 1968.[21]

Events crowded in on each other in the two and a half months after the luncheon with Kitt. North Korea seized the *Pueblo,* the North Viet-namese and the Viet Cong began the Tet offensive, and the number of political challengers to Lyndon Johnson within the Democratic party grew as Eugene J. McCarthy and Robert F. Kennedy entered primaries and sought convention delegates. In her diary entries, Lady Bird Johnson came back again and again to the state of her husband's health and to his fatigue under the burdens of office. On March 10 she noted: "Those sties are coming back on Lyndon's eyes. First one and then the other, red and swollen and painful." Three weeks later, on the weekend of 31 March 1968, they had come to the brink of a withdrawal statement.[22]

On that Sunday evening, Lyndon Johnson was to make a televised speech about the Vietnam War. In the course of going over the text, he showed his wife and their friends Arthur and Mathilde Krim his state-ment of withdrawal at the end of his remarks. They had "talked about this over and over, and hour after hour, but somehow we all acted and felt stunned." Mrs. Johnson asked herself: "And I, what did I feel? . . . so uncertain of the future that I would not dare to try to persuade him one way or the other." As she weighed the desire to run and thus seek vindication or to withdraw and be free, she recalled her husband's fre-quent comment: "I do not believe I can unite this country." How much the president's declining political fortunes were weighed in the balance with his health she did not say. As the moment of the speech neared, "I felt as if I ought to do *something.* I must *do* something—but what? And how did I dare to do anything, with the decision so momentous, one I could by no means implement, or take the responsibility for mak-ing turn out right."[23]

The speech was made, including the withdrawal statement, at 9 o'clock that evening. "Remember—pacing and drama," she said to her husband just before he began. The moments afterward were for her "a great blur of confusion," and then she met with friends on the second floor. "Nearly everybody just looked staggered and struck silent—and then the phones began to ring." Later, for the reporters, Lady Bird Johnson issued a state-ment herself: "We have done a lot; there's a lot left to do in the remain-ing months; maybe this is the only way to get it done." The next day, in a meeting with her staff, she told them that "she hoped to make these next ten months rich and productive ones, dividing her time about half and half between, she used the word environmental quality rather than beautification, and the Johnson Library." Then the group cried a little and spoke about the days ahead.[24]

During her last ten months, Lady Bird Johnson pushed forward with her beautification agenda. In late May, her media advisor, Simone Poulain, said to a friend: "We are almost as busy as before the President announced

Lady Bird Johnson and Liz Carpenter on 19 May 1968.

his big decision. Mrs. Johnson is extremely well admired for her efforts in improving the environment—invitations pour in from all areas of the country." In addition to the April trip to Texas, Mrs. Johnson went first to Connecticut and then on a Discover America tour on the Hudson River in mid May. At the end of the month she visited Phoenix, Arizona, dedicated Camelback Mountain along with Barry Goldwater, and noted "the depth of concern which people everywhere are showing about our environment."[25]

One of her last formal policy statements about the environment came in late June, when she delivered the B. Y. Morrison Memorial Lecture at the annual convention of the American Institute of Architects. She spoke about a "new conservation" in architecture that had "a concern for the total environment—not just the individual building, but the entire community." Her listeners should try to solve such city blights as "unsightly shopping centers" and "the ugly ragged city fringes to metropolis." Her creed came near the end: "The nature we are concerned with, ultimately, is *human* nature. That is the point of the beautification movement—and that, finally, is the point of architecture."[26]

Lady Bird Johnson took particular pleasure in one of the concluding episodes of her husband's conservation policies. On 15 July 1968 the president signed a law that amended the Land and Water Conservation Fund, which had been created in 1964. "The measure that we have come here today to sign," said Lyndon Johnson, "will enlarge the fund—as I requested—with revenues from mineral leases in the outer continental shelf." These oil and gas revenues doubled the annual income of the fund to $200 million. Melville B. Grosvenor of the National Geographic Society called it "an ingenious way of paying for" the wilderness and park acquisitions that would follow the Johnson years. Sixteen years later, Lady Bird Johnson believed that this "little-known" change in the funding for the wilderness buttressed the claims that she and her husband could legitimately make as forerunners of the environmental movement of the 1970s.[27]

She had many other reasons for pride in what she and her husband had accomplished. During the years of Johnson's presidency, nearly three hundred laws relating to some aspect of the environment were signed, and as Martin Melosi has noted, between $12 billion and $13 billion in funds were earmarked for these programs. Lyndon Johnson had led the way by obtaining more environmental legislation than any previous president. In 1968, Stewart Udall told the Johnsons that their contribution went beyond the legislative record: the changes that they had wrought in pursuing the New Conservation would affect values and attitudes about the way that people saw the environment, and this would have a long-range impact on the history of the nation.[28]

On 26 July 1968, Lady Bird Johnson attended an informal White House ceremony at which the president signed an appropriations bill for the Department of the Interior. He gave her a felt board on which were mounted the pens that he had used in signing some fifty laws relating to conservation and beautification during his term of office. Attached to the board was a plaque that read: "To Lady Bird, who has inspired me and millions of Americans to try to preserve our land and beautify our nation. With love from Lyndon." Secretary Udall received a similar present, with a plaque that complimented him for "devotion to preserving the beauties of nature for all mankind."[29]

As the summer of 1968 progressed, with the fights over highway beautification, the Three Sisters Bridge, and other conservation issues, Lady Bird Johnson looked to the completion of those aspects of her beautification work in Washington that could be brought to a conclusion before 20 January 1969. She told Nash Castro on July 11 that she hoped that Walt Whitman Park could be started before they left Washington, and together they went over the other projects in the city that were as yet undone. "I think it behooves us to exert every effort to get them well underway between now and January," Castro informed his superiors. He also suggested that "before the President and Mrs. Johnson leave, we rename Columbia Island after the First Lady." Two weeks later, Mrs. Johnson told Castro that his presence in Washington, along with that of George Hartzog, had convinced her that "her beautification aims will not come to a standstill."[30]

To ensure that her work would be carried on, she appears to have asked the White House staff to explore the possibility of giving her committee a more permanent form before the administration ended. Matthew Nimetz, after talking with Carolyn Fortas, Sharon Francis, Walter Washington, and Sam Hughes, sent Joseph Califano a memorandum about the First Lady's work. In early September, Mrs. Johnson also had Nash Castro look into the question, and he spoke with Mary Lasker, Laurance Rockefeller, and Stewart Udall. By the end of the month, Califano had reached the conclusion that there was no feasible way to give what Mrs. Johnson had done an enduring institutional basis and at the same time to carry out her wish not to "try to bind the next First Lady."

One option was an executive order to make the committee permanent and "make it more likely that the next First Lady will devote time and attention to this area." Presidential action of this kind would also be "recognition" and "added encouragement" for the committee members to keep functioning after the Johnsons had departed. The problem was, of course, that the order would be seen as an effort "by the outgoing Administration" to commit Mrs. Johnson's successor to her campaign and therefore "might be resented." As far as Nimetz could learn, moreover, "the First Lady has never been given official duties by law or executive order, and this would be a break with tradition." In any case, the woman who came after Lady Bird Johnson would determine for herself what she would do as the wife of the president. In his memo to Lady Bird Johnson, Califano concluded that neither an executive order nor making the committee responsible to Mayor Walter Washington would be appropriate. Mrs. Johnson's unwillingness to impose beautification on the next First Lady would remain a consistent theme of her last days in the White House.[31]

Her concern for the substance of her program did not abate. Her interest in the quality of personnel for the advisory committees that related to beautification, historic preservation, and the arts was still strong, and she played a role in appointments to these panels in the autumn of 1968. She also told Carolyn Fortas that she would serve as the honorary chairman of the Society for a More Beautiful National Capital after 20 January

President and Mrs. Johnson with Elizabeth and James Rowe, 29 February 1968.

1969. And she lent her prestige and fame to publications that promoted environmental causes. Writing to the editor of *Reader's Digest* about one of their books, *Our Amazing World of Nature,* she called the volume timely because "as never before in our history has there been such a widespread effort to preserve wild places, to depollute our environment, and to build anew with better ecological sensitivity. Our private passions for imbibing nature have become a crescendo of civic action in conservation."[32]

The key events of these final months would be the meetings of her committee in October, November, and December. As the preparations for the session on October 2 were winding up, Nash Castro told George

Hartzog that "the First Lady has no inkling whatsoever of our plan" to change the name of Columbia Island. She was preoccupied with other thoughts on that busy day. The long struggle to confirm Abe Fortas as chief justice ended in failure, but the Johnsons had the consolation of seeing four conservation measures signed into law on that day. One bill established the North Cascades National Park in Washington State, another created a network of trails in urban and rural areas, and a third set up the National Wild and Scenic Rivers System. Most important of all, there was the law that established the Redwoods Park in California. In his signing statement, President Johnson called his wife an "enthusiastic, tenacious, pugnacious, persistent advocate of conservation every hour in this house." After a luncheon with Laurance Rockefeller, the First Lady and her committee went out to dedicate the Hobart Community Parks and then heard reports on what had been accomplished in Washington during the preceding summer.[33]

In the ensuing month, Jacqueline Kennedy married Aristotle Onassis, an event that left Lady Bird Johnson "strangely freer. No shadow walks beside me down the halls of the White House or here at Camp David." A few days later, her daughter Lynda had her first child. Then Richard Nixon defeated Hubert Humphrey in the presidential election. On 11 November 1968 the president-elect and his wife called on the Johnsons to initiate the process of transition and departure.[34]

It was snowing in Washington on November 12 when Lady Bird Johnson's committee met at the Department of the Interior's auditorium. There were gifts: from the Inaugural Committee, 220 dogwood trees; from the Society for a More Beautiful National Capital, 1 million daffodils, the gift of Mary Lasker; the society and the Park Service, 2,500 dogwoods; and more than a mile of trails through the city. After Mrs. Johnson had spoken, Stewart Udall made the special announcement that Columbia Island in the Potomac River was being renamed Lady Bird Johnson Park. "I was stunned," the First Lady recalled, "but, it can't be denied, pleased that they would want to do this for me." Udall disclosed as well that she had agreed to serve on the National Park Service's Advisory Board in 1969. After they had viewed Columbia Island in the late afternoon and the committee meeting had resumed at a dinner session, Laurance Rockefeller showed her a watercolor of where, on the grounds of the LBJ Library, the committee would sponsor "a high place under the live oak trees, beautifully landscaped, with benches for quiet contemplation." The whole occasion, Mrs. Johnson wrote in her diary, had both "a warm feeling of camaradarie" and a "slightly mournful feeling that the end of our beautification effort—together, at least—was about to take place."[35]

Lady Bird Johnson receiving a plaque from Laurance Rockefeller on behalf of the National Recreation and Park Association, 12 November 1968.

There were still beautification events to be held at the White House. On the following day, Lady Bird Johnson held a luncheon for conservation leaders. "The language of conservation is for me," she said in greeting them, "a language of love." All of them had "helped that word become a more vital part of the political language." One of the two main speakers was Eric Sevareid of CBS News. He said of his hostess that "she has done nothing wrong and so much right, including the stimulation of a new, popular consciousness about the precious American land, a renewed awareness that our psyches are not apt to be well ordered if their physical setting is ordered badly." Paraphrasing Alice Roosevelt Longworth, Sevareid argued that "the plain fact is that there has never been a First Lady to equal Mrs. Johnson."[36]

Sevareid's note of praise echoed through the press analysis of what Lady Bird Johnson had done, which appeared at the end of 1968. On her last beautification trip in late November in the California redwoods, the First Lady was joined by Shana Alexander, who wrote: "Lady Bird in her scarlet coat looked like a jaunty red cardinal." Reviewing a diary of the travels that Mrs. Johnson had made during the preceding five years, Alexander described the individual acts of the First Lady as "modest and rather colorless, like Lady Bird herself." But the forty-seven trips that the "very thick notebook" documented were "in the aggregate a heroic achievement." Alexander "began to sense how much more Mrs. Johnson leaves behind her than daffodils coast to coast. Quite possibly she is the best First Lady we have ever had."[37]

The editors of *Christian Century* reached a similar conclusion: they credited Lady Bird Johnson with being "an inspirer of many movements to save our natural environment." She had, wrote Selwa Roosevelt, "accomplished more with less controversy than any First Lady in history." Mrs. Johnson's "gentler activities," said *U.S. News and World Report,* "are ending in an outburst of public praise." Even the conservative columnist James J. Kilpatrick, who was never friendly to the record of the Johnson administration, wrote a tribute to what Mrs. Johnson had done.[38]

Right to the end of her time in Washington, the First Lady spread the beautification creed. Sharon Francis helped her to plan a meeting on December 9 with trainee engineers in the highway-construction program. It was designed to be "a small shot-in-the-arm—a sort of planting of a last seed on my part for beautification in years to come, because some responsibility for it would rest in the hands of these young engineers." She asked them questions, such as "How do you really take the wishes of the people into account?" and "Will further public hearings such as the 1960 [1968?] Highway Act is providing for bring about participation?" The session went well, and she left convinced that the young men were "aware of the added dimensions of beauty and democracy that ought to be brought to the highway programs of the country."[39]

With the Nixon administration's personnel coming into focus during the transition, the question again arose about seeking the formal continuation of the First Lady's committee. Liz Carpenter suggested that Mrs. Johnson might write a letter to Russell Train, who was slated to become undersecretary of the Interior Department. Train had been involved with Mrs. Johnson's committee through the Conservation Foundation, and Carpenter thought he would be sympathetic to the idea of carrying on the panel. Lady Bird Johnson said to Carpenter: "If you want to have conversations with Judge Train, of course that's all right. But I never want there to be anything on paper that we were instigating any self-perpetuation."[40]

The last meeting of the committee itself was held on 17 December 1968. The First Lady, Mary Lasker, and the others began at the dedication of the two fountains on the Ellipse, donated by Enid Haupt, then they took in Lasker's fountain jet at Hains Point, and they ended back at the site of the fountains that Rose Zalles was purchasing for the Ellipse. They went on to the Yellow Oval Room in the White House, where Mrs. Johnson distributed copies of the committee's "Report to the President." Secretary Udall made some remarks, and then he presented the First Lady with a trowel that she had used at her first planting in March 1965. Plaques identified when the trowel had been used in other beautification ceremonies. President Johnson came in at that point, thanked the members "for returning my wife to me!" and told them that they "brought out the best in people." Nash Castro had the sense as the meeting ended "that this great First Lady had earned many pages in the history of the great American drama."[41]

The echoes of beautification continued right up until 20 January 1969. Four days before the inauguration, a ceremony was held to commemorate the issuance of four beautification stamps in honor of Mrs. Johnson's program. Postmaster General Marvin Watson praised her lavishly on that occasion, but Sharon Francis summed it up best when she said to Lady Bird Johnson: "Well, you made us all better people, Mrs. Johnson." Unhappily, a dispute between the president and Udall, one of the staunchest allies of the Johnson conservation program, over proposed withdrawals of public lands cast a cloud over the final hours. On a more upbeat note, there were Medals of Freedom for her friends in the beautification cause, Laurance Rockefeller and Mary Lasker.[42]

Inauguration Day was hectic and emotional, but finally the former president and his wife were back in Texas, home again. Lady Bird Johnson went to bed after 9:00 that evening, and in her last entry in the diary that she had kept so long and so fully, her thoughts were of a poem: "I seek, to celebrate my glad release, the Tents of Silence and the Camp of Peace." As she conceded, it was not precisely "the right exit line for me because I have loved almost every day of these five years." Part of that affection for the record that she had made as First Lady no doubt arose from a deserved sense of accomplishment that she felt at the work

Lady Bird Johnson among the California redwoods, 25 November 1968.

she had done for the environment of the United States in bringing natural beauty to the nation.[43]

Even before leaving Washington, Lady Bird Johnson had planned to carry on her beautification work on a reduced scale in Texas. "I will continue to be just as interested" in conservation, she said to Washington reporters, and "I think it is quite possible that in my smaller sphere I will at the same time be of some use to conservation." She joined the garden clubs of Stonewall and Johnson City, but she "spent some months resting before taking up new programs."[44]

The most long-lasting commitment of Mrs. Johnson during the early post-presidential years was the annual award ceremony, held at the LBJ Ranch, to honor the highway-beautification programs of the Texas Highway Department. Each of the twenty-five highway districts submitted a nominee, and these would then be reduced to six finalists. In the initial stages, a single first prize was awarded. By 1980, honors were being given to three of the six finalists. The ceremonies included a barbecue luncheon, in addition to the awards themselves. Lyndon Johnson came to the first three occasions, in part, as he said in fun, to see his frugal wife give away money. Others who were associated with Lady Bird Johnson and beautification attended the annual events—Mary Lasker, Laurance Rockefeller, the television host Arthur Godfrey, and cabinet officers from the Carter administration in the late 1970s.[45]

In the introduction to *Texas: A Roadside View,* published in 1980, Lady Bird Johnson surveyed what her awards had done. She was pleased at "the protection of the fall flowers" and at the "planning, imagination, and commonsense the nominees have put to use"; she also hoped that the recognition of the highway officials would encourage in others "a growing sense of the importance of projects that save and use plant material so that we might realize the ecological benefits as well as enjoy the aesthetic results." The ceremonies became part of the ideas that later led her to create the National Wildflower Research Center.[46]

In Austin during the early 1970s, Lady Bird Johnson became identified with the Town Lake Beautification Project along the Colorado River. "My interest in conservation—beautification continues unabating," she wrote Stewart Udall in April 1972, "though now on a very little stage—my current project is the Riverfront in Austin—a hike and bike trail, *many* blooming trees (redbud, crepe myrtle, etc.)." She told an interviewer in 1980 that "we spent a busy five years raising funds," and the handsome parks and extensive running trails through the heart of the city, which were filled with joggers on weekends, reflected what she had accomplished for Austin.[47]

After Lyndon Johnson died in January 1973, his widow pursued diverse business and personal interests throughout the rest of the decade. She served as a regent for the University of Texas, managed the family's extensive television and radio interests, and spent time with the growing families of her daughters. She quietly supported Democratic candidates with campaign contributions, and she spoke out on occasion when the national highway beautification program was under attack. Her own sense of identification with feminism also emerged in the middle of the 1970s.[48]

As Lady Bird Johnson approached her seventieth birthday in 1982, she chose to commit herself to a new project that grew directly out of her own lifelong interest in wild flowers and the beautification experience of the presidential years. On her birthday, 22 December 1982, she announced that for her "last hurrah" she was donating $125,000 and sixty acres east of Austin to establish the National Wildflower Research Center. It was her way, she told reporters, of "paying rent for the space I have taken up in this highly interesting world." Matching gifts from Laurance Rockefeller and others brought the center an initial endowment of $700,000 and enabled it to launch its work over the next year.[49]

By 1986 the Wildflower Center had expanded to a national membership of seventy-five hundred, was the cosponsor of symposia on wildflower research, and had launched projects around the nation on the uses and the scientific value of wild flowers. The center, under the direction of David Northington, also conducted its own inquiries into wild flowers in its 300,000 feet of research space. With highway departments in Texas and other states, it examined how the use of roadside wild flowers might reduce mowing and maintenance costs by millions of dollars per year. "Wildflowers are the stuff of my heart," Lady Bird Johnson said, and the success of the center attested to the endurance of her relationship with the land that had begun decades earlier in East Texas.[50]

During the years since her husband's presidency, the work that Lady Bird Johnson did as First Lady between 1963 and 1969 has not come into sharp focus. Aware that some historians like to portray her as a benign contrast to her husband's darker impulses, she has resisted taking credit for what she had done, lest she seem to be downgrading Lyndon's record. The Johnson Library, responding to the understandable interest in what the president had accomplished, opened his papers in the late 1970s but did not begin to process his wife's Social Files until the mid 1980s. The upsurge of interest in women's history did not awaken a fascination with First Ladies, who were seen, except for Eleanor Roosevelt, as unlikely embodiments of feminist aspirations. As a result, Lady Bird Johnson remained within the shadows of her husband's reputation and historical standing.

Interpretations of what Lady Bird Johnson had achieved tended then to rely on the memoirs of White House staff members and of those in the press corps who had covered her activities. These accounts assigned a large role to Liz Carpenter and Bess Abell in shaping the original beautification program and saw the initiative as a public-relations effort to imitate what Jacqueline Kennedy had done for the renovation of the White House. From the beginning, these writers also raised the issue of how important beautification was in terms of policy. Nancy Dickerson said that the program had a serious purpose, but she believed that "beautification was probably the only subject that LBJ would have let her [Mrs. Johnson] handle without jealousy."[51]

Even during those years there were more positive opinions. Nathaniel Owings wrote in 1969 that "by stressing the social and economic value of beauty," Lady Bird Johnson had "done much to crystallize a positive national point of view toward our environment." Eric Goldman's analytic memoir of the Johnson presidency did not grasp all that Mrs. Johnson had tried to do, but he recognized that she had imparted to the institution of First Lady, in her beautification endeavors, "such organization and so firm a sense of purpose and usefulness that it is doubtful whether it will ever completely return to its traditional aimlessness."[52]

During the first half of the 1980s, Lady Bird Johnson's contributions to environmental issues received a greater recognition. In the spring of 1984, the Johnson Library held a conference to reassess natural beauty and "the nation's unfinished environmental agenda" two decades after the Johnsons had begun their campaign. Speakers such as Wolf Von Eckardt and Henry Diamond looked back at their participation with Lady Bird Johnson in the 1960s. The White House Conference of 1965, Diamond told the audience, was "a bridge from the traditional conservation to the new environmentalism and the start of something grand." In his conclusion, Diamond said: "We need that old time conservationist religion. It was good enough for Lady Bird and Lyndon, and it's good enough for you and me."[53]

Lady Bird Johnson had accomplished much in the 1960s, and her commitment to the beautification of the environment was of lasting importance. The most significant legislative achievement was the Highway Beautification Act of 1965. Twenty years after its adoption, the law had few friends outside of the billboard industry, and congressional efforts to amend it seem likely to prevail in the immediate future. For all the flaws in its drafting, enforcement, and subsequent funding, the law did draw national attention to the problem of junkyards and outdoor advertising. Lady Bird Johnson's identification with this legislation has given the issue of billboard control a visibility and a notoriety that has kept it in the public spotlight among environmental concerns. During her

White House years and since, she has made Americans conscious of the appearance of their roadsides and has spoken out for a standard of regulation that enhances natural beauty.

The other primary focus of Lady Bird Johnson's work was Washington, D.C. The most successful aspect of that campaign was the improved state of the capital city's monuments, parks, and public vistas. The Society for a More Beautiful National Capital and the First Lady's committee represented a creative fusion of private and voluntary resources with governmental agencies to reshape the way that Washington looked. In twenty years the city has maintained and extended many of the plantings and projects that Lady Bird Johnson started. The more difficult and in some ways more ambitious parts of her program—which included the inner-city neighborhoods, the Buchanan School, and the initiatives of Lawrence Halprin—did not have the same enduring impact. They stand as reminders that Lady Bird Johnson saw beautification as a way of addressing the human needs of all sections of the city's population.

Mrs. Johnson's most important legacy was less tangible but no less vital. Having a First Lady who said that the Grand Canyon should be preserved and the redwoods should not be cut down, that parks should be saved and freeways built with urban residents in mind, meant that environmental issues received a statement of legitimacy and value from the White House and the presidency. The generation of Americans who joined Lady Bird Johnson in beautifying the United States during the 1960s was absorbing lessons about the worth of wild places, the need for a balance between humanity and nature, and the power of government to protect natural beauty; and these lessons shaped attitudes and policies during the ensuing decades. As much a celebrity as any other wife of a president, Lady Bird Johnson used her fame to promote the cause that she wished to have identified as the hallmark of her years in Washington.

Mrs. Johnson also became a central figure in the shift from the older style of conservation to the ecological spirit of the 1970s. Her influence on Lyndon Johnson and her interaction with Stewart Udall imparted to the environmental policies of the Johnson years a special tone that spoke to the emerging public concern about the deteriorating quality of the American landscape and the natural setting. She understood what Udall believed the New Conservation of the Johnson years stood for: namely, "the interrelation of every living thing to every other living thing and the relationship of all living things to their environment." In the process she became, as Udall once put it, a second secretary of the interior in the White House. The Johnson presidency laid the foundation for the environmentalism that followed, and Lady Bird Johnson was a powerful and effective champion of these values. The result was an instilling of conservation and ecological ideas in the national mind with a skill and adroitness that put Lady Bird Johnson in the front rank among modern First Ladies and women in American politics.[54]

Mrs. Johnson also represented a culmination of the long tradition of women who were involved in the effort to preserve and enhance the natural environment. There is a direct lineage from the antibillboard campaigns and the City Beautiful movement of the early twentieth century to the Committee for a More Beautiful Capital, to the labors of Mary Lasker, Brooke Astor, Sharon Francis, and Cynthia Wilson, and to the national attention that Lady Bird Johnson stimulated. She deserves a place with Rachel Carson among the leaders of the impressive company of American women who have imparted first to conservation and later to environmentalism more of its energy and substance than men have recognized.

In December 1968, Lady Bird Johnson wrote in her diary: "I came very late and timorously to the uses of power." The tone of self-deprecation was characteristic. It was also wrong. Lady Bird Johnson had taken the amorphous and ill-defined possibilities of the institution of First Lady and had stretched them into a significant campaign for an important national priority. The little girl on Caddo Lake had come far from the flowers and fields of East Texas, but she had never lost the sense of kinship with the land and its natural beauty that she had felt in her youth. When her opportunity came to be an advocate for the preservation and perpetuation of the nation's environment, she seized it with dedication, commitment, and lasting results. She fulfilled her obligation "to keep the beauty of the landscape as we remember it in our youth . . . and to leave this splendor for our grandchildren."[55] She had also amply paid her rent for the space that she had occupied in the world, and she had enriched the history of the United States with her presence.

Bibliographical Essay

The major documentary sources for this study are located in the collections of the Lyndon B. Johnson Presidential Library in Austin, Texas. Though the personal papers of Lady Bird Johnson and the original entries for her White House diary are still in her custody, there is an abundance of information relating to her life and activities at the LBJ Library, amidst the papers and files about her husband. As scholars work through this immense array of primary documentation, new findings about Mrs. Johnson are made regularly. The comments that follow are meant to describe the holdings that proved to be most helpful for this book. A convenient general guide to the Lyndon B. Johnson Papers, the personal papers in the library, and the records of other governmental agencies is "Historical Materials in the Lyndon B. Johnson Library," in *Exploring The Johnson Years,* edited by Robert A. Divine (Austin: University of Texas Press, 1982; reprinted as *The Johnson Years, Volume One: Foreign Policy, the Great Society, and the White House* [Lawrence: University Press of Kansas, 1987]), pp. 251–65.

For a consideration of Lady Bird Johnson's work on beautification the place to start is with the White House Social Files (WHSF) series and the Beautification Files (BF) contained therein, twenty-six boxes in all, with documentary materials located in boxes 1–17. The Beautification Files consist of the records of the First Lady's Committee for a More Beautiful Capital, the various projects in Washington that the First Lady sponsored, and her involvement with national environmental issues, such as highway beautification. All of the records in this file are now open for researchers.

Liz Carpenter maintained her correspondence records in the White House; these are also in the White House Social Files as Liz Carpenter's Alphabetical File (LCAF). Boxes 10–15 have Carpenter's letters on beautification, which I examined thoroughly. I looked at other parts of this file, which consists of 129 boxes in all, for specific items. There is another series of Carpenter material called Liz Carpenter's Subject File (LCSF), relating to the trips and events that Lady Bird Johnson took part in. This file totals 88 boxes. I reviewed specific occasions of importance in this series, and what these files contained often proved to be both important and illuminating. Any of Carpenter's files that are not now open can be reviewed for research.

247

Finally, in the White House Social Files are the general Alphabetical Files. There are 2,142 manuscript boxes in this collection, and they are being reviewed and processed as research requests are made. Such a review of each box, within the procedures of the Johnson Library and the National Archives, takes time, especially when the staff at the library must respond to comparable requests for other subjects and other series in the vast holdings of the Johnson Papers. At a time of budget constraints and staff cutbacks, the library's dedicated personnel do their best to meet all inquiries, but inevitably, choices have to be made in allocating time and energy to the processing of collections. That is why only about one hundred or so boxes are now open for general research.

What has already been processed in the Alphabetical Files is most enlightening about Mrs. Johnson's activities. The files for such friends of the First Lady as Brooke Astor, Orville and Jane Freeman, Mary Lasker, Laurance Rockefeller, James and Elizabeth Rowe, Polly Shackleton, Stewart Udall, and Walter Washington have been opened. Such subjects as beautification, billboards, road signs, the Grand Canyon, the California redwoods, and Washington, D.C., have been reviewed and made available; and by the time this book appears, numerous other topics will have been made ready for research. The Alphabetical Files seem to contain much of Lady Bird Johnson's personal correspondence in the files that I have seen, and the whole series, when ready, should be a major source for her biographer. It will also provide instructive insights into how Americans viewed the First Lady and her work during the 1960s.

On Lady Bird Johnson's part in her husband's life before the presidency, several sections of the Johnson Papers are rich sources of data. The Lyndon B. Johnson Archives (LBJA) for 1931–68, consisting of valuable materials and correspondence with historically important people, contain numerous copies of letters from Lady Bird Johnson to the individuals listed. Her letters show up most often for the months in 1942 when she was operating the congressional office and in 1955, after her husband's heart attack.

The House of Representatives Papers, 1937–49, are a significant source of information on Lady Bird Johnson during those years. For example, box 37, dealing with Personal Correspondence for 1942, contains many letters from those months when she was in charge of the Washington office. She turned up in other files relating to personal matters (box 55), in folders dealing with campaigns (box 110), and in folders marked "Miscellaneous and Personal Correspondence" (box 96). In time a careful perusal of all parts of this collection (which I did not have time to do) should disclose much more about what Lady Bird Johnson contributed to her husband's rise to prominence.

Because of the nature of this book's focus, I looked at the Senate papers only for a few specific items, and I used the LBJA materials for Mrs. Johnson's role during those years. The Vice-Presidential Papers are not yet open for research.

The original manuscript of Lady Bird Johnson's White House diary is also not yet available for research. Only one-seventh of the original has been published, and there will be useful documents in the supporting materials that the First Lady used in compiling her record of the White House years.

The well-organized White House Central Files include much on Lady Bird Johnson's activities as First Lady, but the information about her is scattered throughout a number of topics. The place to start is the President's File, PP5/ Lady Bird Johnson, which provides a general chronological record of those occasions when the First Lady's activities affected the operations of the White House and the presidency. Other categories that I looked at that proved rewarding were Arts (AR), Highways-Bridges (HI), Legislation (LE), Natural Resources (NR), Parks-Monuments (PA), Public Relations (PR), and Transportation (TN). On a selective basis, I looked at individuals in the White House Name Files (WHNF).

Files of the White House Aides were indispensable for an analysis of what Lady Bird Johnson did in regard to beautification. Among the most helpful were Douglass Cater, for highway beautification and other related issues, 1966–68; Richard N. Goodwin, on the origins of the natural-beauty campaign, 1964/65; Mike Manatos, on the legislative struggle over beautification in 1965; Harry McPherson, on all aspects of beautification, 1966–68; and Bill Moyers, a vital collection for the origins of the billboard-control effort in 1964/65. The files of other aides that I consulted as needed were those for Horace Busby, Joseph Califano, James Gaither, Robert L. Hardesty, Charles A. Horsky, John W. Macy, Jr., Matthew Nimetz, Lawrence F. O'Brien, De Vier Pierson, Irvine Sprague, and Henry H. Wilson, Jr.

Where relevant I also used the White House Diaries and the Appointment Logs of Lyndon B. Johnson; I found the Diary Backup file of most help for the questions I had.

The Johnson Library also holds manuscripts and microfilm records from the various governmental departments and agencies. The materials from the Department of Commerce, the Department of the Interior, and the Department of Transportation were the most pertinent for Lady Bird Johnson and beautification.

Former aides of Lyndon B. Johnson's, his friends, and other individuals have deposited their personal papers at the Johnson Library, and these collections proved valuable for this study. The papers of Alan S. Boyd are a rich resource for the highway-beautification program of the Johnson years, especially after Boyd became secretary of transportation. The Barefoot Sanders papers are also important for the billboard-control struggle in 1967 and 1968, when Sanders was a member of the House staff. For an understanding of what Lady Bird Johnson did in Washington, Nash Castro's papers are nearly as important as are her Beautification Files in the White House Social Files. Castro's memorandums to his superiors after his visits with Mrs. Johnson provide almost a running narrative of his collaboration with the First Lady.

The Lewis L. Gould Papers at the Johnson Library contain copies of the legal records in Harrison County about the business career of Thomas Jefferson Taylor, the estate of Minnie Patillo Taylor, and the business transactions of Claudia Taylor Johnson from 1934 to 1964. The collection also has legal records about Lyndon Johnson's personal financial dealings in the Texas Hill Country. Records about Mrs. Johnson and beautification that arose from my research on this book will be added to this collection.

The Oral History project of the Johnson Library has generated numerous memoirs that add significant information about Lady Bird Johnson's beautification campaign and other phases of her life. Of the many oral histories that I consulted, the most useful were those of Bess Abell, Liz Carpenter, Nash Castro, Sharon Francis, Elizabeth Rowe, and Stewart Udall. Interviews that I conducted with Phillip Tocker and Cynthia Wilson will become available to researchers at the library through the Oral History program.

Other libraries and private individuals have manuscript sources that were important for this research. The papers of Katie Louchheim, in the Manuscript Division of the Library of Congress, are very illuminating about the origins of Lady Bird Johnson's campaign in Washington. These papers may be consulted with Mrs. Louchheim's permission. The Nathaniel Owings Papers (LC) have some interesting items about his working relationship with the First Lady in Washington.

At the University of Oregon, Eugene, the Maurine Neuberger Papers provide the perspective of a senator who had close links to the roadside councils during the battle to control billboard advertising. The Lee Metcalf Papers at the Montana Historical Society and the John Sherman Cooper Papers at the University of Kentucky added other data about senators who favored billboard regulation.

The Stewart Udall Papers at the University of Arizona, Tucson, contain ample materials on the interaction of the First Lady with the secretary of the interior during her White House years. The Udall Papers are very valuable for all aspects of resource and conservation policies during the Johnson presidency.

In the course of an interview with Lawrence Halprin in 1984, he kindly allowed me to see and then had copies made for me of the records that bore on those aspects of his professional career regarding his participation in the effort to revitalize neighborhoods in Washington, D.C., from 1966 to 1968.

Similarly, Cynthia Wilson gave me access to her records about how Mrs. Johnson's office answered beautification mail; these items have been deposited in the Johnson Library.

The Ruth Montgomery Papers in the Texas Collection, Baylor University, are useful for the text of the interviews that Lady Bird Johnson and Lyndon Johnson gave in 1963 for Montgomery's biography of Mrs. Johnson.

Interviews with participants in Lady Bird Johnson's work and those who were affected by what she did gave me a sense of how she operated as First Lady; they sometimes added important items of factual information. Bess Abell, Liz Carpenter, Nash Castro, Sharon Francis, Lawrence Halprin, Ruth R. Johnson, Ross Netherton, Spencer Smith, Phillip Tocker, and Walter Washington graciously shared their recollections with me. In September 1984, Lady Bird Johnson also talked with me about her beautification campaign.

Because of the volume prepared by the Lyndon B. Johnson Library staff, *Lyn-*

don B. Johnson: A Bibliography (Austin: University of Texas Press, 1984), pp. 209–24, which contains an extensive listing of the published sources about Lady Bird Johnson, I have not included a formal bibliography of the sources that I used in the preparation of this volume. A second volume of the Johnson bibliography, compiled by Craig H. Roell, will appear soon; it will list even more sources about the First Lady.

Notes

Acronyms and Abbreviated Forms Used in the Notes

AF	Alphabetical File
Barker Texas History Center	Eugene C. Barker Texas History Center, University of Texas at Austin
BF	Beautification Files
Gould Papers	Lewis L. Gould Papers, Lyndon B. Johnson Library
GPO	Government Printing Office
HB	Highway Beautification
HCC	Harrison County Courthouse, Marshall, Texas
HCCR	Harrison County Court Records, Marshall, Texas
JHP	Johnson House Papers
LBJ	Lady Bird Johnson
LBJA	Lyndon B. Johnson Archives
LBJL	Lyndon B. Johnson Library, Austin, Texas
LC	Library of Congress, Washington, D.C.
LCAF	Liz Carpenter Alphabetical Files
LJ	Lyndon Baines Johnson
MC	Meetings-Conferences
MsD	Manuscript Division, Library of Congress
NR	Natural Resources
OH	Oral History. Unless otherwise indicated, oral histories are in the Lyndon B. Johnson Library
Texas Collection	Texas Collection, Baylor University, Waco, Texas
WHCF	White House Central Files
WHNF	White House Name Files
WHSF	White House Social Files

Chapter 1. Introduction: Women in Conservation

1. Garry Wills, *Reagan's America: Innocents at Home* (Garden City, N.Y.: Doubleday, 1987), p. 186; Barbara Howar, *Laughing All the Way* (New York:

Stein & Day, 1973), p. 126; Myra MacPherson, *The Power Lovers: An Intimate Look at Politicians and Their Marriages* (New York: Putnam's, 1975), p. 82. This dismissive tone reappeared in 1987 when Nancy Reagan's work as First Lady came under scrutiny. "Lady Bird Johnson got interested in the gardens of Washington," said the noted political scientist James David Barber, *Houston Chronicle,* 4 Mar. 1987.

2. Abigail McCarthy, "ER as First Lady," in *Without Precedent: The Life and Career of Eleanor Roosevelt,* ed. Joan Hoff-Wilson and Marjorie Lightman (Bloomington: Indiana University Press, 1984), pp. 220–21; June Sochen, *Movers and Shakers: American Women Thinkers and Activists, 1900–1970* (New York: Quadrangle Books, 1973), pp. 244–45; Vaughn Davis Bornet, *The Presidency of Lyndon B. Johnson* (Lawrence: University Press of Kansas, 1983), p. 137.

3. Mary I. Wood, "Civic Activities of Women's Clubs," in *Women in Public Life* (Philadelphia: Annals of the American Academy of Political and Social Science, 1914), p. 80; Imogen B. Oakley, "The More Civic Work, the Less Need of Philanthropy," *American City* 6 (June 1912): 805. Carolyn Merchant, "The Women of the Progressive Conservation Crusade," in *Environmental History: Critical Issues in Comparative Perspective,* ed. Kendall E. Bailes (Lanham, Md.: University Press of America, 1985), pp. 153–75; Marlene Stein Wortman, "Domesticating the Nineteenth-Century American City," in *Prospects: An Annual of American Cultural Studies,* vol. 3, ed. Jack Salzman (New York: Burt Franklin, 1977), pp. 531–72.

4. Suellen M. Hoy, " 'Municipal Housekeeping': The Role of Women in Improving Urban Sanitation Practices, 1880–1917," in *Pollution and Reform in American Cities, 1870–1930,* ed. Martin V. Melosi (Austin: University of Texas Press, 1980), pp. 173–98. The quotations from Hoy appear on pp. 183, 191, and 194 respectively. See also Alan S. Brown, "Caroline Bartlett Crane and Urban Reform," *Michigan History* 56 (Winter 1972): 282–301; and J. Horace McFarland to Caroline Bartlett Crane, 5 Nov. 1906, Meat Inspection Correspondence, box 22, Caroline Bartlett Crane Papers, Western Michigan University, Kalamazoo.

5. Mrs. T. J. Bowlker, "Women's Home-Making Function Applied to the Municipality," *American City* 6 (June 1912): 863; Mary Ritter Beard, *Woman's Work in Municipalities* (New York: D. Appleton, 1915), pp. 297 (last quotation), 307–8 (Levinson quotation); Mary Bronson Hiatt, "Beautifying the Ugly Things," *World's Work* 9 (Feb. 1905): 5859–68; see also Martin V. Melosi, *Garbage in the Cities: Refuse, Reform, and the Environment, 1880–1980* (College Station: Texas A&M University Press, 1981), pp. 117–24.

6. Merchant, "Women of the Progressive Conservation Crusade," pp. 163, 169. Evidence of the general interest of middle-class women in conservation can be seen in Charles Lathrop Pack to Anna J. Pennybacker, 18 Mar., 28 May, and 15 Aug. 1913, and Gifford Pinchot to Pennybacker, 14 Nov. 1913, in box 2M14, Anna J. Pennybacker Papers, Barker Texas History Center.

7. Elizabeth B. Lawton, "Progress in Roadside Legislation," *Nature Magazine,* 22 Nov. 1935, pp. 299–300; idem, "Florida behind the Billboards," ibid., May

1940, pp. 277–84; idem and Walter L. Lawton, "Pennsylvania Tries Cooperation to Solve the Roadside Problem," ibid., Jan. 1942, pp. 35–38; Roger William
Riis, "The Billboard Must Go: II," *Reader's Digest,* Nov. 1938, pp. 81–84, for
biographical data on Lawton; for Hilda Fox see Richard Westwood, "Roadside
Conference: A Report," *Nature Magazine,* Feb. 1941, p. 98.

8. Linda D. Vance, *May Mann Jennings: Florida's Genteel Activist* (Gainesville:
University Presses of Florida, 1985), pp. 127–39, 134 (1st quotation), 138 (2d
quotation).

9. Stephen Fox, *John Muir and His Legacy: The American Conservation Move-*
ment (Boston: Little, Brown, 1981), pp. 174–82, 181 (1st quotation), 344 (2d
quotation).

10. Yale Maxon to Lewis L. Gould, 16 Apr. 1984, discusses Helen Reynolds
and her background; U.S., Senate, "Control of Advertising on Interstate
Highways," *Hearing before a Subcommittee of the Committee on Public Works,* 85th
Cong., 2d sess. (Washington: GPO, 1958), pp. 10, 37; "Lady Philanthropist:
Mrs. Albert D. Lasker," *Congressional Record, Appendix,* 85th Cong., 1st sess.,
17 June 1957, p. A4753; *Beauty for America: Proceedings of the White House Con-*
ference on Natural Beauty (Washington: GPO, 1965), p. 569.

11. Rachel L. Carson, *Silent Spring* (Boston: Houghton Mifflin, 1962), p.
8; Fox, *John Muir,* p. 292.

12. Fox, *John Muir,* pp. 292–95; Paul Brooks, "Rachel Carson," in *Notable*
American Women: The Modern Period, ed. Barbara Sicherman and Carol Hurd
Green (Cambridge, Mass.: Belknap Press of Harvard University Press, 1980),
pp. 139, 140.

13. Frank Graham, Jr., in *Since Silent Spring* (Boston: Houghton Mifflin, 1970),
reviews the reaction to Carson's book in the 1960s from a friendly perspective.
Elizabeth M. Whelan, in *Toxic Terror* (Ottawa, Ill.: Jameson Books, 1985), pp.
64–67, indicates the passion that Carson's work still arouses among her critics.

14. Graham, *Since Silent Spring,* p. 50 (1st quotation); Carson, *Silent Spring,*
p. 297.

15. Fox, *John Muir,* p. 344.

16. Ibid., pp. 341, 345.

Chapter 2. From East Texas to the White House

1. Ruth Montgomery, "Selling the Nation on Beauty," *New York Journal*
American, 30 May 1965, reprinted in U.S., House of Representatives, *Congres-*
sional Record, Appendix, 89th Cong., 1st sess., 23 June 1965, p. A3287.

2. The facts of Mrs. Johnson's birth and the origins of her nickname are given
in a number of places. Nan Robertson, "Our New First Lady," *Saturday Even-*
ing Post, 8 Feb. 1964, pp. 22–23, is representative. The quotation from Antonio Taylor comes from his OH, 23 Nov. 1969, p. 5. Ruth Montgomery's
Mrs. LBJ (New York: Holt, Rinehart & Winston, 1964) was one of the first
biographies of Mrs. Johnson and is the source of much of the other writing

about her. It is based on an interview, the transcript of which is available in the Ruth Shick Montgomery Papers, Texas Collection. Quotations will be to Montgomery's biography unless the interview transcript contains more precise information.

3. Cameron McElroy and Lucille W. McElroy, OH, 11 Mar. 1981, p. 9, discussed T. J. Taylor's romantic reputation. Robertson, in "Our New First Lady," p. 23, quotes Mrs. Johnson about her father. For the comment about the relative size of T. J. Taylor and Lyndon Johnson see Emily Crow Selden, OH no. 2, 16 Jan. 1980, p. 7. T. J. Taylor's business career can be followed in part in the deed records, HCC. Some information about this phase of his life, based on photocopies made by me, has been deposited in LBJL as part of the Gould Papers. For analyses of Taylor's life that do not rest on such evidence see J. Evetts Haley, *A Texan Looks at Lyndon* (Canyon, Texas: Palo Duro Press, 1964), pp. 57–58; and Robert Caro, *The Years of Lyndon Johnson: The Path to Power* (New York: Alfred A. Knopf, 1982), pp. 294–95.

4. General portraits of Mrs. Taylor are available in Montgomery, *Mrs. LBJ*, pp. 8–9, and Robertson, "Our New First Lady," p. 22.

5. For Mrs. Taylor's interest in quail and for her other personal habits see Cameron McElroy and Lucille W. McElroy, OH, 11 Mar. 1981, pp. 3–4, 6; Dorris Powell, OH, 18 Apr. 1978, p. 8, talks about Mrs. Taylor and politics; Antonio J. Taylor, OH, 23 Nov. 1969, p. 5, discusses his memory that the family was rarely together. Haley, in *A Texan Looks at Lyndon*, p. 68, questions the accuracy of stories that Mrs. Taylor was an advocate of civil rights at this time.

6. The quotations are from the transcript of the 1963 interview with Mrs. Johnson, apparently conducted by Blake Clark, in the Montgomery Papers at Baylor University. They have been rendered in edited prose in Montgomery, *Mrs. LBJ*, p. 9. Mrs. Taylor died on 6 Sept. 1918, not 14 Sept. 1918, as Montgomery says on page 9 of her book. The date of death is given on a deed record dated 20 Nov. 1936, vol. 221, p. 183, HCCR, in Gould Papers. Mrs. Taylor seems to have died intestate, which officials at the HCC say was not at all unusual at that time.

7. The record of the guardianship that T. J. Taylor established for his three children can be followed in the Probate Minutes, HCCR; see Index to Probate Record, file 1110, p. 144. All of the documents relating to the guardianship have been copied and are available in the Gould Papers. The quotations about Effie Patillo are from Eugenia B. Lasseter, OH, 10 Mar. 1981, p. 19 (1st quotation); and Montgomery, *Mrs. LBJ*, p. 18 (2d quotation).

8. Mrs. Johnson's remarks in 1976 at the dedication of the LBJ Grove at the Lady Bird Johnson Park in Washington, D.C., are in *Congressional Record*, 94th Cong., 2d sess., 7 May 1976, extension of remarks of Congressman J. J. Pickle, p. 13033; for Caddo Lake see Mrs. Lyndon B. Johnson, "Memories of the Wilderness," *Wild Places of North America: Engagement Calendar, 1984* (Washington: National Geographic Society, 1984), p. 4; Elizabeth Janeway, "The First Lady: A Professional at Getting Things Done," *Ladies Home Journal*, Apr. 1964, p. 64.

9. For Mrs. Johnson's quotation about her nickname see Lady Bird Johnson, *A White House Diary* (New York: Holt, Rinehart & Winston, 1970), p. 74; for her memories of her high-school years see "Lady Bird Johnson's Montage of Memories," *Marshall* (Texas) *News Messenger,* 31 May 1978, copy in Gould Papers; Montgomery, *Mrs. LBJ,* pp. 13–14.

10. The quotation about her boarding-school experience is from Lady Bird Johnson, "When I Was Sixteen," *Good Housekeeping,* Oct. 1968, p. 98; Emily Crow Selden, OH no. 1, 10 Jan. 1980, pp. 4–9, describes Claudia Taylor's theatrical activities at St. Mary's, her social life, and her friends.

11. Montgomery, *Mrs. LBJ,* p. 14 (1st quotation); LBJ to Jack R. Maguire, 18 Apr. 1966, WHSF, AF, box 2022; *The 1932 Cactus: Yearbook of the University of Texas* (Austin, 1932), Alpha Phi listing, has Claudia Taylor as a pledge. Emily Crow Selden, OH no. 1, 10 Jan. 1980, pp. 19, 29, mentions the plane flight and T. J. Taylor's refusal to allow his daughter to join a sorority.

12. LBJ to Frances Davis Miller, 9 Oct. 1964, WHSF, AF, Personal Data–Education –M, box 1621; LBJ, address at University of Texas Centennial Commencement, 21 May 1983, my copy.

13. "The Doors of the World Swung Open," University of Texas Ex-Students Association, *Alcalde,* Nov. 1964, p. 21; Claudia Taylor, "Wrenn Library Shows First Edition of Keats's Poems," *Daily Texan,* 18 Jan. 1933; "The University of Texas Sports Association," *The 1933 Cactus: Yearbook of the University of Texas* (Austin, 1933), p. 134; *Daily Texan,* 20 May 1932, records Claudia Taylor's election as assistant publicity manager, in Scrapbooks, Records of University of Texas Physical Training for Women, box 3R/215, Barker Texas History Center.

14. Eugenia B. Lasseter, OH no. 1, 10 Mar. 1981, p. 5 (1st quotation); Flora Reta Schreiber, "Lady Bird Johnson's First Years of Marriage," *Woman's Day,* Dec. 1967, p. 91 (2d quotation); Emily Crow Selden, OH no. 2, 16 Jan. 1980, p. 10 (3d quotation). The nature of "dating" in the early 1930s was less structured and formal than it would be fifty years later, and not all of Taylor's five or six male friends were "serious" relationships, though two were, according to Schreiber, "Lady Bird Johnson's First Years of Marriage," p. 88. For Taylor's motives in obtaining a journalism degree see Montgomery, *Mrs. LBJ,* p. 18. *Daily Texan,* 6 June 1933 and 5 June 1934, records her two graduations.

15. The quotation is from the interview with Lady Bird Johnson, Montgomery Papers. The edited version is given in Montgomery, *Mrs. LBJ,* p. 16. Lyndon Johnson described the meeting, but not his feelings toward Claudia Taylor, in "Notes Made in Interview with the Vice President, July 3, 1963," Montgomery Papers. A copy of her personalized stationery is on display at LBJL.

16. Marie Smith, *The President's Lady: An Intimate Biography of Mrs. Lyndon B. Johnson* (New York: Random House, 1964), pp. 40–41. Pierre van Paassen and James Waterman Wise, eds., *Nazism: An Assault on Civilization* (New York: H. Smith & R. Haas, 1934). I am indebted to Louis Gomolak for calling this volume to my attention and for kindly sharing with me his work on Lyndon Johnson and Israel.

17. The famous remark is quoted as given in the interview in the Montgomery

Papers. Montgomery, *Mrs. LBJ,* p. 20, changed the second sentence to "This time you've brought home a man," and that is how it has been repeated in the biographical literature on the Johnsons.

18. The correspondence between Claudia Taylor and Lyndon Johnson in the autumn of 1934 is cited from "A National Tribute to Lady Bird Johnson on the Occasion of Her Sixty-Fifth Birthday, 11 Dec. 1977, pp. 4, 6, copy in LBJ Library; Johnson, *White House Diary,* p. 604. Taylor also had some business dealings with her father during these years, which are recorded in HCCR, Deed Records, vol. 193, 24 Oct. 1933, p. 592, vol. 195, 15 Apr. 1933, pp. 499–500, and vol. 199, 25 Oct. 1934, pp. 240–41, copies in Gould Papers. She is listed as a partner in the firm of Taylor and Howard in the 15 Apr. 1933 oil and gas lease.

19. Thomas Jefferson Taylor to Ida McKay, 23 Nov. 1934, in "LBJ as a Determined Suitor," *U.S. News and World Report,* 15 Feb. 1965, p. 11; Lasseter, OH, 10 Mar. 1981, p. 10. Lady Bird Johnson's account of her wedding is given in the interview in the Montgomery Papers.

20. Booth Mooney, *The Lyndon Johnson Story* (New York: Farrar, Straus, 1964), p. 21.

21. Schreiber, "Lady Bird Johnson's First Years of Marriage," p. 89; Barbara Klaw, comp., "Lady Bird Johnson Remembers," *American Heritage,* Dec. 1980, p. 13 (quotation).

22. The "affair" with Alice Glass is chronicled most extensively in Caro, *The Years of Lyndon Johnson: The Path to Power* (New York: Alfred A. Knopf, 1982), pp. 476–92. Ronnie Dugger, in *The Politician: The Life and Times of Lyndon Johnson* (New York: Norton, 1982), p. 254, treats the matter in somewhat more guarded terms. Paul Conkin's *Big Daddy from the Pedernales: Lyndon Baines Johnson* (Boston: Twayne, 1986), pp. 98–99, is balanced. An initial effort to pull together biographical information about Alice Glass is Dorothy Lane's "The Alice Glass Story," seminar paper, University of Texas at Austin, 1987, copy in Gould Papers. Herbert S. Parmet, in *JFK: The Presidency of John F. Kennedy* (New York: Dial Press, 1983), p. 14, alludes to the 1960 involvement.

23. Nancy Dickerson, *Among Those Present: A Reporter's View of Twenty-Five Years in Washington* (New York: Random House, 1976), pp. 138–39.

24. Merle Miller's *Lyndon: An Oral Biography* (New York: Putnam's, 1980), p. 54, contains the quotations from Mrs. Johnson. Lyndon Johnson mentioned her part in the roadside parks in "Remarks at the Unveiling of the 'Plant for a More Beautiful America' Postage Stamp," 5 Oct. 1966, *Public Papers of the Presidents of the United States: Lyndon B. Johnson, 1966,* 2 vols. (Washington, D.C.: GPO, 1967), 2:499, 500; Dugger (*Politician,* p. 186) says that the idea was Mrs. Montgomery's, but Mrs. Johnson was present when the idea was discussed.

25. Miller quotes Carroll Keach on Mrs. Johnson's role (*Lyndon,* p. 60). The other quotations are from Mrs. Johnson's remarks in Katie Louchheim, ed., *The Making of the New Deal: The Insiders Speak* (Cambridge, Mass.: Harvard University Press, 1983), p. 300. The account of Mrs. Johnson's conversation with her father is given in several places: see, e.g., Miller, *Lyndon,* p. 58; Caro, *Years of*

Lyndon Johnson, pp. 396–97. The $10,000 represented part of the $21,000 that T. J. Taylor had promised to pay his daughter as her share of her mother's estate. He was supposed to make three payments of $7,000 each in Nov. 1937, Nov. 1938, and Nov. 1939. Apparently the remaining money was not paid until 1942. See HCCR, Deed Record, 6 Nov. 1936, vol. 221, p. 183, Deed of Trust, 6 Nov. 1936, vol. 49, pp. 261–62, Deed of Trust, 12 Sept. 1939, vol. 54, pp. 409–10, Gould Papers; LBJ interview, Montgomery Papers.

26. Louchheim, *Making of the New Deal,* p. 303, for the quotations from Lady Bird Johnson; Miller quotes Virginia Durr on Mrs. Johnson as a bride (*Lyndon,* p. 65). Caro also describes her, but only alludes in passing to the miscarriages and the attempts by the Johnsons to have children (*Years of Lyndon Johnson,* p. 489).

27. Miller, *Lyndon,* p. 84; Caro refers to her home movies of the campaign (*Years of Lyndon Johnson,* p. 842). All accounts agree that Mrs. Johnson did not campaign in 1941. There is, however, a draft speech prepared for her to deliver, apparently in Brenham, Texas, during the period in May 1941 when Johnson was in the hospital. The speech is in "Miscellaneous Campaign," JHP, box 12; it refers to filling the seat of Morris Sheppard, the senator whose death precipitated the contest in 1941.

28. LBJ to Mrs. Edward M. Cape, 3 Mar. 1942, LBJA, Edward Cape file, Selected Names, box 14. The letters about this period of Mrs. Johnson's life are scattered throughout these files and the Johnson House Papers. See, e.g., LBJ to Buck Hood, 8 May 1942, JHP, Personal Correspondence, 1942, box 37. For the array of problems that she confronted see LBJ to Mayor Tom Miller, 6 Mar., 13 and 25 June 1942, LBJA, Tom Miller file, Selected Names, box 27. Her comment to a friend about her education is in LBJ to Jerry Wilkie, 15 Apr. 1942, JHP, Personal Correspondence, 1942, box 37.

29. LBJ to LJ, 9 Mar. 1942, with his marginal comments, copy in LBJL. J. J. ("Jake") Pickle to LJ, 3 Apr. 1942, JHP, Personal Correspondence, 1942, box 37. She is quoted in Miller, *Lyndon,* p. 93.

30. LBJ to Emily Crow, 12 May 1942, LBJA, Cp-Cz folder, Selected Names, box 14 (1st quotation); LBJ to R. Bonna Ridgway, 6 June 1942, LBJA, Ridgway folder, Selected Names, box 31 (2d quotation); LBJ to Ben Crider, 16 July 1942, LBJA, Ben Crider folder, Selected Names, box 16 (3d quotation); LBJ to Mrs. L. E. Jones, Jr., 11 July 1942, LBJA, L. E. Jones folder, Selected Names, box 21. For her involvement in political decisions see Charles Marsh to LJ, 21 May 1942, "Lyndon B. Johnson, 1942," Charles Marsh Papers, box 8, LBJL. I am indebted to David Humphrey for this reference.

31. Jonathan Daniels, *White House Witness: 1942–1945* (Garden City, N.Y.: Doubleday, 1975), p. 58; Dugger, *Politician,* p. 254.

32. LBJ to Mr. and Mrs. E. H. Perry, 22 Mar. 1943, LBJA, E. H. Perry Folder, Selected Names, box 29 (1st quotation); "Ways to Beautify America," *U.S. News and World Report,* 22 Feb. 1965, p. 72 (2d quotation); Louchheim, *Making of the New Deal,* p. 300 (last quotation).

33. Ken Givens, "A Brief History of the Early Years of one Austin Texas Radio

Station KTBC" (Austin, 1981; typescript in Barker Texas History Center, hereafter referred to as Givens, "Brief History"), pp. 1, 4, for the quotations from Mrs. Johnson.

34. The quotation was conveyed to me in 1964 by Jack Gould during his research on Lyndon Johnson's television interests, and I have reconfirmed its accuracy as a statement of his views at that time. The Ford Motor Co. apparently was a frequent advertiser on the radio station. Industry sources always stressed that the radio aspect of the Johnsons's media holdings was the most lucrative part of their operations. Dugger has the most complete account of the origins of the radio and television business (*Politician*, pp. 266–73). Most discussions of the topic also draw on the important articles by Louis M. Kohlmeier in the *Wall Street Journal*, 23 and 24 Mar. 1964. The Johnson Library has now acquired copies of the reports to the Federal Communications Commission by KTBC during the time when the Johnsons owned the station.

35. Speech Draft, "Future Speeches," JHP, box 54; the quotation from the FCC application appears in Dugger, *Politician*, p. 270; Mrs. Johnson's net worth is in Kohlmeier, *Wall Street Journal*, 23 Mar. 1964; Harfield Weedin comments on the station's condition in OH, 24 Feb. 1983, p. 15.

36. Givens, "Brief History," pp. 4 (1st and 2d quotations), 6 (last quotation); LJ to Willard Deason, 10 May 1943, JHP, Willard Deason file, box 143; Weedin, OH, 24 Feb. 1983, pp. 21–25.

37. The quotation about Lady Bird Johnson and a balance sheet appears in *Wall Street Journal*, 23 Mar. 1964, where the station's growth is also described. For evidence of the Johnsons' activities with the station see LJ to J. C. Kellam, 14 May 1946, JHP, J. C. Kellam file, box 55; Kellam to LBJ, 13 Feb. 1947, and Walter Jenkins to Kellam, 23 Aug. 1954, LBJA, J. C. Kellam file, Selected Names, box 22. For her comment about her years with the station see LBJ to Jesse Kellam, 6 Dec. 1963, WHSF, AF, Personal Data–S, box 1621.

38. The growth of the Johnsons's broadcasting interest can be traced in the Kohlmeier stories in the *Wall Street Journal*, 23 and 24 Mar. 1964, and in the reports of the station to the FCC, copies of which are in the LBJL. See also, for transactions involving the Texas Broadcasting Company, HCCR, Deed of Trust, 18 May 1953, vol. 94, pp. 123–25, and Deed Records, 12 Aug. 1952, vol. 405, pp. 30–33, Gould Papers.

39. LJ to Edward M. Cape, 21 Mar. 1944, JHP, Edward M. Cape file, box 142; LJ to Herman Jones, 2 July 1945, LBJA, Herman Jones file, Selected Names, box 21; Montgomery, *Mrs. LBJ*, pp. 39–40.

40. Lady Bird Johnson is quoted in Speech Draft, JHP, "Future Speeches" file, box 54. On the impact of the 1946 race see Conkin, *Big Daddy*, pp. 113–15; LBJ to T. J. Taylor, Jr., 21 June 1946, and LBJ to Commissioner of Internal Revenue, 26 June 1946, JHP, Mrs. Johnson File, box 55.

41. The newspaper quotation is from the *Wichita Falls Record News*, 24 Aug. 1948, clipping in Thomas R. Edwards Papers, LBJL; LBJ to Mrs. Arthur Becker, 31 July 1948, JHP, Arthur Becker file, box 110 (2d quotation); W. H. Wentland

to LJ, 6 Sept. 1948, JHP, W-Austin, box 91 (3d quotation); Montgomery, *Mrs. LBJ*, pp. 36–37 (last quotation).

42. Montgomery, *Mrs. LBJ*, p. 45; Miller, *Lyndon*, p. 357; for the acquisition of the ranch itself see Conkin, *Big Daddy*, pp. 122–24.

43. News story, "Texas Senator's Wife Has Varied Talents," enclosed with Jack Brooks to LJ, 24 Jan. 1954, LBJA, Jack Brooks file, Congressional, box 40; LBJ to O. F. Garrett, 21 Sept. 1955, LBJA, G folder, Selected Names, box 4 (1st and 2d quotations); LBJ to Mrs. Frank Stanton, 25 Oct. 1955, LBJA, Sm–Sz folder, Selected Names, box 33.

44. Lady Bird Johnson, as told to Jack Harrison Pollack, "Help Your Husband Guard His Heart," *Dallas Morning News,* 12 Feb. 1956, p. 7 (1st and 2d quotations); LBJ to Terrell Maverick, 28 July 1955, LBJA, Maury Maverick file, Selected Names, box 27.

45. Johnson, "Help Your Husband Guard His Heart," p. 9 (1st quotation); LBJ to Styles Bridges, 21 July 1955, LBJA, Styles Bridges file, Congressional, box 40; LBJ to Thomas G. Corcoran, 27 Aug. 1955, LBJA, Thomas G. Corcoran file, Selected Names, box 3.

46. "Mrs. Johnson Laughs at Idea of First Lady," *Washington Evening Star,* 12 Aug. 1956 (1st quotation); Mary V. R. Thayer, "Lyndon's Holding Court," *Washington Post,* 15 Aug. 1956 (2d quotation). I am indebted to Michael Gillette for calling these stories to my attention.

47. Montgomery, *Mrs. LBJ*, pp. 64–67; Gordon Langley Hall, *Lady Bird and Her Daughters* (Philadelphia: Macrae Smith, 1967), p. 154 (1st quotation); Katie Louchheim, *By the Political Sea* (Garden City, N.Y.: Doubleday, 1970), p. 222.

48. Montgomery, *Mrs. LBJ*, p. 75 (quotations); Parmet, *JFK*, p. 14; Miller, in *Lyndon*, pp. 253–54, outlines the events leading up to the 1960 Democratic convention.

49. Alfred Steinberg, *Sam Johnson's Boy* (New York: Macmillan, 1968), p. 529 (1st quotation); Philip Graham's famous memorandum is printed in Theodore H. White, *The Making of the President, 1964* (New York: Atheneum, 1965), pp. 407–15, the quotation appears on p. 414. Mrs. Johnson is quoted in Smith, *President's Lady,* p. 136.

50. The interview is published in U.S. Senate, *Congressional Record,* 86th Cong., 2d sess., 24 Aug. 1960, p. 17397.

51. Montgomery, *Mrs. LBJ*, pp. 89 (1st quotation), 83 (2d quotation); Steinberg, *Sam Johnson's Boy,* p. 540 (last quotation).

52. Montgomery, *Mrs. LBJ*, pp. 85–86; T. J. Taylor's will is in HCC, Probate Minutes, vol. 82, p. 630, copy in Gould Papers.

53. Mrs. Johnson's version of the Dallas episode is given in her interview, Montgomery Papers; Miller, *Lyndon*, pp. 270–71.

54. Smith, *President's Lady,* p. 126 (1st quotation); Miller, *Lyndon*, p. 271 (2d and 3d quotations); Montgomery, *Mrs. LBJ*, p. 101 (last quotation).

55. Hall, *Lady Bird and Her Daughters,* p. 161 (1st quotation); Montgomery, *Mrs. LBJ*, p. 143 (2d quotation); Flora R. Schreiber, "Lady Bird from Texas," *Good Housekeeping,* July 1961, pp. 48–49, 136–42.

56. Liz Carpenter, *Ruffles and Flourishes* (Garden City, N.Y.: Doubleday, 1969, 1970), pp. 28–29; Bess Abell, OH, 28 May 1969, pp. 4–7.

57. Smith, *President's Lady*, pp. 163, 171.

58. Ibid., p. 179; Blake Clark, "Lyndon Johnson's Lady Bird," *Reader's Digest*, Nov. 1963, p. 113.

59. U.S., Senate, *Congressional Record*, 88th Cong., 1st sess., 13 Dec. 1963, p. 24509; Smith, *President's Lady*, p. 185 (1st quotation); Clark, "Lyndon Johnson's Lady Bird," p. 112 (2d quotation).

60. Montgomery, *Mrs. LBJ*, pp. 141 (1st quotation), 160 (last quotation); the *Post* editorial appears in U.S., Senate, *Congressional Record*, 88th Cong., 1st sess., 12 May 1963, p. 9444.

61. Clark, "Lyndon Johnson's Lady Bird," p. 112.

62. Lady Bird Johnson, *Texas: A Roadside View* (San Antonio, Texas: Trinity University Press, 1980), p. xvi.

Chapter 3. Becoming First Lady

1. Lady Bird Johnson, *A White House Diary* (New York: Holt, Rinehart & Winston, 1970), pp. 6, 9.

2. Kathleen J. Turner, *Lyndon Johnson's Dual War: Vietnam and the Press* (Chicago: University of Chicago Press, 1985), pp. 40–41; Johnson, *White House Diary*, pp. 10–12, 14 (quotation); "Agenda for Talking to Mrs. Kennedy," 26 Nov. 1963, LBJL, President's appointment file, Diary Backup, box 1.

3. Mrs. Johnson's notebook page is reproduced in *A White House Diary: The Exhibition* (Austin: Lyndon Baines Johnson Library, 1985), at entries of 26 Nov. and 7 Dec. 1963; Johnson, *White House Diary*, p. 15.

4. Johnson, *White House Diary*, p. 15; Liz Carpenter, *Ruffles and Flourishes* (Garden City, N.Y.: Doubleday, 1969, 1970), p. 114.

5. Johnson, *White House Diary*, p. 37.

6. Carpenter, *Ruffles and Flourishes*, p. 117; Nan Robertson is quoted in Myra Greenberg Gutin, "The President's Partner: The First Lady as Public Communicator, 1920–1976" (Ph.D. diss., University of Michigan, 1983), p. 459; see also Norma Ruth Holly Foreman, "The First Lady as a Leader of Public Opinion: A Study of the Role and Press Relations of Lady Bird Johnson" (Ph.D. diss., University of Texas at Austin, 1971).

7. The process of compiling the diary is described in Johnson, *White House Diary*, pp. vii–x (p. vii for 1st quotation), and Liz Carpenter, "About the Author: A Reminiscence," in *A White House Diary: The Exhibition*, pp. 7–8 (2d and 3d quotations).

8. The president's remark about his older daughter is from Ruth Montgomery, *Mrs. LBJ* (New York: Holt, Rinehart & Winston, 1964), p. 152. Gordon Langley Hall, *Lady Bird and Her Daughters* (Philadelphia: Macrae Smith, 1967), pp. 28–60. I had a chance to observe Mrs. Robb's personal style at the conference on "Modern First Ladies," Gerald R. Ford Museum, Grand Rapids, Mich., 18–20 Apr. 1984.

9. Montgomery, *Mrs. LBJ*, p. 152; Hall, *Lady Bird and Her Daughters*, pp. 61–100. Luci Johnson Turpin also attended the Ford Museum conference and spoke about her youth and years in the White House.

10. Johnson, *White House Diary*, p. 347. Mrs. Johnson visited my seminar on First Ladies in Nov. 1982. A transcript of her remarks was made at the time, but the comments herein are based on my notes and recollections.

11. For the gun-control documents see Michael Manatos to LBJ, 20 Mar. 1968, WHCF, PP5/LBJ, 30 Jan. 1968–22 Mar. 1968, box 63; Harry C. McPherson, Jr., to LBJ, 7 Dec. 1967, LBJ and Harry McPherson files, box 50; LBJ to Mary Lasker, 20 July 1967, WHSF, AF, Presidential Library–L, box 1699; interview with LBJ, 16 Sept. 1984.

12. Johnson, *White House Diary*, pp. 349 (1st quotation) and 351 (2d quotation); memos dated 31 Aug. 1964, WHCF, PP5/LBJ, box 62; LJ notation on memo of 8 Mar. 1966, WHCF, Ex/PR/18, 7 Feb. 1966–6 Apr. 1966, box 358, and memo to LJ, 12 Dec. 1966, WHCF, Ex/PR/18, 12 Nov. 1966–27 Dec. 1966, box 358.

13. Merle Miller, *Lyndon: An Oral Biography* (New York: Putnam's, 1980), pp. 354–55.

14. Marie Smith, *The President's Lady: An Intimate Biography of Mrs. Lyndon B. Johnson* (New York: Random House, 1964), p. 19 (1st quotation); Katie Louchheim, "Her Interest Is People," *Ladies Home Journal*, Mar. 1964, pp. 56, 126; Anne Morrow Lindbergh, "As I See Our First Lady," *Look*, 19 May 1964, p. 105; Ruth Montgomery, "What Kind of Woman Is Our New First Lady?" *Good Housekeeping*, Mar. 1964, p. 44.

15. Lewis L. Gould, "First Ladies," *American Scholar* 55 (Fall 1986): 528–35.

16. Barbara Klaw, comp., "Lady Bird Johnson Remembers," *American Heritage*, Dec. 1980, pp. 7–8; Katie Louchheim, ed., *The Making of the New Deal: The Insiders Speak* (Cambridge, Mass.: Harvard University Press, 1983), p. 304; Johnson, *White House Diary*, p. 106.

17. The standard treatment of Eleanor Roosevelt as First Lady is Joseph P. Lash, *Eleanor and Franklin* (New York: Norton, 1971); but see also the essays in Joan Hoff-Wilson and Marjorie Lightman, eds., *Without Precedent: The Life and Career of Eleanor Roosevelt* (Bloomington: Indiana University Press, 1984).

18. Marianne Means, *The Woman in the White House* (New York: Random House, 1963), p. 248 (quotation); Lewis L. Gould, "First Ladies and the Press: Bess Truman to Lady Bird Johnson," *American Journalism* 1 (Summer 1983): 48–50; Margaret Truman, *Bess W. Truman* (New York: Macmillan, 1986).

19. "I Don't Consider Myself Dull at All: The Real Lady Bird Johnson," *National Observer*, 24 Apr. 1967.

20. Johnson, *White House Diary*, p. 10; Mary Van Rensselaer Thayer, *Jacqueline Kennedy: The White House Years* (Boston: Little, Brown, 1967), p. 34.

21. Gould, "First Ladies and the Press," pp. 52–54; Herbert S. Parmet, *JFK: The Presidency of John F. Kennedy* (New York: Dial Press, 1983), pp. 102–3, 106–11.

22. "Mrs. Lyndon B. Johnson's Remarks at Wilkes College, Wilkes-Barre, Penn-

sylvania, January 11, 1964" (1st quotation), WHSF, Liz Carpenter's subject files, Trip to Wilkes-Barre, box 1; Johnson, *White House Diary,* p. 38 (2d quotation).

23. Johnson, *White House Diary,* pp. 38 (1st quotation), 41 (4th and 5th quotations); "Mrs. Lyndon B. Johnson's Remarks" (2d quotation); William L. Batt to Liz Carpenter, 13 Jan. 1964 (3d quotation), WHSF, Liz Carpenter's subject files, Trip to Wilkes-Barre, box 1; "First Lady on the Move: Schedule Stirs Memories of Eleanor Roosevelt," *U.S. News and World Report,* 27 Jan. 1964, p. 16.

24. Johnson, *White House Diary,* pp. 99, 141, 159–60.

25. *Addresses by the First Lady, Mrs. Lyndon Baines Johnson, 1964,* pamphlet in LBJL, pp. 3, 11.

26. "Lady Bird's Pine Lands and Her Tenants," *U.S. News and World Report,* 4 May 1964, pp. 43–45; Allen J. Matusow, *The Unraveling of America: A History of Liberalism in the 1960s* (New York: Harper & Row, 1984), p. 217; "GOP Probers Report on Johnson Tenants," *Washington Post,* 15 May 1964; Johnson, *White House Diary,* p. 103.

27. Johnson, *White House Diary,* p. 53 (quotation), 60–61, 78–79, 97–98, 134–37; Nash Castro to George B. Hartzog, 5 June 1964, conveying the minutes of the meeting of the Committee for the Preservation of the White House, 7 May 1964, LBJL, Committee for the Preservation of the White House, Nash Castro Papers, box 5.

28. LBJ to L. L. Camp, 11 Feb. 1964, WHCF, Ex/PP16, Trees Planted, box 126; Stewart Udall to LBJ, 24 July 1964, WHSF, AF, Stewart Udall, box 2016; "Mrs. Johnson Opens the American Landmarks Celebration," press release, 4 Aug. 1964, WHCF, PP5/LBJ, box 62.

29. Johnson, *White House Diary,* pp. 112–13, 125, 166.

30. Johnson, *White House Diary,* p. 170; *Addresses by the First Lady,* pp. 5, 18–19.

31. James Reston, Jr., to Richard Goodwin, 4 May 1964, Richard Goodwin Files, Conservation–Natural Beauty, box 28; *Public Papers of the Presidents of the United States: Lyndon B. Johnson, 1963–1964,* 2 vols. (Washington, D.C.: GPO, 1965), 1:357.

32. Charles M. Haar, OH no. 1, 14 June 1971, p. 4 (quotation); Nancy Kegan Smith, "Presidential Task Force Operation during the Johnson Administration," *Presidential Studies Quarterly* 15 (Spring 1985): 320–23.

33. Richard Goodwin, "Preservation of Natural Beauty," 17 June 1964, Stewart Udall Papers, University of Arizona Library, Tucson.

34. Udall to LJ, 27 Nov. 1963, WHCF, Legislation/Natural Resources, 22 Nov. 1963–20 Oct. 1964, box 142; Samuel P. Hays, "From Conservation to Environment: Environmental Politics in the United States since World War II," *Environmental Review* 6 (Fall 1982): 24–25.

35. Lynton Keith Caldwell, *Environment: A Challenge for Modern Society* (Garden City, N.Y.: Natural History Press, 1970), pp. 50–51; Robert Rienow and Leona Train Rienow, *Moment in the Sun: A Report on the Deteriorating Quality of the American Environment* (New York: Ballantine, 1967); Hays, "From Conservation to Environment," p. 20.

36. Senator Kuchel is quoted by James L. Sundquist in *Politics and Policy: The Eisenhower, Kennedy, and Johnson Years* (Washington, D.C.: Brookings Institution, 1968), p. 331; Brower's 1959 remarks are in William Schwartz, ed., *Voices for the Wilderness* (New York: Ballantine, 1969), p. ix; Stewart Alsop, "America the Ugly," *Saturday Evening Post,* 23 June 1962, p. 8; see also "The Creeping Junkyard," *Life,* 20 Mar. 1964, p. 4; James Nathan Miller, "Conservation Is Everybody's Battle," *Reader's Digest,* Aug. 1964, pp. 161–69; for an analytical overview of these developments see Martin V. Melosi, "Lyndon Johnson and Environmental Policy," in *The Johnson Years,* vol. 2 (Lawrence: University Press of Kansas, 1987), pp. 114–17; Hays, "From Conservation to Environment," pp. 20–23.

37. Stewart Udall, *The Quiet Crisis* (New York: Holt, Rinehart & Winston, 1963), p. xii; Sundquist, *Politics and Policy,* pp. 345–46; Melosi, "Lyndon Johnson and Environmental Policy," pp. 118–19.

38. Udall to Bill Moyers, 20 Mar. 1964, WHCF, Natural Resources, 22 Nov. 1963–30 Apr. 1964, box 6; James Reston, Jr., to Udall, 5 Aug. 1964, Udall Papers.

39. Caldwell, *Environment,* p. 54; Melosi, "Environmental Policy," pp. 121–28.

40. Stewart Udall to Lewis L. Gould, 1 Oct. 1984; Gould interview with Udall, 11 Apr. 1984; Gould interview with LBJ, 16 Sept. 1984. Something of the mutual interest of the Johnsons in conservation matters comes through in Lady Bird Johnson, *Texas: A Roadside View* (San Antonio, Texas: Trinity University Press, 1980), pp. xvi–xvii.

41. Reston to Udall, 5 Aug. 1964, Udall Papers.

42. Haar, OH, 14 June 1971, pp. 13, 22.

43. Udall interview, 11 Apr. 1984.

44. For a biographical sketch of Udall see Douglas H. Strong, *The Conservationists* (Menlo Park, Calif.: Addison-Wesley, 1971), pp. 166–68; Arthur M. Schlesinger, Jr., *Robert Kennedy and His Times* (Boston: Houghton Mifflin, 1978), p. 225; see also Barbara Le Unes, "The Conservation Philosophy of Stewart L. Udall, 1961–1968" (Ph.D. diss., Texas A&M University, 1977). Udall is preparing a new edition of *The Quiet Crisis,* and his papers at the University of Arizona are a rich source for his years at the Department of the Interior.

45. Udall, *Quiet Crisis,* p. viii.

46. Udall interview, 11 Apr. 1984; Udall, OH, 19 May 1969, p. 1.

47. Udall, OH, 19 May 1969, p. 7; Melosi, "Lyndon Johnson and Environmental Policy," p. 121.

48. Udall to Liz Carpenter, 23 Apr. 1964, LBJ to Udall, 31 July 1964, Udall Papers; Udall interview, 11 Apr. 1984.

49. *Salt Lake City Tribune,* 16 Aug. 1964 (University of Utah quotation); draft of Park City speech, draft of Flaming Gorge speech, WHSF, Liz Carpenter Subject file, Western Trip, box 9; Udall to LJ, 19 Aug. 1964, LJ to Udall, 24 Aug. 1964, WHCF, Ex/PP5/LBJ, 15 July 1964–1 Oct. 1964, box 62; Udall interview, 11 Apr. 1984 (for the tour de force comment).

50. Udall interview, 11 Apr. 1984 (1st, 2d, and 3d quotations); Udall, OH, 19 May 1969, p. 12.

51. Johnson, *White House Diary,* p. 192 (1st, 2d, and 3d quotations); Miller, *Lyndon,* p. 391 (other quotations).

52. Remarks by Lady Bird Johnson at "Salute to Mrs. Lyndon B. Johnson" Luncheon, Columbus, Ohio, 18 Sept. 1964, WHSF, Liz Carpenter subject file, Akron and Columbus, Ohio, box 11, and "Remarks of the President and Mrs. Johnson in Front of the Hartford Times Building, Hartford, Connecticut," 28 Sept. 1964, WHSF, Liz Carpenter subject file, New England trip, box 11.

53. India Edwards to Carpenter, 9 Sept. 1964, WHSF, Liz Carpenter subject file, Whistle Stop, box 11. For an overview of the whole trip see Elvia Garcia, "Lady Bird Johnson: Whistle Stopping through the South" (Plan II senior essay, University of Texas at Austin, 1986), copy in LBJL.

54. Zephyr Wright recounts the motel episode in OH, 5 Dec. 1974, p.6; Carpenter, *Ruffles and Flourishes,* pp. 143, 147–48.

55. Carpenter, *Ruffles and Flourishes,* pp. 143 (1st quotation), 147–48 (2d and 3d quotations); Johnson, *White House Diary,* p. 195 (quotation about Senator Robertson). For the organization of the trip see Jack Valenti to Walter Jenkins, 4 Sept. 1964, Warren Woodward to LBJ, 1 Oct. 1964, Gerry Sohle to LBJ, n.d. but conveying votes on the Civil Rights bill for her use, WHSF, Liz Carpenter subject file, Whistle Stop, box 11.

56. Woodward to LBJ, 1 Oct. 1964, WHSF, Liz Carpenter subject file, Whistle Stop, box 11; Carpenter, *Ruffles and Flourishes,* pp. 153–58; Miller, *Lyndon,* pp. 396–97.

57. Carpenter, *Ruffles and Flourishes,* pp. 155 (1st quotation), 158 (3d quotation); Gutin, "President's Partner," p. 438 (2d quotation); Foreman, "First Lady as a Leader of Public Opinion," p. 171 (quotation about Boggs).

58. Foreman, "First Lady as Leader of Public Opinion," pp. 173 (1st quotation), 174 (3d and 4th quotations); Carpenter, *Ruffles and Flourishes,* p. 162 (2d quotation).

59. Doris Fleeson, "Mrs. Johnson Draws the Names," *Washington Evening Star,* 8 Oct. 1964; Johnson, *White House Diary,* p. 198.

60. Liz Carpenter, OH, 27 Aug. 1969, pp. 32–39; Miller, *Lyndon,* pp. 399–400, 604 (LBJ's statement); Foreman, "First Lady as Leader of Public Opinion," pp. 179–80.

61. Johnson, *White House Diary,* p. 198.

62. Johnson, *Texas,* p. xviii.

Chapter 4. Ways to Beautify America

1. For Mrs. Johnson's own recollections of her work with Head Start see Edward Zigler and Jeanette Valentine, eds., *Project Head Start: A Legacy of the War on Poverty* (New York: Free Press, 1979), pp. 43–49.

2. The phone call from Lyndon Johnson to Luther Hodges on 6 Nov. 1964

is recorded as having been made, President's Diary, 6 Nov. 1964, box 2; Mrs. Johnson is quoted in Henry Brandon, "A Talk with the First Lady," *New York Times Magazine,* 10 Sept. 1967.

3. Charles Haar to LJ, 17 Nov. 1964, "Report of the Task Force on the Preservation of Natural Beauty," 18 Nov. 1964, first summary page for the quotation, and passim, Task Forces, box 2; Udall to Haar, 27 Nov. 1964 (quotation), Haar to Udall, 2 Dec. 1964, Udall Papers.

4. Udall, "Memorandum for the First Lady," 19 Nov. 1964, Udall Papers (1st quotation); Udall interview, 11 Apr. 1984 (2d quotation); for Udall's ranch visit, President's Diary, 20 Nov. 1964, box 2; Udall noted, on Lewis L. Gould to Udall, 11 Aug. 1985, that Mrs. Johnson had been "briefed" about the Task Force Report and was "keenly interested," copy in Gould Papers.

5. Elizabeth Rowe to LBJ, 8 Dec. 1964, with Rowe to Ashton Gonella, 8 Dec. 1964, Formation of Committee, WHSF/BF, box 1.

6. Katie Louchheim, "Suggested Program for Mrs. Johnson," 20 Nov. 1964, "National Beautification," 20 Nov. 1964, box C33, Stewart Udall, "Memorandum for the First Lady: Proposed Capital Beautification Program," 9 Dec. 1964, Antonia Chayes to LBJ, 9 Dec. 1964—all in Papers of Katherine Louchheim, LC, MsD, box C29; Antonia Chayes to Lewis L. Gould, 6 Oct. 1986.

7. "Informal Notes of Conversation in the White House with Mrs. Johnson," 11 Dec. 1964, and "Luncheon Notes," 15 Dec. 1964, Louchheim Papers, box C29.

8. Udall, 'Memorandum for the First Lady," 9 Dec. 1964, Louchheim Papers, box C29; Wolf Von Eckardt, "Washington's Chance for Splendor," *Harper's Magazine,* Sept. 1963, p. 55.

9. Wolf Von Eckardt, *A Place to Live: The Crisis of the Cities* (New York: Dell, 1967), pp. 260, 261.

10. Andrew Kopkind and James Ridgeway, "Washington: The Lost Colony," *New Republic,* 23 Apr. 1964, pp. 13 (lost colony), 14 (Kennedy remark); Wolf von Eckardt, "New Town in Washington," *Americas,* June 1965, pp. 6–12.

11. For the origins of highway beautification see chap. 7.

12. *Public Papers of the Presidents of the United States: Lyndon B. Johnson, 1965,* 2 vols. (Washington, D.C.: GPO, 1966), 1:8.

13. Maxine Cheshire, "Mrs. Johnson Digs New Landscape Role on Capitol Hill," *Washington Post,* 5 Jan. 1965 (1st, 2d, and 3d quotations); Lady Bird Johnson, *A White House Diary* (New York: Holt, Rinehart & Winston, 1970), p. 215.

14. LBJ to Katie Louchheim, 30 Jan. 1965, Louchheim Papers, box C33; LBJ to Mary Lasker, 30 Jan. 1965, WHSF, AF, Beautification, "L" folder, box 12, are examples of these letters.

15. Johnson, *White House Diary,* p. 234.

16. *Public Papers,* 1:155, 156.

17. Johnson, *White House Diary,* pp. 240–42, provides Mrs. Johnson's account of the meeting. There is another brief account in "Beautification Summary: The Committee for a More Beautiful Capital, 1965–1968," copy in LBJL, hereafter referred to as "Beautification Summary."

18. Johnson, *White House Diary,* p. 241; "Beautification Summary," p. 6 (quotation).

19. "Ways to Beautify America: Exclusive Interview with the First Lady," *U.S. News & World Report,* 22 Feb. 1965, pp. 72, 74, 75, 78.

20. Eileen Boone to LJ, 5 Feb. 1965, WHCF, NR, 1 Dec. 1964–30 Apr. 1965, box 6; Mrs. Clifford Norman to LJ, 22 Feb. 1965, WHCF, NR, 1 Dec. 1964–15 Mar. 1965, box 6; James M. Perry, "Natural Beauty Is a Political Natural," *National Observer,* 1 Mar. 1965, enclosed with Richard Goodwin to LJ, 3 Mar. 1965, WHCF, NR, 1 Dec. 1964–30 Apr. 1965, box 1.

21. Von Eckardt, *Place to Live,* p. 25.

22. Wolf Von Eckardt and Joseph Watterson, 8 Dec. 1964, Udall Papers; William H. Wilson, "J. Horace McFarland and the City Beautiful Movement," *Journal of Urban History* 7 (May 1981): 315 (quotation); Jon A. Peterson, "The City Beautiful Movement: Forgotten Origins and Lost Meanings," *Journal of Urban History* 2 (Aug. 1976): 415–33.

23. Mel Scott, *American City Planning since 1890* (Berkeley: University of California Press, 1971), pp. 43–109, quotation on p. 45.

24. Peterson, "City Beautiful Movement," pp. 423 (1st quotation), 429, for the size of the campaign; Wilson, "J. Horace McFarland," p. 318; see also William H. Wilson, " 'More Almost Than the Men': Mira Lloyd Dock and the Beautification of Harrisburg," *Pennsylvania Magazine of History and Biography* 99 (Oct. 1975): 490–99.

25. Martin V. Melosi, *Garbage in the Cities: Refuse, Reform, and the Environment, 1880–1980* (College Station: Texas A & M University Press, 1981), pp. 127, 128 (quotation), 129–133.

26. Scott, *American City Planning,* p. 119 (Ford); Wilson, "J. Horace McFarland," p. 328 (Gilbert).

27. Barbara Klaw, comp., "Lady Bird Johnson Remembers," *American Heritage,* Dec. 1980, p. 6. For comments that echo this formulation see Victor Gruen, *The Heart of Our Cities: The Urban Crisis: Diagnosis and Cure* (New York: Simon & Schuster, 1964), pp. 168–69; William H. Whyte, *The Last Landscape* (Garden City, N.Y.: Doubleday, 1968), p. 327, on the language of the "anti-prettification critiques" and how the phrase "garden-club ladies" is used.

28. Sharon Francis, OH, 20 May 1969, p. 35; Liz Carpenter, OH, 4 Apr. 1969, p. 11; Charles M. Haar, OH, 14 June 1971, pp. 10, 11.

29. Lady Bird Johnson, "Beautification and Public Welfare," *Social Action* 34 (May 1968): 11; for an example of how men reacted to the term *beautification* see the remarks of William C. Cramer (R, Fla.), in U.S., House, "Highway Beautification," *Hearings before the Subcommittee on Roads of the Committee on Public Works,* 89th Cong., 1st sess. (Washington, D.C.: GPO, 1965), p. 372.

30. "The President's Message on Natural Beauty," *Landscape* 14 (Spring 1965): 1. A good introduction to Jackson's ideas is D. W. Meinig's "Reading the Landscape: An Appreciation of W. G. Hoskins and J. B. Jackson," in *The Interpretation of Ordinary Landscapes: Geographical Essays,* ed. D. W. Meinig (New York: Oxford University Press, 1979), pp. 210–32. For Jackson's own statements of

his views see J. B. Jackson, "Various Aspects of Landscape Analysis," *Texas Conference on Our Environmental Crisis* (Austin: School of Architecture, University of Texas, 1966), pp. 150–57, *Discovering the Vernacular Landscape* (New Haven, Conn.: Yale University Press, 1984), and "The Vernacular City," in *The Land, the City, and the Human Spirit: America the Beautiful: An Assessment,* ed. Larry Paul Fuller (Austin: Lyndon Baines Johnson Library et al., 1985), pp. 48–61.

31. "President's Message," p. 1.

32. Jackson, "Various Aspects of Landscape Analysis," p. 157.

33. LBJ to Sylvia Porter, 28 Dec. 1965, WHSF, LCAF, Beautification–P, box 14.

34. Sharon Francis, OH, 20 May 1969, pp. 2, 7.

35. Ibid., pp. 8–12, 17; LBJ to Francis 10 Mar. 1965, WHSF, AF, Stewart Udall, box 2016.

36. Cynthia Wilson interview, 24 Oct. 1985. The text of this interview will become part of the Oral History Project of the Johnson Library. Ms. Wilson kindly furnished me with copies of the standard letters that she sent out during her White House service. A set of these letters has also been added to the WHSF in the Johnson Library.

37. Johnson, *White House Diary,* pp. 248–49.

38. John Carver to Stewart Udall, 6 Mar. 1965, Victor Gruen to Udall, 10 Mar. 1965, Udall Papers.

39. "Beautification Summary," p. 9, discusses the 17 Mar. 1965 meeting.

40. Transcript, First Lady's Committee for a More Beautiful Capital, 8 Apr. 1965, WHSF/BF, box 1, pp. 4, 5, 36 (Washington); "Beautification Summary," p. 10.

41. Transcript, 8 Apr. 1965, pp. 5–6, 27–42.

42. Sharon Francis to Liz Carpenter, 1 Apr. 1965, Francis to Hilda Burns, 2 Apr. 1965, Francis to Polly Shackleton, 2 Apr. 1965, Meredith S. Conley to Carpenter, 23 Apr. 1965, WHSF/BF, Reader's Digest Event, box 12; "Beautification Summary," p. 10; "Mrs. Lyndon B. Johnson Pleads: Beautify the U.S.!" *Reader's Digest,* May 1965, pp. 131–34.

43. Liz Carpenter, *Ruffles and Flourishes* (Garden City, N.Y.: Doubleday, 1969, 1970), p. 74 (both quotations); Johnson, *White House Diary,* pp. 270–73.

44. Johnson, *White House Diary,* p. 271.

45. Ibid.

46. "Beautification Summary," p. 11; Johnson, *White House Diary,* pp. 272, 273; Nan Robertson, "Mrs. Johnson Leads a Tour to Promote See-America Theme," *New York Times,* 12 May 1965.

47. Johnson, *White House Diary,* pp. 274, 275–76.

48. "Beautification Summary," pp. 12–13; on the "Potomac Pick-up Day" see Kenward K. Harris to Charles Horsky, 4 May 1965, Harris to LBJ, 4 and 7 May 1965, Charles Horsky Files, Potomac River, box 49. The files of White House aides, such as Horsky, are listed in alphabetical order at the Johnson Library; they are consulted separately from the White House Central File.

49. Mary Lasker to Katie Louchheim, 12 Oct. 1965 (quotation), Louchheim

to Lasker, 18 Oct. 1965, box C29, Louchheim Papers; Lasker to LBJ, 25 June 1965, WHSF/BF, Fund Raising for Washington, box 6; "Report to the First Lady's Committee for a More Beautiful Capital," 28 Feb. 1966, WHSF/BF, Beautification Meeting, 28 Feb. 1966, box 2; "Beautification Summary," pp. 13, 15–16, 17.

50. Stewart Udall, Suggestions Concerning the President's White House Conference on Natural Beauty, 19 Jan. 1965, John Macy Files, White House Conference on Natural Beauty, box 891; Johnson, *White House Diary*, p. 234.

51. The best available biographical study on Laurance Rockefeller is by Peter Collier and David Horowitz, *The Rockefellers: An American Dynasty* (New York: Holt, Rinehart & Winston, 1976), pp. 215–22, 292–309, 383–88; the quotation is from Nathaniel Alexander Owings, *The Spaces in Between: An Architect's Journey* (Boston: Houghton Mifflin, 1973), p. 169.

52. Collier and Horowitz, *Rockefellers*, pp. 384–86; James L. Sundquist, *Politics and Policy: The Eisenhower, Kennedy, and Johnson Years* (Washington, D.C.: Brookings Institution, 1968), p. 355 (quotation).

53. Collier and Horowitz, *Rockefellers*, p. 400; Laurance S. Rockefeller, "Business and Beauty: Our Changing Landscape," *Vital Speeches of the Day*, 15 Jan. 1966, p. 220.

54. John R. Churchill to Chief of Office of Legislation and Cooperative Relations, 11 Feb. 1965, Records of the Department of the Interior, reel 30 (1st and 2d quotations); Jack Valenti to LJ, 4 Mar. 1965, Rockefeller to LJ, 19 Mar. 1965, WHCF/NR, MC, box 8; Rockefeller to LBJ, 19 Mar. 1965, WHSF, AF, Laurance Rockefeller, box 1779.

55. *Beauty for America: Proceedings of the White House Conference on Natural Beauty* (Washington, D.C.: GPO, 1965), pp. 20, 68.

56. Ibid., p. 689.

57. Ibid., pp. 17, 19, 21, 22. There are drafts of her speech in LCSF, White House Conference on Natural Beauty, 24/25 May 1965, box 15.

58. Oral Kelly and Roberta Hornig, "Fight for Natural Beauty: Delegates to Ask President," *Washington Evening Star*, 25 May 1965 (quotation); *Beauty for America*, pp. 227, 573; LBJ to Brooke Astor, 1 June 1965, WHSF, AF, Mrs. Vincent Astor, box 45.

59. "Beauty Parley Agrees on Nature of Problem," *Washington Evening Star*, 27 May 1965 (1st quotation); *Beauty for America*, pp. 481–82 (McHarg), 527 (Halprin).

60. *Beauty for America*, pp. 676, 679; Fuller, *The Land, the City, and the Human Spirit*, p.1.

61. *Beauty for America*, p. 681.

62. LBJ to William L. Rutherford, 24 June 1965, WHSF, AF, Beautification–Ford, box 113 (1st and 2d quotations); Joseph Watterson, "Beauty USA: The White House Conference on Natural Beauty," *AIA Journal*, July 1965, pp. 61–62; *National Wildlife* 3 (April/May 1965): 29.

63. Elizabeth Brenner Drew, "Lady Bird's Beauty Bill," *Atlantic*, Dec. 1965, p. 71. See the discussion of the enactment of the Highway Beautification Act in chap. 7 for more on this issue.

64. Fuller, *The Land, The City, and The Human Spirit,* pp. xix, 2.

65. For a recent treatment of these events see Ian Hamilton, *Robert Lowell: A Biography* (New York: Random House, 1982), pp. 320–27. Hamilton's account of the White House side of the issue draws on Eric F. Goldman, *The Tragedy of Lyndon Johnson* (New York: Alfred A. Knopf, 1969), pp. 420–75, which should be supplemented with the very different view of Goldman's role in Bess Abell, OH, 1 July 1969, pp. 24–29.

Chapter 5. Beautifying Monumental Washington

1. Katie Louchheim, *By The Political Sea* (Garden City, N.Y.: Doubleday, 1970), p. 232.

2. "Beautification Summary: The Committee for a More Beautiful Capital, 1965–1968," pp. 46–47 (quotation on p. 47); Nash Castro to Sutton Jett, 1 Mar. 1967, Nash Castro Papers, Mrs. Johnson's File, box 3.

3. There is no full-length biography of Mary Lasker. For general data see "Mrs. Albert D. Lasker," *Current Biography, 1959,* pp. 245–47; Richard Rettig, *Cancer Crusade* (Princeton, N.J.: Princeton University Press, 1977), p. 19; Nadine Brozan, "Health Care Lobbyist on a National Scale: Mary Lasker," *New York Times,* 21 Nov. 1985.

4. John Gunther, *Taken at The Flood: The Story of Albert D. Lasker* (New York: Harper, 1960), pp. 240–41; "Medicine: Fanning the Fire," *Time,* 30 Aug. 1948, p. 41; Rettig, *Cancer Crusade,* pp. 19–20.

5. "Lady Philanthropist: Mrs. Albert D. Lasker," U.S., Senate, *Congressional Record, Appendix,* 85th Cong., 1st sess., 17 June 1957, p. A4754; Carl Bakal, *Charity U.S.A.* (New York: New York Times Books, 1979), pp. 154–55. I am indebted to Clarence G. Lasby for this reference and for his kind willingness to share his knowledge of Mary Lasker's medical-research campaigns.

6. "Lady Philanthropist," *Congressional Record,* p. A4753; Samuel Grafton, "Cities in Bloom," *Reader's Digest,* July 1960, pp. 108–10.

7. "Lady Philanthropist," p. A4753.

8. Anna M. Rosenberg to LJ, 26 Aug. 1948, LBJA, Selected Names, R file, box 8; Joseph Lash, *A World of Love: Eleanor Roosevelt and Her Friends, 1943–1962* (Garden City, N.Y.: Doubleday, 1984), p. 513; LBJ to Mary Lasker, 29 Nov. 1963, WHSF, AF, Mary Lasker, box 1340; Rettig, *Cancer Crusade,* p. 23.

9. Lady Bird Johnson, *A White House Diary* (New York: Holt, Rinehart & Winston, 1970), pp. 146 (2d quotation), 238 (1st quotation), 410–11; Mary Lasker to Richard Goodwin, 24 Feb. 1965, Goodwin to Lasker, 4 Mar. 1965, Richard Goodwin Files, Natural Beauty, box 29.

10. Nash Castro, OH, 25 Feb. 1969, p. 2 (quotation); Johnson, *White House Diary,* p. 318; Castro to Sutton Jett, 12 Jan. 1966, Castro Papers, Mrs. Johnson's file, box 3; my interview with Nash Castro, 28 Sept. 1984.

11. Lasker's phrase, which she often repeated, is given in Johnson, *White House Diary,* p. 238; Sharon Francis, OH, 20 May 1969, p. 24.

12. Castro to Sutton Jett, 17 Mar. 1965, Nash Castro Papers, Mrs. Johnson's file, box 3.

13. Castro to Jett, 20 May 1965, Castro Papers, Mrs. Johnson's file, box 3.

14. LBJ to Philip Harris, 20 Sept. 1965, LBJ to Walter Tobriner, 29 Sept. 1965, LBJ to William F. McKee, 13 Oct. 1965, LBJ to Otis Singletary, 13 Oct. 1965, Castro Papers, Mrs. Johnson's file, box 3.

15. Castro to LBJ, 13 Oct. 1965 (1st quotation), Castro to Sutton Jett, 6 Oct. and 18 Nov. 1965 (3d and 4th quotations), Castro Papers, Mrs. Johnson's file, box 3; Castro to Jett, 22 Oct. 1965, Udall Papers (2d quotation).

16. T. Sutton Jett to Abbie Rowe and Kathryn Simons, 9 July 1965, Castro to Jett, 18 Nov. 1965, Castro Papers, Mrs. Johnson's file, box 3; Udall to LBJ, Dec. 1965, WHSF, AF, Stewart Udall, box 2016; "Beautification Summary," p. 22.

17. Mary Lasker to Katie Louchheim, 26 July and 12 Oct. 1965, Louchheim to Lasker, 18 Oct. 1965, Lasker to Mrs. Tracy Barnes, 17 Feb. 1966, LC, MsD, Katie Louchheim Papers, box C29; Report to the First Lady's Committee for a More Beautiful Capital by Mrs. Albert D. Lasker, 28 Feb. 1966, WHSF/BF, Beautification Meeting, 28 Feb. 1966, box 2; *Washington Post,* 24 Sept. 1965; Castro to Sutton Jett, 24 Sept. 1965, Castro Papers, Mrs. Johnson's file, box 3; Castro to Jett, 22 Oct. 1965, Udall Papers.

18. Castro to Jett, 12 Jan. 1966, Castro Papers, Mrs. Johnson's file, box 3.

19. LBJ to Mary Lasker, 4 and 21 Jan. and 11 Feb. 1966, WHSF, AF, Mary Lasker file, box 1340; Lasker to Liz Carpenter, 6 Jan. 1966, with enclosure, WHSF/BF, Planting, box 7. Lasker's unorthodox methods sometimes strained Castro's working relations within the National Park Service in Washington: see Kathryn Simons to Castro, 28 Apr. 1966, Castro Papers, BF, box 7.

20. LBJ to Russell Page, 22 Feb. 1966, WHSF, LCAF, Beautification–P, box 14; Nash Castro to Sutton Jett, 15 Apr. 1966, Castro Papers, Mrs. Johnson's file, box 3. Russell Page, in the preface to *The Education of a Gardener* (New York: Random House, 1962, 1983), does not mention Lady Bird Johnson.

21. Castro to Jett, 29 Sept. 1966, Udall Papers (quotation); Merelye Secrest, "Beautification Gets a Boost," *Washington Post,* 30 Sept. 1966; Castro to Jett, 13 Oct. 1966, Castro Papers, Mrs. Johnson's file, box 3.

22. Castro to LBJ, 2 Nov. 1966, Castro Papers, Mrs. Johnson's file, box 3.

23. Transcript of Beautification Meeting, 30 Nov. 1966, WHSF/BF, box 2, pp. 11, 13, 15.

24. Notes made as Mrs. Johnson talked during the Asian trip, WHSF/BF, Asian Trip, box 9; Transcript of Beautification Meeting, 30 Nov. 1966, box 2.

25. LBJ to Mary Lasker, 10 Jan. 1967, WHSF, AF, Mary Lasker file, box 1340; Liz Carpenter to LBJ, 10 Jan. 1967, WHSF, LCAF, Beautification–L, box 12; Lasker to Douglass Cater, 30 Jan. 1967, Douglass Cater files, Highway Beautification, box 96.

26. Lasker to Cater, 30 Jan. 1967, Cater files, Highway Beautification, box 96.

27. LBJ to William Walton, 11 Feb. 1967, WHSF, AF, Washington, D.C., file, box 2068; Castro to Jett, 1 Mar. 1967, Castro Papers, Mrs. Johnson's file, box 3.

28. Castro to Jett, 4 Apr. 1967, Castro Papers, Mrs. Johnson's file, box 3.

29. Sharon Francis to Castro, 19 June 1967 (quotation), Castro to Francis, 26 June 1967, Castro Papers, BF, box 7.

30. Castro to Francis, 26 June 1967, BF, box 7; Castro to Jett, 27 June 1967, Mrs. Johnson's file, box 3—all in Castro Papers.

31. U.S., House, *Department of the Interior and Related Agencies Appropriations For 1968: Hearings before a Subcommittee of the Committee on Appropriations,* 90th Cong., 1st sess. (Washington, D.C.: GPO, 1967), p. 345; Castro to Jett, 28 June 1967, and Mary Lasker to Charles Schultze, 28 July 1967, Castro Papers, BF, box 7.

32. "No More Money: Julia Balks Beautification," clipping from Vancouver, Wash., newspaper, dated 12 Aug. 1967, Castro Papers, BF, box 7.

33. Liz Carpenter and Nash Castro to LBJ, 29 Aug. 1967, Castro Papers, Mrs. Johnson's file, box 3.

34. Julia B. Hansen to LJ, 27 Sept. 1967, Barefoot Sanders to Liz Carpenter, 29 Sept. 1967, Sanders to Hansen, 29 Sept. 1967, LBJ to Hansen, 6 Oct. 1967, WHCF, Gen PP5/LBJ, 16 July 1966–, box 65; for another example of how the First Lady tried to reach Hansen see Sanders to Carpenter, 29 Aug. 1967, Barefoot Sanders Papers, Memoranda–Legislation Targeted, box 13; Castro to Jett, 16 Oct. 1967, Castro Papers, Mrs. Johnson's file, box 3.

35. "Beautification Summary," pp. 60–61.

36. Castro to Sutton Jett, 19 Oct. 1967, Castro Papers, Mrs. Johnson's file, box 3.

37. "Beautification Summary," pp. 62–63.

38. "Beautification Summary," pp. 63–64; Minutes of Shade Tree Meeting, 23 Jan. 1968, WHSF/BF, Street Trees, box 8.

39. Mary Lasker to LBJ, 26 Feb. 1968, LBJ to Lasker, 29 Feb. 1968, WHSF/BF, Street Trees, box 8.

40. Nash Castro to George B. Hartzog, 8 Mar. 1968, Castro Papers, Mrs. Johnson's file, box 3; Castro to LBJ, 29 Mar. 1968, Sharon Francis to LBJ, 25 Apr. 1968, WHSF/BF, Shade Trees, box 8.

41. Polly Shackleton to Castro, 15 Apr. 1968, LC, MsD, Katie Louchheim Papers, box C30; Castro to George B. Hartzog, 18 Apr. 1968, Castro Papers, Mrs. Johnson's file, box 3.

42. U.S., House, *Department of the Interior and Related Agencies Appropriations for 1969: Hearings before a Subcommittee of the Committee on Appropriations,* 90th Cong., 2d sess. (Washington, D.C.: GPO, 1968), p. 506.

43. Ibid.; pp. 399, 500, 501.

44. Castro to Hartzog, 1 Apr. 1968, Castro Papers, Mrs. Johnson's file, box 3.

45. Johnson, *White House Diary,* p. 646; "Beautification Summary," pp. 73–74.

46. Castro to Hartzog, 12 July 1968, Castro Papers, Mrs. Johnson's file, box 3.

47. Ibid.; Castro to Hartzog, 25 July 1968, Castro Papers, Mrs. Johnson's file, box 3.

48. Castro to Hartzog, 7 Sept. 1968, Castro Papers, Mrs. Johnson's file, box

3; "Beautification Summary," passim; Sharon Francis to Henry L. Diamond, 7 Nov. 1968, Francis to Louis Reed, 6 Dec. 1968, Francis to Knox Banner, 24 Dec. 1968, WHSF/BF, Report to the President, box 12.

49. Barry Hyams, *Hirshhorn: Medici from Brooklyn* (New York: Dutton, 1979), pp. 142, 143, 144, which is based on Hirshhorn's personal papers.

50. Hyams, *Hirshhorn*, pp. 145–46; Johnson, *White House Diary*, pp. 275–76.

51. Hyams, *Hirshhorn*, pp. 144, 146–48.

52. Ibid., p. 149.

53. Johnson, *White House Diary*, pp. 307–8; Hyams, *Hirshhorn*, p. 149.

54. LJ to Joseph Hirshhorn, 15 Sept. 1965, Harry McPherson to LJ, 14 Sept. 1965, LJ to Hirshhorn, 17 May 1966, Harry McPherson files, "H" Correspondence, box 47; Hyams, *Hirshhorn*, pp. 151, for his response, and 152, for his comments about Mrs. Johnson.

55. "The Joseph H. Hirshhorn Museum and Sculpture Garden," *Weekly Compilation of Presidential Documents, May 23, 1966* (Washington, D.C.: GPO, 1966), pp. 653–55; Hyams, *Hirshhorn*, p. 154; LBJ to Mr. and Mrs. Joseph Hirshhorn, 11 Jan. 1967, WHCF, PP5/LBJ, 24 Sept. 1966–14 Mar. 1967, box 63.

56. Sherman Lee to LBJ, 20 May 1966, Roger L. Stevens to Lee, 1 June 1966, in U.S., House, *Hirshhorn Museum: Hearing before the Subcommittee on Public Buildings and Grounds of the Committee on Public Works,* 89th Cong., 2d sess. (Washington, D.C.: GPO, 1966), pp. 137–38; see also U.S., Senate, *Joseph H. Hirshhorn Museum and Sculpture Garden: Hearing before the Subcommittee on Public Buildings and Grounds of the Committee on Public Works,* 89th Cong., 2d sess. (Washington, D.C.: GPO, 1966); Hyams, *Hirshhorn*, pp. 155–88; Mrs. Johnson is quoted on p. 188.

57. Nathaniel Alexander Owings, *The Spaces in Between: An Architect's Journey* (Boston: Houghton Mifflin, 1973), p. 233; "Remarks by Mrs. Lyndon B. Johnson at a Meeting to Discuss Formation of a Committee for a More Beautiful Capital," 11 Feb. 1965, copy in James Gaither files, Beautification, box 257.

58. Owings, *Spaces in Between*, p. 230; the early history of the Pennsylvania Avenue Commission is well summarized in the testimony of Daniel P. Moynihan in U.S., House, *Pennsylvania Avenue National Historic Site: Hearings before the Subcommittee on National Parks and Recreation of the Committee on Interior and Insular Affairs,* 89th Cong., 2d sess. (Washington, D.C.: GPO, 1966), pp. 45–50.

59. Owings, *Spaces in Between*, p. 233; *Pennsylvania Avenue National Historic Site*, p. 49 (Johnson quotation); Wolf Von Eckardt, "Cheering Up the Capitol," *New Republic*, 13 June 1964, p. 36.

60. LBJ to Nathaniel Owings, 24 Feb. and 16 Sept. 1965, box 20, Owings to E. C. Bassett et al., 28 May 1965, LC, MsD, Nathaniel Owings Papers, box 34; Owings, *Spaces in Between*, pp. 233–34.

61. LBJ to Marjorie Merriweather Post, 14 Oct. 1965, WHSF, LCAF, Beautification–P, box 14.

62. Transcript of Meeting, the First Lady's Committee for a More Beautiful Capital, 24 Sept. 1965, WHSF/BF, box 1, pp. 36, 37–38, 61, 64.

63. LJ to John W. McCormack, 30 Sept. 1965, and Udall's order designating

the avenue, 30 Sept. 1965, in *Pennsylvania Avenue National Historic Site,* pp. 3, 11–13.

64. Harry McPherson to LJ, 13 Sept. 1966, Harry McPherson files, Pennsylvania Avenue, box 43; for the response of the National Capital Planning Commission and the remarks of Congressman Saylor see *Pennsylvania Avenue National Historic Site,* pp. 19 (Saylor), 77 (commission).

65. Udall to Liz Carpenter, 1 Mar. 1966, Udall Papers; Owings to LBJ, 6 May 1966, and Owings to Carpenter, 5 May 1966, Owings papers, box 37.

66. Owings to LBJ, 20 May 1966, box 34, LBJ to Owings, 14 June 1966, box 20, Owings Papers.

67. Owings, *Spaces in Between,* p. 234; Transcript, Meeting of the First Lady's Committee for a More Beautiful Capital, 28 June 1966, WHSF/BF, box 1, pp. 9, 10.

68. Owings to LBJ, 12 Oct. 1966, box 20, Owings to Stewart Udall, 9 May 1967, box 44, Owings Papers.

69. Owings to Udall, 9 May 1967, box 44, Owings Papers (1st quotation); Harry McPherson to Barefoot Sanders, 7 July 1967 (2d quotation), Daniel P. Moynihan to McPherson, 8 July 1967 (3d quotation), draft of Lyndon Johnson to Wayne Aspinall, with Harry McPherson to LJ, 24 July 1967, Harry McPherson files, Pennsylvania Avenue, box 44.

70. Sharon Francis, OH, 4 June 1969, p. 13; Francis to Liz Carpenter, 31 Jan. 1968, WHSF/BF, Pennsylvania Avenue Plan, box 7, recalling Mrs. Johnson's talk with Owings in Nov. 1967. Harry McPherson to LBJ, 2 Oct. 1967, McPherson files, Mrs. Johnson, box 50. For other evidence of Lady Bird Johnson's role see Irvine Sprague to Barefoot Sanders, 15 Sept. 1967, reporting on a phone call to the First Lady, Irvine Sprague files, Memos for Barefoot Sanders, 15 Sept. 1967, box 7.

71. Moynihan to McPherson, 8 July 1967 (Kennedy underground quotation), Udall to McPherson et al., 3 May 1968, McPherson files, Pennsylvania Avenue, box 44; Francis to Liz Carpenter, 31 Jan. 1968, Francis to LBJ, 22 Oct. 1968, WHSF/BF, Pennsylvania Avenue Plan, box 7; Owings, *Spaces in Between,* pp. 241–45.

72. Owings, *Spaces in Between,* pp. 235–36.

73. Nathaniel Alexander Owings, *The American Aesthetic* (New York: Harper & Row, 1969), p. 93.

74. *Report to the President from the First Lady's Committee for a More Beautiful Capital,* WHSF/BF, box 22.

75. Nash Castro to George B. Hartzog, 18 Dec. 1968, Castro Papers, Mrs. Johnson's file, box 3.

76. "Beautification Summary," p. 72.

77. *Gold Medals to the Daughter of Harry S. Truman; Lady Bird Johnson; and the Widow of Roy Wilkins: Hearing before the Subcommittee on Consumer Affairs and Coinage of the Committee on Banking, Finance, and Urban Affairs, House of Representatives,* 98th Cong., 2d sess. (Washington, D.C.: GPO, 1984), pp. 36 (Lederer), 58 (Rowe).

78. Remarks of Mayor Walter Washington at the First Lady's Beautification Luncheon, 17 Apr. 1968, WHSF/BF, Mayor's Remarks, box 6.

Chapter 6. A Pattern of Quality
for Washington's Neighborhoods

1. Antonia Chayes to LBJ, 9 Dec. 1964, "Informal Notes of Conference in the White House With Mrs. Johnson," 11 Dec. 1964, LC, MsD, Katie Louchheim Papers, box C29; Wolf Von Eckardt, "Mrs. Johnson's Call to Beautify City Brings Eager Response of Leaders," *Washington Post,* 3 Feb. 1965.
2. Stewart Udall to Liz Carpenter, 7 January 1965, WHSF/BF, Formation of Committee, box 1.
3. For biographical data on Walter Washington see "Walter Edward Washington," *Current Biography, 1968,* pp. 419–22, and "Walter Washington: Black Mayor, White Mind," in Milton Viorst, *Hustlers and Heroes: An American Political Panorama* (New York: Simon & Schuster, 1971), pp. 250–51 (quotation).
4. "Walter Edward Washington," p. 422; Lady Bird Johnson, *A White House Diary* (New York: Holt, Rinehart & Winston, 1970), p. 249.
5. My interview with Walter Washington, 9 Aug. 1984; Transcript, Meeting of First Lady's Committee for a More Beautiful Capital, 8 Apr. 1965, WHSF/BF, box 1, pp. 35, 36.
6. Transcript, Meeting of First Lady's Committee, 8 Apr. 1965, pp. 36–39; Walter Washington to LBJ, 24 Sept. 1965, WHSF/BF, Beautification Meeting, 24 Sept. 1965, box 1 (quotation).
7. John Hatcher to LBJ, n.d., LBJ to Hatcher, 19 Mar. 1965, and attached clipping, WHSF/BF, Walker-Jones Beautification, box 21; Bill Gold, "The District Line," *Washington Post,* 30 Apr. 1965; Marian W. Hollander to Walter Washington, 24 Apr. 1965, Washington to Liz Carpenter, 4 May 1965, Carpenter to Hollander, 6 May 1965, WHSF, LCAF, Beautification-Special, box 14.
8. "Beautification Summary: The Committee for a More Beautiful Capital, 1965–1968," pp. 12–13; Washington to LBJ, 24 Sept. 1965, WHSF/BF, Beautification Meeting, 24 Sept. 1965, box 1.
9. Washington to LBJ, 24 Sept. 1965, WHSF/BF, Beautification Meeting, 24 Sept. 1965, box 1.
10. LBJ to Milo F. Christiansen, 18 Aug. 1965, WHSF, LCAF, Beautification-C, box 10.
11. Washington to LBJ, 24 Sept. 1965, WHSF/BF, Beautification Meeting, 24 Sept. 1965, box 1; Arthur A. Davis to Washington, 22 Sept. 1965, Louchheim Papers, box C29.
12. Katharine Graham to LBJ, 28 Sept. 1965, Louchheim Papers, box C29.
13. Notes on luncheon meeting with Walter Washington and Charlotte Hubbard, 6 Oct. 1965, Louchheim Papers, box C29.
14. LBJ to Graham, 11 Oct. 1965, Louchheim Papers, box C29.
15. Washington to Liz Carpenter, 20 Oct. 1965, WHSF/BF, Give Till It's

Beautiful, box 6; Nash Castro to Sutton Jett, 18 Nov. 1965, Nash Castro Papers, Mrs. Johnson's file, box 3.

16. Castro to Jett, 18 Nov. 1965, Castro Papers, Mrs. Johnson's file, box 3; "Beautification Summary," p. 22.

17. Ben W. Gilbert to Walter Tobriner, 12 Nov. 1965, Louchheim Papers, box C29.

18. LBJ to Tobriner, 6 Dec. 1965, WHSF, LCAF, Beautification–T, box 15.

19. Castro to Jett, 12 Jan. 1966, Castro Papers, Mrs. Johnson's file, box 3, describes Brooke Astor's early commitment to the Buchanan School. For Mrs. Johnson's comment about Astor see LBJ's speech at the dedication of the Buchanan School playground in 1968, reprinted in U.S., House, *Congressional Record*, 90th Cong., 2d sess., 15 May 1968, p. 13554. The Astor-Johnson friendship had evolved during 1965; see LBJ to Brooke Astor, 10 Feb. and 24 May 1965, Astor to LBJ, 16 Feb., 21 May, and 11 Sept. 1965, WHSF, AF, Mrs. Vincent Astor, box 45; Brooke Astor, *Footprints* (Garden City, N.Y.: Doubleday, 1980), pp. 335–40.

20. Katie Louchheim to Liz Carpenter, 2 Mar. 1966, Castro Papers, BF, box 7.

21. Polly Shackleton to LBJ, 21 Jan. 1966, WHSF, AF, Polly Shackleton, box 1836; for the biographical data on Shackleton see U.S., Senate, *Nominations of D.C. Commissioner, Assistant to Commissioner, and Nine City Council Members: Hearings before the Committee on the District of Columbia*, 90th Cong., 1st sess. (Washington, D.C.: GPO, 1967), pp. 163–65.

22. LBJ to Shackleton, 26 Jan. 1966, WHSF, AF, Polly Shackleton, box 1836.

23. Shackleton to Liz Carpenter, 24 Feb. 1966, LBJ to Shackleton, 1 Mar. 1966, WHSF, LCAF, Beautification–S, box 14. Shackleton noted that what she was proposing was in line with what Senator Abraham Ribicoff of Connecticut had suggested in a Senate speech on 10 Feb. 1966: see U.S., Senate, *Congressional Record*, 89th Cong., 2d sess., 10 Feb. 1966, p. 2951.

24. Shackleton furnished an account of how Project Pride had evolved when the First Lady's Committee met in Oct. 1966: see Transcript, First Lady's Committee for a More Beautiful Capital, 5 Oct. 1966, WHSF/BF, box 2, pp. 22–28.

25. Project Pride, press release, 19 July 1966, Louchheim Papers, box C30.

26. Sharon Francis to Liz Carpenter, with Mrs. Johnson's written comments, 25 Aug. 1966, WHSF/BF, Beautification Meeting, 5 Oct. 1966, box 2.

27. Transcript, First Lady's Committee, 5 Oct. 1966, pp. 23, 24, 34, 35.

28. Shackleton to Carolyn Fortas, 20 Oct. 1966, WHSF, AF, Polly Shackleton, box 1836; Shackleton to Francis, 14 Apr. 1967, WHSF/BF, Trail Blazers, box 8.

29. Laurance Rockefeller to LBJ, 7 July 1967, WHSF, AF, Laurance Rockefeller, box 1779; Shackleton to Rockefeller, 18 July (2d quotation) and 1 Sept. (last quotation) 1967, WHSF/BF, Trail Blazers, box 8.

30. Rockefeller to Shackleton, 24 Aug. 1967, WHSF/BF, Trail Blazers, box 8.

31. LBJ to William R. Manning, 13 Feb. 1968, WHSF, AF, Laurance Rockefeller, box 1779; Sharon Francis to Washington, 27 Sept. 1968, WHSF, AF, Walter Washington, box 2070.

32. Joseph Judge, "New Grandeur for Flowering Washington," *National Geographic,* Apr. 1967, p. 520.

33. "Beautification Summary," p. 38. Astor also announced plans to transform the area around the Arthur Capper housing development at 5th and K streets, S.E.; see LBJ to Astor, 3 Apr. 1967, and LBJ to Astor, 25 Oct. 1967, with attached drafts and Mrs. Johnson's comments, WHSF, AF, Mrs. Vincent Astor, box 45.

34. "Walter Edward Washington"; Viorst, *Hustlers and Heroes,* pp. 242–48; Sharon Francis, OH, 20 May 1969, pp. 37–39.

35. For accounts of these events see the news stories reproduced in *Nominations of D.C. Commissioner,* pp. 135–49, 187–95.

36. McPherson to LJ, 24 Aug. 1967, Harry McPherson files, District of Columbia, box 20; Sharon Francis, OH, 4 June 1969, pp. 18–19.

37. Stephen R. Currier to LJ, 15 Dec. 1965, Francis to Liz Carpenter, 15 Feb. 1966, WHSF/BF, Urban America, box 13. Because of the early deaths of Currier and his wife, there is not much biographical data about him; see "Currier Lawyers Ask Court Ruling," *New York Times,* 1 Feb. 1967, and "800 Attend Rites for the Curriers," *New York Times,* 16 Feb. 1967. Joan Mellen, in *Privilege: The Enigma of Sasha Bruce* (New York: New American Library, 1983), pp. 86–87, suggests a more complex picture of the Curriers' marriage and his motivation.

38. Francis to Carpenter, 6 July 1966, and n.d., WHSF/BF, Currier Offer, box 6.

39. Francis to Carpenter, 27 Sept. 1966, and Victor Weingarten to Francis, 14 Sept. 1966, WHSF/BF, Currier Offer, box 6; Francis, OH, 20 May 1969, pp. 28–29. In her oral recollections, Francis places Currier's offer after Mrs. Johnson's trip to the West Coast in September, but the idea had clearly been discussed before that. For the First Lady's remarks at the Urban America conference see "Beautification Summary," p. 35.

40. Francis to Carpenter, 27 Sept. 1966, WHSF/BF, Currier Offer, box 6.

41. Francis, OH, 20 May 1969, p. 26; Johnson, *White House Diary,* pp. 423–27. For the political dimension of the trip see Ann Alanson to LBJ, 15 June 1966, Carpenter to LBJ, 24 June 1966, Carpenter to Alanson, 5 July 1966, WHSF, LCAF, Beautification–D, box 10.

42. Carpenter to LBJ, Sept. 1966, WHSF/BF, Currier Offer, box 6; Francis, OH, 20 May 1969, pp. 27, 28.

43. Lawrence Halprin, *Cities* (New York: Reinhold, 1964), and *Freeways* (New York: Reinhold, 1966); Pamela Knight, "Pioneer Planner in the Western Wilderness," *Sports Illustrated,* 28 Mar. 1966, p. 52; my interview with Halprin, 5 Apr. 1984; Halprin kindly let me consult relevant parts of his personal archives in San Francisco after the interview; Carpenter to LBJ, Sept. 1966, WHSF/BF, Currier Offer, box 6.

44. Francis, OH, 20 May 1969, pp. 30, 31.

45. Ibid., p. 32.

46. Ibid., pp. 33–34.

47. Francis to LBJ, 4 Jan. 1967, WHSF/BF, Halprin Report, box 6 (quotations); for Halprin's own designs see Taconic Foundation, 7 Dec. 1966, Vic Weingarten, Washington, 13 Dec. 1966, Notes re Washington trip for next week, Dec. 1966—all in Lawrence Halprin Papers, San Franciso.

48. Francis to LBJ, 4 Jan. 1967, WHSF/BF, Halprin Report, box 6; see also Thomas Appleby to Francis, 2 Dec. 1966, Halprin Report, box 6, and Dwight Rettie to Francis, 5 Jan. 1967, Capper Plaza, box 5—both in WHSF/BF.

49. Roberta Hornig, "Stress on Neighborhood Slated in Beautification," *Washington Evening Star,* 12 Jan. 1967 (quotations); Wolf Von Eckardt, "Proposed New Parks Are Badly Needed," *Washington Post,* 13 Jan. 1967.

50. Transcript, Meeting of the First Lady's Committee for a More Beautiful Capital, 12 Jan. 1967, WHSF/BF, Beautification Meeting, 12 Jan. 1967, box 2, p. 5 (Udall quotation).

51. Ibid., pp. 9, 10.

52. Ibid., pp. 12, 18, 21, 39.

53. Ibid., p. 46; Roberta Hornig, "Beauty Planned For Capitol East," *Washington Evening Star,* 13 Jan. 1967 (LBJ's quotation); Eckardt, "Proposed New Parks Are Badly Needed."

54. Francis, OH, 20 May 1969, p. 41, for Rowe's remark.

55. Ibid., pp. 58–62 (Francis quotation on p. 62).

56. LBJ to Mrs. Bruce, 17 Jan. 1967, WHSF/BF, Halprin Report, box 6, expressing her concern to Mrs. Currier's mother about reports that the couple had been lost; Francis, OH, 20 May 1969, p. 64; "800 Attend Rites for the Curriers."

57. Progress Report, Halprin Proposals, 1 Apr. 1967, WHSF/BF, Halprin Report, box 6; Lloyd K. Garrison to Francis, 20 June 1967, Francis to LBJ, 30 June 1967, WHSF/BF, Capitol East–Inner Blocks, box 5.

58. Polly Shackleton, Report on Capitol East to First Lady's Committee, 17 Mar. 1967, Francis to Edward Gruis, 16 Feb. 1967, WHSF/BF, Capitol East–Inner Blocks, box 5.

59. Progress Report, Halprin Proposals, 1 Apr. 1967, WHSF/BF, Halprin Report, box 6; Charles Horsky to Edward Aronov, 15 Feb. 1967, Aronov to Isadore Seaman, 13 Mar. 1967, WHSF/BF, Capper Plaza, box 5; Gerald M. Rubin to Francis, 2 Mar. 1967, Andrew F. Euston, Jr., to Francis, 6 Mar. 1967, WHSF/BF, Capitol East–Inner Blocks, box 5.

60. Francis to Stewart Udall, 7 Apr. 1967, Charles M. Haar to Charles A. Horsky, 11 Apr. 1967, Elmer Atkins to Horsky, 25 Apr. 1967, WHSF/BF, Halprin Report, box 6.

61. Francis to LBJ, 12 May 1967, Francis to Lloyd Garrison, 2 May 1967, WHSF/BF, Halprin Report, box 6.

62. Francis to Liz Carpenter, 23 May 1967, WHSF/BF, Capitol East–Inner Blocks, box 5. The trigger for the committee's action seems to have been an article attacking the administration's domestic programs; see Charles Stevenson, "The Great Society's Wondrous 'War' Budget," *Reader's Digest,* Apr. 1967, p. 51, and the response of the Johnson administration in U.S., House, *Indepen-*

dent Offices and Department of Housing and Urban Development Appropriations for 1968; Hearings before a Subcommittee of the Committee on Appropriations, 90th Cong., 1st sess. (Washington, D.C.: GPO, 1967), pp. 76–79.

63. Douglass Cater to Mike Manatos, 9 June 1967, conveying the memo of Francis to Carpenter of 23 May 1967, Douglass Cater files, Miscellaneous Correspondence, 1967, box 21.

64. Francis to LBJ, 30 June 1967, conveying Lloyd Garrison to Francis, 20 June 1967, WHSF/BF, Capitol East–Inner Blocks, box 5; Francis, OH, 20 May 1969, pp. 98–100.

65. These events are summarized in Interior Block Chronology, 1968, WHSF/BF, Capitol East–Inner Blocks, box 5.

66. Don Hummel to Walter Washington, 11 Mar. 1968, Hummel to Francis, 13 Mar. 1968, WHSF/BF, Capitol East–Inner Blocks, box 5.

67. Francis, OH, 20 May 1969, p. 99.

68. Lawrence Halprin to George B. Hartzog, Jr., 1 Dec. 1967, Halprin Papers.

69. Sharon Francis Notes on Kingman Lake Contract, 1968, WHSF/BF, Anacostia–Kingman Lake, box 4.

70. Francis, OH, 27 June 1969, pp. 8–9; "Beautification Summary," p. 72.

71. Francis to LBJ, 30 July 1968, WHSF/BF, Anacostia–Kingman Lake, box 4; Francis, OH, 27 June 1969, p. 11.

72. Johnson, *White House Diary,* pp. 647–60 (quotations on pp. 647, 649, 660). For an extensive analysis of this trip see Norma Ruth Holly Foreman, "The First Lady as a Leader of Public Opinion: A Study of the Role and Press Relations of Lady Bird Johnson" (Ph.D. diss., University of Texas at Austin, 1971), pp. 210–35.

73. Johnson, *White House Diary,* p. 655; Francis, OH, 27 June 1969, p. 5.

74. Johnson, *White House Diary,* p. 666; LBJ's remarks, WHSF/BF, Luncheon, Bus Tour, 17 Apr. 1968, box 4.

75. Speech of Walter Washington, WHSF/BF, Mayor's Remarks, 17 Apr. 1968, box 6; Francis, OH, 27 June 1969, p. 10; Johnson, *White House Diary,* p. 667.

76. *Congressional Record,* 15 May 1968, p. 13554; Francis, OH, 27 June 1969, p. 21.

77. Johnson, *White House Diary,* p. 667.

78. My interview with Lawrence Halprin, 5 Apr. 1984; my interview with Walter Washington, 9 Aug. 1984.

79. Walter Washington speech, 17 Apr. 1968, WHSF/BF, Mayor's Remarks, box 6. For the society's decline see Carolyn Agger Fortas to the Trustees, 8 Mar. 1973, and Wayne H. Dickson to Conrad Wirth, 15 June 1973, Louchheim Papers, box C31.

Chapter 7. The Highway Beautification Act of 1965

1. John Miller, "You Still Can't See Forest for the Billboards," *New York Times,* 28 Jan. 1985; Charles F. Floyd and Peter J. Shedd, *Highway Beautification: The*

Environmental Movement's Greatest Failure (Boulder, Colo.: Westview Press, 1979), p. 1.

2. The material in this paragraph is drawn from the chapter "The Struggle against the Billboard: Bane of the City Beautiful," by William H. Wilson of North Texas State University. I am indebted to Professor Wilson for his kindness in letting me consult this chapter from his manuscript on the City Beautiful movement during the Progressive Era.

3. Phillip Tocker, "Standardized Outdoor Advertising: History, Economics and Self-Regulation," in *Outdoor Advertising: History and Regulation,* ed. John W. Houck (Notre Dame: University of Notre Dame Press, 1969), pp. 34–35. Chester H. Liebs, in *Main Street to Miracle Mile: American Roadside Architecture* (Boston: Little, Brown, 1985), pp. 41–42, and Phil Patton, in *Open Road: A Celebration of the American Highway* (New York: Simon & Schuster, 1986), pp. 171–74, both look at billboards in the context of larger concerns about the impact of roads on American history; they have relatively little new to add to what the Houck volume provides. Association of National Advertisers, *Essentials of Outdoor Advertising* (New York: Association of National Advertisers, 1952), is an industry manual. For a general history of the Outdoor Advertising Association see *The Outdoor Story* (Chicago: Outdoor Advertising Association of America, 1954).

4. Mrs. Jack Marnie summarized the work of the Outdoor Circle at the 1965 White House Conference on Natural Beauty; see *Beauty for America: Proceedings of the White House Conference on Natural Beauty* (Washington, D.C.: GPO, 1965), p. 257 (quotation). For more on the Hawaiian case see Fred C. Kelly, "Boycott versus Billboard," *Reader's Digest,* Feb. 1937, pp. 39–40; see also Donald Culross Peattie, "The Billboards Must Go," ibid., Oct. 1938, pp. 56–58; Roger William Riis, "The Billboards Must Go: II," ibid., Nov. 1938, pp. 81–84; and Thomas C. Desmond, "The Billboard Lobby," *American Mercury,* Sept. 1947, pp. 344–50; Michael Litka, "The Use of Eminent Domain and Police Power to Accomplish Aesthetic Goals," in *Outdoor Advertising,* pp. 89–98.

5. James L. Sundquist, *Politics and Policy: The Eisenhower, Kennedy, and Johnson Years* (Washington, D.C.: Brookings Institution, 1968), pp. 340–43; Richard L. Neuberger to Dear Friend, 22 Apr. 1957, Lee Metcalf Papers, Montana Historical Society, Helena; Clifton W. Enfield, "Federal Highway Beautification: Outdoor Advertising Control, Legislation and Regulation," in *Outdoor Advertising,* pp. 150–56.

6. R. Neuberger and Thomas Kuchel to LJ, 21 Mar. 1958, LBJA, Thomas Kuchel file, Congressional, box 48; Sundquist, *Politics and Policy,* pp. 344–45.

7. Resolution attached to Lee Metcalf to Garden Department, Century Club, Kalispell, Mont., 4 Apr. 1958, Metcalf Papers; Sundquist, *Politics and Policy,* p. 343; for an example of the work of a roadside council see Yale Maxon to Board of Supervisors of Alameda County, Calif., 21 May 1959, on behalf of the California Roadside Council, copy courtesy of Mr. Maxon.

8. *Beauty for America,* pp. 250–52 (quotation on p. 251); see also M.

Neuberger to Hilda Fox, 17 July 1961, Hugh Scott to Fox, 7 July 1961, Maurine Neuberger Papers, University of Oregon, Eugene.

9. There is no standard scholarly history of the billboard industry. Tocker, "Standardized Outdoor Advertising," pp. 11–56, is a good place to begin; see also Sundquist, *Politics and Policy,* pp. 343–44; Charles Stevenson, "The Great Billboard Scandal of 1960," *Reader's Digest,* Mar. 1960, pp. 146–56; Thomas E. Redard, "The Politics of Beautification in the Johnson Administration" (Master's Thesis, University of Texas at Austin, 1976), p. 26–43.

10. For Johnson's attitude toward billboard control see LJ to George Parkhouse, 15 June 1957, LJ to Phillip Tocker, 26 Mar. 1957, LBJA, Highways, subject file, box 69; Lloyd Hand to LJ, 21 Mar. 1958, Senate subject files, Highways, 1958, box 603; Arthur C. Perry to Paul Middleton, 7 Oct. 1959, Senate subject files, Highways, 1959, with the resolution of the Outdoor Advertising Association of Texas, conveyed with Middleton to LJ, 29 Sept. 1959, box 677; see also Hand to LJ, 3 Mar. 1959, Senate subject files, Highways, 1959, box 677, for more on Tocker and LJ.

11. Special Message to the Congress on the Federal Highway Program, 28 Feb. 1961, *Public Papers of the Presidents of the United States: John F. Kennedy, 1961* (Washington, D.C.: GPO, 1962), p. 132.

12. Maurine Neuberger to Luther Hodges, 28 Feb. and 2 June 1961, M. Neuberger to Mrs. Wallace Baker, 11 May 1961, Hodges to M. Neuberger, 22 Mar. 1963, M. Neuberger to Mrs. Cyril G. Fox, 24 Oct. 1963, Maurine Neuberger Papers, University of Oregon, Eugene. I am indebted to John Simpson of Eugene, Oregon, for making copies of relevant materials from the Neuberger Papers for me.

13. For Connor's comments about the 1958 law see U.S., House, *Highway Beautification: Hearings before the Subcommittee on Roads of the Committee on Public Works,* 89th Cong., 1st sess. (Washington, D.C.: GPO, 1965), p. 4. For an evaluation of the strengths and weaknesses of the 1958 law see Floyd and Shedd, *Highway Beautification,* pp. 71–74. The authors prefer the Bonus Act to what occurred under the Highway Beautification Act of 1965.

14. Ross Netherton, who was involved in the enforcement of the 1958 measure, gave me the benefit of his detailed analysis of the 1958 law in his comments on a paper about Mrs. Johnson and highway beautification that I sent him in early 1986. The quotations are taken from his critique; see also Ross Netherton, "An Anniversary View of Highway Beautification," a paper delivered at the Conservation and Beautification Forum of the Garden Club of Virginia, 7 Nov. 1984, courtesy of Ross Netherton.

15. Peter Blake, *God's Own Junkyard: The Planned Deterioration of America's Landscape* (New York: Holt, Rinehart & Winston, 1964), p. 15; Stevenson, "Great Billboard Scandal of 1960," pp. 146–56.

16. Report of the Task Force on the Preservation of Natural Beauty, 18 Nov. 1964, Task Force Reports, box 1, pp. 9–10; James Reston, Jr., to Goodwin, 4 May 1964, Richard Goodwin files, Conservation–Natural Beauty, box 28, and Natural Beauty and the Public Interest, 28 Oct. 1964, Goodwin files, Natural

Beauty–Background, box 14 (quotation); see also William H. Whyte, *The Last Landscape* (Garden City, N.Y.: Doubleday, 1968), pp. 304–6.

17. The quotation is from Maxine Cheshire, "Mrs. Johnson Digs New Landscape Role on Capitol Hill," *Washington Post*, 5 Jan. 1965; the only phone call from Lyndon Johnson to Luther Hodges during this period was on 6 Nov. 1964, President's Diary, 6 Nov. 1964, box 2; Rex M. Whitton to Bill Moyers, 23 Dec. 1964, WHCF, Highways (HI) 3, 22 Nov. 1963–10 Sept. 1965, box 5; my interview with LBJ, 16 Sept. 1984.

18. Hodges to LJ, with attached statement, 16 Dec. 1964, WHCF, HI3, 22 Nov. 1963–10 Sept. 1965, box 5; see also Lowell Bridwell to Hodges, 16 Nov. 1964, Robert E. Giles to Bridwell, 11 Dec. 1964, Clarence D. Martin to John T. Connor, 25 Jan. 1965, Records of the Department of Commerce, HB, reel 42, LBJL.

19. Hodges to LJ, 16 Dec. 1964, WHCF, HI3, 22 Nov. 1963–10 Sept. 1965, box 5; Clarence Martin to Moyers, 24 Dec. 1964, Bill Moyers files, HB, box 79.

20. The talks between the Kennedy administration and the Outdoor Advertising Association are discussed in B. W. Bordages to Jack Valenti, 21 Dec. 1964, WHCF, HI3, 22 Nov. 1963–17 Feb. 1965, box 6.

21. Donald S. Thomas to LJ, 28 Mar. 1965, Bill Moyers files, HB, box 79.

22. Thomas to LJ, 28 Mar. 1965, and Robert E. Giles to Moyers, 31 Mar. 1965, Moyers files, HB, box 79.

23. My interview with Phillip Tocker, 7 Feb. 1984.

24. For Moyers's reminiscences of his dealings with Tocker, which does not mention their negotiations in the first half of 1965, see Bill Moyers, *Listening to America: A Traveler Rediscovers His Country* (New York: Harper's Magazine Press Book, 1971), p. 267.

25. Tocker interview, 8 Feb. 1984; Lloyd Hand to LJ, 3 Mar. 1959, Senate subject files, Highways, 1959, box 677. The connection between Thomas and the Johnsons is indicated in Plea in Intervention in the Estate of T. J. Taylor, deceased, 21 Oct. 1963, HCCR, Probate Minutes, vol. 97, pp. 195–99, copy in Gould Papers.

26. *Public Papers of the Presidents of the United States: Lyndon B. Johnson, 1965*, 2 vols. (Washington, D.C.: GPO, 1966), 1:18 (1st quotation), 81 (2d quotation). For the drafting of the letter to Connor see Moyers to LJ, 19 Jan. 1965, Bill Moyers files, HB, box 79.

27. LJ to John T. Connor, 19 Jan. 1965, Moyers files, HB, box 79, contains LJ's handwritten copies in typed form, and there is another copy of the letter, with the president's handwriting, in the Department of Commerce Records, HB, reel 42; LJ to Connor, 5 Feb. (quotation) and 2 Apr. 1965, WHCF, HI3, 22 Nov. 1963–10 Sept. 1965, box 5; LJ to Connor, 4 Mar. 1965, Moyers files, HB, box 79; *Public Papers,* 1:54.

28. Lee C. White to ArDee Ames, 13 Apr. 1965, Richard Goodwin files, Natural Beauty, box 29.

29. "Ways to Beautify America," *U.S. News & World Report,* 22 Feb.1965, p. 75; Frank Blake, to Liz Carpenter, 11 Feb. 1965, Carpenter to Blake, 19 Feb.

1965, WHSF, Liz Carpenter's AF, Beautification–O, box 13; LBJ to Mrs. Baker Brownell, 26 Mar. 1965, WHSF, AF, Billboards–B, box 222; Carpenter to Rex Whitton, 15 Apr. 1965, WHSF/BF, Freeways: Routing and Design, box 10.

30. Phillip S. Hughes to Moyers, 7 Mar. 1965, Robert E. Giles to Hughes, 31 Mar. 1965, Bill Moyers files, HB, box 79.

31. Hughes to Moyers, 7 Mar. 1965, Moyers to LJ, 26 Mar. 1965, Moyers files, HB, box 79.

32. Donald S. Thomas to LJ, 28 Mar. 1965, Moyers files, HB, box 79; see also Thomas to Moyers, 28 Mar. and 6 Apr. 1965, WHCF, Legislation/Highways 3, 22 Nov. 1963–15 June 1965, box 63.

33. Giles to Moyers, 31 Mar. 1965, Moyers files, HB, box 79; see also Hughes to Moyers, 1 Apr. 1965, WHCF, HI3, 22 Nov. 1963–10 Sept. 1965, box 5.

34. Paul Southwick to Lawrence O'Brien, 14 Apr. 1965, Moyers files, HB, box 79 (1st quotation); Henry Wilson to O'Brien, 16 Apr. 1965, Michael Manatos files, HB, box 8 (2d quotation).

35. Thomas to Moyers, 14 Apr. 1965, WHCF, HI3, 22 Nov. 1963–10 Sept. 1965, box 5, quotes Tocker; Thomas to Moyers, 23 Apr. 1965, Moyers files, HB, box 79 (remaining quotations).

36. Tocker interview, 7 Feb. 1984. The conclusions about the motives of the OAAA and Tocker are mine.

37. Moyers to LJ, 27 Apr. 1965, WHCF, LE/HI3, box 62; Tocker to Moyers, 22 Apr. 1965, Moyers files, HB, box 79; Hubert Humphrey to Moyers, 3 May 1965, Moyers files, HB, box 79.

38. Moyers to Thomas, 26 Apr. 1965, Tocker to Moyers, 30 Apr. and 7 May 1965 (quotation), Moyers files, HB, box 79.

39. Undated memo conveying message from Tocker, May 1965, memo of 11 May 1965, Mark Evans to LJ, 21 May 1965, Evans to Moyers, 28 May 1965, Bill Moyers files, HB, box 79; Tocker to LJ, 24 May 1965, copy furnished by Tocker. For the phrase in the bill about state control see U.S., Senate, *Highway Beautification and Scenic Road Program: Hearings before the Subcommittee on Public Roads of the Committee on Public Works,* 89th Cong., 1st sess. (Washington, D.C.: GPO, 1965), p. 2.

40. Sharon Francis, OH, 4 June 1969, p. 52.

41. Maurine Neuberger to Hilda Fox, 10 Feb. 1965, box 1, Neuberger Papers; LBJ to Fox, 9 Mar., 2 Apr., and 22 May 1965, Billboards–P, LBJ to Helen Reynolds, 9 Apr. 1965, Billboards–R, WHSF, AF, box 222.

42. Mary Pakenham, "Capital Gets Road Beauty Signals Mixed," *Chicago Tribune,* 7 Feb. 1965; Thomas F. McGarry to Pakenham, 16 Feb. 1965, discussing Rex Whitton to Regional and Division Engineers, 25 Jan. 1965, WHSF, LCAF, Beautification–M, box 13.

43. Laurance Rockefeller to M. Neuberger, 14 May 1965, about her service as a delegate to the conference, and Hilda Fox to M. Neuberger, 11 May 1965, M. Neuberger to Fox, 20 May 1965, Neuberger Papers; *Beauty for America,* pp. 252–54, 266.

44. *Beauty for America,* p. 653.

45. Ibid., p. 681; Tocker interview, 7 Feb. 1984.

46. Helen Reynolds is quoted in Yale Maxon to Lewis L. Gould, 16 Apr. 1984, Gould Papers; Jack B. Robertson and Robert Evans to LJ, 26 May 1965 (2d quotation), Fred Farr to LJ, 27 May 1965, both included with covering memo of Lawrence McQuade to Richard Goodwin, 16 July 1965, Alan Boyd Papers, box 15; Palmer Smith to Douglass Cater, 29 May 1965, WHCF, HI3, 4 June 1965–14 June 1965, box 6; Robertson to M. Neuberger, 13 July 1965, Neuberger Papers.

47. James Schall to LBJ, 19 July 1965 (quotation), Alan Boyd to John T. Connor, 3 Aug. 1965, box 15, John T. Connor to Durward G. Hall, 23 Aug. 1965, box 16, Boyd Papers.

48. For the examples quoted see Bess Abell to Mike Manatos, 9 Jan. 1967, Manatos files, Social/Bess Abell, box 5; Sanders to Abell, 26 Feb. and 6 Mar. 1968 (with chart from which quotations are taken), Barefoot Sanders Papers, Memoranda, Chronological, box 25; for a representative event in 1965 see Johnson, *White House Diary,* p. 251.

49. For the transmittal of the highway bills see *Public Papers, 1965,* 1:582–84. The measured reaction of Senators Randolph and McNamara is reported in Claude Desautels to O'Brien, 26 May 1965, Lawrence O'Brien files, John Kluczynski file, box 16, and is evident in U.S., Senate, *Congressional Record,* 89th Cong., 1st sess., 3 June 1965, pp. 12534–36. For the quotation see Moyers to Richard Goodwin, 22 June 1965, Bill Moyers files, Department of Commerce, box 114.

50. Manatos to Liz Carpenter, 5 Aug. 1965, Paul Southwick to Henry Wilson, 11 Aug. 1965, O'Brien to LBJ, 16 Aug. 1965, Manatos files, HB, box 8; Dowell H. Anders to Alan Boyd, 30 Aug. 1965, HB, Department of Commerce Records, reel 42.

51. Manatos to O'Brien, 14 Aug. 1965, O'Brien to LBJ, 16 Aug. 1965 (quotation), Manatos files, HB, box 8. For criticism of the Highway Trust Fund and its beneficiaries see Helen Leavitt, *Superhighway-Superhoax* (Garden City, N.Y.: Doubleday, 1970), pp. 187–227.

52. *Public Papers, 1965,* 1:545, 546; Joseph W. Barr to LBJ, 17 June 1965, WHSF/BF, Highway Beautification Act, box 14; Manatos to O'Brien, 21 Aug. 1965, Manatos files, HB, box 8.

53. U.S., House, *Highway Beautification,* pp. 89 (1st quotation), 136–38, 143–217, for the complaints of the billboard industry; George H. Fallon to John W. McCormack, 3 Aug. 1965, Manatos files, HB, box 8.

54. Manatos to O'Brien, 3 Aug. 1965 (1st quotation), Manatos to Liz Carpenter, 5 Aug. 1965 (other quotations), Manatos files, HB, box 8.

55. Manatos to O'Brien, 16 Aug. 1965, O'Brien to LBJ, 16 Aug. 1965, Manatos files, HB, box 8; U.S., Senate, *Highway Beautification,* passim.

56. Charles Schultze to LJ, 17 Aug. 1965, Moyers files, HB, box 79 (italics in the original); Alan Boyd to John T. Connor, 6 Aug. 1965, Department of Commerce, Highway Beauty, reel 42.

57. Manatos to O'Brien, 21 and 23 Aug. 1965, Paul Southwick to Henry Wilson, 2 Sept. 1965, Manatos files, HB, box 8.

58. Manatos to O'Brien, 23 Aug. 1965, Paul Southwick to Those Listed Below, 3 Sept. 1965, Manatos files, HB, box 8; John T. Connor to LJ, 26 Aug. 1965, WHCF, HI3, 11 Sept. 1965–31 Mar. 1966, box 5.

59. Walter Reuther to LBJ, 20 Aug. 1965 (1st quotation), LBJ to Reuther, 26 Aug. 1965 (2d quotation), WHSF/BF, Beautification Special, box 15; Tocker to Moyers, 12 and 18 Aug. 1965, Moyers to Tocker, 18 Aug. 1965, WHCF, HI3, 14 Aug. 1965–14 Sept. 1965, box 6.

60. Elizabeth Brenner Drew, "Lady Bird's Beauty Bill," *Atlantic,* Dec. 1965, p. 71; the quotation is from the Johnson slide presentation, courtesy of LBJL.

61. Committee Print, S.2084, 3 Sept. 1965, Phillip S. Hughes to Moyers, 4 and 7 Sept. 1965, Moyers files, HB, box 79; Paul Southwick to Manatos, 7 Sept. 1965, Manatos files, HB, box 8; the origins of the "just compensation" provision are not evident in the materials held in LBJL. The legislative sponsor of this language seems to have been Senator John Sherman Cooper, a Kentucky Republican who had worked with Maurine Neuberger and other billboard-control advocates on earlier legislation; see John Sherman Cooper, "The Highway Beautification Act of 1965," a draft for a speech that the senator made, and other press releases, statements, and legislative materials regarding his authorship of "just compensation," in the John Sherman Cooper Papers, University of Kentucky Library, box 528. I am indebted to Bill Cooper of the University of Kentucky Library for putting this material at my disposal.

62. Joseph W. Barr to Manatos, 7 Sept. 1965, Manatos to O'Brien, 7 and 8 Sept. 1965; Paul Southwick to Manatos, 8 Sept. 1965, Stanley S. Surrey to Manatos, 9 Sept. 1965, Manatos files, HB, box 8.

63. Notes From Mrs. Johnson's Day, WHSF, Liz Carpenter's subject file, Jackson Hole, Wyo., Sept. 1965, box 17, quotes Lady Bird Johnson's reaction; for her speech see "Beautification Summary," p. 17; "Senate Unit Approves Stiff Outdoor Bill," *Advertising Age,* 13 Sept. 1965, p. 8.

64. For Kluczynski's general position see his comments in U.S., House, *Highway Beautification,* pp. 241–68; and for his initial views on the bill see Jake Jacobsen to LJ, 11 Sept. 1965, WHCF, HI3, 11 Sept. 1965–30 Mar. 1966, box 5.

65. Manatos to Jack Valenti, 10 Sept. 1965, Manatos files, HB, box 8.

66. Joseph Califano to LJ, LBJ, et al., 11 Sept. 1965, WHCF, Legislation/Natural Resources, 22 Nov. 1963–20 Oct. 1964, box 142, summarizes the results of the conference; Liz Carpenter conveyed the information and the quotation about Kluczynski during an interview with her and Mrs. Johnson, on 16 Sept. 1984; Jake Jacobsen to LJ, 11 Sept. 1965, WHCF, HI3, 11 Sept. 1965–30 Mar. 1966, box 5.

67. Tocker interview, 7 Feb. 1984, Tocker to Donald S. Thomas, 12 Sept. 1965, O'Brien to LJ, 13 Sept. 1965, 10:45 A.M., WHCF, LE/HI3, box 63; O'Brien to LJ, 13 Sept. 1965, 7:20 P.M., WHCF, HI3, 11 Sept. 1965–30 Mar. 1966, box 5; John T. Connor to Tocker, 26 Aug. 1965, Boyd Papers, box 16.

68. LJ to Patrick McNamara, 15 Sept. 1965, Manatos to O'Brien, 17 Sept. 1965, O'Brien to LJ, 18 Sept. 1965, Manatos files, HB, box 8; U.S., Senate,

Congressional Record, 89th Cong., 1st sess., 14 Sept. 1965, pp. 23784, 23791, 15 Sept. 1965, pp. 23868–85, and 16 Sept. 1965, pp. 24087–24144. The amendment is printed on p. 24111; the crucial vote on it appears on p. 24126.

69. U.S., Senate, *Congressional Record,* 89th Cong., 1st sess., 15 Sept. 1965, p. 23872 (Cooper quotation), and 16 Sept. 1965, p. 24141 (final passage); Manatos to O'Brien, 17 Sept. 1965, Manatos files, HB, box 8.

70. O'Brien to LJ, 17 Sept. 1965, Manatos files, HB, box 8.

71. U.S., House, *H.R. Report 1084,* 89th Cong., 1st sess. (Washington, D.C.: GPO, 1965), p. 45; Boyd to Moyers and O'Brien, 23 Sept. 1965, Alan Boyd Papers, box 17; O'Brien to LJ, 23 Sept. 1965, WHCF, LE/H13, box 63; James C. Rettie to Director, Resources Program Staff, 24 Sept. 1965, file 103, Records of the Department of the Interior, box 5, reporting on the meeting of the National Highway Beautification Committee.

72. Boyd to Moyers and O'Brien, 23 Sept. 1965, Alan Boyd Papers, box 17. The figure about the mail on highway beauty comes from Helen Reynolds to Editor, *Atlantic Monthly,* 15 Dec. 1965, with Sharon Francis to Helen Reynolds, 8 Jan. 1966, WHSF/BF, Highway Beautification Act, box 14.

73. For the lobbying effort see Helen Reynolds to John T. Connor, 20 Sept. 1965, Boyd to Reynolds, 28 Sept. 1965, Boyd Papers, box 17; Paul Southwick to Hayes Redmon, 28 Sept. 1965, Wayne Phillips to Redmon, 29 Sept. 1965, Bill Moyers files, HB, box 79; Activities on Behalf of Highway Improvement Bill, 5 Oct. 1965, WHSF/BF, Highway Beautification Act, box 14; Henry Wilson to Carpenter, 27 Sept. 1965, WHSF, Liz Carpenter's subject file, Buffalo and Syracuse, N.Y., Sept. 1965, box 18; LBJ to Mrs. Leonard Fox and family, 17 Sept. 1965, WHSF, AF, Beautification–Fox, box 113.

74. *Washington Post,* 30 Sept. 1965 (1st and 2d quotations), 1 Oct. 1965 (3d quotation); Carpenter to LBJ, 4 Oct. 1965 (last quotations), WHSF/BF, Highway Beautification Act, box 14.

75. LBJ to Helen Reynolds, 7 Oct. 1965, WHSF, AF, Billboards–C, box 222.

76. Carpenter to LJ, 6 Oct. 1965, WHCF, HI3, 11 Sept. 1965–30 Mar. 1966, box 6; *Washington Post,* 6 Oct. 1965 (last two quotations).

77. Jack Anderson, in "Sharp Battle on Beautification Bill," *Washington Post,* 15 Oct. 1965, covers these events; Johnson, *White House Diary,* pp. 324–28; *Washington Post,* 8 Oct. 1965 (1st quotation); President Johnson's comments can be heard on "A Salute to Congress, The White House," 7 Oct. 1965 (Washington: The White House Historical Association, 1965), a phonograph record, at the end of side two.

78. U.S., House, *Congressional Record,* 89th Cong., 1st sess., 7 Oct. 1965, pp. 26288 (1st quotation), 26307 (2d quotation), 26302 (3d quotation), 26306 (Dole amendment).

79. *Congressional Record,* pp. 26295 (Tuten amendment), 26300 (vote on Tuten amendment), 26321–22 (vote on bill); Tocker interview, 7 Feb. 1984.

80. Robert E. Giles to John T. Connor, 8 Oct. 1965, Bill Moyers files, HB, box 79; Wilson to O'Brien, 12 Oct. 1965 (quotation), Henry Wilson files, HB, box 8; U.S., Senate, *Congressional Record,* 13 Oct. 1965, p. 26864.

81. Paul Southwick to Connor, 22 Oct. 1965, Department of Commerce Records, reel 1; *Public Papers, 1965,* 2:1073.

82. LBJ to W. Robert Amick, 19 Nov. 1965, WHSF, AF, Beautification–Four H Clubs, box 113; *Washington Evening Star,* 8 Oct. 1965; "Highways Not Low Ways," *Christian Science Monitor,* 20 Oct. 1965; for the cartoon see LBJ to William H. Crawford, with a copy of the drawing as it appeared in the *Pittsburgh Press,* 11 Oct. 1965, LCAF, Beautification–P, box 14.

83. Lee Ray Page to LJ, 10 Sept. 1965, WHCF, NR, 1 Oct. 1965–8 Dec. 1965, box 7; Page operated the Dallas Outdoor Sign Co., in Dallas, Texas; "Apologies to Lady Bird Johnson," U.S., Senate, *Congressional Record,* 13 Oct. 1965, p. 26860, discusses the Montana sign; the Bill Mauldin cartoon appears in "Signs along the Road," *New Republic,* 2 Oct. 1965, p. 7. For the aftermath of the Dole episode and his remarks in the House see U.S., House, *Congressional Record,* 8 Oct. 1965, p. 26423. Senator Richard Russell of Georgia sent President Johnson information about Dole's actions in the House debate; see Russell to LJ, 15 Nov. 1965, WHCF, NR, 1 Sept. 1965–16 Jan. 1966, box 4.

84. Johnson, *White House Diary,* p. 325.

85. Hilda Fox to M. Neuberger, 3 Nov. 1965, Maurine Neuberger Papers; Drew, "Lady Bird's Beauty Bill," p. 68.

86. Francis, OH, 20 May 1969, pp. 49–50.

87. Drew, "Lady Bird's Beauty Bill," pp. 68, 70; Tocker interview, 7 Feb. 1984. For the use of "generalists" in the Johnson White House see Emmette S. Redford and Richard T. McCulley, *White House Operations: The Johnson Presidency* (Austin: University of Texas Press, 1986), pp. 60–61.

88. Rex M. Whitton to Phillip A. Conrath, 23 Aug. 1965, box 16, Whitton to Helen Reynolds, 23 Dec. 1965, box 20, Boyd Papers; Hilda Fox to M. Neuberger, 11 May 1965, Maurine Neuberger Papers. There is no evidence in the Neuberger Papers, for example, that the senator was brought in on the lobbying campaign of the White House in Oct. 1965.

89. Lawrence F. O'Brien, in *No Final Victories: A Life in Politics from John F. Kennedy to Watergate* (Garden City, N.Y.: Doubleday, 1974), pp. 170–71, stresses Lady Bird Johnson's involvement in the legislative process.

Chapter 8. Protecting Highway Beauty, 1966–69

1. Lawrence Jones to Liz Carpenter, 23 and 24 Nov. 1965, WHSF, LCAF, Beautification–H, box 12.

2. Boyd to John T. Connor, 19 Jan. 1966, Alan Boyd Papers, box 21, describes the procedures that had to be followed in implementing the new law.

3. Connor to LBJ, 19 Jan. 1966, LBJ to Connor, 22 Jan. 1966, WHSF, AF, John T. Connor, box 101. The report that she read was the Alan Boyd memo cited in n. 2. The draft standards were printed in U.S., Senate, *Congressional Record,* 89th Cong., 2d sess., 25 Mar. 1966, pp. 6809–13, as part of a speech by Senator Warren Magnuson.

4. Ibid., p. 6809.

5. U.S., House, *Congressional Record,* 89th Cong., 2d sess., 9 Feb. 1966, p. 2810 (1st quotation); Senate, *Congressional Record,* 4 Feb., pp. 2139–41 (Randolph), and 16 Feb. 1966, p. 3127 (Muskie); Paul Southwick to Bill Moyers, 10 Feb. 1966, WHCF, H13, 11 Sept. 1965–30 Mar. 1966, box 5, discusses Tocker; see also Tocker to Connor, 10 Feb. 1966, Department of Transportation Records, reel 98; S. Frank Rafferty to Connor, 10 Feb. 1966, Alan Boyd Papers, box 22.

6. "Special Message to the Congress on Transportation," 2 Mar. 1966, *Public Papers of the Presidents of the United States: Lyndon B. Johnson, 1966,* 2 vols. (Washington, D.C.: GPO, 1967), 1:250, and "Annual Budget Message," ibid., 1:53; for the background on the Highway Trust Fund proposal see Boyd to John K. Carlock, 28 Feb. 1966, Boyd Papers, box 22.

7. C. J. Ternand to Everett M. Dirksen, n.d., enclosed with Dirksen to Connor, 8 Mar. 1966, and Boyd to Dirksen, 19 Apr. 1966, Boyd Papers, box 25; Boyd to Connor, 30 June 1966, ibid., box 26; U.S., Senate, *Federal Aid Highway Act of 1966: Hearings before the Subcommittee on Roads of the Committee on Public Works,* 89th Cong., 2d sess. (Washington, D.C.: GPO, 1966), pp. 87–88, 321–23.

8. Connor to Nicholas Katzenbach, 27 July 1966, Boyd Papers, box 26. For the documentation see Lawrence C. McQuade to James Jones, 19 Sept. 1966, WHCF, Highways 2/ST/42, box 5; Rex. M. Whitton to Helen Reynolds, 10 Nov. 1966, WHSF/BF, Highway Beauty Act, box 14.

9. The revised guidelines are summarized in Whitton to Connor, June 1966, Transportation Records, reel 98. For Tocker's lobbying see Boyd to Tocker, 15 June 1966, ibid., reel 98, and also Boyd to Senator Fred Harris of Oklahoma, 6 June 1966, and Boyd to Herbert Wiltsee, 30 June 1966, Boyd Papers, box 26.

10. Sharon Francis Notes of Conversation with Rex Whitton, 12 Aug. 1966, and Francis to Liz Carpenter, with draft letter to Lawrence Jones, Aug. 1966, WHSF/BF, Freeways: Routing and Design, box 10.

11. Lowell Bridwell to Boyd, 8 July 1966, Boyd Papers, box 27; U.S., House, *Congressional Record,* 89th Cong., 2s sess., 11 Aug. 1966, pp. 19082–84.

12. *Congressional Record,* 11 Aug. 1966, pp. 19100 (quotation), 19103 (vote on amendment), 19105 (vote on Ford's motion). On the position of the administration see Henry Wilson to Wilfred H. Rommel, 11 Aug. 1966, and Rommel to Wilson, 18 Aug. 1966, Charles Roche files, Federal-Aid Highway, box 2.

13. Lowell Bridwell to Paul Southwick, 19 Aug. 1966, Boyd Papers, box 28; Al Keefer to Southwick, 18 Aug. 1966, Henry Wilson Files, Federal-Aid Highway, box 13; House, *Congressional Record,* 31 Aug. 1966, pp. 21338–39, 21340 (Harsha quotation), and 2 Sept. 1966, p. 21724 (Wilson quotation).

14. Liz Carpenter and Sharon Francis to LBJ, 7 Oct. 1966, WHSF/BF, Highway Beauty Act, box 14.

15. For Lady Bird Johnson's previous acquaintance with Fred Farr see Lady Bird Johnson, *A White House Diary* (New York: Holt, Rinehart & Winston, 1970), pp. 270, 424, 425; Carpenter to Farr, 7 Dec. 1965, Farr to LBJ, 6 Apr.

1966, LBJ to Farr, 27 Apr. 1966, WHSF, LCAF, Beautification–F, box 11; Bridwell to Farr, 21 Nov. 1966, Alan Boyd Papers, box 31; Boyd to LBJ, 9 Jan. 1967, WHSF/BF, Highway Beauty Act, 1967, box 15.

16. Boyd to Francis, 28 June 1966, Boyd Papers, box 26; Francis to LBJ, 9 Jan. 1967, WHSF/BF, Highway Beauty Act, 1967, box 15; see also Boyd's testimony in U.S., Senate, *Highway Beautification and Highway Safety Programs: Hearings before the Subcommittee on Roads of the Committee on Public Works,* 90th Cong., 1st sess. (Washington, D.C.: GPO, 1967), pp. 3–8.

17. Boyd to LBJ, 4 Jan. 1967, WHSF/BF, Highway Beauty Act, 1967, box 15. President Johnson asked for a Highway Beauty Trust Fund on 30 Jan. 1967; see *Public Papers of the Presidents of the United States: Lyndon B. Johnson, 1967,* 2 vols. (Washington, D.C.: GPO, 1968), 1:98.

18. The standards were published on 10 Jan. 1967 as *1967 Highway Beautification Program,* Senate Document no. 6, 90th Cong., 1st sess. (Washington, D.C.: GPO, 1967); see also Francis to LBJ, 9 Jan. 1967, WHSF/BF, Highway Beauty Act, 1967, box 15; *Washington Post,* 12 Jan. 1967.

19. Boyd to LBJ, 4 Jan. 1967, WHSF/BF, Highway Beauty Act, 1967, box 15, discusses the contrasting positions in detail.

20. Ibid.

21. Jennings Randolph to Boyd, 16 Jan. 1967, Boyd Papers, box 33; Francis to Douglass Cater, 25 Jan. 1967, WHCF, HI3, 31 Mar. 1966–, box 5.

22. Russell Train to Francis, 26 Jan. 1967, conveying the Highway Beautification Report, 23 Jan. 1967, of the Conservation Foundation, with the quotations from pp. 3 and 4 of the report, WHSF/BF, Highway Beauty Act, 1967, box 15; for the Washington State amendments see U.S., House, *Congressional Record,* 90th Cong., 1st sess., 9 Mar. 1967, pp. 6053–57. The leading sponsor was Thomas M. Pelly, a Democrat.

23. Liz Carpenter to LJ and LBJ, 30 Jan. 1967, WHSF/BF, Highway Beauty Reception, box 16. There is a news story attached to the memo from which Lyndon Johnson's remarks to the Congressional leaders are taken.

24. Boyd to LJ, 7 Feb. 1967, Boyd, Memorandum of Conversation Re: Highway Beautification, 8 Feb. 1967, Cater to LJ, 8 Feb. 1967, Douglass Cater files, HB, box 96.

25. Remarks of Mrs. Lyndon B. Johnson at Reception Honoring Citizens Advisory Committee on Recreation and Natural Beauty, 16 Feb. 1967, Francis to Carpenter, n.d. but Feb. 1967, WHSF/BF, Highway Beauty Reception, box 16; see also Cater to LJ, 15 Feb. 1967, Cater files, Memos to the President, Feb. 1967, box 16.

26. These events are discussed in and the quotations are taken from the remarks of William Cramer in U.S., House, *Review of Highway Beautification: Hearings before the Subcommittee on Roads of the Committee on Public Works,* 90th Cong., 1st sess. (Washington, D.C.: GPO, 1967), p. 4.

27. Boyd to LJ, received 27 Mar. 1967, with Cater to LJ, 27 Mar. 1967, Cater files, HB, box 96.

28. Cater to LJ, 27 Mar. and 4 Apr. 1967, Cater files, HB, box 96.

29. Cater to LJ, 4 Apr. 1967, Cater files, HB, box 96.

30. Inez Robb, "Billboard Lobby Like Lola in That Song," *New York World Journal Tribune,* 5 Apr. 1967, Cater files, HB, box 96.

31. *Review of Highway Beautification,* pp. 2, 4; Francis, Notes on House Hearings, 5 Apr. 1967, WHSF/BF, Highway Beauty Act, box 14 (Wright and Francis quotations).

32. *Review of Highway Beautification,* pp. 121, 393, 660.

33. Boyd to LJ, 6 May 1967 (Boyd quotations), Boyd Papers, box 43; *Review of Highway Beautification,* pp. 968 (Wright), 992 (Cramer), 1021 (Kluczynski); Wilson to Lawrence O'Brien, 3 May 1967, Henry Wilson files, Memos to the Postmaster General, box 14.

34. Richard D. McCarthy to Carpenter, 12 May 1967, Cater files, HB, box 96; Charles Vanik to LBJ, 25 Aug. 1967, WHSF/BF, HB, Implementation, box 16; Marjorie Hunter, "Road Beauty Law Menaced in House," *New York Times,* 4 May 1967.

35. Boyd to Joseph Califano, 24 May 1967, Boyd to Kluczynski, 24 May 1967, WHSF/BF, Highway Beauty Act, 1967, box 15.

36. Califano to LJ, 24 May 1967, WHCF, Highways, 23 Nov. 1963–31 Aug. 1967, box 1.

37. Helen Reynolds to Spencer M. Smith, 16 June 1967, WHSF/BF, Highway Beauty Act, 1967, box 15.

38. See William Pearce to Culp Kruger, 28 Feb. 1966, WHCF, HI3, 15 Sept. 1965–, box 5, for reports on the rumors about the Johnsons; Carpenter to Lou Canaly, 28 Mar. 1967, Ashton Gonella to Cynthia Wilson, 6 May 1967, WHSF, LCAF, Beautification–C, box 10.

39. Bess Abell to Secretary of Defense, 5 Oct. 1966, John Steadman to Abell, 14 Oct. 1966, WHSF/BF, HB, Implementation, box 16; Wilson to Carpenter, 21 Mar. 1967, WHSF/BF, Highway Beauty Act, 1967, box 15.

40. Peter L. Bakker to LBJ, 28 Mar. 1967; Paul J. C. Friedlander, "Everybody's out to Discover America," *New York Times,* 9 Apr. 1967; Mrs. James F. Graves to LBJ, 10 Apr. 1967; Carpenter to Cater, 19 Apr. 1967—all in Cater files, HB, box 96.

41. Cater to Boyd, 16 July 1967, enclosing a clipping from the *Pittsburgh Press,* 9 July 1967, with an article by John J. Williams, WHCF, H13, 15 Sept. 1965–, box 6; Boyd to Cater, 29 Aug. 1967, Cater files, HB, box 96.

42. Carpenter to Cater, 31 Aug. 1967, WHSF/BF, Highway Beauty Act, 1967, box 15.

43. Carpenter to Bill Connell, 23 Jan. 1968, WHSF, LCAF, Beautification–C, box 10.

44. U.S., Senate, *Highway Beautification,* pp. 3–8 (Boyd), 85 (Tocker), 146 (Roadside Business Association), 363 (Mrs. Waller).

45. Cynthia Wilson to LBJ and Carpenter, 22 Aug. 1967, WHSF/BF, Highway Beauty Act, 1967, box 15.

46. Carpenter to Cater, 30 Aug. 1967, Francis to Carpenter, 8 Sept. 1967,

WHSF/BF, Highway Beauty Act, 1967, box 15; Drew Pearson, "The Lobby against Beauty," *Washington Post,* 10 Sept. 1967.

47. James R. Jones to LJ, 21 Sept. 1967, WHCF, LE/NR, 21 Oct. 1964–, box 142; U.S., House, *Highway Beautification Programs,* Report no. 713, 90th Cong., 1st sess. (Washington, D.C.: GPO, 1967), p. 13.

48. Sanders to LBJ, 2 Oct. 1967, WHSF/BF, Highway Beauty Act, 1967, box 15; Bridwell to Sanders, 30 Oct. 1967, enclosing Bridwell to Boyd, 30 Oct. 1967, Beautification, Barefoot Sanders Papers, box 16.

49. Sanders to LJ, 2 Nov. 1967, with cover remarks by the president, Beautification, Sanders Papers, box 16.

50. Sanders to John Gonella, 6 Feb. 1968, Chronological Memoranda, box 28; Carpenter to De Vier Pierson, 13 Mar. 1968, Beautification, box 16—both in Sanders Papers.

51. Sanders to Gonella, 8 Mar. 1968, Chronological Memoranda, Sanders Papers, box 25.

52. U.S., House, *Congressional Record,* 90th Cong., 2d sess., 5 Apr. 1968, pp. 9162, 9163; Helen Reynolds to Sharon Francis, 3 June 1968, WHSF/BF, HB, 1968, box 15.

53. Francis to LBJ, 20 June 1968, WHSF/BF, HB, 1968, box 15; Irvine Sprague to Sanders, 28 June 1968, Irvine Sprague files, Highway Beauty, box 2.

54. Sanders to LBJ, 29 June 1968, WHSF/BF, HB, 1968, box 15; John L. Sweeney to Sanders, 3 July 1968, Beautification, Sanders Papers, box 16, for the quotation about Cramer.

55. U.S., House, *Congressional Record,* 90th Cong., 2d sess., 3 July 1968, pp. 19917 (Cramer), 19919 (Wright).

56. Ibid., pp. 19919, 19920.

57. Carpenter and Francis to LBJ, 10 July 1968, WHSF/BF, HB, 1968, box 15.

58. U.S., Senate, *Congressional Record,* 90th Cong., 2d sess., 24 June 1968, p. 8369, gives the language of the 1966 law creating the Department of Transportation and discusses the proposed changes; Helen Leavitt, *Superhighway-Superhoax* (Garden City, N.Y.: Doubleday, 1970), p. 221; for Alan Boyd's position see Boyd to Thomas S. Baker, 16 Jan. 1968, Boyd Papers, box 44.

59. The Three Sisters Bridge controversy generated a large amount of coverage in the Washington press and elsewhere. Among the helpful sources are Mathilde D. Williams, "The Three Sisters Bridge: A Ghost Span over the Potomac," *Records of the Columbia Historical Society of Washington, D.C., 1969–1970* (Washington, D.C.: Columbia Historical Society, 1970), pp. 489–509; U.S., House, *Major Highway Problems in D.C.: Hearings before the Subcommittee on Roads of the Committee on Public Works,* 90th Cong., 1st sess. (Washington, D.C.: GPO, 1967); Leavitt, *Superhighway,* pp. 93–99.

60. *Major Highway Problems in D.C.,* pp. 18 (Boyd), 208 (Cramer); Leavitt, *Superhighway,* p. 107.

61. Francis to Carpenter, 8 Apr. 1965, Rex M. Whitton to Carpenter, 14 May 1965, WHSF/BF, Freeways: Routing and Design, box 10.

62. "Rte 87 Foes Hoot Mrs. Johnson Note," *New York Times,* 9 Jan. 1966, with Elizabeth Rowe to LBJ, 11 Jan. 1966, WHSF, AF, Mr. and Mrs. James Rowe, box 1792.

63. Ian McHarg to LBJ and Francis, 22 Feb. 1966, Boyd to Francis, 28 Feb. 1966, William F. Lipman to Francis, 22 Mar. 1966, WHSF/BF, Freeways: Routing and Design, box 10; Carpenter to Farr, 7 Dec. 1965, WHSF, LCAF, Beautification–F, box 11; for LBJ's speech see U.S., Senate, *Congressional Record,* 89th Cong., 2d sess., 25 Feb. 1966, pp. 4176–78, 4177 for quotation.

64. Note to File, 12 Aug. 1966, Francis to Rai Okamoto, 1 Feb. 1967, WHSF/BF, Freeways: Routing and Design, box 10; W. Marvin Watson to Robert Stein, 17 July 1967, quoting LBJ, WHCF, PP5/LBJ, box 63.

65. Francis to LBJ, 2 Feb. 1968, WHSF/BF, D.C. Freeways, box 6.

66. Carpenter and Francis to LBJ, 10 July 1968, WHSF/BF, HB, 1968, box 15; U.S., Senate, *Congressional Record,* 90th Cong., 2d sess., 29 July 1968, p. 24031.

67. Carpenter to LBJ, 24 July 1968, WHSF/BF, HB, 1968, box 15.

68. Sanders to Mike Manatos, 24 July 1968, Sanders to LJ, 24 July 1968, Beautification, Barefoot Sanders Papers, box 16; Manatos to Ashton Gonella, 26 July 1968, WHCF, WHNF, Jennings Randolph, box 34.

69. U.S., House, *Congressional Record,* 90th Cong., 2d sess., 26 July 1968, p. 23713; Sanders to LJ, 27 July 1968, Chronological Memoranda, Sanders Papers, box 25.

70. U.S., Senate, *Congressional Record,* 90th Cong., 2d sess., 29 July, p. 24038, and 2 Aug. 1968, p. 24951.

71. Udall to LJ, 12 Aug. 1968, WHSF, AF, Stewart Udall, box 2016.

72. Notes, Sharon Francis, 31 July and 1 Aug. 1968, WHSF/BF, D.C. Freeways, box 6.

73. Randolph to LJ, 31 July 1968, Manatos to LJ, 20 and 21 Aug. 1968 (21 Aug. for the quotation about his telephone call to the White House), WHCF, WHNF, Jennings Randolph, box 34; Randolph to LBJ, 22 Aug. 1968, WHSF, AF, Beautification, Randle, box 171.

74. Randolph to LBJ, 22 Aug. 1968, WHSF, AF, Beautification, Randle, box 171.

75. Califano to LJ, 22 Aug. 1968, Joseph Califano files, Memos to the President, Aug. 1968, box 22; Francis, OH, 27 June 1969, pp. 44–45, 49 (quotation); Sanders to LBJ, 3 Aug. 1968, Beautification, Barefoot Sanders Papers, box 16; *Public Papers of the Presidents of the United States: Lyndon B. Johnson, 1968–1969,* 2 vols. (Washington, D.C.: GPO, 1969), 2:908–10.

76. "Ban the Bridge?" *Newsweek,* 3 Nov. 1969, p. 68; "Remnants of Interstate Going Away," *New York Times,* 29 July 1985.

77. Lady Bird Johnson, *Texas: A Roadside View* (San Antonio, Texas: Trinity University Press, 1980), p xxiii; I attended the award ceremonies in Oct. 1984 through the kindness of Liz Carpenter and Lady Bird Johnson.

78. U.S., Senate, *Federal Highway Beautification Assistance Act of 1979: Hearings before the Committee on Transportation of the Committee on Environment and*

Public Works of the United States Senate, 96th Cong., 1st sess. (Washington, D.C.: GPO, 1979), p. 42.

79. "Senator Stafford Calls Highway Beautification Act a Failure," press release, 9 Jan. 1985, Office of Senator Robert T. Stafford, courtesy of Senator Stafford; "The Outdoor Advertising Program Needs to Be Reassessed," *Report of the General Accounting Office to the Chairman, Committee on Environment and Public Works, United States Senate* (Washington, D.C.: General Accounting Office, 1985), p. 44; Charles F. Floyd, "Requiem for the Highway Beautification Act," *Journal of the American Planning Association,* Autumn 1982, pp. 441–53.

80. U.S., Senate, *Federal Highway Beautification Assistance Act of 1979,* p. 21, testimony of Charles F. Floyd. For Floyd's writings on this period see Charles F. Floyd, "Billboards, Aesthetics and the Police Power," *American Journal of Economics and Sociology* 42 (July 1983): 369–84; "How the Billboard Industry Beats the Law," *Planning* 45 (Apr. 1979): 14–16; and "Billboard Control under the Highway Beautification Act: A Failure of Land Use Controls," *Journal of the American Planning Association,* Apr. 1979, pp. 115–26.

81. U.S., Senate, *Federal Highway Beautification Assistance Act of 1979,* pp. 310, 311.

82. Neal Peirce, "Billboard Blight," *San Francisco* (Calif.) *Examiner,* 19 May 1985; Tim Kennedy, "Billboard Removal Will Dress Up City," *Houston* (Texas) *Post,* 1 June 1985; Philip Shabecoff, "Beauty Is Found Slipping," *New York Times,* 9 Jan. 1985; John Miller, "You Still Can't See the Forest for the Billboards," *New York Times,* 28 Jan. 1985. For a more sweeping critique of the rationale of the Highway Beautification Act see John J. Costonis, "Law and Aesthetics: A Critique and a Reformulation of the Dilemmas," in *Land Use and Environment Law Review, 1983,* ed. Stuart L. Deutsch (New York: Clark Boardman, 1983), pp. 89–195.

83. For the telegram from LBJ and Laurance Rockefeller to Senator Slade Gorton see U.S., Senate, *Congressional Record,* 99th Cong., 2d sess., 23 Sept. 1986, p. S13263; Tom Kenworthy, "How the Highway Beautification Act Went by the Billboards," *Washington Post National Weekly Edition,* 9 Mar. 1987, pp. 31–32; for the Senate debates on the amendment see U.S., Senate, *Congressional Record,* 100th Cong., 1st sess., 3 Feb. 1987, pp. S1543–54, with the vote on p. S1554; see also "Surface Transportation and Uniform Relocation Assistance Act of 1987," Report 100-27, U.S., House, 100th Cong., 1st sess., copy courtesy of Senator Robert T. Stafford.

Chapter 9. Natural Beauty for the Nation

1. Matthew Nimetz to Joseph Califano, 11 Dec. 1967, James Gaither files, Task Force on Quality of the Environment, box 196. Martin V. Melosi brought this item to my attention.

2. Bess Abell to Marvin Watson, 13 July 1965, WHCF, EX/PP5/LBJ, box

62, about office space; Christine Stugard to James Jones, 22 Aug. 1966, WHCF, HI3, 31 Mar. 1966–, box 5, also about space considerations.

3. Carpenter to Watson, 4 Aug. 1965, and accompanying documents, WHSF, Liz Carpenter subject files, Jackson Hole, Wyo., box 17.

4. Sharon Francis, in OH, 20 May 1969, pp. 19–20, describes her part in drafting LBJ's speeches.

5. Wolf Von Eckardt to Carpenter, 18 Sept. 1965, Carpenter to LBJ, 19–20 Sept. 1965, WHSF, Liz Carpenter subject files, Buffalo and Syracuse, box 18; Eckardt to LBJ, 7 Oct. 1965, WHSF/BF, Give Till It's Beautiful, box 6; "Beautification Summary: The Committee for a More Beautiful Capital, 1965–1968," pp. 19–20.

6. "Beautification Summary," p. 16–18 (Sept. 1965 speech); 'First Lady Addresses Williams College," U.S., House, *Congressional Record*, 90th Cong., 1st sess., 9 Oct. 1967, p. 28166.

7. Lady Bird Johnson, "Beautification and Public Welfare," *Social Action* 34 (May 1968): 11–17, for the Yale address.

8. *Congressional Record*, 9 Oct. 1967, p. 28166.

9. Lady Bird Johnson, *A White House Diary* (New York: Holt, Rinehart & Winston, 1970), p. 381.

10. Liz Carpenter, OH, 15 May 1969, pp. 19 (1st and 2d quotations) and 15 (3d quotation).

11. Norma Ruth Holly Foreman, "The First Lady as a Leader of Public Opinion: A Study of the Role and Press Relations of Lady Bird Johnson" (Ph.D. diss., University of Texas at Austin, 1971), p. 142; for the song see Carpenter to Castro, n.d., Nash Castro Papers, "This Is Our Country," box 11.

12. Johnson, *White House Diary*, pp. 376–83, quotation on p. 379.

13. Ibid., p. 382 (1st and 2d quotations), 381 (Udall quotation); Liz Carpenter, *Ruffles and Flourishes* (Garden City, N.Y.: Doubleday, 1969, 1970), p. 88. For press accounts of the Texas trip see Shana Alexander, "Lady Bird's Boat Ride," *Life*, 15 Apr. 1966, p. 34; Frances Koltun, "Let's Travel: With Mrs. LBJ to Big Bend," *Mademoiselle*, July 1966, p. 26.

14. Carpenter, in *Ruffles and Flourishes*, pp. 74–83, 125, 206–19, discusses the trips, and the files on specific trips in Carpenter's subject files, WHSF, are illuminating for individual episodes.

15. Carpenter, OH, 4 Apr. 1969, pp. 27, 28.

16. Johnson, *White House Diary*, pp. 575, 576, 577, 578.

17. Ibid., pp. 579, 581; Carpenter, OH, 4 Apr. 1969, p. 29.

18. Johnson, *White House Diary*, p. 582; Francis, OH, 4 June 1969, p. 24. U.S., Senate, *Congressional Record*, 90th Cong., 1st sess., 7 Nov. 1967, p. 31260.

19. Francis to Carpenter, 22 Mar. 1965, Francis to Lee Udall, 9 Apr. 1965, Francis to Mary Connor, 11 Aug. 1965, WHSF/BF, Speakers Bureau, box 13; LBJ to Trudye Fowler, 19 Feb. 1966, WHSF, LCAF, Beautification–F, box 11.

20. Francis to Carpenter, 2 Dec. 1965, Francis to Mrs. Robert McNamara, 6 Jan. 1966, Simone Poulain to LBJ, 7 Feb. 1966, Francis to Members of the

Beautification Speakers Bureau, 2 Mar. 1966, WHSF/BF, Speakers Bureau, box 13; Francis et al. to LBJ et al., 24 Feb. 1967, WHSF/BF, Governors and Mayors, box 10.

21. Carpenter, OH, 4 Apr. 1969, p. 12; Sylvia Porter, "Beautification Is Big Business," attached with LBJ to Porter, 28 Dec. 1965, WHSF, LCAF, Beautification–P, box 14.

22. Adam Rumoshosky recalled his remark when he spoke to the First Lady's Committee on 28 Feb. 1966, Transcript of the Meeting, 28 Feb. 1966, p. 34, WHSF/BF, box 1; J. Howard Rambin to LBJ, 17 May 1965, WHSF/BF, Service Stations, box 12.

23. Nash Castro to Sutton Jett, 6 Dec. 1965, Stewart Udall Papers, University of Arizona, Tucson.

24. Charles A. Vanik to Jack Valenti, 2 Feb. 1966, Bess Abell to Vanik, 9 Feb. 1966, WHCF, PP5/LBJ, 29 Dec. 1965–15 July 1966, box 65.

25. Francis to Carpenter, 9 Nov. 1966, Rumoshosky Report, 6 June 1967, William O. Hermann to Carpenter, 20 June 1968, WHSF/BF, Service Stations, box 12.

26. Notes of Meeting, 17 Oct. 1966, Francis to Carpenter, 23 Feb. 1967, Francis to George V. Whitford, 8 Mar. 1967, WHSF/BF, Reliance Insurance Event, box 12.

27. Paul S. Forbes to Francis, 15 Oct. 1968, WHSF/BF, Report to the President, box 12, reviewed the collaboration with Giant Foods.

28. LBJ to William K. Coors, 6 Oct. 1965, WHSF, Cynthia Wilson files; LBJ to Fred J. Borch, 19 Aug. 1965 (General Electric), WHCF, NR, 29 June 1965–31 Aug. 1965, box 6; Coal for a Better America to LBJ, with LBJ to Udall, 9 Sept. 1966, WHSF, AF, Stewart Udall, box 2016.

29. Castro to Francis, 26 June 1967, Nash Castro Papers, Beautification file, box 7; Laurance S. Rockefeller, "Business and Beauty: Our Changing Landscape," *Vital Speeches of the Day,* 15 Jan. 1966, pp. 219–21.

30. Nand Burnett to John B. Connally, 9 Sept. 1965, LBJ to Connally, 15 Sept. 1965, WHSF, AF, Coney, box 101; *Texas Conference on Our Environmental Crisis* (Austin: School of Architecture, University of Texas at Austin, 1965), p. 11.

31. Ibid., pp. 157 (Jackson), 200 (Diamond); LBJ to Patrick Horsbrugh, 4 Feb. 1966, WHSF, AF, University of Texas–H, box 2022.

32. Castro to Sutton Jett, 28 June 1966, Nash Castro Papers, Mrs. Johnson's file, box 3, quotes the First Lady. For the arrangements of the conference see George Fox and Jacqueline Sharp to M. Neuberger, 10 June 1966, Maurine Neuberger Papers, University of Oregon, Eugene; Francis to Elizabeth Mason, 11 May 1966, WHSF, LCAF, Beautification–M, box 13; "Beautification Summary," pp. 31–32; Johnson, *White House Diary,* pp. 390–91.

33. McPherson to Jacqueline Sharp and George Fox, 5 Aug. 1966, enclosed with McPherson to LJ, 16 Dec. 1966, Harry McPherson files, Beautification Program, box 19.

34. Edward C. Crafts to John T. Connor, 14 Nov. 1966, with accompanying

documents, Connor to McPherson, 25 Nov. 1966, McPherson files, Beautification Program, box 19.

35. Crafts to Connor, 25 Nov. 1966, Liz Carpenter to LJ and LBJ, 8 Dec. 1966, McPherson files, Beautification Program, box 19.

36. *Public Papers of the Presidents of the United States: Lyndon B. Johnson, 1966,* 2 vols. (Washington, D.C.: GPO, 1967), 2:1457; *Weekly Compilation of Presidential Documents* (Washington, D.C.: National Archives & Record Service, 1967), p. 1834; Diana MacArthur to LBJ, 8 Jan. 1967, WHCF, NR, 1 Jan. 1967–7 July 1967, box 5; MacArthur to Sharon Francis, 1 Feb. 1967, MacArthur to LBJ, 15 Jan. 1968, with report on "Youth Wants a Piece of the Action!" WHSF, AF, Diana MacArthur, box 1394.

37. For LBJ's Foreword see National Trust for Historic Preservation, *With Heritage So Rich* (Washington, D.C.: Preservation Press, 1966, 1983), pp. 17–18; Albert Rains to LBJ, 7 Dec. 1965, Francis to Carpenter, 17 Dec. 1965, with draft foreword, WHSF/BF, Historical Preservation, box 11; Elizabeth D. Mulloy, *The History of the National Trust for Historic Preservation* (Washington, D.C.: Preservation Press, 1976), pp. 136–37.

38. *Weekly Compilation of Presidential Documents* (Washington, D.C.: National Archives & Records Service, 1966), pp. 607–8, for Lyndon Johnson's remarks and the executive order. Laurance Rockefeller expressed his views on the Recreation Advisory Council in Rockefeller to Orville Freeman, 9 July 1965, WHSF, LCAF, Beautification–L, box 12.

39. Edward C. Crafts to Milton P. Semer, 25 Aug. 1966, Crafts to Sharon Francis, 10 Aug. 1966 (quotation), WHCF, Federal Government (FG) 738, 22 Nov. 1963–3 Sept. 1966, box 404.

40. Henry L. Diamond to Douglass Cater et al., 28 Apr. 1967, Cater to Manatos, 8 May 1967, Manatos to Cater, 9 May 1967, Michael Manatos files, Beautification 1967, box 6.

41. Summary Minutes, Joint Meeting, President's Council on Recreation and Natural Beauty and Citizens' Advisory Committee on Recreation and Natural Beauty, 29 June 1967, Harry McPherson files, Beautification Program, box 19.

42. Edward C. Crafts to Phillip S. Hughes and McPherson, 12 Mar. 1968, Douglass Cater to John Macy, 13 Mar. 1968, WHCF, FG738, 1 Jan. 1968–30 June 1968, box 404.

43. Francis to Bess Abell, 15 Mar. 1968, WHSF/BF, Citizens' Advisory Committee, 29 Mar. 1968, box 9; for LBJ's comments see "Beautification Summary," p. 67; *Public Papers of the Presidents of the United States: Lyndon B. Johnson, 1968–1969,* 2 vols. (Washington, D.C.: GPO, 1969), 2:596, 599.

44. Macy to LBJ, 22 Mar. 1968, Dewitt C. Greer file, box 227; Matthew B. Coffey to Macy, 4 May 1967, Coffey to LBJ, 28 June 1968, John W. Macy files, box 815; LJ to Marvin B. Durning, 23 Oct. 1968, WHCF, FG738A, box 404.

45. Summary Minutes, Joint Meeting, 29 June 1967, Harry McPherson files, Beautification Program, box 19.

46. The President's Council on Recreation and Natural Beauty, *From Sea to*

Shining Sea: A Report on the American Environment (Washington, D.C.: GPO, 1968), pp. 6, 85; De Vier Pierson to LJ, 23 Oct. 1968, WHCF, FG738, 1 July 1968–, box 404.

47. Jay K. Kruster to LBJ, 3 Apr. 1966, WHSF, AF, Grand Canyon–K, box 866; LBJ to Mrs. Robert Fox, 7 May 1966, WHSF, AF, Beautification–Fox, box 113; Stephen Fox, *John Muir and His Legacy: The American Conservation Movement* (Boston: Little, Brown, 1981), pp. 329–31.

48. Orren Beatty to Udall, 16 July 1966, Sharon Francis to Udall, 18 Aug. 1966, Stewart Udall Papers.

49. U.S., House, *Congressional Record*, 89th Cong., 2d sess., 5 Aug. 1966, p. 18443.

50. LBJ to Susan Frey, 1 July 1965, WHSF, AF, Redwood National Park, box 1734. The best analysis of the controversy about the redwoods is Susan R. Schrepfer, *The Fight to Save the Redwoods: A History of Environmental Reform, 1917–1978* (Madison: University of Wisconsin Press, 1983), pp. 130–39.

51. LBJ to Mrs. William F. Bade and Mary G. Marston, 30 Sept. 1966, WHSF, AF, Redwood National Park, box 1734; Johnson, *White House Diary*, p. 424.

52. Francis, OH, 4 June 1969, p. 3.

53. Ibid., pp. 3–6; Francis to John B. DeWitt, 29 June 1967, WHSF, AF, Redwood National Park, box 1734.

54. Francis, OH, 4 June 1969, p. 6; Francis to Mrs. Morse Erskine, 12 Sept. 1967, Francis to Joe Carithers, 17 July 1968, WHSF, AF, Redwood National Park, box 1734; Schrepfer, *Fight to Save the Redwoods*, p. 160.

55. Francis to Newton Drury, 9 Oct. 1968, LBJ to Mrs. Richard Codman, 23 Dec. 1968, WHSF, AF, Redwood National Park, box 1734; Schrepfer, *Fight to Save the Redwoods*, p. 161.

56. Meg Greenfield, "The Lady in the East Wing," *Reporter*, 15 July 1965, pp. 28–31.

57. "Claudia the Beautician: Beautifying the Cities," *Time*, 1 Oct. 1965, p. 29; Hugh Sidey, " 'Lady Bird,' Says L.B.J., 'Will Beautify Us out of Existence,' " *Life*, 22 July 1966, p. 30b; "America the More Beautiful," *Time*, 30 Sept. 1966, pp. 53–54.

58. James B. Craig, "The Quickening Tick of the Conservation Clock," *American Forests* 72 (Nov. 1966): 10–13; "American Forest Association's Distinguished Service Award for 1967: Mrs. Lyndon B. Johnson," ibid., 73 (Nov. 1967): 76; "Beautification Summary," p. 29.

Chapter 10. Her Space in the World

1. LJ To M. Neuberger, 9 Aug. 1965, Maurine Neuberger Papers; Kermit Gordon to Heads of Departments and Agencies, 6 May 1965, WHCF, NR, 1 Dec. 1964–30 Apr. 1965, box 1; Bill Moyers to Hayes Redmon, 3 Sept. 1965, WHCF, NR, 1 Sept. 1965–16 Jan. 1966, box 4.

2. *Public Papers of the Presidents of the United States: Lyndon B. Johnson, 1965,* 2 vols. (Washington, D.C.: GPO, 1966), 2:939, 1074.

3. *Public Papers of the Presidents of the United States: Lyndon B. Johnson, 1966,* 2 vols. (Washington, D.C.: GPO, 1967), 1:195, 203.

4. Ibid., 1:264.

5. Ibid., 2:930–31.

6. Ibid., 2:1115–16.

7. Ibid., 2:1173–74.

8. *Public Papers of the Presidents of the United States: Lyndon B. Johnson, 1967,* 2 vols. (Washington, D.C.: GPO, 1968), 1:5; Lady Bird Johnson, *A White House Diary* (New York: Holt, Rinehart & Winston, 1970), pp. 472, 480–81.

9. Douglass Cater to Emilio Jaksetic, 13 Oct. 1967, WHCF, NR4, 15 Apr. 1966–, box 12.

10. Johnson, *White House Diary,* pp. 317–18.

11. Sharon Francis, OH, 20 May 1969, p. 32; Johnson, *White House Diary,* pp. 518–19.

12. Johnson, *White House Diary,* pp. 565–67; Lyndon Baines Johnson, *The Vantage Point: Perspectives of the Presidency, 1963–1969* (New York: Holt, Rinehart & Winston, 1971), pp. 427–28.

13. Johnson, *White House Diary,* pp. 573–74.

14. Ibid., pp. 583–84.

15. Ibid., pp. 596–97, 604.

16. Ibid., pp. 611–12.

17. Ibid., p. 616–21.

18. Johnson, *White House Diary,* pp. 620–22; Liz Carpenter, *Ruffles and Flourishes* (Garden City, N.Y.: Doubleday, 1969, 1970), pp. 202–3; Eartha Kitt, *Alone with Me* (Chicago: Henry Regnery, 1976), pp. 237–41; Norma Ruth Holly Foreman, in "The First Lady as a Leader of Public Opinion: A Study of the Role and Press Relations of Lady Bird Johnson" (Ph.D. diss., University of Texas at Austin, 1971), pp. 195–208, covers the Kitt episode in detail. Janet Mezzack, in "Mrs. Johnson and Eartha Kitt: The Women Doer's Luncheon of January 18, 1968" (seminar paper: University of Texas 1987, copy in LBJL), skillfully uses the Social Office Files on the incident.

19. Johnson, *White House Diary,* p. 622; Kitt, *Alone with Me,* pp. 243–46; Francis, OH, 4 June 1969, p. 36.

20. Johnson, *White House Diary,* pp. 622–23; Kitt, *Alone with Me,* pp. 246–47.

21. Johnson, *White House Diary,* pp. 623–24; Carpenter, *Ruffles and Flourishes,* p. 204; Kitt, *Alone with Me,* pp. 248–66; "A Word from Miss Kitt," *Newsweek,* 29 Jan. 1968, pp. 23–24; Elise K. Kirk, *Music at the White House: A History of the American Spirit* (Urbana: University of Illinois Press, 1986), p. 314.

22. Johnson, *White House Diary,* p. 638.

23. Ibid., pp. 642–45.

24. Ibid., pp. 645–46; Francis, OH, 4 June 1969, p. 58.

25. Simone Poulain to Paul Weeks, 27 May 1968, WHSF, LCAF, Weathers,

box 123; "Beautification Summary: The Committee for a More Beautiful Capital, 1965–1968," p. 77.

26. "Beautification Summary," pp. 79–80.

27. *Public Papers of the Presidents of the United States: Lyndon B. Johnson, 1968–1969*, 2 vols. (Washington, D.C.: GPO, 1969), 2:808–9; Melville B. Grosvenor to LJ, 20 Sept. 1968, LJ to Grosvenor, 25 Sept. 1968, WHCF, Parks 3, 1 Jan. 1968–, box 16; LBJ interview, 16 Sept. 1984; Dyan Zaslowsky and the Wilderness Society, *These American Lands: Parks, Wilderness, and the Public Lands* (New York: Henry Holt, 1986), p. 36.

28. Martin V. Melosi, "Environmental Policy," in *The Johnson Years*, vol. 2, ed. Robert A. Divine (Lawrence: University Press of Kansas, 1987), p. 114; Udall interview, 11 Apr. 1984.

29. "Beautification Summary," pp. 80–81.

30. Castro to George B. Hartzog, 12 and 25 July 1968, Nash Castro Papers, Mrs. Johnson's file, box 3; Francis, OH, 27 June 1969, p. 59.

31. Matthew Nimetz to Joseph Califano, 31 July 1968, James Gaither files, Beautification, box 257; Califano to LBJ, 30 Sept. 1968, WHCF, NR, 1 July 1968–, box 6.

32. Carolyn Fortas to Mary Lasker, 1 Oct. 1968, WHSF/BF, Society for a More Beautiful Capital, box 7; LBJ to Edward S. Barnard, 15 Nov. 1968, WHSF, AF, Beautification–R, box 184; see also Lady Bird Johnson, "America Can Be More Beautiful with Your Help," *Reader's Digest*, Nov. 1968, pp. 142–49.

33. Castro to George B. Hartzog, 1 Oct. 1968, Nash Castro Papers, Mrs. Johnson's file, box 3; Johnson, *White House Diary*, pp. 714–15; Francis, OH, 27 June 1969, p. 60.

34. Johnson, *White House Diary*, p. 725.

35. Ibid., pp. 735–37.

36. Eric Sevareid, Remarks at Conservation Luncheon, and LBJ, Remarks at Conservation Luncheon, 13 Nov. 1968, WHSF/BF, Conservation Luncheon, box 9.

37. Shana Alexander, "Best First Lady," *Life*, 13 Dec. 1968, p. 22b; "With the First Lady on Her Farewell Tour," *U.S. News and World Report*, 9 Dec. 1968, pp. 46–47.

38. "Lady Beautiful," *Christian Century*, 27 Nov. 1968, p. 1523; Selwa Roosevelt, "Straight As for Lady Bird," U.S., Senate, *Congressional Record*, 91st Cong., 1st sess., 15 Jan. 1969, pp. 877–78; James J. Kilpatrick, "A Stirrup Cup for Lady Bird," ibid., p. 880.

39. Johnson, *White House Diary*, pp. 748–49; Francis, OH, 27 June 1969, pp. 65–66.

40. Francis, OH, 27 June 1969, pp. 66–67.

41. Ibid., pp. 68–72; Castro to George B. Hartzog, 18 Dec. 1968, Nash Castro Papers, Mrs. Johnson's file, box 3. The Johnsons discussed their work together in the White House with Howard K. Smith of ABC News on 27 Dec. 1968; see *Public Papers, 1968–1969*, 2:1222–31.

42. U.S., House, *Congressional Record*, 91st Cong., 1st sess., 22 Jan. 1969, p.

1536; Francis, OH, 27 June 1969, p. 80; Johnson, *White House Diary,* pp. 772–76; John P. Crevelli, "The Final Act of the Greatest Conservation President," *Prologue* 12 (1980): 173–91.

43. Johnson, *White House Diary,* p. 783.

44. U.S., Senate, *Congressional Record,* 91st Cong., 1st sess., 15 Jan. 1969, p. 878; Lady Bird Johnson, *Texas: A Roadside View* (San Antonio, Texas: Trinity University Press, 1980), p. xviii.

45. Johnson, *Texas,* pp. xix–xx.

46. Ibid., p. xxiii.

47. Barbara Klaw, comp., "Lady Bird Johnson Remembers," *American Heritage,* Dec. 1980, p. 6; LBJ to Udall, 18 Apr. 1972, Stewart Udall Papers, University of Arizona, Tucson.

48. Klaw, "Lady Bird Johnson Remembers," pp. 5, 10–11, 17; Lady Bird Johnson, "Comment," *Discovery: Research and Scholarship at The University of Texas at Austin* 7, no. 3 (1982): 2–4.

49. Lee Kelly, "Lady Bird Renews Commitment at 70," *Austin* (Texas) *American-Statesman,* 22 Dec. 1982; Cheryl Coggins, "70th Birthday Blooms in Joy for Lady Bird," ibid., 23 Dec. 1982.

50. Helen Hayes to Lewis and Karen Gould, 7 Nov. 1986, enclosing memo of David Northington to Helen Hayes, a fund-raising document in my collection; see also *Wildflower: The Newsletter of the National Wildflower Research Center* 3 (Fall 1986).

51. James B. West, with Mary Lynn Kotz, *Upstairs at the White House: My Life with the First Ladies* (New York: Coward, McCann & Geoghegan, 1973), pp. 331–32; Traphes Bryant, with Frances Spatz Leighton, *Dog Days at the White House: The Outrageous Memoirs of the Presidential Kennel Keeper* (New York: Macmillan, 1975), p. 106; Nancy Dickerson, *Among Those Present: A Reporter's View of Twenty-Five Years in Washington* (New York: Random House, 1976), pp. 106, 136; see also Barbara Howar, *Laughing All the Way* (New York: Stein & Day, 1973), p. 126.

52. Nathaniel Alexander Owings, *The American Aesthetic* (New York: Harper & Row, 1969), p. 93; June Sochen, *Movers and Shakers: American Women Thinkers and Activists, 1900–1970* (New York: Quadrangle Books, 1973), pp. 244–45; Eric F. Goldman, *The Tragedy of Lyndon Johnson* (New York: Alfred A. Knopf, 1969), p. 375.

53. Abigail McCarthy, "ER as First Lady," in *Without Precedent: The Life and Career of Eleanor Roosevelt,* ed. Joan Hoff-Wilson and Marjorie Lightman (Bloomington: Indiana University Press, 1984), pp. 220–21; Vaughn Davis Bornet, *The Presidency of Lyndon B. Johnson* (Lawrence: University Press of Kansas, 1983), p. 137; Larry Paul Fuller, ed., *The Land, the City, and the Human Spirit: America the Beautiful: An Assessment* (Austin: Lyndon Baines Johnson Library et al., 1985), pp. 7, 11. In 1984, Congress voted Mrs. Johnson a gold medal for her achievements: see "Gold Medals to the Daughter of Harry S. Truman; Lady Bird Johnson; and the Widow of Roy Wilkins," *Hearings before the Subcommittee on Consumer Affairs and Coinage of the Committee on Banking, Finance and Urban*

Affairs, U.S. Congress, House, 98th Cong., 2d sess. (Washington, D.C.: GPO, 1984), pp. 12–58; Bob Krueger, "Lady Bird Brings Beauty to Texas," *Dallas Morning News,* 18 Apr. 1987.

54. Stewart Udall to Robert B. White, 11 Oct. 1965, WHCF, NR4, 5 June 1965–14 Apr. 1966, box 12.

55. Johnson, *White House Diary,* p. 752; Lady Bird Johnson, Introduction to *Texas in Bloom: Photographs from Texas Highways Magazine* (College Station: Texas A & M University Press, 1984), p. 10.

Index

303